C000218252

# Old Testament Wisdom Literature

## A THEOLOGICAL INTRODUCTION

### CRAIG G. BARTHOLOMEW
### & RYAN P. O'DOWD

IVP Academic

An imprint of InterVarsity Press
Downers Grove, Illinois

Apollos
Nottingham, England

InterVarsity Press, USA
P.O. Box 1400
Downers Grove, IL 60515-1426, USA
World Wide Web: www.ivpress.com
Email: email@ivpress.com

APOLLOS (an imprint of Inter-Varsity Press, England)
Norton Street
Nottingham NG7 3HR, England
Website: www.ivpbooks.com
Email: ivp@ivpbooks.com

InterVarsity Press®, USA, is the book-publishing division of InterVarsity Christian Fellowship/USA® <www.intervarsity.org> and a member movement of the International Fellowship of Evangelical Students.

Inter-Varsity Press, England, is closely linked with the Universities and Colleges Christian Fellowship, a student movement connecting Christian Unions throughout Great Britain, and a member movement of the International Fellowship of Evangelical Students. Website: www.uccf.org.uk

Unless otherwise indicated, Scripture quotations are the authors' own translation.

The poem on p. 229 is from THE HOCUS POCUS OF THE UNIVERSE by Laura Gilpin, copyright ©1977 by Laura Gilpin. Used by permission of Doubleday, a division of Random House, Inc.

Design: Cindy Kiple
Images: The Prophet Job by Fra Bartolommeo at Accademia, Florence, Italy. Scala/Ministero

USA ISBN 978-0-8308-3896-7
UK ISBN 978-1-84474-537-1

Printed in the United States of America ∞

**Library of Congress Cataloging-in-Publication Data**

Bartholomew, Craig G., 1961-
    Old Testament wisdom literature: a theological introduction / Craig
G. Bartholomew and Ryan P. O'Dowd.
        p. cm.
    Includes bibliographical references and index.
    ISBN 978-0-8308-3896-7 (hardcover: alk. paper)
    1. Wisdom literature—Criticism, interpretation, etc. 2. Bible.
O.T.—Theology. I. O'Dowd, Ryan. II. Title.
    BS1455.B27 2011
    223'.061—dc22

                                                                    2010052972

**British Library Cataloguing in Publication Data**

A catalogue record for this book is available from the British Library.

P   20   19   18   17   16   15   14   13   12   11   10   9   8   7   6   5   4   3   2   1

Y   28   27   26   25   24   23   22   21   20   19   18   17   16   15   14   13   12   11

*We dedicate this book to*

*Gary and Claire O'Dowd, Ryan's parents,*

*whose wisdom has for many years*

*nurtured him and his family*

*along the paths of life.*

*And*

*Wayne and Anne Barkhuizen,*

*longtime friends of Craig's*

*and fellow seekers of wisdom*

*amid the challenges of life.*

# Contents

# Preface

Now well into the twenty-first century, we are aware that we need wisdom as much as ever, at the personal, national and international levels. As Job 28 alerts us, the crucial question is where wisdom is to be found. The Bible contains a rich wisdom tradition, which, after a long period of neglect, has found its way back onto biblical and theological agendas. We welcome this recovery, but it is important to note that we have a long way to go to recover a full biblical theology of wisdom.

In this book our focus is on the theological interpretation of Old Testament wisdom. Nowadays books dealing with different aspects of Old Testament wisdom appear on a regular basis but rarely with deep theological engagement. The recent renaissance of theological interpretation in biblical studies has still to mature and certainly still to excavate the riches awaiting us in Old Testament Wisdom literature. Our hope is that this volume will contribute to just such an excavation.

As Proverbs tells us, Lady Wisdom calls out to us amid all the challenges of public and private life. All the while Dame Folly stands as a symbol for our unwillingness to attend to her call. In our view the time is ripe for renewed attention to Lady Wisdom's voice as we encounter it in Proverbs, Job and Ecclesiastes. If Scripture is indeed God's Word to us, then much is at stake in attending to his address through these remarkable books. They present the real possibility of finding wisdom amid the great challenges of the twenty-first century.

Many people have contributed in different ways to this volume. We are grateful to Brian Zegers and Jane Haanstra of Redeemer University

College for their administrative help in a variety of ways. Amy O'Dowd has read and commented on countless passages, helping us to improve the clarity and relevance of our message. Dan Reid of InterVarsity Press has been a pleasure to work with, and we are delighted to see this book published with InterVarsity Press. The Paideia Centre for Public Theology has generously provided for Ryan to have time to work on this manuscript, and Redeemer University College, where we both work, has provided a congenial context in which to work together in completing it.[1]

Our hope is that our book will be of use in churches as well as in the academy. Resources for using the book as a text in Old Testament courses can be found on the InterVarsity Press website at <www.ivpress.com>.

Wisdom is a journey, and we remain grateful to God, who at different points in our lives brought us to Christ, wisdom incarnate. He is the one through whom and for whom the creation was made, and our prayer is that this volume will lead both readers and authors ever more deeply into him.

*Ryan and Craig*
*Pentecost 2010*

---

[1]Ryan now teaches at Cornell University.

# Abbreviations

| | |
|---|---|
| ANE | Ancient Near East |
| BHS | Biblia Hebraica Stuttgartensia |
| LXX | Septuagint |
| OT | Old Testament |
| AB | Anchor Bible |
| AnBib | Analecta biblica |
| *ANET* | *Ancient Near Eastern Texts Relating to the Old Testament.* Edited by J. B. Pritchard. 3rd ed. Princeton: Princeton University Press, 1969. |
| *ARAB* | *Ancient Records of Assyria and Babylonia.* Edited by Daniel David Luckenbill. 2 vols. Chicago, 1926-1927. |
| BCBS | Believers Church Bible Commentary |
| BCOTWP | Baker Commentary on the Old Testament Wisdom and Psalms |
| BETL | Bibliotheca ephemeridum theologicarum lovaniensium |
| *BTB* | *Biblical Theology Bulletin* |
| BZAW | Beiheft zur Zeitschrift für die alttestamentliche Wissenschaft |
| *CD* | Karl Barth, *Church Dogmatics.* Edited and translated by Thomas F. Torrance and Geoffrey Bromiley. Edinburgh: T & T Clark, 1936-1969. |
| FRLANT | Forschungen zur Religion und Literatur des Alten und Neuen Testaments |
| ICC | International Critical Commentary |
| *JBL* | *Journal of Biblical Literature* |
| JSOTSup | Journal for the Study of the Old Testament Supplement Series |

| | |
|---|---|
| NIBC | New International Biblical Commentary |
| NCB | New Century Bible |
| NICNT | New International Commentary on the New Testament |
| NICOT | New International Commentary on the Old Testament |
| NIGCT | New International Greek Testament Commentary |
| NYRB | New York Review of Books |
| OBO | Orbis Biblicus et Orientalis |
| OTL | Old Testament Library |
| SBLDS | Society of Biblical Literature Dissertation Series |
| SNTSMS | Society for New Testament Studies Monograph Series |
| TOTC | Tyndale Old Testament Commentary |
| *VT* | *Vetus Testamentum* |
| VTSup | Supplements to Vetus Testamentum |
| WBC | Word Biblical Commentary |
| *ZAW* | *Zeitschrift für die alttestamentliche Wissenschaft* |

# Introduction

## WISDOM AND THE LOSS OF WONDER

There is group in the United Kingdom called the Cloud Appreciation Society whose aim is . . . to spot clouds![1] What may sound escapist and strange is also intriguing and, we would argue, necessary for us today. As the book of Job reminds us, counting clouds is a matter of godly wisdom (Job 38:37).

For most of the world's history, people have lived their lives in close touch with the creation. Some farmers and monks still maintain this discipline of natural wonder, as does much of the developing world. Yet we in the West have lost touch with nature in any kind of meaningful way. Anthropologist and ethnobiologist Wade Davis notes that "one of the intense pleasures of travel is the opportunity to live amongst people who have not forgotten the old ways, who still feel their past in the wind, touch it in stones polished by rain, taste it in the bitter leaves of plants."[2] For us in the West such experiences are rare. Few of us take time in the day to spot clouds, count stars or watch the sun rise or set. Few of us change the pace of our day or month as the weather changes. Almost none of us stores up food for winter or goes to bed when the sun

---

[1]<www.cloudappreciationsociety.org>. See Gavin Pretor-Pinney, *The Cloudspotter's Guide* (London: Hodder & Stoughton, 2006).

[2]Wade Davis, *The Wayfinders: Why Ancient Wisdom Matters in the Modern World,* CBC Massey Lectures (Toronto: Anansi, 2009), p. 1. See also idem, *Light at the Edge of the World: A Journey Through the Realm of Vanishing Cultures* (Vancouver: Douglas and McIntyre, 2001). Davis's writing is more pantheistic than we would like, but his exploration of diverse cultures casts an illuminating light on secular Western culture.

goes down. Most of us wake in the morning to radio news and advertising jingles rather than dim light, birds singing and crickets chirping.
This is not to suggest that all cultural development is bad but to highlight the extent to which our modern, Western world has lost touch
with the vast and miraculous fact of God's created reality that surrounds us, sustains us, quite often threatens us and yet is in the process
of being renewed to sustain us for all eternity. In sum, we have the lost
the capacity to wonder at the power and order of the creation.

For evangelical Christians our culture's disconnect with creation has
not been helped by what Gordon Spykman refers to as "the eclipse of
creation" in evangelical theology. He rightly says of much evangelical
theology,

> In its passionate concern to proclaim Jesus Christ as Savior, it sidelines
> a fundamental concern with the work of God the Father in creation. It
> gives the impression of bypassing creation in a hasty move to take a
> shortcut to the cross. . . . This is a faulty and shortsighted approach. For
> the full biblical import of our sinful predicament, of the call to conver-
> sion and sanctification, and of our future hope comes to its own only
> against a backdrop of a solidly based commitment to the work of God
> in creation.[3]

This is because the cross and resurrection do more than save us from sin;
they also restore the creation as the place where we will live forever with
God. The Wisdom literature of the Bible, which teaches us to orient our
experiences to the creation and the Creator, has been prized apart from
the doctrine of salvation and nudged off the Christian radar.

In sum, the increasingly insulating power of our large, comfortable,
sheltered, and gas-heated homes; electricity; clock radios; luxury auto-
mobiles; microwaves; computers; and cell phones have distanced us
from the creation, helped along by our narrow theology with its focus
on personal salvation. Large swaths of our generation of Christianity
have never thought to embrace or develop a theology of wisdom, with
its comprehensive focus on creation. The eclipse of creation and the

---

[3]Gordon J. Spykman, *Reformational Theology: A New Paradigm for Doing Dogmatics* (Grand
Rapids: Eerdmans, 1992), p. 176.

marginalization of the biblical Wisdom literature have left us bereft of sheer wonder at God's ways with his world.

## HEARING ANCIENT WISDOM TODAY

But this has not, of course, always been so. In his classic book *The Discarded Image*, C. S. Lewis tells us that to understand the medieval view of the world, books will not help us; we need to "go out on a starry night and walk for about half an hour trying to see the sky in terms of the old cosmology."[4] Lewis presents a contrast between the wonder of the medieval view with the lostness of our modern view of the world: "The 'space' of modern astronomy may arouse terror, or bewilderment or vague reverie; [but] the spheres of the old present us with an object in which the mind can rest, overwhelming in its greatness but satisfying in its harmony."[5]

Old Testament Israel had this same embrace of the *old* sense of harmony and wonder. Like her ancient neighbors in Egypt and Mesopotamia, Israel lived in close touch with the creation. Just think of the repetition of the Genesis creation stories in Hebrew homes and the countless psalms that sing of God's works in the skies, seas, earth, animals and crops. Not only did these cultures live in touch with creation, but their religion was also woven into their view of the world. Israel was unique in that it saw all of the creation as coming from its God, Yahweh, the Creator of heaven and earth. To live in this world that God has made is to live in communion with its maker. To touch the soil and breathe the air and watch a cloud is a religious act because all of creation matters to God. And to hope for salvation meant a renewal of the human race *with* the world and all of its beauty.

How might we recover such wonder at God's intricately fashioned world today? What will save us from the eclipse of creation in so much of our theology? Doubtless there are many resources in Scripture that would bring about such healing; however, a—perhaps *the*—major resource is the Old Testament Wisdom literature.

---

[4]C. S. Lewis, *The Discarded Image: An Introduction to Medieval and Renaissance Literature* (Cambridge: Canto, 1994), p. 98.
[5]Ibid., p. 99.

According to Proverbs it was by *wisdom* that Yahweh founded the earth (Prov 3:19). The result is that his wisdom is woven into the warp and woof of the very fabric of creation. And it is only as we are deeply in touch with the *Lord* that our eyes are opened to witness the marvel of his wisdom. Contrary to popular opinion and much modern theory, therefore, wisdom is not the same as "natural law" or "good technique"— as if we only need basic disciplines of getting in touch with ourselves and nature in order to be wise. Israel's wisdom *begins* distinctively with "the fear of the Lord" (Job 28:28; Prov 1:7; Ps 111:10). Her wisdom, therefore, does not start with us or even with nature but with the Creator-Redeemer himself. And the starting point makes all the difference. History demonstrates that every human culture has a tendency to distort and misuse the created world (its water, its creatures, its land and its cultures) for its own interests. *Genuine wisdom will be found only when we recover God's designs for his world.*

Because it is "*by* wisdom" that the LORD fashioned the earth (Prov 3:19; cf. Ps 104:24), it is the gift *of* wisdom that leads us back to living in harmony with God's created world. And, as we will find throughout this book, that "harmony" is quite often very different from what we might conclude if left to our own devices. Who would ever think that suffering is important for becoming wise? Or that death on a cross is the way to life and redemption? Or that the last will be first? And yet the Bible points to all of these as God's wisdom, which stands over against the "wisdom of this world." Thus we need to pursue God's wisdom and its natural grounding in wonder.

Our overall aim in this book is to open a dialogue about what it means to embrace and embody a theology of the Old Testament Wisdom literature today. Through engagement with the biblical text and the best of ancient and modern scholarship we articulate our views in every chapter. But at the end of each chapter we also reference the most important sources that raise questions to extend the dialogue beyond the pages here. In this way the book not only presents a theology of wisdom but also serves as a textbook, which points the way to further study.

Our exploration of Old Testament wisdom proceeds as follows. Chapters one through three establish the context for the book. Chapter one introduces wisdom and the Wisdom literature. Chapter two provides an introduction to the world of ancient wisdom. Examining wisdom in Egypt, Mesopotamia and Israel, we seek to show what was common to the thinking of that day and yet also what makes Israel's wisdom distinct. In chapter three we introduce the genre of poetry. Poetry was the most common way of writing wisdom in the ancient world, and so we examine how ancient people understood this genre and its purposes. We also reflect on why Israel found poetry such a useful genre for conveying wisdom and what this might mean for us today.

The next six chapters (4-9) are the heart of the book, working steadily through Proverbs, Job and Ecclesiastes—the three major Old Testament wisdom writings—to accomplish the following three goals. First, these chapters provide an overview and theological interpretation of each wisdom book. Here our aim is to orient our scholarship to listen for God's address in and through these books. Second, these chapters draw out the history of reception—how each book, or even part of a book, has been read and heard throughout the history of the church. Finally, we provide a close exegetical and theological reading of a piece of poetry from each Old Testament wisdom book. Because of the uniqueness of each book, these three goals are accomplished in different ways.

The last three chapters move toward a full theology of wisdom for today. In chapter ten we examine wisdom in the books of the New Testament; chapter eleven serves as a summary and full statement of an Old Testament theology of wisdom; and chapter twelve leads us to consider how we can embrace a comprehensive Christian theology of wisdom today.

As you will discover in this book, wisdom is nothing if not practical. Before plunging into the first chapter, we have a suggestion. Why not take C. S. Lewis's advice and go for a walk at night, slow down after your busy day and contemplate the starry sky. Allow yourself to *experience* the intricacy and wonder of God's creation.

# 1

# An Introduction to
# Old Testament Wisdom

*There is a central quality which is the
root criterion of life and spirit in a man,
a town, a building, or a wilderness.
This quality is objective and precise,
but it cannot be named.*

—CHRISTOPHER ALEXANDER,
*THE TIMELESS WAY OF BUILDING*

THE QUOTATION IN THE EPIGRAPH ABOVE comes from Christopher Alexander's award-winning approach to architecture, which he says centers on a quality that "cannot be named." We think, however, that there are good reasons to identify this quality as something close to biblical "wisdom." For one, it is a quality of *the whole of things:* it applies to *everything* in the creation, both living and inanimate. Second, it is the "root criterion of life and spirit." Wisdom, as we will argue throughout this book, is about the paths that lead to life, shalom (peace) and flourishing—whether among humans, creation, cities, farms, families, schools, governments or whatever else we can imagine. And this is precisely the quality Alexander is looking for to inform our architecture.

But when speaking of biblical wisdom we need to qualify Alexander's unnamed quality. First, the quality that the Old Testament calls wisdom finds its meaning only in relation to the one true God and

Creator of the world. Scripture is emphatic that its approach to wisdom is the only right one. Wisdom, therefore, must begin with the fear of the LORD (Ps 111:10; Prov 1:7; 9:10). Second, true wisdom is a part of one, *particular religious tradition* and is thus found within the covenant community of God's people and their story of salvation—first in Israel and now in the church. And third, wisdom is not always readily apparent. As we said in the introduction, wisdom is sometimes the very opposite of what our human reason and intuitions conclude.

Below we will give a fuller definition of this wisdom, but first it is important to understand the history of wisdom in the Christian church and how that history influences our own understanding.

## WISDOM IN THE HISTORY OF THE CHURCH

It is likely that the Wisdom literature boasts the most unusual history of all the genres in the Old Testament (law, prophets, history, prophecy, poetry and wisdom). With only a few exceptions, wisdom in the first fifteen hundred years of the church was interpreted allegorically.[1] Whether wisdom was interpreted as the church, the Spirit, the mind, Mary the mother of Jesus or as some other spiritual ideal, it was rarely understood as a literal way of life in the world.

This was largely because of the dualistic way the early church was inclined to oppose spiritual things to physical things. The third and fourth centuries A.D. were critical for this Neo-Platonic development in the church. During this time, churches at Antioch practiced what we would call a more literal reading while the churches at Alexandria practiced spiritual, moral and allegorical reading. The differences between the two are subtle, and it would be a mistake to think of "literal" and "allegorical" in only their modern senses today. For example, in the last century it has been common to think of literal in a scientific or mathematic way. Thus, when the Bible speaks of God "coming in the clouds," contemporary literal readings often believe that this must mean

---

[1]See Al Wolters, *The Song of the Valiant Woman: Studies in the Interpretation of Proverbs 31:10-31* (Carlisle: Paternoster, 2001), pp. 57-154; Craig Bartholomew, *Reading Ecclesiastes: Old Testament Exegesis and Hermeneutical Theory*, AnBib 139 (Rome: Editrice Pontificio Istituto Biblico, 1998), pp. 32-41; idem, *Ecclesiastes*, BCOTWP (Grand Rapids: Baker Academic, 2009), pp. 21-43.

those physical sources of rain in the sky.

In the ancient world, literal carried more of a liter*ary* meaning, with a broader appreciation for poetic and symbolic ideas. The clouds could be the literal ones we see, but they could also be a sign of God coming from a higher place that we cannot see. We believe this broader literary interpretation is better suited to biblical interpretation.

That said, even the literalist schools in the ancient churches would have practiced allegorical interpretation when it seemed appropriate. Such Neo-Platonic allegorism, however, sought to find in many of the physical things in the Bible some kind of spiritual, symbolic or disembodied meaning. This was based on the Neo-Platonic belief that the body, the world and all physical things are less important and to be shunned in favor of spiritual things and ideas. While allegorical interpretation has largely disappeared in the Western church, Neo-Platonic ways of reading the Bible have not.

Jerome (A.D. 347-420) was a pivotal character in this history. He gained his popularity through his translation of the Latin Vulgate—the Bible that would stand as the church's main text for one thousand years. Although Jerome favored a broad variety of reading methods, his own exegesis typically followed the more allegorical or spiritual meaning. So, for example, he reads Ecclesiastes as encouraging us to spurn the world and focus on the "spiritual." The passages in Ecclesiastes that speak of eating and drinking Jerome reads allegorically as referring to the sacraments. Jerome's interpretation of Ecclesiastes dominated the book's interpretation for a thousand years. Together, Christian dualism, the allegorical method of interpretation and the growing asceticism of the Middle Ages made literal readings of wisdom rare.

In the sixteenth century, Martin Luther (1483-1546) and Philipp Melanchthon (1497-1560) were the first to write widely read commentaries and sermons that adopted a literal approach. In the process they recovered a vibrant doctrine of creation and broke the back of Jerome's type of approach to Old Testament wisdom. Their understanding of the Song of Songs, the meaning of Ecclesiastes and the identity of the woman in Proverbs 31 provided fresh new ways of thinking about wisdom and creation. But, largely because of a focus on justification and personal salvation, it would be several centuries before these literal readings of the Wisdom literature would come to fruition.

A number of radical shifts in wisdom research began at the end of the Enlightenment era, when critical historical investigation became the dominant approach to the study of the Bible. Scholars sought less of a religious and humanistic use of wisdom than a reconstruction of the social, religious and cultural history behind the writing of the Bible. While this led to a wealth of new insights into the background of the Old Testament literature,[2] the emphasis on history had terrible consequences for wisdom studies for over a century. Because the wisdom books (Job, Proverbs and Ecclesiastes) appeared to make no mention of Israel's covenants, the patriarchs, the law or her redemptive history, they were largely neglected from 1800 to 1940, as scholars, perplexed about how to fit these books into their reconstructions of Israel's history and theology, ended up generally ignoring their contributions altogether.

An exception was Franz Delitzsch (1813-1890), who was one of the first modern writers to pursue wisdom in literal terms that connected it to living in tune with God's creation. His work, plus the many discoveries of ancient Near Eastern wisdom texts in the early twentieth century, initiated a return to wisdom studies, a return that is overflowing in the academic literature today. What is most significant about the discoveries of ancient wisdom, as we will see in the next chapter, is the deeply religious connection between wisdom and creation order.

## WISDOM AND WISDOM LITERATURE

Biblical Wisdom literature is a modern convention and arouses controversy when it is applied to the books of the Bible. Scholars agree that wisdom material is written in both poetry and prose, and is found throughout the Old Testament. The wisdom theology, language and metaphors we will study throughout this book show up especially in places like Deuteronomy, 1-2 Kings, many of the psalms, the Song of Songs, and prophets like Isaiah and Jeremiah. Scholars have therefore disagreed for decades about how to draw a line between what we call

---

[2]See here the essays in John Day, Robert P. Gordon and H. G. M. Williamson, eds., *Wisdom in Ancient Israel* (Cambridge: Cambridge University Press, 1995).

"wisdom" and other genres.[3] But in our opinion much of this debate is shortsighted. For one, it is unlikely—or certainly inconclusive—that the ancient Israelites would have drawn such sharp lines as they wrote and read their literature. Furthermore, because wisdom is a universal concept, we would expect it naturally to arise in all areas of life—in legal, historical, poetic and prophetic situations alike.[4] But when wisdom shows up in these other books there is often, even usually, another genre that would be more appropriate for a description. Song of Songs is perhaps one exceptional book that seems to fit equally into several of these categories. But apart from Song of Songs, there is little debate that Job, Proverbs and Ecclesiastes show the most distinctive traits of what we could call Wisdom literature. This will be borne out in the chapters that follow.

The first three chapters, in fact, look at the ways Israel's history and literary culture allowed her to express wisdom in so many diverse ways. This will help us understand wisdom and its relationship to other theological themes in the Bible, as well as alerting us to the different ways in which the wisdom vocabulary is used. It is important at this stage to recognize that "wisdom" (Hebrew *ḥokmâ*) finds its home above all else in the *poetical books*—among metaphors, wordplay and more imaginative literature. Wisdom is not primarily interested in relating a list of theological truths, an account of history or a picture of the future. Wisdom is about the *ways* of things—how they are meant to exist and work—and so we find it popping up all over the Bible.

In fact, the word *ḥokmâ* and its synonyms in the Wisdom literature (knowledge, understanding, discretion) express a range of ideas associated with order, justice, discretion, and both moral and skillful types of behavior. As we will see in the next chapter, the poetic style, which is so common in Old Testament Wisdom literature, even creates symbolic images of wisdom that arouse in the reader a desire for wisdom. Ger-

---

[3]In our opinion James Crenshaw's "Method in Determining Wisdom Influence Upon 'Historical Literature,'" *JBL* 88 (1969): 129-42, fails to lead us forward primarily because he works on the assumption that wisdom and Wisdom literature can only appear in a very narrow form.
[4]Here the ancient legal expert David Daube is particularly insightful. See *David Daube's Gifford Lectures*, vol. 2, *Law and Wisdom in the Bible*, ed. Calum Carmichael (West Conshohocken, Penn.: Templeton Press, 2010).

hard von Rad observes the problems of scientific theories of language when encountering these words in poetic contexts:

> Obviously one would not arrive at this form of speech if one insisted on taking the words, at all costs, in accordance with their various shades of meaning. A differentiation in meaning certainly comes into play, but one must also take into consideration a certain ceremonial quality in the speech, a circumstantiality in speech which has become game. If one asks what emerges from this stylization, then it is certainly not so much nuances appropriate to the perception being expressed as a desire to convince.[5]

Wisdom thus refers to a very wide range of desires, behaviors, skills and beliefs—all of which, like the spokes of a wheel, find their hub in the order God has created into our world. Raymond van Leeuwen's work on wisdom is particularly helpful in articulating the range of wisdom's meaning. He observes that wisdom is a "totalizing" concept. Hebrew wisdom is not just about activities like sewing, farming, building or reasoning on their own. It is about how all such activities find their meaning in the whole of God's created order. Mending a garment, cooking a meal and plowing a field are wise when they are in harmony with God's order for the world. Van Leeuwen suggests four major categories to help us draw out this totalizing nature of Hebrew wisdom.[6]

***Wisdom begins with the "fear of Yahweh."*** First, as we will note in our study of the book of Proverbs, the phrase "the fear of Yahweh" has been carefully embedded in the structure and theology of the wisdom books. Not only does the phrase introduce Proverbs as the beginning of knowledge (wisdom) in Proverbs 1:7; but it also appears thirteen more times, at key places in the structure of the book:

Beginning: in Proverbs 1:7 as the introduction to wisdom

Middle: in Proverbs 9:10, marking the major division between Proverbs 1–9 and Proverbs 10–29

---

[5]Gerhard von Rad, *Wisdom in Israel*, trans. James D. Martin (London: SCM, 1970), p. 54.
[6]Raymond van Leeuwen, "Wisdom Literature," in *Dictionary for Theological Interpretation of the Bible*, ed. Kevin J. Vanhoozer, Craig G. Bartholomew, Daniel J. Treier and N. T. Wright (Grand Rapids: Baker Academic, 2005), pp. 847-50.

End: in Proverbs 31:30, closing the book as the prized quality of the valiant woman

The "fear of Yahweh" also appears in modified forms in Job 28:28 and Ecclesiastes 12:13. Throughout the rest of the Old Testament, the "fear of Yahweh" similarly represents total devotion to God as the heart of Israel's "true" religion. To fear Yahweh is to sense his power and holiness (Ex 20:20) and yet, at the same time, to embrace him in love and obedience (Deut 10:16). Walther Eichrodt rightly observes that the fear of Yahweh simultaneously combines the *mysterium tremendum* ("repulsive mystery") and *mysterium fascinans* ("mysterious attraction") of God.[7] True wisdom exists in a relationship with a God who is both gracious in his embrace and severe in his judgment.

What must be recognized above all else about this phrase—the fear of *Yahweh*—is the radical nature of Israel's *ethical monotheism* among her polytheistic neighbors. Nothing else existed like this in the ancient world, and no other ethical system has had a greater impact on the development of Western civilization.[8] The implications for Israel's view of wisdom are profound. Gerhard von Rad's description of the fear of Yahweh and its grounding in ethical monotheism is still the best work on this topic since he wrote it forty years ago. We highlight just two of his major insights.

First, the fear of Yahweh shapes Israel's theory of knowledge (epistemology). While epistemology deals with a wide range of issues, we define it in terms of three questions: *What* is knowledge? *How* do we get knowledge? How to we *test* the results of our knowing? Von Rad draws out Israel's unique answer to these questions:

---

[7] Walther Eichrodt, *Theology of the Old Testament*, trans. J. A. Baker (Philadelphia: Westminster Press, 1967), 2:269. Eichrodt cites Rudolf Otto, but the phrase originally goes back to the mystics.

[8] Rodney Stark has produced an abundance of works in this area. For a fine introduction to monotheism in history, see his *One True God, Historical Consequences of Monotheism* (Princeton: Princeton University Press, 2001). There continues to be much discussion about monotheism in the OT and among the ANE. See, for example, Mark S. Smith, *The Origins of Biblical Monotheism: Israel's Polytheistic Background and the Ugaritic Texts* (Oxford: Oxford University Press, 2001); Johannes Cornelius de Moor, *The Rise of Yahwism: The Roots of Israelite Monotheism*, rev. ed. (Leiden: Peeters, 1997); Jan Assmann, *Of God and Gods: Egypt, Israel and the Rise of Monotheism*, (Madison: University of Wisconsin Press, 2008); idem, *The Price of Monotheism* (Stanford: Stanford University Press, 2010); as well as the extensive bibliographies in these works.

The thesis that all human knowledge comes back to the question about commitment to God is a statement of penetrating perspicacity. . . . It contains in a nutshell the whole Israelite theory of knowledge. . . . There lies behind the statement an awareness of the fact that the search for knowledge can go wrong . . . because of one single mistake at the beginning. To this extent, Israel attributes to the fear of God, to belief in God, a highly important function in respect of human knowledge. She was, in all seriousness, of the opinion that effective knowledge about God is the only thing that puts a man into a right relationship with the objects of his perception.[9]

As we will see in future chapters, wisdom and knowledge are indeed the product of a human search, but one conducted in a deep communal and spiritual abiding in God. Von Rad argues that wisdom is in fact "self-evident" but "only within the sphere of a specific world order"[10] or what some would call a specific worldview. In this world order, knowledge has moral conditions. It is distorted by sin and disobedience. And, whatever the intensity of our obedience or the power of our search, our knowledge will always be limited by God's own decrees and wisdom.

Second, this ethical monotheism, which believed in a single creator and author of order, focused Israel more intently on the one source of all reality. Egypt's understanding of Ma'at as a permanent *guarantee* of world order has no parallel in Israel in this respect. Instead, Israel's theology continually reinforces the limitations of human wisdom and the need for a category of wonder. Von Rad explains:

Did not Israel, in all her attempts to perceive the course of human experience, always come back to Yahweh who comprehended all things in power? . . . This means that Israel was obliged to remain open, in a much more intensive way, to the category of the mysterious. When she spoke of mystery . . . she did not mean something vague and inexpressible which defied being put into words. . . . [Mystery] refers rather to something perceived by the understanding rather than by the feelings.[11]

---

[9]Von Rad, *Wisdom in Israel*, pp. 67-68.
[10]Ibid., p. 115.
[11]Ibid., pp. 72-73.

In other words, mystery was not a matter of giving up trying to know and understand when things get hard. Mystery refers to a specific discipline of wisdom where we hold our gaze on the wonder of God's designs and his works in the world. It is an attitude whereby we remember our form as created beings and our status as subjects of a king and the priority of both of these truths in shaping our approach to life, knowledge and worship.

***Wisdom is concerned with the general order and patterns of living in God's creation.*** Second, wisdom is always alert to Yahweh's position as ruler and wise creator. The patterns of the planets, animals and seasons are all used as teaching examples for the grooves God has built into the world order. Life has places for us to walk and ways for us to live, just as much as there are places and ways that must be avoided.

The earliest Wisdom literature was written and spoken to equip its hearers with a sense of the day-to-day patterns needed to play our role in an orderly but fallen world. Wisdom thus always gazes out and in. It gazes out toward the general order built into creation: the limits to the waters, circuits for the sun and moon, the work of the creatures and the change of seasons. And it gazes in to tune the patterns of our daily lives to the musical score of God's created order: hard work, adequate rest, humble speech, good counsel and moral behavior.

As we will see in the next chapter, every known form of ancient Near Eastern wisdom believed in this kind of rhythm and world order. But Israel's faith declares that only Yahweh's wisdom is able to guide humanity along the true path to *his* creative desire for the world—the world has a personal quality tied to a single God that other nations did not share. Biblical wisdom thus leads us into true religion; into the love of God and neighbor; and into the proper care for animals, land and our ecological surroundings.

***Wisdom provides discernment for the particular order and circumstances of our lives.*** Third, naturally wisdom's view of the general order also provides a framework for the particular order and direction of life, family and nation. God has given wisdom to us to guide us through the unique challenges facing each of us each day of our lives—what we could refer to as historical particularity. Old Testament wisdom provides a bridge between the general order and the particular order for every event and every created object. Wisdom is both for kings, to lay down laws, make treaties and care for the oppressed; and it is also for individuals: where to go to school, who or whether to marry, what profession to seek, when to have children, whether to buy a house, how to love my neighbor.

Indeed, it is precisely because wisdom is attuned to the patterns in *creation* that it can give guidance in making good decisions in unique circumstances. Whatever the seeming randomness of life before us, wisdom assures us that there is still an order created by God for the very dilemma we face. Wisdom provides freedom within form and life within limits.[12] In other words, wisdom affirms that God has established both an overall, dynamic world order and that this order provides for every moment and every person.

When we take this particular focus of wisdom together with its view of the general cosmic order, we can see it as God's wonderful gift for humanity to help us navigate our lives within the general morality and order expected of all of us and with regard to the specific decisions we have to make based on our unique gifts and calling. If this is true, shouldn't we all daily follow James's advice: "If any of you lacks wisdom, you should ask God, who gives generously to all without finding fault, and it will be given to you" (Jas 1:5)?

***Wisdom is grounded in tradition.*** Fourth, the word *tradition* has taken on pessimistic overtones in the last two centuries. Yet wisdom, like the rest of the Old Testament, is aware of the fact that stories, customs, laws and values are passed on from generation to generation. Like Moses' teaching on the great commandment (Deut 6:4-9), and like Paul's instruction to Timothy (2 Tim 2:2), proverbs are memorable ways for parents and teachers to pass wisdom on to children and students (e.g., Prov 1:8-10; 2:1; 3:1). Those who dare to venture out on their own, apart from the counsel of the family, community and church, stray away from wisdom into folly and thus away from God's orderly design for humanity and into the interests of selfish desire.

---

[12]Raymond van Leeuwen, "Proverbs," in *The New Interpreter's Bible,* ed. Leander Keck (Nashville: Abingdon, 1997), 5:31.

But not just any tradition will do. Biblical Wisdom literature establishes *its* tradition in the imagery and theology of the creation account in Genesis, which begins with two striking contrasts: a glorious creation scene of life, beauty, and harmony, and a tragic scene of rebellion, suspicion, shame, and judgment. The tree of the knowledge of good and evil and the tree of life become the two symbols of these two scenes and two competing traditions. When confronted with the serpent's distorted version of the truth, Adam and Eve appeal to their selfish, prideful, and foolish interests and reject God's tradition: "When the woman saw that the fruit of the tree was good for food and pleasing to the eye, and also desirable for gaining wisdom, she took some and ate it. She also gave some to her husband, who was with her, and he ate it" (Gen 3:6). Eve's decision highlights the link between our desire, our search for wisdom and God's way of revealing it. The threefold repetition of the "tree" in this verse reminds us of the other trees in the garden and especially of the "tree of life" and its unfulfilled potential. The end of the scene depicts the closing of the garden to separate humanity from the tree of life (Gen 3:22-24). As in other cultures, the trees become a powerful symbol: for Israel they evoke a memory of the loss of life and divine intimacy—of another possible story to the one we live in now.

The wisdom tradition picks up these themes and language from Genesis 1–3. The book of Proverbs prominently features the cosmic Woman Wisdom, who not only witnessed the events of the creation (Prov 8:22-31) but herself now represents the "tree of life" to those who will take hold of her (Prov 3:18)—a clear image of healthy desire in contrast with Adam and Eve's rebellious passions. The sexual, intellectual and agricultural impulses of Genesis 1–3 are picked up in the language of Woman Wisdom in order to present herself as God's gift of a path to living obediently within the grooves of his world. Adam, Eve and the serpent demonstrate the complex task of living out the way of wisdom from day to day. Flowing from the mouths of parents (Prov 1:8; 2:1; 3:1) and written in books to be read (Job and Ecclesiastes), wisdom is inseparable from life in family, community and the traditions that unite them.

For our own part it is worth noting that since the fall, humanity has constantly found itself in a "tournament" of stories and traditions.[13] We are endlessly bombarded with peer pressure, political action groups, the news media, "expert testimony," and the seductive appeal of entertainment and advertising. We are left with the task of interpreting right from wrong and true from false in the midst of countless opinions. As we will see in future chapters, wisdom calls out to the "son" (and daughter) to follow the right path, to seek the tree of life and to dwell in the house of righteousness. This can only be found within the community of God's people and their story and account of the world.

## CONCLUSION

Neither Craig nor Ryan—sadly!—has much interest in science fiction. But when Ryan's son Patrick got his grandmother to buy him Orson Scott Card's science fiction novels about a young boy called Ender, his grandmother got hooked and read them all. Ryan then got hooked and couldn't put them down. And then Craig got hooked . . . and so it continues. Our hope is that this introduction has whetted your appetite for Old Testament wisdom. We hope it gets you hooked! Wisdom is wonder-full and far bigger than we generally imagine. And the Christian church urgently needs to recover a robust theology of wisdom today. Such a recovery requires us to journey deep into Old Testament wisdom. In the next chapter we will examine wisdom in the context of other ancient Near Eastern wisdom traditions.

## RECOMMENDED READING

### Introductory studies

Bartholomew, Craig G. "Wisdom Books." In *New Dictionary of Biblical Theology*, ed. T. Desmond Alexander et al., pp. 120-22. Leicester, U.K.: Inter-Varsity Press, 2000.

———. "A God for Life and Not Just for Christmas! The Revelation of God in the Old Testament Wisdom Literature." In *The Trustworthiness of God*, ed. Paul Helm and Carl Trueman, pp. 39-57. Grand Rapids: Eerdmans, 2002.

---

[13]This phrase comes from C. Stephan Evans.

————. *Reading Proverbs with Integrity.* Cambridge: Grove, 2001.

Leeuwen, Raymond C. van. "Wisdom Literature." In *Dictionary for Theological Interpretation of the Bible,* ed. Kevin J. Vanhoozer, Craig G. Bartholomew, Daniel J. Treier and N. T. Wright, pp. 847-50. Grand Rapids: Baker Academic, 2005.

### *Advanced studies*

Rad, Gerhard von. *Wisdom in Israel,* trans. James D. Martin. London: SCM, 1970.

Whybray, R. N. *The Intellectual Tradition in the Old Testament.* BZAW 135. Berlin: Walter de Gruyter, 1974.

## 2

# The Ancient World of Wisdom

*Israel's fearless and trustful attitude toward the world was
possible only on the basis of its trust in Yahweh. Without this trust, Israel
would only have had the deified world as the basis of its experience with
reality; and it would have been forced to feel insecure in it and
fear it. . . . Israel trusts in Yahweh, and not the world order. . . .
We should not underestimate the high degree of hermeneutical
sophistication of texts such as Psalm 104; 148; Genesis 1,
and many others. These texts portray the presence of the
universal world order in the daily lives of the creatures.*

—ROLF P. KNIERIM,
*THE TASK OF OLD TESTAMENT THEOLOGY*

WISDOM IS THE COLLECTION OF LEARNING we build from
our experiences in the world.[1] In the modern West, children learn about
the danger of busy traffic and hot stoves, the importance of obeying
parents, and the joy of birthday parties. Adults learn the ways of married life, how to succeed at work, cook, clean, find a shortcut in rush-
hour traffic and manage a complicated financial world. But as basic as
these things are, it is also important to recognize the great complexity
and vulnerability of such learning.

Wisdom is complex if nothing else because of the great breadth and
seeming randomness of events in daily life. And it is vulnerable both

---

[1]See Gerhard von Rad, *Wisdom in Israel,* trans. James D. Martin (London: SCM, 1970), pp. 3-4.

because of our limited experience and because of the forces of sin and evil within us and around us. Clouds don't always mean rain. A stove may or may not be hot. One person's generosity may encourage greedy manipulation for another. Telling the truth may get you in trouble. By its very nature, therefore, the wisdom of experience is pliable; it requires us to refine our understanding and adapt our knowledge to each new person and circumstance.

From our study of the ancient world, we find that almost every culture in the Near East produced collections of this kind of experiential wisdom. On the one hand, we have to recognize that Israel is very much like her neighbors with their parallels in literature, worship, politics, languages and customs. In fact, all signs indicate that these nations all influenced one another, particularly in their study of wisdom. On the other hand, Israel's wisdom was inspired by Yahweh's unique identity as the *one* Creator and ruler of all reality, and this makes it different—sometimes radically so—from any other ancient form of wisdom. In order to appreciate the uniqueness in Israel's wisdom, we need to set it in the context of the wisdom of her nearest neighbors, Egypt and Mesopotamia.

## ANCIENT VERSUS MODERN WORLDVIEWS

As residents of the modern world, we first have to recognize how differently we have come to think and live when compared to ancient cultures. In our Western, postindustrial context we interpret human experience primarily through the authority of the scientific mind, and we are assured that our "neutral" and "objective" observations will give us truth about the world we live in. Our mechanistic, sterile view of the world with its critical lens orients us to our experience through psychological, social or scientific concepts. When reason and observation rule in this way, anyone who speaks seriously of mystery, the transcendent or the spiritual seems increasingly out of touch with reality.[2]

The ancients, however, viewed human life in the world as a personal,

---

[2]For a marvelous narrative on this move from ancient to modern worldview, see Charles Taylor, *A Secular Age* (Cambridge, Mass.: Belknap Press of Harvard University Press, 2007).

holistic and nonscientific relationship with nature.[3] Instead of the "it" of the world *out there,* humans existed in an "I-Thou" relationship with the world in and around them. To have a dream of a dead relative was not a subconscious experience of the mind but was a real part of relating to the human experience of life and death. Where our modern science theorizes about the meaning of space and time, the ancient world sought meaning in mythical and poetic images of nature, with its life, death and seasons. Time was primarily a matter of the long rhythms of nature, not the physics and exactitude of clocks and day planners. Rather than reducing the problem of death to a need for medical advances, as we do today, ancient cultures naturally turned to the seas, the deeps, the darkness and creatures like the Leviathan to relate in natural ways to death, mystery and chaos. Personifications like Israel's Woman Wisdom and Egypt's female goddess Ma'at were used to create a personal and sensual relationship to the order and rhythm of life in the world.

## THE GOD-KING-CREATION-WISDOM NEXUS

Ancient wisdom's holistic and personal view of the world thus allowed for a unique understanding of the order and structure of the world. Wisdom, rather than science, was the key to unlocking the living structure and order in creation; the key to a well-lived life was a well-developed sense of wisdom. Figure 2.1 is a helpful way to picture the unity and structure in the ancient world.

**Figure 2.1**

[3]The now dated collection of essays in Henri Frankfort, H. A. Frankfort, John A. Wilson, Thorkild Jacobsen and William Irwin, *The Intellectual Adventure of Ancient Man: An Essay on Speculative Thought in the Ancient Near East* (Chicago: University of Chicago Press, 1946), remains one of the most important sources on the ancient mind.

For most of us, God, kings, creation and wisdom do not belong in the same phrase let alone the same sentence. God belongs to worship, the king to politics, creation to theology and/or science, and wisdom to ethics or the practical life. But that signals the radical shifts that have taken place in western culture. In the ancient Near Eastern world, these four concepts were woven together into a single fabric.[4] Their writings are infused with symbolic images of reality. Othmar Keel notes: "We tend to work almost exclusively with concepts either concrete (tree, door, house) or abstract (being, kingship, mentality). The ancient Near East, on the other hand, has a preference for concepts which are in themselves concrete, but which frequently signify a reality far larger than their concrete meaning."[5] So, for example, heaven and earth, waters, seas, hills, and deeps are all concrete symbols that imagine the powerful political, religious and philosophical realities of the ancient world. These places in nature are where the gods dwell, where the powers threaten humanity and where the conflicts occur that will influence the course of human life on earth. Kings were usually given divine status as political and religious representatives of the gods on earth. A king's job was to apply wisdom against the forces of chaos and thus preserve the harmony and order of the human world.

The remainder of our journey in this chapter will take us through the writings and religions of ancient Egypt and Mesopotamia. These two major cultures constitute the main groups that surrounded Israel for centuries as her wisdom and poetic literature was written. Understanding how they wrote, thought and worshiped will go a long way toward helping us comprehend the context and motivation of Israel's ancient writings.

## EGYPTIAN WORLDVIEWS

We know of Egypt's powerful stature in the ancient world not only

---

[4]See Raymond C. van Leeuwen, *Context and Meaning in Proverbs 25–27*, SBLDS 96 (Atlanta: Scholars Press, 1988), p. 74, who says, "In my judgment, Judean royal ideology and creation theology are two sides of one ideological complex: God-king-world-order and justice go together."

[5]Othmar Keel, *The Symbolism of the Biblical World: Ancient Near Eastern Iconography and the Book of Psalms* (New York: Seabury, 1978), p. 8.

because of the vast riches of modern historical discoveries, like the pyramids and mummies, but also because of the way the writers of the Old Testament constantly testified to its influence on Israel. From the stories of Abraham and Joseph and the prophecies in Jeremiah, it is clear that the Israelites were constantly influenced by this commanding presence to her south. As we will see below, her many years spent among the Egyptians are evident throughout Job, Ecclesiastes and especially Proverbs.

Egypt had a strong tie between the natural and religious world order. We must of course note that Egypt's three major kingdoms spanned over two-thousand years (2800-100 B.C.), amassing a whole range of religious and political views. The result is that many of her myths, laws, poetry and histories contradict one another.

Still, we can identify some of the fundamental ways that ancient Egyptians understood wisdom. What is most unique about this Egyptian cosmology is its "consubstantial" view of reality. Gods, humans, animals, water and nature are all part of one spectrum of being or substance. One can become more like a god or more like a mountain, even in attitudes or particular actions, and thus move back and forth through this substance. But both gods and plants are no less bound to this same sphere of reality.

The many and varying creation stories in Egypt generally view creation as coming from "Nu" (sometimes "Nun"), the primordial waters. There are also stories of self-creation and stories where Atum, Ptah or Ra created the world. Most scholars agree that the details of creation were not that important to the Egyptians; it was simply a natural and harmonious movement to higher order. Thus, unlike other ancient Near Eastern cultures, and especially Israel, Egypt was not nearly as concerned with the creation event as it was with maintaining the harmony and order of the creation in the present.

In this respect, Nu's connection to water is significant, for Egypt understood water as creation's life-giving power for each new growing season. The annual rising of the Nile River represents both the primary source of human life and the rhythms that humans are meant to pursue for themselves. Ra (sometimes Re) was the god of the sun and perhaps the most important God for Egypt. He was the father of the lesser gods and the god of justice. Here we can already see many parallels with the images we find in the creation account in Genesis, but also in Job, Proverbs and Psalms, which frequently appeal to the waters, the sun, moon and the stars as ways to relate to wisdom, knowledge, justice, chaos, death and lament.

Ra gave birth to a goddess known as Ma'at. Egypt's understanding of Ma'at shares many parallels with biblical wisdom *(hokmâ)*, and in future chapters, we will consider the relationships between Ma'at and "Lady Wisdom" (Prov 1–9). J. A. Wilson says that Ma'at was "the cosmic force of harmony, order, stability, and security . . . and the organizing quality of created phenomena."[6] In this way, Ma'at was similar to biblical wisdom. But it was also less vulnerable than Israelite wisdom. Ma'at's ability to provide justice and order was sure, and it only needed to be sought out to be achieved in the individual life. Many scholars have noted strong periods of humanism and extraordinary optimism in human achievement throughout Egypt's later history. On the contrary, biblical wisdom, as we will see throughout this book, is a gift from the Creator and can only be acquired through humility and reverence (Prov 1:7).

Here we must make careful note of the pharaoh (king) as the Egyptian god of the created order. He was, therefore, also the god of Ma'at, meaning that he had the ethical responsibility to maintain agricultural, economic and social stability in Egypt. Here we see Egypt's belief in a kind of king-god-creation-order nexus. It cannot be overstated that the Nile River was the central feature in Egypt's understanding of life and order. As the sole source of life in a vast desert, it determined the pharaoh's strength; it revealed the favor of the gods; it explained the life of the sun in each new day; and it explained the tendency to see the world through a symmetric balance between water and desert.

When Israel's God came to deliver his people from Pharaoh's reign, the battle was quite appropriately carried out in the context of Ma'at. In the plagues, Yahweh declared his authority over snakes, rivers, animals and the mighty waters of the sea. As creation brought death to Egypt,

---

[6]J. A. Wilson, *The Burden of Egypt* (Chicago: University of Chicago Press, 1951), p. 48, quoted in John D. Currid, *Ancient Egypt and the Old Testament* (Grand Rapids: Baker, 1997), p. 118.

it brought life to Israel (Exod 5–12). But it is the waters that are perhaps most significant. From the first curse, where the Nile turned to blood, to the drowning of Pharaoh in the Red Sea, redemption from Egypt was a distinctive claim by Yahweh to be the true owner of creation, its only ruler and its sole source of life and renewal.

## EGYPTIAN WRITINGS

Here we will look at three major groups of writings in ancient Egypt to help us appreciate the strength of the holistic worldview and the power of the god-king-creation-wisdom nexus in their sense of structure and order.

The first important group of writings in Egypt consists of many hymns and prayers, which in some ways parallel the book of Psalms. These Egyptian songs, however, show far less unity in their purpose. Among other things, hymns are sung to the gods, the pharaohs, the sun (Re) and the Nile. Like the book of Psalms, praise is given for victory in battle, for mercy to creatures and for strength. A series of songs also shows evidence of a period of "monotheistic" worship of "the one," but also sometimes the "three" of Egypt's many gods.[7]

Second, it is likely that Egypt produced more wisdom writings than perhaps any other ancient Near Eastern culture. The Egyptians developed schools, often attached to temples, whose main purpose was to produce "full-scale manuals of behavior" in collections known as *sb3yt* (instruction or teaching).[8] The genres of this collection vary widely but are still a close parallel to Israelite Wisdom literature. The Instruction for Merika-re (fifteenth century B.C.), the Instruction of Ani (ca. eleventh to eighth century B.C.) and writings by Ptahotep are wisdom documents that attest to a world of creation similar to the account in Genesis 1–2. In Egypt the power of "the water monster"[9] is portrayed in the origin of created life and order. Furthermore, like the book of Proverbs,

---

[7]See *ANET* 368-69. In all reality, Egypt recognized the existence of many gods. These hymns are, therefore, technically "henotheistic," elevating the worship of one god despite the existence of others.

[8]J. D. Ray, "Egyptian Wisdom Literature," in *Wisdom in Ancient Israel*, ed. John Day, Robert P. Gordon and H. G. M. Williamson (Cambridge: Cambridge University Press, 1995), p. 18.

[9]*ANET* 417.

the "son" or reader is the common recipient of the advice and is encouraged to use wisdom to be successful in life and often kingship. Like Israel's wisdom, Egyptian wisdom was grounded in creation, tied to the king and handed down through family tradition (cf. Prov 1:1-7; 3:19-30; Ps 104:19).

It is increasingly clear to scholars today that Egypt's writings have more parallels with the Proverbs than any other ancient source. In fact, large portions of Amenemope's writings have impressive parallels in the material in Proverbs 22:17–24:22. Consider the examples in table 2.1.

**Table 2.1**

| Amenomope[a] | Proverbs |
|---|---|
| Do not carry off the landmark at the boundaries of the arable land, Nor disturb the position of the measuring chord; Be not greedy after a cubit of land, Nor encroach upon the boundaries of a widow. (7.15) | Do not move the ancient landmark that your fathers have set. (Prov 22:28)<br><br>Do not move the ancient boundary-marker or go into the field of orphans. (Prov 23:10) |
| Do not eat bread before a noble, Nor lay on thy mouth at first. If thou are satisfied with false chewings, They are a pastime for thy spittle. Look at the cup which is before thee, And let it serve thy needs. (23.15) | When you sit down to eat with a ruler, Observe carefully what is before you, and put a knife to your throat if you have a big appetite. Do not desire the ruler's delicacies, for they are deceptive food. (Prov 25:1-3) |

[a] *ANET* 421-24.

Throughout this book we will argue that these parallels invite us to look for the critical differences between the two forms of wisdom. As Ray observes, Egyptian wisdom developed "from the pragmatic rules of Ptahhotep, through the disillusionment of some Middle Kingdom teaching, to the synthesis of moral behavior and divine will which is seen in Amenemope . . . to the divorce between ethics and providence which is argued in parts of Insinger."[10] While Israelite wisdom developed too, Yahweh's sovereign rule over the creation provides for a unique form of wisdom.

---

[10]Ray, "Egyptian Wisdom Literature," p. 28.

Finally, many ancient Egyptian wisdom writings resemble the auto-biographical form of instruction that we find in Ecclesiastes. Examples include the Instruction of King Amenemhet, the Instruction of Prince Hor-Dedef and Amenemope, which we mentioned above.

From these and many other parallels with Egyptian wisdom, it is clear that Hebrew wisdom and poetry were written with similar language and images and with the same kinds of social concerns as ancient Egypt. The justification and motivation for attending to wisdom in both cultures came from their theology of creation and the desire of the gods (kings) to maintain its order.

## MESOPOTAMIAN WORLDVIEWS

The strong relationship between god, king, creation, houses and wisdom is also evident throughout ancient Mesopotamia. Like Egypt, Mesopotamia did not have a single creation myth, nor does it seem to have had an emphatic concern with the details of creation.

The general sense of the universe lies with three gods who emerged out of the chaos: Anu, the most supreme and god of the sky; Enlil, the god of the storm; and Enki, the god of water and creativity. In some stories Anu is the author of the order in creation. Ea (in Babylonian) or Enki (in Sumerian) is the god of water, order, creation and the wise counselor of the other gods.

Whereas Egypt had a consubstantial worldview—all reality is in one harmonious spectrum of substance—Mesopotamia's lived by what William Irwin calls a "polytheistic naturalism."[11] Probably because of the unpredictable climate in Mesopotamia, the cultures there viewed creation in a much less harmonious and settled way. There is a pervasive sense of violence and force, both in what we know of their climate and their mythologies.[12] The *Enuma Elish*, the Babylonian creation story, and the Gilgamesh epic are all well-known myths distinctive for their impulsive sexuality and the violent battles that precipitate the creation of the rest of the universe.

In this way it is helpful to understand that Mesopotamia viewed the

---

[11]William A. Irwin, "The Hebrews," in *Intellectual Adventure*, p. 224.
[12]Thorkild Jacobsen, "Mesopotamia" in *Intellectual Adventure*, p. 128.

universe through an "integration of wills"; the gods represent the social forces from which these wills emerge. Thorkild Jacobsen concludes that the cosmic order in Mesopotamia is best viewed as a "state."[13] Creation order is not a given, but something that must be pursued amid the natural chaos and competitive social forces in life.[14] The confidence natural to Egyptian Ma'at has no real parallel here. Instead, a sense of legal order, justice and social responsibility drive these cultures to rise above the unexpected to achieve a state of human flourishing.

Van Leeuwen probes the Mesopotamian sense of a state-ordered world further still. He draws out its distinctive representation in the architectural terms of houses—*building* and *filling* them in particular.[15] Here the "house of the father functioned materially and culturally to organize the life world of ancient societies."[16] For the gods, the house symbolizes the entire cosmos or universe, whereas for the human the house represents the full breath of life, from agriculture to food and material goods. Here we can begin to see the importance both of building and filling or "provisioning" houses. A text from the Esarhaddon Chronicle exemplifies this well:

> The house I built, I completed, with splendor I filled it. . . . I built and completed it. For my life, for length of days, for the stability of my reign, for the welfare of my posterity, for the safety of my priestly throne, for the overthrow of my enemies, for the success of the harvest of Assyria, for the welfare of Assyria, I built it.[17]

Note especially the way this passage begins and ends with the phrase, "I built it," and the description of his filling it. By constructing and filling his house, King Esarhaddon establishes his status as a ruler who makes wise use of the created order.

Many scholars have identified this same building and provisioning imagery in Genesis 1. Days one through three build the skies, waters

---

[13]Ibid., p. 127.

[14]Ibid., pp. 126-27.

[15]Raymond van Leeuwen, "Cosmos, Temple, House: Building and Wisdom in Mesopotamia and Israel," in *Wisdom Literature in Mesopotamia and Israel*, ed. Richard J. Clifford (Atlanta: Society of Biblical Literature, 2007), pp. 67-90.

[16]Ibid., p. 68.

[17]*ARAB* 2:702, quoted in Van Leeuwen, "Cosmos, Temple, House," p. 71.

and earth while days four through six fill each of these in sequence. Two passages from the book of Proverbs also demonstrate the importance of understanding the relationship between creation, house provisioning and wisdom.

> By wisdom the LORD laid the earth's foundations,
>     by understanding he set the heavens in place;
> by his knowledge the deeps were divided,
>     and the clouds let drop the dew. (Prov 3:19-20)

> By wisdom a house is built,
>     and through understanding it is established;
> through knowledge its rooms are filled
>     with rare and beautiful treasures. (Prov 24:3-4)

Like the Mesopotamian worldview, Israelite theology understood wisdom as a common necessity for God and his creatures. God built his world with wisdom, and humans live in that world—build houses—through the wisdom that God gives. But Israel's theological distinctive is in the monotheistic conception of this world order.[18] Yahweh is the true creator of the world and only by fearing and obeying him do we find the path to true wisdom.

## MESOPOTAMIAN WRITINGS

We turn now to a brief survey of the ancient Mesopotamian writings. Like Egypt, they date to as early as 2700 B.C.[19]

*Wisdom and poetic writings.* Shurappak (versions from 2500, 1800 and 1100 B.C.) is the collected sayings of a wise man to his son, Ziusudra, who is a biblical parallel to Noah.

Shube'awilum (second millennium B.C.) is another collection of sayings from a father to a son (cf. lines 31-55 with Prov 24:17-18; 25:21-22).

Ahiqar (sixth century B.C.) was a vizier who delivered a number of counsels and sayings that are very similar to the proverbs. He also

---

[18]Ibid., p. 80.
[19]These summaries are taken largely from Karel van der Toorn, "Why Wisdom Became a Secret: On Wisdom as a Written Genre," in *Wisdom Literature*, p. 27; Michael V. Fox, *Proverbs 1–9*, AB (New York: Doubleday, 2000), p. 23; as well as the translations in *ANET.*

praises heavenly wisdom, writings that parallel parts of Job, Psalms and Proverbs 8.

*Theodicy.* Theodicies are texts that seek to vindicate the goodness of God in the face of evil and injustice. Many of the Mesopotamian theodicies resemble the book of Job. The Worm and the Toothache (*ANET* 100-101), like much of Job, depicts an appeal to the created order to understand suffering. Man and His God is a Sumerian variation of the book of Job (*ANET* 589-91). In both stories the main character calls out to gods, friends and his wife. The Babylonian Theodicy (*ANET* 601-4) is a poem between a man and his friends that resembles the dialogues between Job and his "comforters" (Job 3–37).

*Poetry.* Like Egyptian poetry, there are many Sumerian and Akkadian hymns and prayers. These include praises of gods and creation, lamentations, and psalms.

The language and images in these ancient writings are evident in Egypt and in Israel's poetic works. In all of these cultures, political-creational-social images dominate their way of thinking and writing about the world: cosmic battle, kingship, theophany, lament and theodicy, cosmogony, redemption, wisdom, and order. It is also significant that the mountain or the hilltop was often considered the origin of creation and the dwelling place of the gods (cf. Mount Sinai and Zion in the Old Testament). This is especially illuminating when we consider the power of God descending to Mount Sinai and the Psalms returning so often to the greatness of Mount Zion in Jerusalem.

*Legal writings.* It is likely that Egypt's sense of justice and equilibrium in the individual life as well as the divinity of pharaoh discouraged the need to produce legal codes.[20] The Mesopotamian region, however, had an unpredictable climate paired with instability at its national borders. The constant sense of chaos in life encouraged them to write many law codes and treaties. In this way, law plays a much more explicitly integrated role with wisdom than in Egypt. This is important in that it demonstrates the way kings used their wisdom to enact and

---

[20]Especially in Egypt's Old Kingdom. The first is probably Boccharis from 715 B.C. See Enrique Nardoni, *Rise Up, O Judge: A Study of Justice in the Biblical World*, trans. Sean Charles Martin (Peabody, Mass.: Hendrickson, 2004), p. 21.

enforce laws that would maintain social and creational order for the gods—what the Old Testament refers to as "peace" (shalom) and "justice and righteousness" (cf. Ps 33:4-5; Prov 1:3).

In sum, the "minds" in ancient Egypt and Mesopotamia linked gods, kings, creation, wisdom and order together. Humanity is joined with the gods and nature, and wisdom serves as the key both to survival and to flourishing. Kings, sages and parents all bring wisdom from the gods to humanity.[21] Through many generations of retelling these stories, these cultures viewed themselves as living within one integral matrix of life, work and worship.

## WISDOM AND WORLDVIEW IN ISRAEL

Israel's relationship with her Egyptian and Mesopotamian neighbors is indisputable. She traveled with them, lived with them, fought with them, hosted them and traded economic goods with them. They studied in one another's schools and heard one another's stories.

In other words, while Israel's poetic and wisdom writings look very much like those of her neighbors, the places where they differ are the most important. Israel's unique transformation of these ancient forms of literature highlights the distinctiveness of her theology, religion, worldview, politics and ethics. Although the main chapters of this book are devoted to investigation, reflection and integration of these distinctive aspects of Israel's wisdom, it will help us here to outline the major contours of Israel's social, religious and political ways of life.

Most importantly, Israel's wisdom begins with "the fear of Yahweh" (Prov 1:7; 9:10; cf. Job 28:28; Eccles 12:13). Israel's monotheism, we argue, not only sets apart her wisdom but also her whole way of life. Wisdom has a singular origin and a single, religious path. For this reason, the idea of chaos takes on a different sense than in Egypt or Mesopotamia. No longer is chaos an all-powerful, fearful thing in itself or something caught up in some battle between competing gods; rather, chaos is understood as the mysterious parts of the world, which are fully within the power and control of the one and only wise God. Rolf

---

[21]See Richard J. Clifford, *The Wisdom Literature* (Nashville: Abingdon, 1998), p. 26.

**Table 2.2**

|  | ANE Wisdom | Israelite Wisdom |
|---|---|---|
| Divinity | Henotheism—many gods, often in competition; pantheism—gods are nature or are within nature and worshiped as such | Monotheism—only one God; monolatry—worshiping only that God |
| View of Creation as nature | Consubstantialism and naturalism—all is one | God set apart from all reality |
| View of Creation as Act | Chaotic, violent, sexual, purposeless | Ordered and purposeful. A generous Creator shares his creative rights with humanity |
| King | Usually has divine status, origin of law and wisdom, omnipotent | Rules on Yahweh's behalf, under Yahweh's law and wisdom. A humble exemplar for the people |
| Wisdom | Tremendous cultural variety; strong humanistic overtones | Begins with fear of Yahweh, ethical, religious |
| Sexuality | Fertility cults, tied to pagan myths, not monogamous | Grounded in creation, free but monogamous[a] |

[a]Certainly polygamy appears to be tolerated in the OT, but the vision from creation in Genesis, the laws against adultery, and the failures of Israel's polygamous patriarchs and kings seems to point to an ideal of monogamy.

Knierim notes that this view of the world "let Israel understand both the mystery of the world as creation at home in Yahweh and the meaning of Israel itself as the witness to this fact."[22] Israel's religious view of wisdom thus critiqued the naturalism and pantheism of her neighbors by encouraging lives of faith and obedience that testified to Yahweh as the one true God of all.

Monotheism also provides for new views of sexuality and violence. Whereas other ancient creation myths combine various degrees of chaos, sexuality and divine battles,[23] Hebrew wisdom is an act of a single God

---

[22]Rolf P. Knierim, *The Task of Old Testament Theology* (Grand Rapids: Eerdmans, 1995), p. 205.
[23]See Paul Ricoeur, *The Symbolism of Evil* (Boston: Beacon, 1967), especially pp. 161-74.

bringing the world from chaos to order. Sexuality is a gift to humans as they take up roles as fruit-producing co-creators under Yahweh.

Yahweh is not only the sole creator in Israel's wisdom, he is also the supreme ruler. Israel's king is never favorably portrayed as the source of law, wisdom or of ultimate authority. Rather, kings and judges are constrained to rule under the wisdom and authority of Yahweh, the true king of Israel (Ps 72:1-2; Prov 16:11-15).

These distinctive features in Israel's wisdom are not always absolute; many cultures viewed wisdom as ethical and religious. However, the combination of these features helps us to appreciate how they frame Israel's religion, worship and wisdom within a unique worldview. Table 2.2 summarizes Israel's particular worldview.

With these distinctions in mind, it becomes clear that the Old Testament wisdom books set out to frame a worldview for Israel—one grounded in the theology of Genesis and the law. God intended these creative and highly memorable writings to become a way of life for his people.

## RECOMMENDED READING

Brown, William P. "*Creatio Corporis* and the Rhetoric of Defense in Job 10 and Psalm 139." In *God Who Creates*, ed. William P. Brown and S. Dean McBride, pp. 107-24. Grand Rapids: Eerdmans, 2000.

Clifford, Richard J. "The Hebrew Scriptures and the Theology of Creation." *Theological Studies* 46 (1985): 507-23.

Day, John, Robert P. Gordon and H. G. M. Williamson, eds. *Wisdom in Ancient Israel*. Cambridge: Cambridge University Press, 1995.

Frankfort, Henri, H. A. Frankfort, John A. Wilson, Thorkild Jacobsen and William Irwin. *The Intellectual Adventure of Ancient Man*. Chicago: University of Chicago Press, 1946.

Keel, Othmar. *The Symbolism of the Biblical World: Ancient Near Eastern Iconography and The Book of Psalms*. New York: Seabury, 1978.

Simkins, Ronald A. *Creator and Creation: Nature in the Worldview of Ancient Israel*. Peabody, Mass.: Hendrickson, 1994.

# 3

# The Poetry of Wisdom
# and the Wisdom of Poetry

*But the whole question . . . is one of knowing whether wisdom, if it is*
*taken as something more than a mere catalogue of utilitarian guidelines*
*and techniques, can take root anywhere but in the same soil from*
*which poetry originates and draws its nourishment.*

—GABRIEL MARCEL, *TRAGIC WISDOM AND BEYOND*

*The poet affirms and collaborates in the formality of the Creation. This I*
*think is a matter of supreme, and mostly unacknowledged, importance.*
*A poem reminds us also of the spiritual elation that we call*
*"inspiration" or "gift."* . . . *Hence, it reminds us of love.*
*It is amateur's work, lover's work.*

—WENDELL BERRY, "THE RESPONSIBILITY OF THE POET"

## A PLEA FOR POETRY

Poetry, like wisdom, has a rich, renewing, healing and unifying power,
which largely goes unnoticed or unappreciated today. Aside from a few
select psalms, few of us give much attention to biblical poetry. It might
surprise readers to realize just how much of the Old Testament is written in poetry. We encounter it in unexpected places such as small passages in Genesis, Exodus and Deuteronomy, and in some lengthier

prayers in Samuel.[1] In other places it dominates. Poetry is the overriding form of writing in the Major and Minor Prophets, from Isaiah to Malachi, and it is used almost exclusively in what we call the "poetic" books of the Bible: Job, Psalms, Proverbs, Ecclesiastes,[2] Song of Songs and Lamentations. All told, the massive corpus of poetry in the Old Testament greatly exceeds all of the writings of the New Testament, which, incidentally, has its own share of poetry in places like John 1, Hebrews 1, Philippians 2, Revelation and elsewhere. Clearly, to read and interpret the Bible we must understand what poetry is and how it functions.

What then is poetry? Consider the famous aphorism from Samuel Taylor Coleridge:

> Prose,—words in their best order;
> Poetry,—the best words in the best order.

Coleridge's distinction celebrates the human ability to innovate and create with language. In a collected anthology, editor Helen Vendler offers a similar introduction to poetry as a blend of the imagination and the "mastery of language."[3] Terry Eagleton meanwhile defines a poem as "a fictional, verbally inventive moral statement, in which it is the author, rather than the printer or word processor, who decides where the lines should end."[4]

Such definitions are helpful and true as far as they go. Poetry *does* contain a masterful mix of imagination and language, but historically it has played a far more significant cultural role. Historically poetry may precede literacy. The oldest surviving poem is the epic of Gilgamesh, from the fourth millennium B.C. in Sumer (in Iraq/Mesopotamia). The oldest love poem, found on a clay tablet now known as *Istanbul #2461*,

---

[1]As Robert Alter, *The World of Biblical Literature* (London: SPCK, 1992), p. 172, notes, "It is only in our century that scholars have begun to realize to what extent the prose narratives of the Bible are studded with brief verse inserts, usually at dramatically justified or otherwise significant junctures in the stories."

[2]As we will see in our examination of Ecclesiastes, there is no agreement about how much of it is prose or poetry.

[3]Helen Vendler, *Poems, Poets, Poetry: An Introduction and Anthology* (Boston: Bedford, 1997), p. ix.

[4]Terry Eagleton, *How to Read a Poem* (Oxford: Blackwell, 2007), p. 25.

was also a Sumerian poem. It was recited by a bride of the Sumerian king Shu-Sin, who ruled from 2037-2029 B.C. The oldest epic poetry besides the epic of Gilgamesh are the Greek epics the *Iliad* and the *Odyssey* and the Indian Sanskrit epics *Ramayana* and *Mahabharata*.

One only has to reflect on the significance of the *Iliad* and the *Odyssey* to realize that historically poetry was far more influential then than it is today. "If you were giving a compliment to an ancient Greek, the highest praise possible was to compare him or her to Homer."[5] Today we might compare someone to a rock star or great intellectual or sportsman, but it is unimaginable that we would reach for the name of a contemporary poet to provide the highest praise possible. Indeed, many of us probably have trouble even naming five major poets of our day. This is because poetry has become part of high art, an elite activity for the contemplation of a privileged few.

As we will see below, such views—though recent in their emergence on the historical scene—significantly inhibit our reading of the Bible and our understanding of life and language before the living God. Below we will trace some formative periods in the history of poetics so that we can see how the institution of high art emerged and how to escape from it.

## A HISTORY OF POETRY

Perhaps not surprisingly there is no clear line between poetry and prose. In fact, the desire to make a sharp distinction is a very recent convention.[6] But how did we get to that point? As we noted above, poetry originated very early. Among the Greek philosophers, views of poetry varied. Plato was suspicious of the arts. Because of their imitative function he thought they were dangerous because they took one further away from the realm of ideas and forms, where truth was located. Aristotle had a more positive attitude toward poetry, and in his *Poetics* (335 B.C.) he describes the three genres of poetry—the epic, comic and

---

[5]Charlotte Higgins, *It's All Greek to Me* (London: Short Books, 2008), p. 21. See Eagleton, *How to Read a Poem*, pp. 18-41.
[6]See Charles Taylor, "Language and Human Nature," in *Human Agency and Language: Philosophical Papers 1* (Cambridge: Cambridge University Press, 1985), p. 233.

tragic—and develops rules to distinguish the highest-quality poetry of each genre. Aristotle's analysis of poetry remains important today, but he was also the father of logic and thus sowed the seeds for the triumph of logical propositions over poetry, seeds that eventually came to fruition in the Enlightenment.

From the time of Greek and Roman literature until the Enlightenment (400 B.C.–A.D. 1700) the writing in most cultures spanned a broad spectrum of forms in which poetic and prose styles overlap. Robert Alter says, "In fact, it is rare to find anywhere a poetic style that does not bear some relation to the literary prose of the same culture; rather it turns out in many instances that literary prose is influenced by contemporary or antecedent poetry in the same language, often seeking knowingly or unwittingly to achieve for itself a quasi-poetic status without the formal constraints of verse."[7] The distinction between the prose and verse can only be limited to a broad, gray area.

Furthermore, poetry in this time was written almost exclusively from a religious perspective. Writings and works of art were often produced anonymously so as not to draw attention to the artist. For almost two thousand years poetry played a central role in the life and worship of the church: in the church fathers, the medieval church, the mystics, the Eastern Church, the Celtic and Welsh churches and their poets, the Christian renaissance and the Anglican divines. For them, the poetry of the Bible and of their own writings served as materials for memorization; a model for hymn writing, arts and artisanship; and an impetus for obedient Christian living. As far as we can tell, debates about the formal systems in poetic lines are almost nonexistent until at least the Renaissance if not the nineteenth-century age of aesthetics.[8]

The scientific revolution and the Enlightenment sparked the beginning of a long movement, going back to Aristotle, which elevates reason and science over literature, philosophy and religion. Sir Philip Sydney's *Defense of Poetry* in the late sixteenth century is evidence of the efforts during the Renaissance to uphold the cultural importance of the arts against these trends. He says that those who

---

[7]See Robert Alter, *The Art of Biblical Poetry* (New York: Basic, 1985), pp. 6-7.
[8]See ibid., pp. x-xi.

seek to deface that which, in the noblest nations and languages that are known, hath been the first light-giver to ignorance and first nurse, whose milk by little and little enabled them to feed afterwards of tougher knowledges. And will they now play the hedgehog that, being received into the den, drave out his host? Or rather the vipers, that with their birth kill their parents?[9]

Sydney points out the absurdity of the exclusive new turn to science and naturalism in the search for meaning. European culture had gained its position at the head of the world over the course of a thousand years of Christian humanist tradition. Children were taught religion, litera-ture, politics, ethics and logic as part of a balanced worldview. Poetics has its own role in giving us a nuanced understanding of people, lan-guage and culture.

Sydney's voice sinks into the background in this new modern age, where knowledge gained through scientific theory is elevated over knowl-edge gained through art and poetry. In biblical studies the fruit of the Enlightenment legacy was the historical-critical method of interpreting the Bible. This has been a major attempt to read the Bible "scientifically." As Alter notes, an effect of the historical-critical method has been to detract from the poetic form of much of the Old Testament:

> The critical-historical investigation of Scripture, in the process of pro-viding genuine illumination for much that was long obscure, has tacitly assumed a kind of Lockean distinction between primary and secondary qualities of the Bible. . . . The literary features of the text . . . have by and large been relegated to the status of secondary qualities, suitable mainly for discussion in the effusive appreciations of aesthetes and ama-teurs, but hardly worthy as objects of scholarship.[10]

During this time, Alexander Baumgarten (1714-1762) emerged as the author of a new modern "aesthetic" theory that attempted to recon-nect rational knowledge with art; he argued that art contributed to ra-tional knowledge by providing a sensible image of perfection.[11] Im-

---

[9]Sir Philip Sidney, *A Defence of Poetry*, ed. J. A. Van Dorsten (New York: Oxford University Press, 1991), p. 18.

[10]Alter, *World of Biblical Literature*, p. 26.

[11]"Aesthetic," in Howard Caygill, *A Kant Dictionary* (Oxford: Blackwell, 1995), p. 53.

manuel Kant (1724-1804) made a judgment of taste central to his aesthetic: "it is a judgment that pleases 'apart from any interest.' . . . In a judgment that something is beautiful, the subject is neither charmed by the object . . . nor instructed by its perfection."[12]

The history of aesthetics is complex, and we cannot explore it in any detail here. Suffice it to say that the disinterestedness central to Kant's aesthetic is at the heart of the development of the institution of high art. As Jerome Stolnitz says,

> We cannot understand modern aesthetic theory unless we understand the concept of "disinterestedness." . . . It is, in our time, so much a common place that the work of art and the aesthetic object generally is "autonomous" and "self-contained," and must be apprehended as such, that we have to catch ourselves up. This has not always been a common place. Indeed throughout most of the history of Western art, this notion would have seemed not so much false as incomprehensible. During these periods the values of art are iconic or otherwise cognitive, or moral, or social, with nothing left over that art can call its own. To repudiate this conception of art is "the most tremendous change . . . in the whole history of art."[13]

The problem with rationalism that Baumgarten experienced became pronounced in the Romantic period of the nineteenth century. The Romantics reacted to the disenchantment of the world resulting from an overemphasis on reason by looking to the arts to reenchant the world.[14] This is the age of Mozart, Wordsworth, Emerson and Darwin and the rapid shifts in culture their works produced. Art began to matter solely for the sake of beauty and form and the genius of the artist. Crucially, the Romantic reaction remained within the human-centered framework of the Enlightenment humanism. Thus poetry, in the Romantic age, gradually lost its role of uniting the world before a Creator and instead became a means to glorify humans as the ultimate creators

---

[12]Ibid., p. 55.

[13]Jerome Stolnitz, "On the Origins of 'Aesthetic Disinterestedness,'" *Journal of Aesthetics and Art Criticism* 20, no. 2 (1961): 131-43, quoted in Nicholas Wolterstorff, *Art in Action* (Grand Rapids: Eerdmans, 1980), p. 34.

[14]See Charles Taylor, *A Secular Age* (Cambridge, Mass.: Belknap Press of Harvard University Press, 2007), pp. 352-61.

within nature. As Charles Taylor says of this time,

> In the Romantic period, artistic creation comes to be the highest do-
> main of human activity.
>
> If we reach our highest goal through art and the aesthetic, then this
> goal, it would appear, must be immanent. It would represent an alterna-
> tive to the love of God as a way of transcending moralism. But things
> are not so simple. God is not excluded. . . . The important change is that
> this issue must now remain open. This is what marks us off from earlier
> times. In pre-modern times, the beauty of art was understood in terms
> of mimesis: the imitation of reality which was set in an ordered cosmos,
> with its levels of being, which was further understood as God's creation.
> . . . It went without saying that great art refers us to the correspon-
> dences, to the order of being, to sacred history. With the fading of these
> backgrounds, with the coming of a buffered self, for whom this larger,
> spiritual environment was no longer a matter of untheorized experience
> . . . we have the growth of what I have been calling, following Wasser-
> man, "subtler languages." . . .
>
> These languages function, have power, move us, but without having
> to identify their ontic commitments. "Absolute" music expresses being
> moved by what is powerful and deep, but does not need to identify where
> this is to be found, whether in heaven, or on earth, or in the depths of our
> own being—or even whether these alternatives are exclusive.
>
> And this is what offers a place to go for modern unbelief. As a re-
> sponse to the inadequacies of moralism, the missing goal can be identi-
> fied with the experience of beauty, in the realm of the aesthetic. But this
> is now unhooked from the ordered cosmos and/or the divine. [15]

The Romantic defense of poetry in the nineteenth century had been
grounded in the need to balance the growing hegemony of science in
Western culture. Although the Romantics had moved away from what
they saw as the naiveté of a religious and enchanted world, they still
believed that both science *and* the arts were necessary to get in touch
with truth and reality. This high view of art and poetry made it very
fragile; what if poetry was to become flattened and lose its power?[16]

---

[15]Ibid, pp. 359-60.
[16]See ibid., pp. 748-61.

And, indeed, this confident search for meaning has been undermined in the twentieth century. From Friedrich Nietzsche, William James and John Dewey at the beginning of the century to Jacques Derrida, Michel Foucault and Richard Rorty at its end, the search for truth and reality, in poetry and art as well as in science, are exchanged for pragmatism or the play of nihilism. Most postmodern literary critics abandon the search for what a text means and seek instead to show either that it has no meaning or that its meaning is whatever we want it to be.[17]

Out of this increasingly fragmented world arise the definitions of poetry cited in this chapter's introduction: poetry is valued for the power of its language: either to be contemplated or to be critiqued and judged, but rarely to be connected to a deeper theology or spiritual reality. What has been lost is a concern for what Nicholas Wolterstorff calls the original "flux of purposes and uses"[18] poetry had throughout most of history. Amid the fragmentation of postmodernism, art either remains confined to the institutions of high art for disinterested contemplation or reduced to pop art.

In the West, poetry in particular has become a marginal pursuit among the populace and a hobby among the elite. Local bookshops retain poetry sections, but they are small and marginal, symbolic of the role of poetry in our cultures today. It is hard to imagine schools in which poetry would be seen as an indispensable and major part of the curriculum. And in our churches we have lost the practice of memorizing Scripture, a practice for which poetry is particularly well-suited. Of course we still sing hymns and choruses, but we would be surprised if our church held a songwriting class with a view to using the best new songs in our worship. And yet in the Bible, poetry virtually dominates the Old Testament "curriculum." The poetry of the Bible was often written by and for the lower classes, grounded in a strong belief in the spiritual nature of truth and meaning. It served to inspire faith and action in its readers. To understand ancient poetry, therefore, we must set aside modern notions of art and retrieve its original functions. Essen-

---

[17]See Roger Lundin, *Believing Again: Doubt and Faith in a Secular Age* (Grand Rapids: Eerdmans, 2009), pp. 61-99.
[18]See Wolterstorff, *Art in Action.*

tially, we need a Christian aesthetic for our day if we are to plumb the resources of Old Testament wisdom. A Christian aesthetic will help us understand Old Testament wisdom's preference for poetry, and at the same time, a rich, thick analysis of Old Testament wisdom will help us recover a Christian aesthetic. Fortunately, some good work has been done on a Christian aesthetic,[19] and in what follows we will draw in particular on the fertile work of Nicholas Wolterstorff.

## POETRY FOR LIFE

Poetry and art can evoke contemplation, not least of God. This is the value of the institutions of high art like museums; they provide a comfortable space in which to slowly explore works of art. But inspiring contemplation is only one of the functions of poetry, and, especially in our day, it is the many other functions of poetry that need to be recovered. Witnessing the power of ancient art, the poet Rainer Maria Rilke said that it leads one to conclude that "you must change your life."[20] Similarly, Wolterstorff says that art's power confronts us and prepares us for action; it exists not for escape from the world into contemplation—as is the growing trend with modern art—but to move us to act in the world.[21] Because biblical poetry was written far from the critical or analytical impulses of modern art, we must reorient ourselves to its purposes and uses within ancient Israel as it evoked a world "charged with the grandeur of God" and invited readers and listeners to make that world their own.

Wolterstorff's reflections on the functions of art and poetry in human cultures are particularly helpful to us in this process of reorientation. He suggests that "world-projection" is the "most pervasive and

---

[19]See, e.g., Calvin Seerveld, *A Christian Critique of Art and Literature* (Toronto: Tuppence Press, 1995); idem, *Rainbows for a Fallen World: Aesthetic Life and Artistic Task* (Toronto: Tuppence Press, 1980); idem, *Bearing Fresh Olive Leaves* (Toronto: Tuppence Press, 2000); Craig Bartholomew, ed., *In the Fields of the Lord: A Seerveld Reader* (Carlisle, U.K.: Piquant, 2000); Michael Edwards, *Towards a Christian Poetics* (London: Macmillan, 1984); Nicholas Wolterstorff, *Works and Worlds of Art* (New York: Oxford University Press, 1980); idem, *Art in Action*.

[20]Quoted in Mary Rose O'Reilly, *The Garden at Night: Burnout and Breakdown in the Teaching Life* (Portsmouth, N.H.: Heinemann, 2005), p. 44.

[21]Wolterstorff, *Art in Action*, pp. 4-5.

important of the actions that artists perform by means of their artifacts."[22] "World-projection" is a metaphor for the way we see the world and discern its meaning and truth. Poets are writers who create images, fiction or even creative retellings of history to influence our perspective or point of view. Wolterstorff lists several such points of view that we encounter in art:

A world with varying degrees of reliability or unreliability,

A presentation of the temporal or time-related dimensions of the world,

A presentation of knowledge or ignorance,

A focus on something particular in the world,

An evaluation and exhibition of attitudes and values toward the world,

A presentation of a symbolic or allusive character in the world, and

An expression of beliefs and attitudes about our actual world.[23]

As we read and see the world through the artist's lens, we are challenged to change our life in one way or another. Wolterstorff lists seven functions of art that artists often aim to achieve in their audience:

1. a confirmation of truth, religion or our national history.

2. an illumination, typically a characteristic of modern, higher art

3. an alteration of our convictions or confirmation of them to be true based on the question of reliability in the art

4. in some way to provoke or move our emotions

5. modeling a certain belief or set of behaviors

6. communicating a message

7. providing consolation[24]

While this is an overview of actions in art in general, it gets at the many actions poetry can perform. This list is especially helpful for the

---

[22]Ibid., p. 122.
[23]Ibid., pp. 139-44.
[24]Ibid., pp. 144-50.

way it allows Old Testament poetry come to life in our own reading. The remaining chapters of this book will draw this out in detail, but it will help us a good deal to consider Old Testament wisdom books in this language of action and world-projection that we have just reviewed.

## OLD TESTAMENT WISDOM AS ACTION-FORMING POETRY

Proverbs, Job and Ecclesiastes are all uniquely designed to shape the worldview and behavior (theology and life) of their readers. What are we to make of their artistry? We should first recognize that, although all ancient religious poetry has this formative ability, biblical poetry has a unique way of operating.[25] Harold Fisch argues that Old Testament poetry always creates its point of view in distinct opposition to the cultures and religions of Israel's ancient neighbors. Thus, while it shares the aesthetic traits of beauty, form, plot and rhythm of the best ancient Near Eastern writing, its use and purpose are what he calls "unepic" and "anti-literature" by comparison.[26] While this may overstate the case, the insight that Hebrew poetry sought to oppose competing worldviews is no less valid.

But Old Testament poetry is not simply a cultural critique. It also projects a world. Alter expresses this character of Old Testament poetry well:

> The covenantal urgency of the biblical authors impelled them on a bold and finally impossible project: they sought to use literature to go irrevocably beyond itself, but, being writers of genius enamored, as writers always are, with how they could tap the endless resources of their medium, they could not avoid producing in their work an enchanting affirmation of the free-playing logic of literary expression.[27]

Indeed, the "covenantal urgency" of evoking a world awash with God should not be seen as being in tension with the delight of literary play. If we remember that covenant is rooted in creation and concerned

---

[25]Jewish literary scholars have done the best work on the poetics of the OT. On the poetics of OT narrative, Meir Sternberg, *The Poetics of Hebrew Narrative* (Bloomington: Indiana University Press, 1987), is in a class of its own. The best work on the poetics of OT poetry is Alter, *Art of Biblical Poetry.*

[26]Harold Fisch, *Poetry with a Purpose: Biblical Poetics and Interpretation* (Bloomington: Indiana University Press, 1988).

[27]Alter, *World of Biblical Literature*, p. 46. For Alter's critique of Fisch, see pp. 28-46.

with the recovery of God's purposes with creation, any such tension is undermined. The delight of literary play amid the urgency of a world-view aflame with a sense of God is entirely congruent.

Old Testament poetry and especially Old Testament wisdom evoke a world charged with God's grandeur as the Creator and redeemer. In the process of evoking this world, Old Testament wisdom invites, cajoles and even commands us to live our lives consciously in this world. Biblical poetry is never poetry for poetry's sake. Yet it is still aesthetic and to be savored as such. Its creativity with words, sounds and images gives it its evocative and memorable powers. All of these wisdom books naturally became a part of the traditions in the home, the community and at festival gatherings. Each book thus generated a formative presence in the cultural consciousness of God's people. In sum, we simply will not hear God's address through Old Testament wisdom if we fail to attend closely to its poetic character. Here is a brief look at each of the books studied in the following chapters.

***Proverbs.*** Proverbs 1–9 is a highly symbolic collection of sayings from two very different sources: Woman Wisdom and the parents of a maturing son. The son is a realistic but fictional character entering the actual world adults encounter day to day. Woman Wisdom, however, is a fictional and cosmic character who, as wisdom personified, beckons the son to desire her ways and paths. This may be a complex way of getting at what's going on in all of the imagery, but it alerts us to the great power of biblical art. The mysterious woman character creates the symbolic and allusive points of view introduced above. The point is not for the young man to believe that this woman is a human; rather, he is drawn to make the theological and experiential connections between God's created purpose and the world he will soon enter as an adult. The woman's cosmic, feminine character attaches urgency and emotion to the simple actions of life in this world, for they will be played out before God within the deep, mysterious, cosmic order he has formed.

Furthermore, Alters says that "in Proverbs, didactic points are frequently made through sharp thrusts of wit in the metaphors."[28] An

---

[28]Robert Alter, *The Book of Psalms: A Translation with Commentary* (New York: Norton, 2007), p. xxiv.

example of this is the two houses of Proverbs 9. Like Lady Wisdom, Dame Folly also calls out to passersby, offering wisdom and feasting. But there is a sting in her tale! Her guests are the dead, those in the depths of Sheol. In this way, Proverbs 1–9 aims to instruct its readers in the urgency and ultimacy of wisdom before moving on to more advanced instruction in Proverbs 10–31.

Proverbs 10–29 moves away from this cosmic imagery to a collection of proverbial sayings. These are wisdom for daily life. The poetry and pithiness of these sayings make them memorable, while their seemingly random arrangement mimics actual life in the world[29]—the way we move almost unpredictably from one event and its set of decisions to the next. The first nine chapters prepared us for the point of view essential to living this mundane life: we must constantly refresh our belief in God's eternal and cosmic design for the world, no matter how tragic, mysterious or random it may seem to us. The proverbial form of Proverbs 10–29 is particularly suited to the particularities of daily life and the challenge they present to actually living wisdom.

Catching a vision of a world aflame with God is one thing; incarnating the vision can be quite another. But how wonderful if we can incarnate the vision! And this is what we find in the hymn of Proverbs 31: a carefully crafted song celebrating the life of a woman who did succeed in practicing wisdom in her daily life. Poetic form is thus a central component to taking the reader of Proverbs on the journey from the ABCs of wisdom to the tough practical realities of life and through to a celebration of a life well lived.

*Job.* Job is poetry fitted to a story. The first two chapters and the last 11 verses (Job 1:1–3:1 and Job 42:7-17) are written in prose. But even here the language is intensified in a way that is similar to poetry. Their purpose is to set up the story in a way that echoes familiar Old Testament images of justice, righteousness, and our legal standing before God and creation. The cosmic images of the Satan (accuser) and the heavenly courts in these chapters, while like Proverbs in their symbolic

---

[29]Once proverbs are "reduced" to writing, it is inevitable that literary connections develop between them, whether intended by the author or not. See, for example, Raymond van Leeuwen, *Context and Meaning in Proverbs 25–27*, SBLDS 96 (Atlanta: Scholars Press, 1988).

and allusive power, serve instead to emphasize the ambiguity and mystery in God's order rather than strong optimism experienced in reading Proverbs 1–9. The bulk of the story (Job 3:2–42:6) is written entirely in poetry that plays on the story formed in the prose introduction.

And the story is one of excruciating suffering, the depths of which only poetry can evoke. Unlike the Psalter, which draws on a stock of traditional language for worship, Job is surprisingly inventive in its use of language.[30] "Job makes constant disruptive departures in the images he uses, in the extraordinary muscularity of his language line after line. The poetry Job speaks is an instrument forged to sound the uttermost depths of suffering, and so he adopts movements of intensification to focus in on this anguish."[31] The role of Job's friends is illuminated by their poetic speech; in contrast to Job they string together "beautifully polished clichés (sometimes virtually a parody of the poetry of Proverbs and Psalms)."[32]

And then, of course, there are God's speeches. They share the intensity of Job's speeches, but whereas Job's words are inwardly focused and egocentric, God's words

> carry us back and forth through the pulsating vital movements of the whole created world. The culmination of the poem God speaks is not a cry of self or a dream of self snuffed out but the terrible beauty of the Leviathan, on the uncanny border between zoology and mythology, where what is fierce and strange, beyond the ken and conquest of man, is the climactic manifestation of a splendidly providential creation that merely anthropocentric notions cannot grasp.[33]

The extraordinary poem in Job 28 is thought by many scholars to be a late addition to Job because of its assured content that wisdom can be found—but only in God—and its fitting, symmetrical style. Attention to poetic form is again helpful here. Job 28 is jarring in its context, but precisely because it is meant to be. The symmetry, which speaks of closure, comes amid Job's terrible struggles for meaning and some degree of closure to his suffering. But where is this to be found and how? Job 28

---

[30]Alter, *Book of Psalms*, p. xxiv.
[31]Alter, *World of Biblical Literature*, p. 188.
[32]Ibid.
[33]Ibid., p. 189.

anticipates God's speech, which is to come, but without giving away its content. It assures the reader that there is a way through this terrible suffering, but it is a path that God alone knows. And thus the reader, like Job and anyone amid suffering, must wait to see how God manifests himself. Little wonder that Alter describes Job as "in many respects the most astonishing poetic achievement in the biblical corpus."[34]

***Ecclesiastes.*** Ecclesiastes is more like Job than Proverbs: it guides readers through alternative perspectives on meaning, truth and reality amid its central character's desperate struggle for meaning in life. An introductory narrator presents us with the autobiography of another character with the unusual title "Qohelet." Qohelet is never given a name, only a title, though we have some signs that he might be Solomon the king. Qohelet's words are extremely complex and just as elusive as his identity but are studded with repetitions of signs on how one might resolve the struggle. The poetry, with its characteristic intensification, mirrors the intensity of Qohelet's struggle. In search of some sense of meaning and reliability in the narration, we naturally pose questions of clarification: Who is Qohelet? What is Qohelet saying? Who is the narrator? What is he telling us about Qohelet? How are these related? We will argue in future chapters that the book gradually leads us to understand these questions and how they communicate an overall message. In all this the poetic character of Ecclesiastes serves as a powerful enactment of the struggle involved in coming to terms with meaning in a broken world.

## THE TECHNIQUES OF HEBREW POETRY

Having considered the history of poetry and the poetics of the wisdom books, we will now examine the techniques or mechanics of ancient Hebrew poetry. However, a word of caution is necessary. As Umberto Eco perceptively notes,

> Poetics becomes entangled in a paradox; in trying to capture the essence of poetry it misses its most essential feature, namely, its uniqueness and the variability of its manifestations.

---

[34]Ibid., p. 188.

> Every Poetics that proposes ideal structures, and chooses to ignore the particularities specific to the individual works is always in the end a theory of the works that the theorist judges best.[35]

There is considerable value in becoming aware of the smorgasbord of techniques available to the Old Testament poet, but we must always subordinate these to the actual poetry we are reading. Poetry specializes in bending rules to suit its purposes, and we will miss the power of Old Testament poetry if we only focus on techniques.

Michael Travers, among other scholars, discerns the three distinct features of Hebrew poetry as parallelism, terseness and figures of speech.[36] We will add a fourth, poetic structures, to complete our toolset for exploring the poetry of the Old Testament.

*Parallelism.* Scholars almost unanimously agree that parallelism is the surest mark of Hebrew poetry. Simply put, parallelism is a dynamic relationship between two or more lines of poetry. In the Old Testament, parallelism can be carried out for several lines in a row and involve various levels of parallels between words, phrases and whole sentences. Here are a few examples.

**Psalm 24:1**
The *earth* is Yahweh's
    and *the fullness thereof,*
the *world*
    and *all those who dwell in it.*

**Deuteronomy 32:30**
How could *one*
    *pursue a thousand?*
And *two*
    *put a myriad to flight?*

**Proverbs 10:5**
The *one who gathers* in summer

---

[35]Umberto Eco, "The *Poetics* and Us," in *On Literature* (Orlando: Harcourt, 2002), p. 241.
[36]See Michael E. Travers, "Poetry in the Bible," in *Dictionary for Theological Interpretation of the Bible,* ed. Kevin J. Vanhoozer, Craig G. Bartholomew, Daniel J. Treier and N. T. Wright (Grand Rapids: Baker Academic, 2005), p. 595.

is a *wise son*;
The *one who sleeps* in harvest
is a *shameful son*.

Notice that each of these parallel verses achieves its message in different ways: sometimes reinforcing, sometimes comparing and other times contradicting. Robert Lowth, writing in the eighteenth century, was the first to suggest three types of parallelism: synonymous, antithetic and synthetic.[37] These divisions stood for some time but gradually gave way to the reality that the categories are too narrow to capture every parallel. James Kugel was perhaps the first of several scholars to suggest expanding the categories to a simpler convention "A, and what's more, B."[38] In other words, the stress is on the addition—the "more"—that line B adds to the parallel. Alter's work in the *Art of Biblical Poetry*, published in 1985, takes poetic studies in this same direction. Adele Berlin, meanwhile, also builds on Lowth, as she demonstrates how parallelism functions at all levels of language and discourse. She thus reminds us that the B line can also send us back to an expanded understanding of line A.[39]

The work of these three major scholars moves us very close to capturing the extraordinary nuance that is achieved between the poetic words, clauses and lines. In fact, Hebrew poetry may include two, three, or more lines and have a number of effects that result from their parallel structure and word choices. Michael Fox has very recently shown that there can even be a "disjunctive" type of parallel, which is technically a "violation" of parallelism—that is, at least at first. "Disjointed parallelism leaves a gap between the lines and invites the reader to fill it," often enriching the meaning of each saying.[40]

In sum, as readers, we have to be prepared to listen and look for the ways the text brings about a heightened or intensified meaning be-

---

[37]Robert Lowth, *Lectures on the Sacred Poetry of the Hebrews* (Whitefish, Mont.: Kessinger, 2004). Available online at <http://books.google.com/books?id=V0AAAAAAYAAJ&dq=lectures%20on%20the%20sacred%20poetry%20of%20the%20hebrews%20robert%20lowth&pg=PP1#v=onepage&q&f=false> (accessed May 13, 2010).

[38]James L. Kugel, *The Idea of Biblical Poetry: Parallelism and its History* (New Haven: Yale University Press, 1981), pp. 1-58.

[39]Adele Berlin, *The Dynamics of Biblical Parallelism* (Grand Rapids: Eerdmans, 2008).

[40]Michael V. Fox, *Proverbs 10–31*, Anchor Yale Bible (New Haven: Yale University Press, 2009), p. 494.

tween the lines. If poetry were predictable or reducible to a system, it would not be poetry.

As a final note on parallelism, Fox has also demonstrated that many proverbs in the Bible emerge from folk sayings of individual lines, not parallel pairs.[41] We find examples of this throughout the Old Testament; for example: "Wickedness issues from the wicked" (1 Sam 24:13), and, "The fathers have eaten sour grapes and the sons' teeth stand on edge" (Ezek 18:2).[42] We believe this is a helpful nuance to the discussion of technique presented here: parallelism seems to be the *dominant* form of poetic presentation in the Bible, but—if proverbs are essentially poetry—then there are exceptions to the rule.

***Terseness.*** Second, Travers suggests that, as opposed to prose or narrative, poetry usually communicates its message with the briefest and most careful choice of words: "the best words in the best order," as Coleridge said. This helpful insight points us to the way poetry often uses metaphors, figures of speech, images, and rhythm or meter. Ellipsis, or hidden repetition, is a form of terseness where a noun or verb is used once but "distributed" to two or more lines. The two parallels in Genesis 4:23 provide a good example. The first line provides two sets of perfect parallels:

> (1a) Adah and Zillah
>> (2a) Hear my voice
> (1b) Wives of Lamech
>> (2b) Give ear to my speech.

The second line introduces an ellipsis:

> (1a) A man I have killed [*hāragtî*]
>> (2a) For wounding me
> (1b) And a boy (I have killed)
>> (2b) For bruising me.

The verb "I have killed" *(hāragtî)* occurs only in the first line (1a), but it is understood in the second line (2b) by way of ellipsis or distribution. Verbless clauses like this occur frequently in Hebrew poetry. This brevity limits

---

[41]Ibid., p. 485.
[42]Ibid.

the words and sounds surrounding the main idea, thus adding intensity to the parallel structures and making them more memorable in the process.

*Figures of speech.* We have already noted the tendency for poetry to be paralleled and terse. This is usually accomplished through figures of speech. Figures of speech arise from the imaginative use of sounds, images or a combination of the two. Of course, prose is full of figures of speech too, but there is a sense in which poetry just uses a lot more. If we were to list all the different figures of speech, it might go on forever. Here we make note of some of the most important ones.

*Metaphor.* Metaphor is probably the most significant building block in all language and especially in poetry. C. S. Lewis notes, "All language about things other than physical objects is necessarily metaphorical."[43] In fact, many, if not most, of the figures of speech below use or play off the power of metaphor. It is thus essential that readers of poetry understand them well.

Metaphors describe one thing by characterizing it as something else; this includes similes, which use the words "like" and "as" to make a metaphor. Metaphors *vibrate* in their dynamic tension between what is and what is not alike between the two images or objects. When we say, "God is our rock," we are saying something about God's stability, but we are not making him a geological artifact. The movement between the "is" and the "is not" in the comparison stalls us in contemplation of what Paul Ricoeur calls an endless "surplus of meaning." N. T. Wright's use of metaphor to define metaphor is apt indeed: "Metaphor consists in bringing two sets of ideas close together, close enough for a spark to jump, but not too close, so that the spark, in jumping, illuminates for a moment the whole area around, changing perceptions as it does so."[44] Here are some familiar biblical examples:

They waited for me as rain. (Job 29:23)

---

[43]C. S. Lewis, "Is Theology Poetry?" in *The Weight of Glory and Other Addresses*, ed. Walter Hooper (New York: Simon & Schuster, 1996), p. 102. Recent decades have seen an explosion of literature on metaphor and language, including the view that all language is metaphorical. For a useful introduction see Dan R. Stiver, *The Philosophy of Religious Language: Sign, Symbol and Story* (Oxford: Blackwell, 1996), pp. 112-33.

[44]N. T. Wright, *The New Testament and the People of God* (Minneapolis: Fortress, 1992), p. 40.

Yahweh is my Shepherd. (Ps 23:1)

The tongue is also a fire. (Jas 3:6)

*Synecdoche.* This involves referring to a part of something to communicate the whole: "hands and feet" or "the heart" for the whole person.

*Metonymy.* In metonymy, one word is substituted for another that is closely associated: "the White House" for the President and staff.

*Merism.* Merism involves using two terms to convey a single idea: "the knowledge of good and evil" for all knowledge;[45] "night and day" for endless or continual time.

*Personification.* Giving personal characteristics to a concept or to non-human matter is called personification:

Wisdom cries out in the open,
  (She) raises her voice in the market. (Prov 1:20 [note the ellipsis
    here too])

*Paronomasia.* Paronomasia, or puns, use words that sound similar but have different meanings: in English poetry, "son" often plays on "sun."

*Alliteration.* Alliteration is the repetition of a consonantal sound: "beaded bubbles winking at the brim" (Keats).

*Assonance.* Assonance is the repetition of a vowel sound: go with the flow.

**Poetic structures.** As we will observe in the following chapters, poetry also makes use of a range of literary structures, which it combines with its parallel lines. Some examples are inclusio (or inclusion), frame narratives, proverb clusters and proverb poems. Many of these will be discussed in chapters below. We will also discuss the alphabetic acrostic in chapter five. This is where a series of poetic lines are organized by beginning each line with a subsequent letter of the Hebrew alphabet. There are both complete in incomplete acrostics.

The chiasm, another major literary device, requires a little more of an introduction. The word *chiasm* comes from the shape of the Greek litter *chi* which looks like the English *x*. The image is meant to depict the intersection or coming together of two lines. Chiasms are typically

---

[45]We are aware that many uses of this phrase may not be a merism.

represented with letters to depicts the progress of ideas in the lines. A simple example is:

a
    b
        c
    b'
a'

In this example, a and a' and b and b' sit in parallel or antithetical relationship, and c is the place of intersection. One can probably imagine a seemingly infinite number of ways to see a chiasm in a passage or book text, and scholarship in recent centuries seems to have tried them all. As such, the nature of chiasm is highly debated. Questions range from whether the chiasm has to be perfect or intact to how one is supposed to interpret the structure in the search for emphasis and meaning. We cannot begin to attend to all these issues, but we do address some of them in chapters ahead.

Clearly, reading poetry requires attentive looking, listening and imagining. And there will always be limits and grey areas in our search to understand. For one, to see many of these figures of speech and structures (especially paronomasia, alliteration, rhyme, rhythm, assonance, chiasm and acrostic) usually requires knowledge of ancient Hebrew. And even then, ancient Hebrew pronunciation is somewhat of a mystery to us. Rhythm, rhyme and assonance will often be very difficult to gauge.

Still, while it may not be realistic for most readers of the Old Testament to understand the original language, it is helpful to know that many of the senses of the original poetry were embedded in the sounds, feelings and images of another culture. So, rather than relying solely on three broad characteristics of poetry to read and understand these Old Testament texts, we must remember that poetry is an encounter with an imaginative new world of sights, sounds and meaning. As readers, therefore, we must develop prayerful habits of expecting God to speak through the variety and richness of poetic language.

## POETRY IN LIFE

At the outset of this chapter we quoted the Catholic philosopher Gabriel Marcel, who poses the question as to whether the wisdom we so need can take root anywhere else than in the soil from which poetry draws its nourishment. Wisdom, as we have seen, comes from God, and certainly this is the soil from which biblical poetry draws its nourishment. But perhaps we can reframe the question by asking: is there something about the poetic form that makes it particularly useful for evoking wisdom?

We do not wish to elevate poetry above other forms of biblical literature, but God has chosen to use poetry in particular to instruct us about the paths of wisdom; and in this concluding section we reflect on why poetry is so fitting for this task.

Poetry, we suggest, is uniquely able to evoke wonder. We marvel at the power and diversity of God's creation. We also stand in awe that God has charged this world with his presence and that he has made us in his image as participants in his work to bring about the full potential of his designs. Poetry thus restores the connections between the mind, the nature of being human and our place in nature, connections we badly need restored. In *Living by Fiction*, Annie Dillard describes the way our world tends to look at literature for "biography, ethics, cultural anthropology, psychology . . . aesthetics, linguistics, art criticism . . . [and] history." This is what she calls the very happy world of the "mind," but she warns her readers that "one day," in the "thick" of the happy life, we will meet the story and its ability to do all of these things with more than just the head.[46] Like art in general, poetry has the ability to address and evoke our human nature as *embodied* creatures. As Wendell Berry says, "The poet affirms and collaborates in the formality of the Creation."[47] The poet reminds us of the goodness of food, drink, sleep, skies, nature, seas and lands—the healing power of outdoor

---

[46]Annie Dillard, *Living By Fiction* (New York: HarperCollins, 1988), p. 12. Dillard is addressing fiction writers, but the point applies to nonfiction and poetry readers also.
[47]Wendell Berry, "The Responsibility of the Poet," in *What Are People For?* (San Francisco: North Point, 1990), p. 89.

walks, pottery in our hands, toes in the water and fingers in the soil. If these poetic books are right, our minds, bodies, communities and human health depend on a proper embrace of the material world and our own materiality. The seventeenth-century English poet Thomas Traherne aptly captures this holistic embodiment:

> You will never enjoy the world aright, till the sea itself floweth in your veins, till you are clothed with the heavens and crowned with the stars . . . till your spirit filleth the whole world, and the stars are your jewels, till you are familiar with the way of God in all ages as with your walk and table . . . till you delight in God for being good to all: you never enjoy the world.[48]

The embodied world is also fallen, dirty and difficult. Poetry is able, as in Job, to evoke the multidimensional brokenness of our world and the possibilities of restoration. As Michael Edwards says of a Christian aesthetic: "To phrase it in dialectical terms, literature begins in the perception of a conflict between *grandeur* and *misère*, and of a disparity between things as they are in a fallen world and things as they might be. It is the patterning of past, present and future, the attempt to deliver a new world out of the loss of an old."[49] Literature and poetry are uniquely positioned to enable us to imagine what was and what could be, as well as to find meaning in the broken present.

Today poetry is, very often, our truest link with reality. Our modern age has tended to prefer facts and reason to imagination. Such an emphasis can misrepresent, underestimate, flatten and distort reality. To say that God is "transcendent" or "omniscient," while it has noble aims, is qualitatively different than declaring that God rules "the raging sea" (Ps 89:9) or asking, "Can you draw in Leviathan with a hook?" (Job 41:1). Both are appropriate for different contexts, but one is not more "true." In this way, biblical poetry alerts us to the limitations of abstract language. Poetry, in fact, is at its best an ethical way of preserving the mystery, ambiguity, power, tragedy and sublimity of our world. It

---

[48]Thomas Traherne, *Poems, Centuries and Three Thanksgivings*, ed. Anne Ridler (Oxford: Oxford University Press, 1966), p. 177, quoted in A. M. Allchin, *The World Is a Wedding* (Oxford: Oxford University Press, 1978), p. 83.
[49]Edwards, *Towards a Christian Poetics*, p. 147.

should be clear to us that our modern preference for the concrete, certain and measurable hardly matches with our daily experiences of God, life and reality. Metaphors, stories and poems, however, meet us in this gap between God's power and goodness and the strangeness of everyday life.

An example of the ways in which poetry affirms our embodiment is its playfulness—and play is necessary. C. S. Lewis notes that "our leisure, even our play, is a matter of serious concern. There is no neutral ground in the universe; every square inch, every split second, is claimed by God and counterclaimed by Satan. . . . It is a serious matter to choose wholesome recreations."[50] Alter speaks of the "play of literary invention" in (Old Testament) poetry; wisdom plays before God in Proverbs 8; Leviathan plays before God in Job 41.

Anyone who has handled poetry with children knows that something mysterious happens when poems come into play. Children love to hear it, read it and write it. Poetry gives them a unique place to experiment with language as they learn to understand themselves through their experiences and perceptions. Poetry inspires their imaginations, and it should ours too because it connects us with the creativity and mirth and rhythmical order of the Creator himself. Without play, our lives become flat, overworked and dull. With poetry, we imitate God in his own creative rhythms (Ps 104:26) and we participate partially in the joy of eternal life that awaits us. So while not all poetry is playful, some of it must be.

Furthermore, as embodied creatures we are always in relationship. And poetry is a means for connecting us to our human counterparts throughout the ages. Rather than recalling the past through a chronicle of facts and dates, poetry joins us with our ancestors through mysterious, dreadful, and beautiful images and sounds. If our first point above is about poetry facilitating a *sacramental* approach to the world, then we could call this function of poetry its *catholicity*, in the sense of connecting us with the human race throughout history. As A. M. Allchin notes, the two are closely connected:

---

[50]C. S. Lewis, *Christian Reflections* (Grand Rapids: Eerdmans, 1967), pp. 33-34.

We are called to embody in the English-speaking world a certain vision of the wholeness and balance, the Catholicity of the Christian tradition. We are called to witness to the sacramental quality of all things through the specifically sacramental nature of our life together. And in some special way we are called to remind the West of the almost forgotten world of the Christian East, of the heritage and experience of the fathers of the Church.[51]

We need, therefore, to recover a sense of the power of poetry. Poetry can serve a great many redemptive actions in the world: consolation, praise, thanksgiving, lament, as well as verbal expressions of love, cultural critique, anger, hope, my stery and repentance. Biblical poetry in particular can renew our vision of God and of his good but fallen world, and it can invite us again to align ourselves wisely with him and his purposes.

Such is the power of poetry that it can also be terribly misdirected, as in the case of the second poem in the Bible, Lamech's poem of vengeance (Gen 4:23-24). But we should not make the modern mistake of marginalizing poetry as harmless and unimportant for real life.

## CONCLUSION

As we examine the individual Old Testament wisdom books in the coming chapters, we must remain alert to their predominantly poetic form. As Patrick Miller notes, "Meaning and beauty, the semantic and the aesthetic, are woven together into a whole, and both should be received and responded to by the interpreter. To ignore the beauty in pursuit of the meaning is, at a minimum, to close out the possibility that the beauty in a significant fashion contributes to and enhances the meaning."[52] In Old Testament wisdom, form and content come together to invite us to participate in the wisdom journey.

## RECOMMENDED READING

### *Introductory studies*
Alter, Robert. *The Art of Biblical Poetry.* New York: Basic, 1985.

---

[51]Allchin, *The World Is a Wedding*, p. 31.
[52]Patrick D. Miller, *Interpreting the Psalms* (Philadelphia: Fortress, 1986), p. 30, though we would not equate "beauty" with "aesthetic," as Miller does here.

Berry, Wendell. "The Responsibility of the Poet." In *What Are People For,* pp. 88-92. San Francisco: North Point, 1990.

### *Advanced studies*

Berlin, Adele. *The Dynamics of Biblical Parallelism.* Grand Rapids: Eerdmans, 2008.

Kugel, James L. *The Idea of Biblical Poetry: Parallelism and Its History.* New Haven: Yale University Press, 1981.

Seerveld, Calvin. *Rainbows for a Fallen World: Aesthetic Life and Artistic Task.* Toronto: Tuppence Press, 1980.

Wolterstorff, Nicholas. *Art in Action.* Grand Rapids: Eerdmans, 1980.

**4**

# Proverbs

*Proverbs are not passé and definitely not dead. . . . Proverbs, those old*
*gems of generationally tested wisdom, help us in our everyday life*
*and communication to cope with the complexities*
*of the modern human condition.*

—WOLFGANG MIEDER,
*PROVERBS ARE NEVER OUT OF SEASON*

P ROVERBS EXPERT RAYMOND VAN LEEUWEN tells the story
about a conversation he once had with a friend who specialized in psychology. When he told her that his research was on Proverbs, she replied: "Whatever turns you on." Van Leeuwen comments, "Ironically, she dismissed proverbs with a proverb whose origin was in her own turned-on sixties generation."[1] Indeed, whatever lack of respect we might have for proverbs today, the proverb is, as van Leeuwen rightly notes, the "workhorse" of language. "Look before you leap"; "you reap what you sow"; "you get what you pay for"; "don't pour the baby out with the bathwater"; "no pain, no gain"; "different strokes for different folks," and on and on. Television, magazines and popular speech are absolutely full of them. And yet few of us give any attention to where they come from or how they work.

It shouldn't surprise us that the book of Proverbs has fallen on hard

[1]Raymond van Leeuwen, "In Praise of Proverbs," in *Pledges of Jubilee: Essays on the Arts and Culture, in Honor of Calvin G Seerveld*, ed. Lambert Zuidervaart and Henry Luttikhuizen (Grand Rapids: Eerdmans, 1995), pp. 308-9.

times in our own day. We use proverbs everywhere, but we don't give them the same cultural significance as recent medical and scientific discoveries. That is not to say that we can't find lots of books, pamphlets and studies on character and morality in Proverbs, but—in our opinion—that is a long, long way from retrieving the immense power of the biblical proverbs. This chapter seeks to do just that.

Scholars sometimes label the book of Proverbs as "early" or "traditional wisdom." The dating of Proverbs is actually very complicated, but the idea of "traditional" wisdom is true in that Proverbs is the foundation for wisdom in the Old Testament. In the first chapter of this book we outlined wisdom in four categories. These stand at the heart of Proverbs and thus of Israel's view of wisdom as a whole:[2]

1. Wisdom is grounded in the "fear of the LORD [Yahweh]."

2. Wisdom is concerned with discerning the order that the LORD has built into the creation.

3. Wisdom focuses on discerning God's ways in *particular* circumstances.

4. Wisdom is grounded in tradition.

While Job and Ecclesiastes deal specifically with how to live when life appears to have turned upside down, as we will see in following chapters, Proverbs represents the ABCs of wisdom when life is generally going right.

## OUTLINE OF PROVERBS

In the outline below, we provide a basic framework for the book of Proverbs. To understand the theology in Proverbs, it is especially important to recognize the three major divisions in the book: chapters 1-9, 10-29, and 30-31.

    I.    Proverbs 1:1–9:18 Admonitions and Interludes

        a.  1:1-7 Title and Prologue

---

[2]Raymond van Leeuwen, "Wisdom Literature," in *Dictionary for Theological Interpretation of the Bible,* ed. Kevin J. Vanhoozer, Craig G. Bartholomew, Daniel J. Treier and N. T. Wright (Grand Rapids: Baker Academic, 2005), pp. 847-50.

b. 1:8-19 First Admonition: Parental Warning Against Sinners

c. 1:20-33 First Interlude: Woman Wisdom's Prophetic Warning

d. 2:1-22 Second Admonition: Search for Wisdom

e. 3:1-12 Third Admonition: Instruction in the Fear of the Lord

f. 3:13-20 Second Interlude: Cosmic Wisdom: Creation, Wisdom, Blessings

g. 3:21-35 Fourth Admonition: Warning and Admonitions

h. 4:1-9 Fifth Admonition: Tradition and Wisdom

i. 4:10-27 Sixth Admonition: Wisdom and Ways

j. 5:1-23 Seventh Admonition: Adultery and Folly; Marriage and Wisdom

k. 6:1-19 Third Interlude: Examples of Folly in Money, Sloth, Good and Evil

l. 6:20-35 Eighth Admonition: Warning Against Adultery

m. 7:1-27 Ninth Admonition: Folly Lurking to Catch a Fool

n. 8:1-36 Fifth Interlude: Cosmic Woman Wisdom—Final Speech

o. 9:1-18 Sixth Interlude: Two Houses, Two Women, Two Ways

II. Proverbs 10:1–22:16 The First Collection of Solomon

a. 10:1–15:33 Proverbs of Antithesis

b. 16:1–22:16 Proverbs of Royalty

III. Proverbs 22:17–24:34 Collected Sayings for a Son

a. 22:17–23:35 Instructions for Justice, Upright Living and Warnings

b. 24:1-22 Wisdom as a Son's Hope and Treasure

c. 24:23-34 Wisdom, Justice and Order in Society

IV. Proverbs 25:1–29:27 The Second Collection of Solomon: Concerns of the Ruler

    a. 25:1–27:27 Kings, Fools and Friends

    b. 28:1–29:27 Justice, Torah and Warnings About Fools

V. Proverbs 30:1-33 Agur and Wisdom in the World Upside Down

VI. Proverbs 31:1-31 King Lemuel and the Valiant Woman

    a. 31:1-9 King Lemuel's Wisdom

    b. 31:10-31 The Valiant Woman of Wisdom

It is fair to say that the book moves from symbolic and ideal wisdom (Prov 1–9), to wisdom in the random events of daily life (Prov 10–29), and then to wisdom in two extreme conditions (Prov 30–31). Our study of these sections begins in the first verse.

**PROVERBS 1:1: THE AUTHORSHIP OF PROVERBS**

The proverbs of Solomon son of David, king of Israel. (Prov 1:1)

Proverbs is introduced as a collection of Solomon, King David's son and the king over Israel. As we saw in chapter two, royal figures in the ancient world were distinguished by their expertise in areas of wisdom, justice and law. Solomon was Israel's only king to reign in a time of prolonged peace, and he embodied all of these traits more than anyone, wisdom most of all. In Israel's historical writings, he is remembered not only for his wisdom but also for his building of the temple (1 Kings 3–6).[3] In the ancient Near East this was a task typically associated with wise kings. It makes sense, then, that his reputation for wisdom is codified in the Old Testament by his association with Proverbs, Ecclesiastes and the Song of Songs (and the Wisdom of Solomon).

The Gospel writers also remember Solomon for the combined achievements of wisdom and temple-building (Mt 12:42; Lk 11:31;

---

[3]But also for his fall into rebellion and disobedience. See chapter eight below for more discussion on Solomon.

Acts 7:47). And yet David, on his deathbed, clearly charged Solomon
to adhere to the Torah, or law of Moses (1 Kings 2:3). In fact, the king
in the Old Testament was preeminently required to be a student of the
Torah (Deut 17:17-20) in order to maintain justice and righteousness in
Israel. Here we arrive at the wonderful, interdependent relationship between wisdom and the law.[4] Law leaves large areas of life in need of
particular direction on how to be faithful to God. Solomon, as the
prime example of the wise king, also faced many situations in which
there were no obvious solutions; it is in such *particular* situations that
wisdom is required.

We know from 1 Kings 2–11 that Solomon was gifted with wisdom
and had a special interest in accumulating wisdom of all sorts. Proverbs
1:1 clearly associates Proverbs with Solomon, but at the same time, sections like Proverbs 22:17–24:34 and Proverbs 30:1–31:31 suggest that
several sources, perhaps over many centuries, were brought together to
build the final book of Proverbs. Still, it is interesting to note that while
the sections ascribed to Hezekiah (Prov 25:1), Agur (Prov 30:1) and
Lemuel (Prov 31:1) are all very commonly accepted as historically valid,
the sections assigned to Solomon are frequently questioned by modern
authors, though without good reason.[5] Solomon's great wisdom—and
his failure to live it out—plays a central role in the theology of wisdom
and of the Old Testament. It is therefore important for theological and
historical reasons to take seriously the origin of much of Proverbs from
Solomon while recognizing other sources in the book and the editing
of the whole into its final form by another hand.

### PROVERBS 1:2-6: THE GREAT BENEFITS OF WISDOM

Not only are proverbs necessary for day-to-day conversation; but they
also communicate the very basic sense we need to orient our lives in a
constantly changing world. Proverbs 1:2-6 offers a long list of wisdom's

---

[4]See David Daube, *Law and Wisdom in the Bible* (West Conshohocken, Penn.: Templeton Press,
  2010), especially pp. 26-55, 85-104.
[5]Bruce K. Waltke, *Proverbs: Chapters 1–15*, NICOT (Grand Rapids: Eerdmans, 2004), pp. 31-
  36, helpfully explores the range of issues relating to authorship and, we think, rightly concludes
  that there are more reasons to believe that Solomon wrote or gathered these sayings than there
  are reasons to believe otherwise.

benefits so as to leave the reader no doubt that wisdom is of great value.

> For attaining wisdom and discipline;
>> for understanding words of insight;
> for acquiring a disciplined and prudent life,
>> doing what is right and just and fair;
> for giving prudence to the simple,
>> knowledge and discretion to the young—
> let the wise listen and add to their learning,
>> and let the discerning get guidance—
> for understanding proverbs and parables,
>> the sayings and riddles of the wise.

This prologue urgently wants the reader to appreciate the many benefits of wisdom and to excite the reader about the possibilities it presents. Proverbs will enable one to gain wisdom and understanding (Prov 1:2), a disciplined and just life (Prov 1:3); it will enable the immature to become mature (Prov 1:4) and the wise to become wiser (Prov 1:5). Proverbs not only provides wisdom instruction; but it will also teach one how to interpret the sayings of the wise (Prov 1:6)—reading the proverbs requires wisdom too.

One is meant to leave this prologue salivating at the prospect of all that wisdom has to offer. Such optimism and confidence in wisdom's rewards are consistent with the whole of Proverbs 1–9.

> For the Lord gives wisdom,
>> and from his mouth come knowledge and understanding.
> He holds victory in store for the upright,
>> he is a shield to those whose walk is blameless,
> for he guards the course of the just
>> and protects the way of his faithful ones. (Prov 2:6-8)

> I guide you in the way of wisdom
>> and lead you along straight paths.
> When you walk, your steps will not be hampered;
>> when you run, you will not stumble. (Prov 4:11-12)

The ethical instruction in Proverbs 1–9 thus imagines a strong connection between action and reward. What has come to be known as the *character-consequence* structure of Proverbs emphasizes the reliable outcomes that will result from obedience to the path of wisdom. Those who obey will be blessed with safety, riches and long life:

> For the upright will live in the land;
>> And the blameless will remain in it. (Prov 2:21)

> My son do not forget my teaching
>> But keep my commands in your heart
> For they will prolong your life many years
>> And bring you prosperity *[šālôm]*. (Prov 3:1-2)

> Honor the LORD with your wealth,
>> with the firstfruits of all your crops;
> then your barns will be filled to overflowing,
>> and your vats will brim over with new wine. (Prov 3:9-10)

> Do not forsake wisdom, and she will protect you;
>> Love her, and she will watch over you. (Prov 4:6)

The first nine chapters seek to build our confidence in the rewards of living wisely—of following in the ways of wisdom. Indeed, "wisdom in the Old Testament is about how to negotiate life successfully in God's good but fallen world."[6] Thus, while in Proverbs 1–9, the book sets out the principles basic to such a wise life, Proverbs 10–30—as we will see below—explores the character-consequence structure in a more nuanced way by focusing, among other things, on exceptions to the rule. However, as any good teacher knows, before you can run you must learn to walk, and thus Proverbs 1–9 inducts the student into the overarching principles of wisdom; only then will one be ready for the more complex nuances of day-to-day life.

### PROVERBS 1:7: THE FOUNDATION OF WISDOM

> The fear of the LORD is the beginning of knowledge,
>> but fools despise wisdom and discipline.

---

[6]Craig G. Bartholomew, *Reading Proverbs with Integrity* (Cambridge: Grove, 2001), p. 8.

God gives wisdom generously (Prov 2:6-7), but not unconditionally. One must "fear" him first and foremost in order to obtain wisdom. The Old Testament theology of "fear" is a much richer concept than our modern notion of trembling and terror. In Deuteronomy fearing God is equated with loving him, obeying his commands and walking in his ways (Deut 10:12-16). In fact, the use of the "fear of the LORD" in Exodus to Deuteronomy is always in the context of the redeemer and lawgiver "Yahweh" (the LORD), who loved Israel and redeemed her from slavery so as to become his people over whom he rules (cf. Ex 3; 6). Fearing God was the appropriate response to salvation (Ex 20:20). Fearing God thus refers to a loving reverence for the LORD, the Creator God who has brought us to himself (Ex 19:4), and to a lifestyle that fits with such an attitude.

The fear of the LORD is the "beginning" of wisdom in two ways. The Hebrew word for beginning is *r'ēšît*, a poetic figure of speech that is often translated as "the head" or "first thing." In the search for wisdom, fearing the LORD thus involves both the *starting point* of the journey and the *foundation*, or ground, on which a life of wisdom is built. One must commit to Yahweh and his plan for creation to begin attaining wisdom. Then, obeying and loving Yahweh become the means to continue a lifelong journey of using wisdom to find his ways in life in every area of God's good creation.

## THE FEAR OF THE LORD AND THE STRUCTURE OF PROVERBS

The fear of the LORD is so foundational to wisdom that it shows up as a thematic refrain, not only in Proverbs but also in Job and Ecclesiastes. The "fear of Yahweh" is repeated fourteen times in Proverbs, having been carefully placed throughout the book to alert us to wisdom's strong emphasis on loving allegiance to the covenant God of Israel. Its placement also illumines the main divisions in the proverbial material. Thus, while most scholars today attribute the divisions in the book to a different historical or theological movement, in our view they contribute to the crafted literary and poetic unity and aesthetic genius of the book. These literary divisions, indicated by "the fear of Yahweh," are as follows:

I. Proverbs 1–9

Introduction: Fear of the LORD as the Beginning of
Knowledge (Prov 1:7)

Fear of the LORD in the Father's First Speech (Prov
1:29)

Fear of the LORD as the Knowledge of God (Prov 2:5)

Fear of the LORD in Lady Wisdom's Call from
Creation (Prov 8:13)

Woman Wisdom's Last Speech: Fear as the Beginning of
Wisdom (Prov 9:10)

II. Proverbs 10–29

Fear of the LORD in the Proverbial Sayings (Prov 10:27;
14:27; 15:16, 33; 16:6; 19:23; 22:4; 23:17)

III. Proverbs 30–31

Traits of the Valiant Woman: Fear as Her Preeminent Virtue
(Prov 31:30)

Thus, not only is this phrase a refrain in the book of Proverbs; but its placement at the beginning and end of Proverbs also functions as an *inclusion*, bookends indicating the centrality of the fear of the LORD to wisdom. Indeed in Proverbs 31:10-31, the book concludes with a hymn to the valiant woman, a wonderful portrait of Proverbs 1:7 in human form. As this woman feeds and clothes her family, cares for the poor, and participates in the local marketplace, she *is* the embodiment of wisdom; by her works she shows us that she fears the LORD.

Cultures in ancient Egypt and Mesopotamia, as we have seen, also had very well-established wisdom traditions, schools and collected sayings, most of which predated Israel's wisdom writings.[7] What makes Hebrew wisdom unique among her peers, more than anything else, is its loyalty to the one true God of Israel, her covenant with him and *his* way of wisdom. This is signified emphatically and poetically by the

---

[7]Roland E. Murphy, *The Tree of Life: An Exploration of Biblical Wisdom Literature* (Grand Rapids: Eerdmans, 1997), pp. 151-75.

repetition of the "fear of Yahweh" at the main "seams," or shifts, in the forms of poetry in the book (Prov 1:7; 9:10; 22:4), thus accentuating Israel's unique theology of wisdom.

Much like the book of Psalms, however, Proverbs is a collection of several, perhaps even dozens, of ancient writings. As such it does not have a logical narrative-type structure, and this has led most recent scholars away from giving attention to it as a true literary and poetic whole.[8] Instead, scholars treat it in a piecemeal fashion, dissecting it into various strands and groups of sayings. We believe, however, that the book's poetic repetitions and many nuanced groupings of proverbs yield countless literary and thus theological patterns and a thematic unity that strengthens and integrates each of the discrete sections of proverbs. Proverbs is not a disconnected group of sayings, but a highly memorable body of teachings with a consistent message about life in God's world—but only when it is read as a whole.

## PROVERBS 1–9

Chapters 1–9 introduce us to the first major grouping in Proverbs. As the introduction to the book, they serve to construct a foundation for Israelite wisdom by giving us a sense of the order and meaning of the world. This sense of order provides the basis for interpreting the whole of life in all its particularities—which we will see is represented by the individual proverbs in Proverbs 10–29. It is thus essential to get a good understanding of the material in these first nine introductory chapters in order to understand the book as a whole.

Even without looking closely for detailed structure, we get the general sense that these nine chapters share a combination of images, rhetorical voices and theological allusions to creation. This mixture is intended to package the more familiar instructions within the structure of the persuasive voices from the family. This makes the theological teaching feel tangible and urgent. Most significantly, they address the "son," or young man, through the frequent repetition of the phrase, "Hear, my son" (Prov 1:8; see also, e.g., Prov 2:1; 3:1; 4:1). This frequent

---

[8]The next chapter presents a fuller history of interpretation of Proverbs.

use of the "son" does not make Proverbs exclusive to men; rather, it is a way of heightening what we have called the liminal urgency in wisdom with the image of an adolescent becoming a man.

The human movement between stages of life is often referred to by the term "liminality."[9] Liminality is the sociological event of crossing "thresholds" and "barriers" (liminals) in life, also referred to as "rites of passage."[10] Religious conversion,[11] graduation, marriage, moving, retirement and, significantly, the entry into adulthood are all liminal moments. Because these moves are filled with both promise and danger, wisdom is needed to make the transition carefully. Proverbs captures this exciting stage of life in its rhetorical use of the parents' voices. But the larger effect is to make its message of wisdom urgent to all who read it. Thus wisdom is not for the young alone; it also exhorts the "wise" to "increase" in their own wisdom (Prov 1:5) with the same urgency as young men and women becoming adults in society. These chapters are a collection of warnings and invitations—whether we are young men and women at the vital stage of life between childhood and adulthood or young children, ruling kings, parents or even trades people—who all alike face the unlimited variety of small and large decisions that arise day to day.

This liminal setting gives the voices and poems in Proverbs their rhetorical power. We can almost feel these voices straining to make these proverbs more than just simple ethical guidelines for behavior. Proverbs ties these teachings into a whole story or view of the world. In other words, the wisdom sages knew that the stories, religions, laws and customs of the cultures around Israel constantly threatened to distort her *larger* picture of the world—her sense of reality and faith in God. Israel's story told them who God is, why he created the world, how humans rebelled against him and where God will take the world

---

[9]Liminality as a sociological category was most significantly used by Arnold van Gennep, *The Rites of Passage*, trans. Monika B. Vizedom and Gabrielle L. Caffee (London: Routledge, 1977); and Victor Turner, *The Ritual Process* (Ithaca, N.Y.: Cornell University Press, 1967).

[10]For an excellent study of liminality in Proverbs, see Raymond van Leeuwen, "Liminality and Worldview in Proverbs 1–9," *Semeia* 50 (1990): 111-44.

[11]See Ronald Clements, *Wisdom for a Changing World: Wisdom in Old Testament Theology* (Berkeley, Calif.: Bibal, 1990), pp. 25-27. Here he connects the liminal nature of Israel's national salvation with the individual growth in wisdom in Proverbs 10–25.

in the future. The story gave Israel her purpose and the motivation for her ethics as she became a light to the nations (Gen 12:1-3). Because every new Israelite generation faced challenges to its faith, these instructions were forcefully delivered to remind them of the importance of teaching them and learning them.

As we turn now to a closer examination of these chapters we will focus in on two important groups of material. The first is a basic set of instructions from parents to children about wise living—what we will call "admonitions." The second group shares similar language with the first but can be distinguished by their theological poems or "interludes," whose major concern is the symbolic and metaphorical world of woman, houses, ways and creation.

***Admonitions and interludes.*** There are nine sets of admonitions from the parents to the son: Proverbs 1:8-19; 2:1-22; 3:1-12, 21-35; 4:1-9, 10-27; 5:1-23; 6:20-35; 7:1-27. Looking at a typical example, Proverbs 4:1-9, helps us to appreciate the urgent tone in their voices.

> Listen, my sons, to a father's instruction; (1a)
>> pay attention and gain understanding. (1b)
> I give you sound learning, (2a)
>> so do not forsake my teaching. (2b) (Prov 4:1-2)

The use of poetic parallelism gives these verses their persuasive tone: "hear" (1a) and "pay attention" (1b) are complementary to "instruction" (1a) and "understanding" (1b), while "I give you sound learning" (2a) sits in contrast to "*do not forsake* my teaching" (2b). This pattern continues through Proverbs 4:9. We can thus characterize the overall style of an admonition as a flowing narrative style of speech from a parental figure with a strong confidence in the ordered, reliable sense of moral actions in the world (the character-consequence motif).

Meanwhile, a more cosmic, almost mystical, view of wisdom emerges in the six interludes (Prov 1:20-33; 3:13-20; 6:1-19; 7:1-27; 8:1-36; 9:1-18). Here wisdom is understood through the metaphors of two ways, two houses and two cosmic feminine figures: *Lady Wisdom* and *Dame Folly*. These women appeal to the young man erotically, sensually, emotionally, socially and economically to walk in their ways and abide in their houses. As we saw in chapter two, a house in ancient Near Eastern literature is a metaphor for the direction and quality of one's life.[12] As young men (and women) prepare to leave home and "build a house," these two women represent two worldviews, or two ways of interpreting the world: the way of wisdom and the way of folly.

Dame Folly's appeal to the young man is driven at his heathen and sensual appetite. She makes no reference to God or his good plans for the man in creation. In fact, as her portrait in Proverbs 9:13-18 demonstrates, her language is overtly devious:

> The woman Folly is loud;
>> she is undisciplined and without knowledge.
> She sits at the door of her house,
>> on a seat at the highest point of the city,
> calling out to those who pass by,
>> who go straight on their way.
> "Let all who are simple come in here!"
>> She says to those who lack judgment.
> "Stolen water is sweet;
>> food eaten in secret is delicious!"
> But little do they know that the dead are there,
>> that her guests are in the depths of the grave.

Notice her desire to command the house, the ways and appetites of the young man, all for selfish gain. In this way Dame Folly's interpretation of the world embodies common views of women and pleasure in the ancient world. Overcome with a heathen appetite, she lies to the young man about the world and its purpose. Yet in this way her character also reflects the dangerous beliefs behind the stories of non-Israelite cultures. In order to counter Dame Folly's rhetoric and her alluring power, these interludes constantly return to Woman Wisdom, her experience, her origin with the LORD and her account of the "created order." We will discuss each of these below.

---

[12]On the important religious and symbolic character of "houses" in the ancient world, see Raymond van Leeuwen "Cosmos, Temple, House: Building and Wisdom in Mesopotamia and Israel," in *Wisdom Literature in Mesopotamia and Israel*, ed. Richard J. Clifford (Atlanta: Society of Biblical Literature, 2007).

But before we do, we pause first to summarize how these cosmic women reinforce the message of the parental admonitions. The cosmic imagery reminds us that what appears to us to be the mundane activity of our daily life has, in reality, been structured by God to fit the architectural plans he made for our world in the beginning of time. If we are obedient in the way we build houses, pursue vocations, and make families and nations, we not only "walk in right paths," as commanded by our parents, but in doing so we follow the path of one of the deep structures in the order of creation, either to death or to life. Theologically, the cosmic imagery is thus meant to convince us that wise living involves walking harmoniously along the grain of the created order. In terms of the character-consequence structure referred to above, good behavior has its rewards because *creation was designed for it from the beginning.*

***Israel's understanding of creation and creation order.*** To understand the theological richness of creation order in Proverbs, we need to recall the historical understanding of wisdom presented in chapter two. The ancient worlds of Egypt, Israel and Mesopotamia viewed their lives as participating in a great created order, a great living harmony of all things. Thus, for these ancient theologies, justice and wisdom are a matter of creating and restoring a sense of societal, political, economic and religious order. Many of these cultures, in fact, have just one or two words that can mean "wisdom," "justice" or "creation order," all signifying the ability to live fittingly in this world order. Our material in chapter two also highlights the significant role of the king. Outside of Israel, the king is the divinely chosen office with primary responsibility for achieving this order. The biblical account, as we will see, shares some of these beliefs and themes about order but is also carefully nuanced in order to construct its own theology of *Yahweh* as king, and wisdom is his gift to his subjects.

Aware of this ancient cultural theology of creation order, it should not surprise us to find the metaphor of creation uniting the wisdom material in Proverbs 1–9. In the interlude in Proverbs 3:18, the narrator equates Woman Wisdom with "the tree of life":

> She is a tree of life to those who embrace her;
> those who lay hold of her will be blessed.

This, of course, echoes the famous "tree of life" passage in Genesis 2–3. The "tree of life," alluded to in places like Psalm 1 and Jeremiah 17:8, finds its richest expression in three places: Genesis 2–3, Proverbs[13] and Revelation, all passages that deal with the cosmic order of God's creation. In the ancient Egyptian and Mesopotamian creation stories, the gods or kings use wisdom to oppose the forces of chaos and build their own houses. But the immediate context in Proverbs 3 connects the wisdom and knowledge God uses to found and establish the creation (3:19-20) to the wisdom available to all humans (Prov 24:3-4), not just gods and kings!

Again, recalling our discussion from chapter two, Genesis 1–2 similarly depicts God's work in creating a home and equipping it as the best environment for humankind. His work is creative, *making* and then *filling*—or *provisioning*—each day.

Day 1 Light
Day 2 Heavens and waters
Day 3 Land

Day 3 Light bearers, sun, moon, stars
Day 4 Birds and fish
Day 5 Beasts and humans

God's creation is also generous, inviting the land, animals and humans each to "be fruitful," "multiply" and "fill the earth" (Gen 1:22, 26; 6:11, 13), just as God had done in his six days of work. Thus, in Genesis, God communicates his creative work and his generosity and care for others to everything else he creates. The same language of wisdom, knowledge and creating is also ascribed to Bezalel and Oholiab in Exodus 35:30–36:7 with the building and provisioning of the tabernacle. With the Spirit of God upon them (a creative allusion to the spirit hovering over the deep in Gen 1:2), these men prepare the tabernacle as the new house for God's dwelling. This language and imagery appears yet again in Proverbs 24:3-4, where wisdom and knowledge are needed for humanity to "build" and "establish" *(kûn)* a house and "fill" *(mālē')* its rooms. Raymond van Leeuwen helpfully explains:

> Though the language of house building is used metaphorically to portray divine creation, the conceptual message runs implicitly in the other

---

[13]Prov 3:18; 11:30; 13:12; 15:4.

direction. The divine building of the cosmic house by wisdom is the model for human house building; human culture is a form of the *imitatio dei*, especially with reference to God's creation of the cosmos as the house in which all houses are contained.[14]

Note too the role of the priests (Ex 28:5) and women who are "wise of heart" and build God's "house" in Exodus 35:25 and use the same rare materials as the valiant woman of wisdom who cares for her own house in Proverbs 31 (Prov 31:13, 19-25).[15] House-building by wisdom stands as the key metaphor for human culture making in the Old Testament. What could be more important, even urgent, than getting this wisdom?

Above all, these intertextual clues all point to the extraordinary *care* and *love* with which God forms the world in which humans are to dwell. At every point the creation bears the marks of the handiwork of the LORD, who created the world by wisdom and offers wisdom to humans so that they might live life to the full in his very good creation (Gen 1:31). As with Genesis 1–3, creation in Proverbs contrasts starkly with other ancient Near Eastern creation stories in its loving, other-person centeredness of the Creator, who is none other than the LORD. True wisdom always results in filling the earth with creativity, generosity, concern for the other and a longing for all of creation to flourish before God.

The most intense expression of creation order appears in the extended interlude by Lady Wisdom in Proverbs 8:1-36. In this long speech, Wisdom attributes her origins to the beginning of God's creative work:

The LORD brought me forth as the first of his works,
    before his deeds of old. (Prov 8:22)

---

[14]Van Leeuwen, "Cosmos, Temple, House," 81.
[15]For detailed discussions of these texts, see J. Richard Middleton, *The Liberating Image: The Imago Dei in Genesis 1* (Grand Rapids: Brazos, 2005), pp. 85-87; Meredith G. Kline, *The Structure of Biblical Authority* (Grand Rapids: Eerdmans, 1972), p. 85; and Raymond C. van Leeuwen, "Building God's House: An Exploration in Wisdom," in *The Way of Wisdom: Essays in Honor of Bruce K. Waltke*, ed. J. I. Packer and Sven K. Soderlund (Grand Rapids: Zondervan, 2000), pp. 204-11.

Wisdom, because she was around before creation, is able to proclaim her expertise, having witnessed and even enjoyed the events of creation (Prov 8:23-31). The many allusions to the created order in this speech express her appreciation for the order and fittingness in all that God has made. Here we modify the NIV in order to highlight the repetition of the words "establish," "boundary" and "mark" in Proverbs 8:27-29, which echo the crafts of house building elsewhere in Proverbs:

> When he **established** a place for the heavens
>> I was there
>>> When he **marked** out the horizon on the face of the deep
> When he **established** the clouds above
>> When he **established** the fountains of the deep
> When he gave the sea a **boundary**
>> So that the waters would not transgress his command
>>> When he **marked** out the foundations of the earth.

The poetry in this passage moves from the heavens (Prov 8:27) to the earth (Prov 8:29) in order to encompass everything created. As it does so, Lady Wisdom describes the order and place that God has made for everything. She goes on to boast of all that she has seen and then appeals to humankind to "listen to my teaching and be wise" (Prov 8:33). God has built, or etched, an order into the world, and wisdom, personified as a woman, is the key to discerning it. Wisdom thus offers us the key to interpreting our world: its beginnings, its purpose, its shape and its direction. She can guide us in walking wisely in this life because she knows the places that God carved out for us. Notice, too, her response to all that she sees:

> When I was the craftsman[16] at his side.
>> I was filled with delight day after day,
>>> rejoicing[17] always in his presence. (Prov 8:30)

In this verse, we can see that wisdom is involved as God fashions the

---

[16]Cf. "the king's architect advisor" or "fashioner" as suggested by Raymond van Leeuwen, *Context and Meaning in Proverbs 25–27*, SBLDS 96 (Atlanta: Scholars Press, 1988), p. 94. See also Michael V. Fox, *Proverbs 1–9*, AB (New York: Doubleday, 2000), pp. 285-88, 414-15.

[17]Or better, "frolicking," following Fox's reading, *Proverbs 1–9*, pp. 287-88.

heavens and the earth. More importantly, we witness a reciprocal relationship, in which God delights in wisdom and she rejoices and frolics
before him. With her unique view, she communicates to us that creation is not only good but "very good" (Gen 1:31). Psalm 104 is a long
poem expanding this same message of the order and goodness of creation—perhaps most significantly in Psalm 104:26, where we read that
the great Leviathan is made to "frolic" in the sea, which God has made.
Our house-building, or culture-forming, task in creation is a vocation
of joy as we take pleasure in God its Creator.

There is a particularly comforting tone to Lady Wisdom's message. She assures us that there are patterns and norms within the
human story—an order and reliability in creation that we can fall
back on in life. Many voices in the Christian tradition portray life as
a dangerous tightrope—a straight-and-narrow line where we dare
not misstep. But this woman testifies to the harmony and order of a
large, open landscape—a *freedom within form and life within boundaries;* it is less a matter of straight lines than winding grooves. Every
day is a new adventure, which may be explored joyfully with wisdom
as our map.

Lady Wisdom's response to her experience of creation, humanity
and the order in God's world emphasizes joy. The end of the passage
leaves us with three salient images: (1) that God delights in her, (2) that
she dances or frolics before him and (3) that she delights in humanity.
The whole poem is full of love, compassion, intimacy, and exuberant
joy and playfulness. This response is evocative of David and Israel's
response when they brought the ark up to Jerusalem—dancing, shout-
ing and celebrating (2 Sam 6:14-15). Cosmic wisdom assures us that
the good life is one of joy and love for the creation.

It is with this long, grand poem that these nine chapters begin to
draw to a close. Proverbs 9 offers one last appeal to value wisdom over
folly before the book restates the motto that "the fear of the LORD is the
beginning of wisdom" (9:10) and turns to the individual proverbs.

From Proverbs 1–9 it is clear that wisdom for ancient Israel was designed to speak to a broad range of concerns in daily life: ethics, family,
work, community, justice, government and more. Thus it is particularly

telling that Lady Wisdom calls out in the public places, where all the activities of social life converge.

Thus, as the first nine chapters come to a close, we are left with a picture that will guide our reading of the next twenty chapters. Wisdom is concerned with life lived according to the grain of creation; the sages are not philosophizing just about ethical concepts but are also seeking to draw our lives into harmony with the created order. The key to such wise and harmonious living is the fear of the LORD—faith in and obedience to Yahweh preconditions our access to God's cosmic designs. As such Proverbs does not lead us into a natural theology or simple oneness with nature but into a faith seeking understanding of the creation and its limits. We alternate our gaze between God and his creation. The benefits for those who hearken to the call of wisdom are immense, sending us confidently and expectantly into the following chapters.

## PROVERBS 10–29

Proverbs 10–29 contains the most familiar type of wisdom: individual proverbs. Whereas Proverbs 1–9 emphasizes the benefits, motivation and created design of wisdom, these chapters embody wisdom at work in the real world. In this way, each of these short sayings is a way of *fitting* wisdom into the changing circumstances of daily life. As Michael Fox, commenting on Carole Fontaine's research to explain a proverb, notes: "In every new use, Fontaine says, a proverb must meet a particular need, and this imbues it with ever fresh 'performance-meaning.' A proverb receives its full meaning only in application, when it is spoken to a particular end."[18] Proverbs demand a new and different discipline of thinking and acting than we are typically used to. They are not concerned primarily with world philosophies, ethical theories or timeless truths but rather with relating a theology of creation to the conditional, local, particular and timely[19]—the right things and the best

---

[18]Michael V. Fox, *Proverbs 10–31*, Anchor Yale Bible (New Haven: Yale University Press, 2009), p. 484. ·

[19]On the loss of concern for the local and particular in modern society, see Stephen Toulmin, *Cosmopolis: The Hidden Agenda of Modernity* (New York: Free Press, 1990), p. 34.

action in the right times and places—what we call *fittingness*.

One can imagine that such practical, daily concerns would work their way into every area of Israel's life. Much like the way we thread lines from popular books and movies into our daily conversations, wisdom showed up in all sorts of times and places. As we said in chapter one above, this leads us to expect wisdom to show up throughout the Old Testament.[20] Nevertheless, as we also pointed out in chapter one, thematic or theological allusions to wisdom do not make every book in the Old Testament a "wisdom book"; each retains its own unique genre and style. The wisdom books, as we argue throughout this chapter, have their own particular literary character and theological and philosophical concerns. The dominant way to express these concerns is, of course, the proverb.

Granted, proverbs in any culture are usually passed on orally, whenever the moment fits, and not in lists. But Proverbs is a collection of these timely sayings, all put into one place. One of the consequences of living in our Western, science-dominated culture is that we live with the tendency to approach these proverbs by reordering them into topics like speech, honesty, diligence and laziness, thus undoing the collectors' work. Yet, by reordering the sayings in this way, some crucial dimensions are lost in the message and theology of the book. If instead we attend to what at times seems to be a random arrangement, we find all new possibilities. First, we find a strong parallel between the proverbs and the reality of life, lived out as it is day to day. As much as we might try to resist it, our lives are not orderly and topically arranged; rather, they jump from this event to that experience with little warning of what will come next. The proverbs mirror this reality by stringing together groups of proverbs that sometimes have only vague interconnections. "Proverbs are diverse and contradictory because human life is contradictory and diverse."[21]

Second, we are attuned to the many connections between proverbs that are situated near one another. That is, when proverbs are collected

---

[20]For an excellent discussion of wisdom influence throughout the OT, see R. N. Whybray, *The Intellectual Tradition in the Old Testament* (Berlin: Walter de Gruyter, 1974). Cf. also Murphy, *Tree of Life*, pp. 97-110.

[21]Van Leeuwen, "In Praise of Proverbs," p. 318.

and arranged as in the book of Proverbs, a new dynamic literary potential is added. Using semantic, structural and poetic tools, we are able to gain a real appreciation for the literary connections between proverbs, with their evocative, connective metaphors, which make them so memorable. On the one hand, we find a prevailing trend in these chapters to present "clusters" of proverb pairs and triads—groups of two or three proverbs in a row that provide a variety of perspectives on a single theme.[22] But on the other hand, we will also be able to identify several longer sections of proverb poems whose organization bring new relationships and meanings to the individual sayings.[23]

When we encounter these groupings and proverb poems, we have to remember that proverbs are in no way universal sayings that hold true in all cases; in fact, in a moment, we will address the freedom of the proverbs and their many intentional contradictions. Proverbs are sayings that apply at a particular time and a particular place. In this way, they illuminate for us the variety within the order of creation; an ordered life is one that navigates changing circumstances, dilemmas and quandaries with wisdom. The proverbs supply basic instructions and extended metaphors to help us interpret these constantly changing events and to respond well. In this way, the book of Proverbs attests to the provisional nature of human life; in our life we will never attain *final* order or *final* justice for the world.[24] God's final, redemptive work alone will do that. But Proverbs does invite us confidently, in the "fear of the LORD," to work for that perfect world in the moment with the wisdom God gives us. In the process our lives become reflections of the perfect order and beauty of the new creation that awaits us.

The book of Proverbs thus urges us to develop the wit, imagination, mystery, ambiguity and the kind of prudent living most appropriate to the particulars of our daily experience. Paremiology—the study of proverbs—is an extraordinary and undervalued field of study both within biblical research and in the modern study of human language.

---

[22]See Fox, *Proverbs 10–31*, pp. 478-80.

[23]Van Leeuwen, *Context and Meaning*, pp. 39-40.

[24]See Oliver O'Donovan, *Resurrection and Moral Order: An Outline for Evangelical Ethics* (Grand Rapids: Eerdmans, 1986), pp. 74-75. Miroslav Volf, *Exclusion and Embrace* (Nashville: Abingdon, 1996), p. 217.

We wish we could say far more than we have here, but space does not allow it. We refer readers to the works by Mieder, Taylor and Fox at the end of this chapter. In what follows, we will examine two types of proverbs that help demonstrate the significance of wisdom and fittingness as presented in Proverbs 10–29.

***Contradiction and hermeneutics.*** In the contradictory proverbs, we witness their distinct power to speak to the constantly changing circumstances of each particular moment. Proverbs 1:6 tells us that wisdom will teach us how to understand a proverb and a saying, especially a contradictory one. Proverbs thus assumes that it is not always giving us the most straightforward word on life—reading, like living, requires wisdom. Because the proverbs are often contradictory in their content, they constrain us into this learning curve. Take two popular pairs of proverbs from modern culture:

The early bird gets the worm.
Look before you leap.

Money talks.
Money isn't everything.

These proverbs communicate two contradictory approaches to our behavior. In the first pair we find both a warning against procrastination and laziness and a reminder of the danger that initiative and spontaneity can become impulsive recklessness. The key is applying the proverbs fittingly in different circumstances.

The proverb poem about "fittingness" in Proverbs 26:1-12 is an excellent example of discerning the appropriate response in different situations.[25] The first verse introduces the theme for the rest of the poem: "honor is not fitting for the fool." Proverbs 26:3 gives several other examples of things that *fit:*

A whip for the horse, a bridle for the donkey,
    and a rod for the backs of fools!

In Proverbs 26:4-5 we are presented with what is clearly a contradiction:

[25]See van Leeuwen, *Context and Meaning*, pp. 87-106.

> Do not answer a fool according to his folly,
>     or you will be like him yourself.
> Answer a fool according to his folly,
>     or he will be wise in his own eyes.

These contrary sayings stop us in our tracks and remind us about the great variety of people and circumstances we meet in life. They constrain us to think carefully about when one should answer a fool "according to his folly" and when not to! Speech, like wisdom in general, requires attention to every new and particular situation. The final verse in the poem issues this warning:

> Do you see a man wise in his own eyes?
>     There is more hope for a fool than for him. (Prov 26:12)

Echoing the warning in Proverbs 3:5, "Do not be wise in your own eyes," this verse reminds us how easy it is to think we are wise when we are acting like fools and how quickly we think we know what a proverb means. The conclusion to this poem is that it is fitting for wise people to be humble and know that they always need more wisdom.

The focus on the fool in this poem is only exemplary—fittingness or making the appropriate response applies to all areas of life. In this way, wisdom is the hermeneutical key to interpreting the ambiguities we face. Fittingness always assumes that some order has been set down around us. Wisdom thus compares scenarios of behavior to what we know of the whole order and guides us into appropriate action. Oliver O'Donovan helpfully explains: "Wisdom is the perception that every novelty, in its own way, manifests the permanence and stability of the created order, so that, however astonishing and undreamt of it may be, it is not utterly incommensurable with what has gone on before."[26] This definition connects the proverbs back to the theology of the created order. Because we know that God fashioned the world with boundaries, grooves and carved places for everything, we can be confident that he has a way for us to negotiate life with all of its dilemmas. Grounded in the fear of the LORD, wisdom looks to the creation and finds the

---

[26]O'Donovan, *Resurrection and Moral Order*, p. 189.

patterns that are meant to give order to our moral, social, economic and political living.

**Wealth and poverty, justice and righteousness.** Another way to understand the contradictory nature of some of the proverbs is in terms of what van Leeuwen calls "contradictions" within a larger "system."[27] Proverbs 1–9 is filled with confident sayings that affirm the goodness of creation, but in Proverbs 10–29, contradictions have been intentionally inserted to teach us to accept the disorder and mystery that meets us in real life. In his exploration of the theme of wealth and poverty, van Leeuwen has collected the relevant proverbial sayings into the four quadrants displayed in table 4.1.[28]

**Table 4.1**

|          | Righteousness | Wickedness |
|----------|:-------------:|:----------:|
| Wealth   | 1             | 3          |
| Poverty  | 2             | 4          |

This table helps us to analyze the perspectives in the various proverbs on justice and the character-consequence structure in the created order. The most familiar perspectives communicated in the book of Proverbs are those where the righteous prosper (quadrant 1) and those where the poor suffer due to laziness or wickedness (quadrant 4). Both quadrants reaffirm the approach to the character-consequence structure in Proverbs 1–9. But there is also evidence of differing perspectives and of the disorder in the world through which Proverbs seeks to guide us. Consider Proverbs 11:16:

> A kindhearted woman gains respect,
>     but ruthless men[29] gain only wealth.

---

[27]See Raymond C. van Leeuwen, "Wealth and Poverty: System and Contradiction in Proverbs," *Hebrew Studies* 33 (1992): 25-36.

[28]Ibid., pp. 28-29.

[29]This is the reading from the Masoretic Text. Given the disjunction between the two halves of the verse, many follow the reading of the Septuagint (LXX) as "vigorous."

While most of the proverbs would fall into quadrants 1 and 4, passages like this one in Proverbs 11:16 express the reality in quadrant 3, that there is disorder and injustice in our world (cf. Prov 13:23; 19:10; 28:15-16; 30:14). This will become important when we examine Job and Ecclesiastes in the chapters below. As with most religions in the ancient Near East, wisdom is the king's primary resource for attaining creation order to include social, natural and economic harmony. The book of Proverbs is like these ancient forms of wisdom as it expresses Yahweh's similar concern for justice and order. But as we have been emphasizing throughout this book, Israel's wisdom forces it to deal much more seriously with mystery. Wonder is not an absence of wisdom but is, rather, wisdom responding humbly and humanly to the Creator's world.

This perspective on injustice emerges in the proverbs in quadrant 2 (Prov 10:2; 11:4; 12:7; 15:25). While humans cannot make sense of all the ambiguity we face in life, we look forward to a day when God will judge all people with his own justice: "The sages' stance is to maintain faith in God's justice, even when the recorded past does not verify it."[30] While this message is central to Job, its roots are clear in Proverbs as well. When we meet mystery in this life, we must have faith in the LORD.

In sum, the proverbs that deal with the exceptions to the character-consequence structure are all found in Proverbs 10–30. Thus they must be read against the background of Proverbs 1–9, which is the hermeneutical key to the book as a whole. The general principle of wisdom is that righteousness and wisdom do lead to blessing and wealth but, as Proverbs 10–29 makes clear, in a fallen broken world there are many exceptions to this rule. Thus Proverbs is aware of and works with this retributive paradox without presenting a final solution to the problem. Proverbs hopes that the LORD's justice will finally come but leaves it open as to how that will take place.

## THE END OF PROVERBS: CHAPTERS 30–31

The final two chapters of Proverbs revert from short individual sayings

---

[30]Van Leeuwen, "Wealth and Poverty," p. 34.

back to more organized proverb poems as found in Proverbs 1–9. Agur's poem, which begins in Proverbs 30:1, has no clear ending; some think it ends in Proverbs 30:9 and others in verse Proverbs 30:33. What is clear is that the wisdom in this chapter flows like a speech that makes strong statements about the perplexity humans must face in trying to live a wise life. In the introduction, Agur is "weary" (Prov 30:1) and almost despairing:

> I have not learned wisdom,
>     nor have I knowledge of the Holy One. (Prov 30:3)

This is a fairly clear contradiction of Proverbs 2:5, which promises that wisdom leads to "understanding" and "the knowledge of God." Agur seems skeptical about his own search. In fact, van Leeuwen's reading of Proverbs 30 leads him to label it the biblical "world upside down," corresponding to a similar way of depicting future hope in other ancient Near Eastern wisdom.[31] In other words, when wisdom sages, trained with the goodness of upright living, observed the fallenness and corruption in the world around them, they often responded with proverbs that depicted a world upside down. It is worth asking how this kind of skeptical or ironic writing influences our understanding of the worldview created by the book of Proverbs. Besides depicting the world in its strangeness, Agur also communicates its incomprehensibility as he discovers things that surpass human understanding. These give us a sense of our finitude and dependence on God and a hope for his future restoration of all things (Prov 30:18-31).

Proverbs 31 (specifically Prov 31:10-31) is a sophisticated poetic hymn to a "valiant woman" and a remarkable conclusion to Proverbs. The chapter actually begins with instructions from a mother to her son King Lemuel (Prov 31:1-9). These instructions consist of a fairly traditional group of wisdom sayings from a mother to her royal son concerning modesty, humility, temperance and justice. More importantly, perhaps, the book turns from the ambiguity in Proverbs 30 to the figure of a wise king. As we have seen, in the ancient Near East the king was the

---

[31]Raymond C. van Leeuwen, "Proverbs 30:21-23 and the Biblical World Upside Down," *JBL* 105 (1986): 599-610.

cultural exemplar of wisdom and a model for the subjects of the kingdom. And the mother's voice reminds us of the admonitions in Proverbs 1–9 and the liminal rhetoric of parents pleading with children to get wisdom. Together, these prepare us for the final climactic poem.

This poem in Proverbs 31:10-31 fits very naturally in this context of the cosmic-parent matrix of Proverbs 1–9. Woman is highlighted as the focus of wisdom, but unlike her role as a cosmic figure, here she is a local activist, wife and mother of a home. In this way, Proverbs achieves something brilliant and rather remarkable in the light of our own culture. The echoes of eternal cosmic Lady Wisdom are merged with the mundane, concrete figure of a woman we could meet anywhere on an average day. Wisdom thus breaks down the common divisions between practice and theory, secular and sacred. We now encounter the eternal, cosmic, organizing power in creation embodied, not only in an earthly woman, but also consequently in the home, the field, the market and in all realms of human life. We will explore the hymn to the valiant woman in more detail in the following chapter.

## RECOMMENDED READING

### Introductory studies
Bartholomew, Craig G. *Reading Proverbs with Integrity*. Cambridge: Grove, 2001.

Brown, William. *Character in Crisis: A Fresh Approach to the Wisdom Literature of the Old Testament*. Grand Rapids: Eerdmans, 1996.

Leeuwen, Raymond C. van. "Proverbs." In *Dictionary for Theological Interpretation of the Bible*, ed. Kevin J. Vanhoozer, Craig G. Bartholomew, Daniel J. Treier and N. T. Wright, pp. 638-41. Grand Rapids: Baker Academic, 2005.

Murphy, Roland. *The Tree of Life: An Exploration of Biblical Wisdom Literature*. 2nd ed. Grand Rapids: Eerdmans, 1996.

### Commentaries
Fox, Michael V. *Proverbs 1–9*. AB. New York: Doubleday, 2000.

———. *Proverbs 10–31*. Anchor Yale Bible. New Haven: Yale University Press, 2009.

Leeuwen, Raymond C. van. "Proverbs." In *The New Interpreter's Bible*, ed.

Leander Keck, 5:17-264. Nashville: Abingdon, 1997.

Murphy, Roland. *Proverbs*. WBC 22. Nashville: Thomas Nelson, 1998.

Waltke, Bruce K. *Proverbs: Chapters 1-15*. NICOT. Grand Rapids: Eerdmans, 2004.

————. *Proverbs: Chapters 15-31*. NICOT. Grand Rapids: Eerdmans, 2005.

### Scholarly resources

Leeuwen, Raymond C. van. "Liminality and Worldview in Proverbs 1–9." *Semeia* 50 (1990): 111-44.

————. "In Praise of Proverbs." In *Pledges of Jubilee: Essays on the Arts and Culture, in Honor of Calvin G Seerveld*, ed. Lambert Zuidervaart and Henry Luttikhuizen, pp. 308-27. Grand Rapids, Eerdmans, 1995.

————. "Wealth and Poverty: System and Contradiction in Proverbs." *Hebrew Studies* 33 (1992): 25-36.

Rad, Gerhard von. *Wisdom in Israel*, trans. James D. Martin. London: SCM, 1970.

### Paremiology

Mieder, Wolfgang. *Proverbs Are Never Out of Season: Popular Wisdom in the Modern Age*. New York: Oxford University Press, 1993.

Taylor, Archer. *The Proverb*. Cambridge, Mass.: Harvard University Press. 1931.

# 5

# Women, Wisdom and Valor

*Only woman is capable of nourishing within her an
unsubstantiated hope, and inviting us to a doubtful future, which we
would have long ceased to believe in were it not for women.*

—MILAN KUNDERA, *IMMORTALITY*

IN THE LAST CHAPTER, WE EXPLORED the ornate, poetic fabric of Proverbs 1–9, with its two powerful and cosmic women, Lady Wisdom and Dame Folly, alongside the more practical teachings from a mother and a father. The resounding motto throughout these chapters is that "the fear of the LORD is the beginning of wisdom" (Prov 1:7; 9:10). Proverbs 10–29, meanwhile, collects hundreds of individual proverbs and proverb poems to teach us patterns for living wisely in God's creation. We have already suggested that Proverbs 31 offers a fitting end to the book in that it combines the guiding motto of the fear of the LORD (Prov 31:30) with the daily works of wisdom in the life of a remarkable but anonymous woman (Prov 31:10-29). These connections between this poem and the material in Proverbs 1–9 and Proverbs 10–29 are essential to the poem's interpretation, as we will demonstrate below.

Most of us encounter this chapter with preconceptions or misgivings that make it hard for us to listen to its message. Indeed, this woman's unbelievable energy and activity have inspired a wide range of interpretations throughout history. Al Wolters's research suggests that, prior to the Reformation, this passage was almost exclusively read spiritually or allegorically—primarily as a result of a dualist worldview that divided nature and grace (or matter and spirit). Since the Reformation, most interpreters have favored a more "literal" reading of an exemplary wife.[1] We'll have more to say on this history below.

Two extreme interpretations seem to prevail today. The one, a literal, more conservative reading, imagines such perfection in this woman that it is unattainable, and the other, a feminist reading, praises this woman's strengths over against the male-dominated cultures of the ancient world. This is a good example of how our social and cultural background influences our reading of the Bible. Often these interpretations fail to attend to this chapter as a carefully crafted poem that concludes the book of Proverbs. Our aim here is to ask how the book as a literary whole would have us understand this woman's long days, her active "hands" and her extraordinary success in everything she touches. Might she have something to teach us about our God, about salvation, life in his world, and faith in the midst of sin, grief and brokenness? We believe that she does. Not only does she give us a theological insight into the hope a woman can bring to a family and a culture; but she also reinforces virtues of beauty, compassion, diligence, creativity, vision, purpose and love, all of which God has woven into the creation for both women and men to embrace and embody.

## OUTLINE

Proverbs 31 is the last of seven sections in the book of Proverbs, each of which is marked by a major heading (Prov 1:1; 10:1; 22:17; 24:23; 25:1; 30:1; 31:1). This final section has two parts: the instructions of King Lemuel's mother, in Proverbs 31:1-9, and the song about the wise woman who "fears the LORD," in Proverbs 31:10-31. Most scholars also see the poem of the valiant woman as further divided into two halves—Proverbs 31:10-18 and Proverbs 31:21-31—separated by a chiastic couplet in Proverbs 31:19-20. Each half is made up of seven sentences—likely a symbol of completeness or perfection. We have adapted this outline slightly in order to draw attention to key words within the wisdom vocabulary to provide a further analysis of structure and repetition.

---

[1]See Al Wolters, *The Song of the Valiant Woman: Studies in the Interpretation of Proverbs 31:10-31* (Carlisle, U.K.: Paternoster, 2001), pp. 59-115.

I.  31:1-9 The Instructions of King Lemuel, Which He Received from His Mother

II. 31:10-31 The Hymn of the Valiant Woman

    a. 31:10-12 Introduction

    b. 31:13-20 Her Wise Works

       i.   31:13-15 She Seeks Worth: Hands, Food, Time, Eyes and Industry

       ii.  31:16-17 She Knows Value: Land, Agriculture, Hands, Physical Strength

       iii. 31:18-20 She Tests Merchandise: Taste, Time, Hands and Textiles

    c. 31:21-26 Her Work at Home and Her Praise in the Gates

       i.   31:21-22 At Home: No Fear of the Cold

       ii.  31:23-25 At the Gates: Her Work and Her Husband's Praise

       iii. 31:26 Wisdom in Her Mouth and Lovingkindness in Her Teaching

    d. 31:27 Watching *(ṣôpiyyâ)* the Ways of Her House

    e. 31:28-31 Conclusion, A Final Hymn: Praise Her Not for Charm, Power or Beauty but for Her Fear of the LORD

Interestingly, the Septuagint (LXX), or Greek version of the Old Testament, places Proverbs 31:1-9 before Proverbs 25, separating them from the poem in Proverbs 31:10-31 by a considerable distance. We believe that there are many good reasons to accept the Hebrew, Masoretic Text (MT)—also represented in almost all English Bibles—which holds both of these poems together. For one, as R. N. Whybray observes, the song in Proverbs 31:10-31 is the only major division in Proverbs without an introduction.[2] Thus, even if the section by King Lemuel's mother was written at a different time by another author, it now

---

[2]R. N. Whybray, *The Composition of the Book of Proverbs*, JSOTSup 168 (Sheffield, U.K.: JSOT Press, 1994), p. 159.

serves as an introduction to the song, which would otherwise sit awkwardly alone in the text. Furthermore, the two passages share important parallels, most notably that they both honor wisdom through the life of an earthly woman. Other common features will be discussed below. Suffice it for now that we recognize the literary and theological unity of the chapter and its two parts.

## FORM AND GENRE

From Aristotle to C. S. Lewis, literary scholars have long cautioned us to read literature through the lens of its genre and form—to ask, what *type* of literature is this and how does that influence its meaning? Genre is especially important with the poem of the valiant woman. Is it meant to be a biography? an exemplary poem for women? a feminist critique of male-dominated culture? What's more, while the question of form is increasingly raised in biblical studies today (even in Proverbs), the common tendency is to stop short of answering these questions in Proverb 31, with most scholars concluding merely that it is a "poem" or a "song." This fails to capture the very peculiar design and purpose of the poetry.

First, the text has been arranged in an alphabetic *acrostic* form;[3] its twenty-two lines follow the Hebrew alphabet from ʾālep to tāw (A to Z), thereby indicating the completeness of wisdom as embodied in this woman. There are as many as fourteen of these acrostic poems in the Old Testament, most of them in the Psalms and others in Lamentations, Nahum and here in Proverbs 31. Very much like the acrostic in Psalm 112, Proverbs 31:10-31 is focused on the *benefits* of wisdom. Psalm 112 calls the man who fears the LORD, "blessed" (Ps 112:2) and draws an antithesis between the "righteous" and the "wicked" (Ps 112:3, 6, 9-10). Proverbs 31 also praises the woman who "fears the LORD" (Prov 31:30), while drawing an antithesis between "beauty" and "vanity" and the one who "fears the LORD." Psalm 112 and Proverbs 31 share several other parallels, which suggests that perhaps the Psalm provided the template for the author of this proverb poem. More importantly, as Wolters notes, the most significant parallel is that they are

---

[3]For a full study of the form, see Wolters, *Song of the Valiant Woman*, pp. 3-14.

both "hymns" that seem to play off one another. Thus, whereas Psalm 112 *begins* with the familiar doxology "Praise the LORD," Proverbs 31 *ends* with the declaration: "Let her works *praise* her at the city gate" (Prov 31:31, emphasis added). The Hebrew *wîhalĕlûhā* ("praise her") sounds nearly identical to the beginning of Psalm 112: *halĕlû yāh*. So, while Psalm 112 praises the LORD as it describes the wise man, Proverbs 31 borrows its familiar structure to pay tribute to a wise woman.

Wolters identifies several common features of hymnic poetry that can be found in this poem. First, this woman is described as "valiant" or "heroic" *(ḥayil)* at both the beginning (Prov 31:10) and the end of the poem (Prov 31:29). This is a hymnic term typically reserved for gods, kings or great warriors and, as far as we know, only elsewhere used of a woman when referring to Ruth (Ruth 3:11; 4:11). The term is also applied to Boaz in the same book (Ruth 2:1)—possibly an allusion to a military background. David's mighty men are also lauded as valiant (e.g., 2 Sam 23:20; cf. 1 Sam 18; 21). These are all important connections we will touch on below.

Wolters also makes two less certain arguments for this poem being a hymn. First, he argues that *ṣôpiyyâ* in Proverbs 31:27, which is translated in the first three words of the phrase "*she looks well* to the ways of her household," is a familiar hymnic participle, which plays on the Greek work for wisdom, *sophia*. We will expand on this below. Wolters, along with others like Roland Murphy, Richard Clifford and Raymond van Leeuwen, all translate Proverbs 31:31 as "praise her for the fruit of her hands." This follows the very familiar form of hymns in the Psalter, but it depends on their translation of the first Hebrew word in the sentence *(tĕnû)* as coming from the root *tānâ* ("praise," "sing," "repeat") rather than the more common root *nātan*, "give" or "ascribe."[4] From this perspective, following her husband and children in Proverbs 31:28-29, the whole audience is called to sing to this woman for her excellence.

As is often the case, it is hard to be sure on these issues. Fox rejects both of these connections, saying that Wolters's arguments for the

---

[4]See our comments on verse 31 below.

translation are "weak."[5] Fox argues instead that the hymn form is used only for God and that this passage is an encomium comparable to Psalms 1; 15; 112; and 128.[6] Fox's literary connections are enlightening, but we find his critique less than convincing. For one, Fox does not believe the form of the hymnic participle ṣôpiyyâ (Prov 31:27) is unusual because he is able to find a similar form in Proverbs 7:11. This is a judgment about what is rare, but twice in a book of 31 chapters seems rare to us. Fox also rejects Wolters's suggestion that the hidden meaning is, "The ways of her house are sophia, wisdom," because it "makes poor sense." "The ways of her household," Fox says, are the actions of "members" of her family and not the woman whom the psalm praises. But the logic in his argument is not clear to us. The parallel in Proverbs 31:27b praises the woman's industry: she "does not eat the bread of idleness." Extending Wolters's suggestion, the hidden meaning is that "the ways of her house are wisdom because of her leadership and service." Though Fox recognizes that "Wolters is right that some of the imagery has heroic or martial overtones," he still believes it is "distant from heroic poetry which eulogizes the exploits of a warrior" with "nothing to be gained from stretching the hymn beyond its usual use [of praising God]."[7] These kinds of distinctions are simply a matter of perspective, and Fox appears to us to limit poetry's power to be allusive in just this way.

Thus we are still persuaded that this poem is a hymn, a form normally reserved for God but now used to esteem a heroic, wise woman. The form has been intentionally used to place this wise woman in a small class of elite Hebrew women like Jael, Deborah and Ruth.

### THE SONG'S MESSAGE IN THE HISTORY OF INTERPRETATION

Clearly this is unusually strong praise of a woman, and the challenge of what to make of her is reflected in the countless allegorical, literal and postmodern readings from ancient rabbinic and patristic times to today.

---

[5]See Michael V. Fox, Proverbs 10–31, Anchor Yale Bible (New Haven: Yale University Press, 2009), pp. 897-99, 902-5.
[6]Ibid., p. 903.
[7]Ibid.

The heroic hymn, after all, could be used to support literal and allegorical readings. Historically, the allegorical interpretation is by far the best attested, dominating interpretations from 100 B.C. to A.D. 1500. In ancient rabbinic interpretation, the woman in Proverbs 31 was generally interpreted allegorically as the Torah, but also as Moses, Joseph and Boaz. For the first fifteen centuries of Christian interpretation, she was read allegorically as the church (Augustine, Gregory the Great and Venerable Bede among many others), but also as intellectual wisdom (Origen), the mind and Mary (Vezelay and Perseigne), yet never as an actual, earthly woman.

It was not until Martin Luther and Philipp Melanchthon in the sixteenth century that we find a challenge to the long history of allegorical interpretation. Dissatisfied with what they regarded as inattentiveness to the linguistic and literary clarity of the text,[8] they read this passage as a poem about the vocation of a wife and mother. Melanchthon's two commentaries on Proverbs were the first to oppose the allegorical interpretation, followed by Luther's careful translation of the literary forms into German. Together these set a new trajectory for Protestant interpreters after the Reformation. Catholic writers, meanwhile, largely continued to defend the allegorical reading.

Even as literal interpretations were on the increase, connections between the woman's works and religion and faith remained unaddressed. To this day commentators are perplexed as to why a woman who fears the LORD is never described as engaging in "religious activities." In other words, she remained a good example for women at home and a vague encouragement to be spiritual and do good work to honor God. Franz Delitzsch, in the nineteenth century, was the first to really break the stronghold of allegorical and spiritualized interpretation, arguing instead that this woman's works were in fact the evidence and outworking of her fear of the LORD. Delitzsch rejected the medieval dualism between the secular and sacred/nature and grace and argued that this woman's spirituality (religion) motivates her works *in the world*. Delitzsch was clearly indebted to the growing tradition of Reformed Prot-

---

[8]See chapter 2 above for our discussion of literal and literary in ancient and modern understandings.

estant writers who, inspired by the rise of more and more historical and literary questions, resisted the Catholic and Anabaptist traditions, which held earthly works to be inferior to the higher spiritual calling of worshiping God.[9]

The move by Delitzsch and others to more literary and historical readings created new opportunities to ask theological questions about this woman's role in Proverbs and in Old Testament theology. What has emerged from this long history is insight into a poem that originally provided both a critique of prevailing elitist, rational forms of wisdom and of demeaning views of woman in the ancient world. At the same time, the poem encourages us to affirm *vocation*, the human calling to inhabit God's world in our full culture-making potential.

### THEOLOGICAL INTERPRETATION OF PROVERBS 31

The remainder of this chapter will unfold these critiques and the positive theology of the chapter.

#### Proverbs 31:1-9.

The sayings of King Lemuel—an oracle his mother taught him.

It is surprising to encounter a woman in the center of the portrait at the start of this chapter. The cosmic feminine theme that dominated Proverbs 1–9 had since largely disappeared, but here a woman is again in a concrete, practical and productive setting.

The words of King Lemuel's mother in Proverbs 31:1-9 are a rare phenomenon. Bruce Waltke points out that, while mothers of kings show up in ancient literature, giving advice on policymaking and theology, no parallel exists for a mother's wise sayings to her royal son.[10] Furthermore, mothers in the ancient world were typically expected to lead quiet lives in the home. This rare mother has knowledge of political, social and moral affairs, which suggests she has gained extensive experience in public life. In the ancient world, kings, gods and male warriors were the common targets of such praise. Yet in a creative turn,

---

[9]See Wolters, *Song of the Valiant Woman*, p. 131.
[10]Bruce Waltke, *Proverbs: Chapters 15–31*, NICOT (Grand Rapids: Eerdmans, 2005), p. 505.

this established king writes an oracle of praise about his own mother and her great wisdom. This has a subversive effect on typical views of wisdom, kingship and women.

Also noteworthy is this woman's first caution to her royal son not to give his "strength" *(ḥayil)* or his "ways" to women (Prov 31:3). This warning echoes the warnings about the adulteress in Proverbs 1–9. But the vocabulary also works to tie the whole book together. The root *ḥayil* ("strength") is rare in Proverbs,[11] and yet it appears three times in this chapter alone, once in King Lemuel's words (Prov 31:3) and twice in the hymn to the valiant woman (Prov 31:10, 29). This is one of many signs that these two passages have been intentionally woven together with the message of the book of Proverbs as a whole. Added to this, the references to "ways" and the strong emphasis on feminine wisdom and kingship connect these admonitions with the parents' voices in Proverbs 1–9. Thus it seems clear at this point that the reader should connect these two concrete women in Proverbs 31 to the cosmic women in Proverbs 1–9 and the wisdom sayings in Proverbs 10–29 (most of which are attributed to King Solomon). The teaching of King Lemuel's mother thus prepares us for the climactic poem in Proverbs 31:10-31.

***Proverbs 31:10-31.*** Recalling the context of Proverbs 31:1-9, Wolters suggests that the heroic hymn in Proverbs 31:10-31 continues the work of cultural critique, this time of ancient wisdom hymns. Not only does the profeminine motif carry over from Proverbs 31:1-9; but the hymn in Proverbs 31:10-31 also clearly symbolizes the public *activity* of a woman of wisdom, which undercuts the moods of antifeminism and rationalist wisdom in these ancient cultures. Wisdom is not a rational or spiritual retreat from the world, nor does it celebrate the musings of male scholars above all other professions. This wisdom is for everyone and applies to everything. As it glories in the essential goodness of women in the creation it sanctifies the concrete, practical lives of all humans—male and female, adult and child, politician and farmer, Wall Street broker and artist.

---

[11]It only appears elsewhere in Prov 12:4; 13:22; 25:23.

The introduction to the hymn begins with a heavily charged rhetorical question:

> A wife of noble character who can find?
>   She is worth far more the rubies. (Prov 31:10)

Finding a wife or woman was a common wisdom theme in the ancient world,[12] and this particular search has an allusive purpose that must be drawn out. First, as we noted before, the neutral translation of "noble character" in the NIV of a Hebrew word *(hayil)*, which is reserved almost exclusively for masculine or divine feats of military accomplishment, is inadequate. "Valiance" is a much more appropriate translation, suggesting that this woman—worthy of masculine, godlike praise—is really something to see. Added to that, the rhetorical effect of the question, "Who can find?" plays on the pervasive vocabulary of *finding wisdom* throughout the Wisdom literature. Using the verb *māṣāʾ* ("to find"), Proverbs speaks endlessly of finding wisdom and knowledge—for example, Proverbs 1:28; 2:5; 3:4, 13; 8:12, 17, 35; 10:13. Other references speak of *finding* the father's words, *finding* the path of life or of Dame Folly's *finding* the young man. It is highly likely that the language in Proverbs 12:4 and Proverbs 18:22 provides the language and imagery for Proverbs 31:10:

> A wife of noble character *[hayil]* is her husband's crown,
>   but a disgraceful wife is like decay in his bones.

> He who finds *[māṣāʾ]* a good wife, finds *[māṣāʾ]* what is good
>   and receives favor from the LORD.

Women, wives and wisdom constitute the central grain of Proverbs 1–9, giving these chapters the liminal urgency young men should feel for finding and loving wisdom. The assurance of finding wisdom in a fallen world, however, will be a complicated one. Elsewhere in Wisdom literature, Job's long, memorable dialogue in Job 28 asks provocatively,

> But where can wisdom be found *[māṣāʾ]*?
>   Where does understanding dwell?

---

[12]See Whybray, *Composition*, p. 155.

An even more extreme expression of finding wisdom appears in Ecclesiastes 7. This chapter repeats the verb *māṣā'* ("to find") a remarkable eight times, and in the chapter's climax the speaker, Qohelet, declares:

> While I was still searching
>> but not finding *[māṣā']*—
> I found *[māṣā']* one *upright* man among a thousand,
>> but one *upright* woman among them all I did not find *[māṣā']*.
>> (Eccles 7:28)[13]

Given all of these references to women, wisdom and finding, Qohelet's despair clearly has symbolic implications for his own search for wisdom. We will take this up in future chapters.

In any case, the question in Proverbs 31:10, like the rest of Proverbs 31 and Proverbs 1–9, has a rich intertextual connection with the many allusions in Old Testament wisdom to searching and finding wives, woman and wisdom.[14] The answer to who can find such a woman, then, is not obvious or simple, and the description of the wife (woman) that follows is one to be studied and considered carefully.

Waltke points out that as the hymn develops it progresses outwardly, starting with domestic work, then to community activity and finally to broader international and economic activity.[15] We would add that it also returns to the home in Proverbs 31:27-29. The introduction thus begins at home, where her husband's heart "trusts" in her for the good she will bring to him (Prov 31:11-12). The next fifteen verses lead us through the full range of her work—at home, in the community, in economics, with the poor and on her own. The nature, attitude and place of these activities, and her resulting praise, naturally give way to rich theological insights, which we will draw out below. Just think of the constant reference to her "hands" in her work; the intensity of her eyes in *looking* and

---

[13]Our translation. See on this more in chapter eight below.
[14]Whybray, *Composition*, p. 161, notes that the Hebrew word for woman (*'iššâ*) occurs only 13 times in 10:1–31:9 but is in more than half of all the verses (256) in Proverbs 1–9, identifying several female figures: "mother, bride, wife, adulteress, prostitute, personified Wisdom and Folly."
[15]Waltke, *Proverbs: Chapters 15-31*, p. 515.

*valuing;* and the joy, laughter and absence of anxiety in her attitude. These are all rich mines for exploration. We can hear overtones of the ideal garden in Genesis 2, with a woman vigorously and happily engaged in the work of tending and developing God's creation.

> She selects wool and flax
> and works with eager hands. (Prov 31:13)

The root word for "selects" is the Hebrew *dāraš,* which might appropriately be translated "she seeks." More importantly, the verb signals a pattern in this poem, focusing on the *value* she places on the commodities of human culture. As we will see again and again in this poem, she knows how to judge *the value of material things:* food, land, clothing and more. Not only does this critique the rationalist or elitist tendencies in ancient wisdom, which treasured ideas and great learning over material things; but it also confronts our culture in the West, both Christian and non-Christian, in the loss of the aptitude to know true quality.

Carlo Petrini gives a trenchant critique of the modern agro-industry, which mass produces, mass preserves and mass distributes food until there is no quality left.[16] Over the last century, foods, along with cars, clothes, homes, furniture, investments and more, have all been excessively labeled as quality products—luring us to value them. But what exactly does it mean to have quality? safe? comfortable? organic? clean? local? These advertisements never give precise answers, leaving us convinced that it must be there somewhere. On the contrary, quality, Petrini argues, is a discipline that must be studied, honed and passed down from generation to generation, from culture to culture—a process that has been totally lost in our postindustrial age.[17]

The psalmist invites us to "taste and see that the LORD is good" (Ps 34:8). Here too, in the tireless efforts of this woman nurturing the creation to bring out its most fruitful and creative products, this woman beckons us back to learn the challenging disciplines of knowing what and how and who to assess as "good" in this world.

---

[16]Carlo Petrini, *Slow Food Nation: Why Our Food Should Be Good, Clean, and Fair* (New York: Rizzoli Ex Libris, 2007).
[17]Ibid., pp. 91-143.

She is like the merchant ships,
  bringing her food from afar.
She gets up while it is still dark;
  she provides food for her family
  and portions for her servant girls. (Prov 31:14-15)

While Proverbs 31:14-15 speaks specifically to the benefits of the woman's house; the imagery overflows with industriousness in the realms of time and place. For one, we witness how her efforts range from the local to the international—like the merchant ships that come from "far away." We also gain a sense of her diligence, which begins "while it is still night" or early morning (Prov 31:15). In Proverbs 31:18 we find that she also works well into the night. In contrast to the weariness of our modern yuppie culture, or indeed to depressed or developing cultures where such long days are often unavoidable, this woman evokes an energy that can't get enough of all the good work there is to do. There are no signs of weariness, despair or burnout. One must proceed with caution at this point. No human could do everything this woman can do! That is not the point of the poem. The point, as we see it, is that true wisdom—when oriented to the goodness of God's creation—has no limit to the material, temporal and geographical regions in which it finds the joys of good work. Wisdom loves all of creation all of the time. The next verse reinforces this:

She considers a field and buys it;
  out of her earnings she plants a vineyard. (Prov 31:16)

This short couplet implies the extraordinary intelligence and vision that this woman has. For one thing, she has saved her money carefully. And, as with so many other sections in this poem, she "considers" (Hebrew *zāmam*) or has the insight and the immense delight in the creation (cf. Prov 8:30-31) to be able to value a piece of land. Here is quality: to a woman of wisdom, good land means good soil, good grapes, a profitable harvest for fermentation, and a community blessed and transformed by the results.

This mix of food and wine in Proverbs 31:15-16 is a theme throughout this poem. Our heroic woman, while attentive to the poor—likely with food—(Prov 31:20) also appreciates the beauty and necessity of celebration in a fallen world. Wine, together with bread and oil, are the most symbolic of foods, what food historian Maguelonne Toussaint-Samat calls the "three sacramental foods" and the "fundamental trinity."[18] As Leon Kass argues, eating is perhaps the most powerful act we do as physical creatures: "Compared to wisdom, eating may be a humble subject, but it is no trivial matter. It is the first and most urgent activity of all animal and human life: We are only because we eat."[19] Food reminds us of our dependency as creatures and wine of the mystery and richness of creation. In the New Testament, with the arrival of the Messiah, the kingdom (John 2) and the Lord's Supper, bread, wine and oil feature centrally as we feast on the Lord himself as our entrance into the redeemed human life. These foods stand as signs against the evil, injustice and poverty in the world while also affirming the place of celebration. Thus, not only does the Supper celebrate that the king of creation reigns; but it also reminds us that God sustains our physical bodies now and will do so for all eternity.

Most of the poetry in this hymn, in fact, describes physical work that leads to meeting the need for clothes and food. But on several occasions these two literal images (clothing and eating) are reversed and used figuratively to praise the woman's strength (Prov 31:17, 25) and her diligent work (Prov 31:27).

> She girds herself with strength;
> she makes her arms strong. (Prov 31:17)[20]

The Hebrew word "girds" (ḥāgar) above is typically used to describe a warrior donning armor for battle. The same imagery appears again in Proverbs 31:25, where "she is clothed with strength and dignity." Here the heroic genre is undeniable, reminding us that this woman deserves the praise of Israel's best warriors and of God himself! The fact that this is a woman, who is otherwise pictured as inferior in the ancient world, reflects positively on all human endeavors in

---

[18]Maguelonne Toussaint-Samat, *A History of Food* (Oxford: Wiley-Blackwell, 2009), p. 183.

[19]Leon Kass, *The Hungry Soul: Eating and the Perfecting of Our Nature* (Chicago: Chicago University Press, 1999), p. 2.

[20]Our translation.

this world—whether done by men or women.

> She sees that her trading is profitable,
>     and her lamp does no go out at night. (Prov 31:18)

Proverbs 31:18 again emphasizes the economic and aesthetic sophistication involved in her work. Quite literally, she "tastes" that her merchandise is good. Those skilled in the visual arts or music, food, clothing or agriculture know that the sense of a product's worth is a skill developed through study and experience. This poem constantly runs against the grain of our fast-food, box-store, technological culture, with its love of speed, affordability and convenience over quality and durability. Slow tasting, measuring, considering and contemplating dominate the wise woman's market sense.

> In her **hand[s]** she holds the distaff;[21]
>     and grasps the spindle with her fingers [**palms**].
> She opens her arms [**palm**] to the poor
>     and extends her **hands** to the needy. (Prov 31:19-20)

These verses, at the center and peak of the chapter, draw our attention to her hands once again, as is shown visually in the passage above. Wolters points out the following chiastic structure in the couplet:

Hands—Reaches
    Palms—Grasps
    Palm—Spreads
Hand—Reaches[22]

To reach or "put out the hands" is another military term, reinforcing her valiant character. Furthermore, fulfilling the words of his mother to Lemuel (Prov 31:9), she provides mercy to the poor and needy. Given the linguistic ties, it seems likely that these verses (Prov 31:19-20) should be taken together. Her tireless industry at home and her keen sense of aesthetic quality and beauty (see Prov 31:21-22) are poured out

---

[21]See Wolters's extended treatment of this verse in *Song of the Valiant Woman*, pp. 42-55, where he shows that "distaff" cannot be found as a tool in literature of the ANE and that a better translation would be some kind of "grasped spindle" nearly synonymous with the tool in Prov 31:19b.

[22]Wolters, *Song of the Valiant Woman*, p. 46.

among oppressed classes in her local culture. This is the opposite of our second-hand culture, where we give away our unwanted stuff. While there is nothing wrong with giving away used things, this woman elevates the dignity of the poor by treating them like her own children. She also confronts our tendency to political and theoretic activism, which yields no benefit to the poor; she readily gets down to the business of caring for the needy with her hands.

> When it snows, she has no fear for her household;
>      for all of them are clothed in scarlet.
> She makes coverings for her bed;
>      she is clothed in fine linen and purple.
>
> She makes linen garments and sells them;
>      and supplies the merchants with sashes.
> She is clothed with strength and dignity;
>      she can laugh at the days to come. (Prov 31:21-22, 24-25)

Proverbs 31:21 begins the second half of the poem, marked by the appearance of the thematic word "fear"—in this case, "she fears not." In fact, in the Hebrew, the verb "fears not" begins the sentence, emphasizing the nature of the attitude she carries into her work. In Proverbs 31:25 we are told that "she laughs at the days to come." In the ancient world, the weather and the unknown course of future events (invasion, corrupt kings, crime, famine and death) were the major threats to local and national well-being. Like the ant who prepares its food in the summer (Prov 6:6-8; 30:25), this woman has prepared herself for the unforeseeable. But she also trusts in God as she works. Her fear, as we will see below, is submitted obediently to Yahweh, the Creator, and her wisdom enables her to face the future fearlessly and joyfully.

These four verses are also important for the way they again emphasize the exceptional quality of this woman's work. The Walmart, mass-market economy, which pursues rapid production at the lowest prices, sets its economic hopes on the abstract values of profit, market share and capital growth. This woman has an old-fashioned sense of the good land (Prov 31:16), good merchandise (Prov 31:18) and, here, in good clothing—a skill of patient and careful reflection. The references to "scarlet," "linen" and "purple" as well as the "linen garments" and "sashes" in Proverbs 31:24, may not be immediately clear to a modern culture, but in the ancient Near East they would be indications of luxury and quality.

> Her husband is respected at the city gate,
> where he takes his seat among the elders of the land. (Prov 31:23)

> She speaks with wisdom,
> and faithful instruction is on her tongue. (Prov 31:26)

In these two verses we find a strong connection between the advice from King Lemuel's mother in Proverbs 31:1-9 and the valiant woman's song. In the song, the husband gains a kind of celebrity status because of his wife's great wisdom. In Lemuel's situation, he is making a public, national statement about the wise words his own mother used to prepare him for a successful kingship. In both cases, women are elevated as foundations of a successful culture by virtue of their great wisdom. Wisdom, we are reminded, is not exclusively or primarily for male kings, as many cultures would have believed. In fact, this is a strong reversal of those values; in Proverbs any ordinary person who embodies wisdom can become the worthy object of royal praise.

> She watches over the affairs of her household
> and does not eat the bread of idleness. (Prov 31:27)

Before the song begins its closing praise (Prov 31:28-31), Proverbs 31:27 provides a summary statement of the entire passage. This is only clear if we make special note of the verb "she watches over," which is translated from the Hebrew *ṣôpiyyâ*. Making careful reference to the probable date of the song and the pronunciation of ancient Hebrew, Wolters has convincingly argued that this verb plays on the Greek word for wisdom, *sophia*.[23] The words sound the same but mean entirely different things. No doubt this would have reinforced the poem's unabated critique of other ancient views of wisdom. Her "wisdom," or *sophia*, is not an intellectual or abstract form of wisdom reserved for philosopher

---

[23]In the introduction above we cited Michael Fox's rejection of Wolters's reading, though we regard it as unsatisfying in many ways.

kings but a particular, active and loving way of living in the world made by the one true God.

> Her children arise and call her blessed;
>     her husband also, and he praises her:
> "Many women do noble things,
>     but you surpass them all." (Prov 31:28-29)

The conclusion to the song requires four full verses. These first two begin with the praise that flows from the home, just as her work started there in Proverbs 31:10-12. This woman is what we would call "im-placed." Her work is not abstract; it is particular in its location and its group of familiar people. She does not just wander the village doing good works, helpful as that would be; she works out of the strength and security of those she loves and those who love her. As Edward Casey observes,

> We care about people as well as places, so much so that we can say that *caring belongs to places*. We care about places in many ways, but in building on them—*building with them*, indeed, *building them*—they become the ongoing "stars of life," that to which we turn when we travel and to which we return when we come back home.[24]

While the woman's success in and outside the home was a common value across ancient cultures, it is less so today. More and more couples live most of their lives outside the home, sometimes by necessity, sometimes in search of identity and affirmation, and often in response to the job market. With the new standard of the two-income household and the single working mother, the family and the home have paid the price. We cannot help but take note of the recent explosion of a whole new set of cultural realities at once: daycare centers, children's television, a plethora of toys and video games, parenting books, countless youth sports programs, extended summer camps, all-day kindergarten and even junior kindergarten. These were rare just thirty years ago. Everywhere we look we find increasing signs that parents and grandparents, aunts and uncles, and siblings and neighbors—all of whom

---

[24]Edward Casey, *Getting Back into Place: Toward a Renewed Understanding of the Place-World* (Bloomington: Indiana University Press, 1993), pp. 175-76.

constituted the "family" in the ancient world of Proverbs—are no longer the dominant context for raising a child. A new economic child-raising conglomerate reigns, while the traditions and the familiarity of the home are lost.

We are not arguing that woman's liberation is to blame. The problems are much larger and far more complex than that. In his classic work *Until Justice and Peace Embrace*, Nicholas Wolterstorff argues that the overwhelming power of the new global economy has driven individuals to break their loyalties to the family, to the church and to anything that doesn't feed individual comfort and survival.[25] Everything in our culture tell us to build careers and economic security, but almost nothing tells us to build homes and to nurture a sense of being grounded in a particular place belonging to a particular people. The family, according to Proverbs 31, is the core building block of a culture—the place where our day begins and ends and the source of our truest affirmation and sense of identity. The valiant woman encourages men and women to ground their loyalty with the people and in the place where they begin and end their day.

> Charm is deceptive and beauty is fleeting;
> but a woman who fears the LORD is to be praised. (Prov 31:30)

Once again, the countercultural thrust of this song comes through. Neither women nor men are to be cherished for physical beauty alone; their deepest worth is in their capacity to embody wisdom. In this way the poem ends where the book of Proverbs began—with the fear of the LORD. What is it that enables this woman to embody wisdom so beautifully? She orients her life to the Creator of the world and lives out her faith to the full in her daily activities. The audience is rightly called to praise her following the example set by the family in Proverbs 31:28-29. Their refrain:

> Honor her for all that her hands have done,
> And let her works bring her praise at the city gate.

---

[25]Nicholas Wolterstorff, *Until Justice and Peace Embrace* (Grand Rapids, Eerdmans, 1983), p. 103.

The translation above comes from the NIV 2010, which takes the first Hebrew word in verse 31, "Honor," as coming from the Hebrew root *tānâ*, "sing," "recite" or "commemorate." The 1984 edition of the NIV had understood the first Hebrew word as coming from *nātan*, "give." The point is that we are to "extol" her for "the fruit of her hands."[26] Fruitfulness is a rich biblical image. Like the tree of life in Proverbs 3:18 and the multiple trees throughout the Bible (Gen 2:9; Ps 1:1-6; Jer 17:8, Ezek 47:11-12; Rev 22:2), this woman's life brings forth the full potential of God's creation. And for this she deserves to be praised by all readers of this song. The imagery of the city gate is a call to praise in the local community. What a striking ending to the book: wisdom receives its rewards not in public media but among the people we see and touch day by day. This woman has created life and vibrancy in her neighborhood.

## THEOLOGICAL REFLECTIONS

The hymn to the valiant woman is a rich resource for theological reflection, some of which we have already developed above. She is so fully human and so alive that it is hard to resist moving from exegesis to application. In conclusion we unpack some of the many theological resources in this chapter.

First, *wisdom is neither purely masculine nor primarily philosophical.* Here we return to the importance of the ancient countercultural intentions of this song. Claire Gottlieb shows that Sumerian texts evidence very similar praises to "treasured" women. Yet in the Sumerian praises, the focus is on the physical beauty and erotic benefits of these women, whereas Proverbs speaks of her intelligence, industry and moral qualities.[27] Similarly in Akkadian and Roman cultures women were often praised for their industry, but only in the home[28] and not in the public square, where the valiant woman is active. Her public industry and her acceptance among merchants, traders and the local culture at the gates

---

[26]See Waltke, *Proverbs: Chapters 15-31*, pp. 514, 536.
[27]Claire Gottlieb, "The Words of the Exceedingly Wise: Proverbs 30-31," in *The Biblical Canon in Comparative Perspective*, ed. K. L. Younger Jr., W. W. Hallo and B. F. Batto, Ancient Near Eastern Texts and Studies 11 (Lewiston, N.Y.: Edwin Mellen, 1991), pp. 284-85.
[28]Ibid., pp. 286-87.

are a strong contrast to common views of women—ancient and modern—that limit their vocations to the home. Wolters shows, by way of the play between the Hebrew *ṣôpiyyâ* and Greek *sophia*, that this woman personifies true wisdom, a symbolic critique of the elitist rationalism of Greek culture.[29]

Furthermore, the song teaches us that the creation, though fallen, is *good*. The valiant woman constantly appraises the essential goodness of clothing materials, land, crops and food. On the one hand we in the Western Christian world suffer from a "left behind" apathy toward the physical creation. We're headed for a heavenly, spiritual realm, so we're told, with no bodies, food, land, houses or games, so why not eat processed food and shop at Wal-Mart? The Bible nowhere teaches such an escapist mentality; rather, it teaches that we are waiting to be surprised by a new creation, where God's will is done on earth as it is in heaven.[30] This good creation is the very stuff of redemption.

The goodness of the creation helps us to appreciate this woman's focus on *particular goods and local neighborhoods*. While she lived in a totally different world and economy, her actions nevertheless persuade us to reflect critically on the costs of the move to global capitalism. Wendell Berry laments that we've been barraged by our secular modern version of a "total economy," which encourages us to work away for the vaporous ideals of money, stock shares, net worth, gross domestic product and the luxurious convenience of unlimited access to food and natural resources.[31] All of these are achieved today at the expense of creational goods, "the health of watersheds, the integrity of ecosystems, the wholeness of human hearts . . . timber and food, clean water and clean air," not to mention the loss of reasonable wages, just trade and the long-term recreational use of the land.[32] All the while we lay an

---

[29]Wolters, *Song of the Valiant Woman*, pp. 13, 34-41.

[30]See N. T. Wright, *Surprised by Hope: Rethinking Heaven, the Resurrection, and the Mission of the Church* (San Francisco: HarperOne, 2008), for an extensive argument for the future eternal hope that awaits the Christian.

[31]For a critical reflection on energy and modern human behavior, see Wendell Berry, "The Use of Energy," in *The Unsettling of America: Culture and Agriculture* (San Francisco: Sierra Club, 1977), pp. 81-95.

[32]Wendell Berry, *Citizenship Papers* (Washington, D.C.: Shoemaker and Hoard, 2003), pp. 36-37, 46-47.

insurmountable agricultural, social and financial debt on the next generation. In all our thinking about shares and capital we have lost track of real people, their true happiness and their ultimate livelihood.

The wise woman's work and values start and end in the home, not in the international marketplace. And, while her trade extends to faraway places, her industry is centered in her local community, signaled clearly by her care for her house, the way she attends to her employees (servant girls), her compassion for the poor and needy, and her praises at the local town gates.

The great diversity of her work also teaches us that *no enterprise or human calling should be regarded as a lower or less-spiritual aspect of God's world*. All of creation is good and calls us to develop its hidden potentials to God's glory.

Wisdom also affirms that *work itself is good* and not just necessary. In the garden, before the fall, God charged Adam and Eve with keeping and tending his whole creation. Tending gardens in the ancient world was a task connected with royalty and great wealth. We are meant to imagine Adam and Eve as God's human king and queen, overseeing all that he has made. The rebellion and fall in Genesis 3 leaves a dark stain on this royal privilege. Yet Proverbs spreads a ray of hope on the plight of the world. Wisdom lovingly provides a path back to the tree of life (Prov 3:18). Wisdom allows this woman, in the midst of the broken and sick realities of the world, to laugh at the future (Prov 31:25) and have no fear of the wildness of nature (Prov 31:21). Rather than work beating her down, as it would do for Adam after the fall (Gen 3:17-19), wisdom sets her eyes on the eternal purposes of the Creator and steadfast desire to redeem and renew the world. In response, she pursues her work with vigor and joy. Woman wisdom's joy and frolicking in Proverbs 8:30-31 is a significant parallel to her attitude here.

Wisdom also teaches us that we live amid a *diverse creation*. The poem's beauty stems largely from its reach into almost every sphere of ancient economic and social life. The point of Proverbs 8, and passages like Psalms 8, 19, 104 and 139, is to teach us that God made the world with endless depth, goodness, variety and breadth. Just think of the billions of species of plants and animals and the hundreds of climates around the world. In human cultures, this has led to an endless range of approaches to economics, social structures, politics, leisure, education and aesthetics. Driven by a love for wisdom, the valiant woman has developed expertise in many different spheres of life. Her creativity thus invites us to explore God's world and develop it as enthusiastically as she does. In this way, she embodies the creation mandate to "be fruitful and increase in number; fill the earth and subdue it. Rule over the fish of the sea and the birds of the air and over every living creature that moves on the ground" (Gen 1:28). Like Noah's dove that returns with olive branches from a new world, this woman ultimately reminds Christians that Jesus has risen with the good news that the creation is safe for humanity to rule again—and not just some of it, but the world in its fullness.[33]

Finally, the song upholds the *vocational richness of humanity*. Because the whole creation is good in its beautiful diversity and because human work is godly, we should affirm a rich variety of vocations. As Eugene Peterson poignantly notes, "We are all in holy orders." Note that we did not say "jobs." Vocation, in contrast to a job, signals *the call* for us each to cultivate our unique gifts as we go out to rule and develop the world. Both our conservative and liberal forms of government in the West rate the workforce by job growth and the employment rate. But how many people are working for a paycheck, sadly separated from their personal gifts and sense of call? Again and again Wendell Berry writes about the goodness of work and the urgent need for Christians to develop and renew the vocations that are necessary for healthy people, communities and nations. Berry mourns the modern devaluation of calling, where "one does not do the work that one chooses to do because one is called to it by Heaven or by one's natural abilities, but does instead the work that is determined and imposed by the economy."[34] We have lost a biblically rooted vision for integrating humanity with its created surroundings.

---

[33]Andy Crouch's book *Culture Making* is a hopeful call for Christians to get about the business of developing the full diversity of creation (Downers Grove, Ill.: InterVarsity Press, 2008). Cf. also Michael Goheen and Craig G. Bartholomew, *Living at the Crossroads: An Introduction to Christian Worldview* (Grand Rapids: Baker Academic, 2008).

[34]Berry, *Citizenship Papers*, p. 71.

In Genesis 2:19-20, when God tells Adam to name the animals, he gives us the freedom to exercise individual creativity in caring for the world he made. When we talk about jobs without reference to vocation we commit an injustice to the way God has made each of us individually to flourish in unique ways. We also carelessly underestimate God's wisdom in giving us a diversity of gifts for the diversity of creation he intends us to keep. As a result, we suffer not just as individuals and communities but as national global economies as well. Only those vocations that are encouraged and supported by our market economy are deemed worthy of pursuing.

In this sense, the renewal of vocations must also give attention to the distortions and corruptions that have come to otherwise good callings. The cultural background of the song reminds us that good callings often go wrong: artists who produce pornography, athletes and businesses dominated by greed, and politicians motivated by narcissism and power. Today, humanist and individualist ideals are often cherished over values like justice, humility, peace and service. But like the resurrected Christ, this woman calls us into our broken cultures to pursue a renewed order in the world where all of God's creatures are freed to flourish and develop their own creativity.

## CONCLUSION

As we end our theological reading of the song, we recall the many reasons this woman is worthy of a hymn, most of them described by verbs like feeding and clothing and not by adjectives like beauty or wit.[35] She serves her husband well (Prov 31:12); she rises early to provide for her household (Prov 31:15); she is successfully involved in real estate ventures and agriculture (Prov 31:16); she shows mercy to the needy and poor (Prov 31:20); and, among other things, she clothes her family in scarlet, fine linen and purple (Prov 31:21-22). Like the cosmic Lady Wisdom in Proverbs 1–9, this woman joyfully embraces the goodness of the created order, burying herself in every sphere where wisdom can go: family, economics, religion, agriculture (winemaking!), marriage,

---

[35]See Wolters, *Song of the Valiant Woman*, p. 11.

mercy to the poor, artistic creations and more. Wisdom is not some intellectual climb to brilliance or a moral growth to perfection. It is about navigating all of life joyfully and faithfully in God's good but fallen world. The description of this woman is the perfect bookend to that of Woman Wisdom in Proverbs 1–9. Where the "fear of Yahweh" is the beginning of wisdom (Prov 1:7; 9:10), it is also the chief reason to praise the valiant woman of great works (Prov 31:30).

In our English Bibles, which follow the order in the Greek Septuagint, Ecclesiastes follows Proverbs. But in many Hebrew manuscripts,[36] Proverbs 31 is followed by the book of Ruth. This story is the only other place where the Hebrew word "valiant" *(hayil)* is used of a woman. This story is about a "valiant" (Ruth 3:11) woman who meets a "valiant" man (Ruth 2:1), who together are expected to bring about "valiance" in all they do (Ruth 4:11). The powerful and all-too-frequently neglected nature of farming, food, houses, service and mercy in the context of fearing the LORD (Ruth 2:4) makes Ruth a fitting narrative to follow this song. As men and women we are called to imitate the heroism of Boaz, Ruth and this woman of wisdom.

### RECOMMENDED READING

#### *Commentaries*

Leeuwen, Raymond C. van. "Proverbs." In *The New Interpreter's Bible,* ed. Leander Keck, 5:17-264. Nashville: Abingdon, 1997.

Waltke, Bruce K. *Proverbs: Chapters 1–15.* NICOT. Grand Rapids: Eerdmans, 2004.

———. *Proverbs: Chapters 15–31.* NICOT. Grand Rapids: Eerdmans, 2005.

#### *Scholarly resources*

Gottlieb, Claire. "The Words of the Exceedingly Wise: Proverbs 30–31." In *The Biblical Canon in Comparative Perspective,* ed. K. L. Younger Jr., W. W. Hallo and B. F. Batto, pp. 277-98. Ancient Near Eastern Texts and Studies 11. Lewiston, N.Y.: Edwin Mellen, 1991.

Wolters, Al. *The Song of the Valiant Woman: Studies in the Interpretation of Proverbs 31:10-31.* Carlisle, U.K.: Paternoster, 2001.

---

[36]The Leningrad Codex, for example.

Whybray, R. N. *The Composition of the Book of Proverbs.* JSOTSup. Sheffield, U.K.: JSOT Press, 1994.

### Practical works

Berry, Wendell. *Sex, Economy, Freedom, Community.* New York: Pantheon, 1993.

Kass, Leon. *The Hungry Soul: Eating and the Perfection of Our Nature.* Chicago: University of Chicago Press, 1994.

Visser, Margaret. *The Rituals of Dinner: The Origins, Evolution, Eccentricities, and Meaning of Table Manners.* Toronto: HarperPerennial, 2008.

# 6

# Job

*We don't receive wisdom; we must discover it for ourselves*
*after a journey that no one can take for us or spare us.*

—MARCEL PROUST, *IN SEARCH OF LOST TIME*, VOL. 2

JOB'S STORY IS ONE OF THE MOST PUZZLING in the Old Testament.[1] There are mysterious divine courts, a nameless accuser, an
incomprehensible turn of events in a righteous man's life and an unexpected conclusion. The book's long speeches and many unanswered
questions take the reader on an extraordinary journey, requiring us to
reflect seriously on a whole range of issues from justice, knowledge,
righteousness and suffering, to forgiveness, community and the sovereignty of God. Not surprisingly many readers throughout the ages have
found Job something of an enigma.[2] Unraveling an enigma is hard
work, but as we hope to show by the end of this chapter, when it comes
to Job the hard work is well worthwhile, indeed, essential.

## ORIGIN AND HISTORY OF THE BOOK

The origin, meaning and integrity of the book of Job have been debated
from the ancient rabbis[3] to the present.[4] The earliest recorded debates

---

[1]We are grateful to Paul Edgar for providing background research for this chapter.
[2]For the ancient history of interpretation of Job, see Hananel Mack, *Job and the Book of Job in Rabbinic Literature* (Ramat Gan, Israel: Bar Ilan University Press, 2004). A comprehensive list of
works on Job is found in David J. A. Clines, *Job 1–20* (Nashville: Nelson, 1989), pp. lxii-cxv.
[3]See Mack, *Job and the Book of Job*.
[4]For a good overview, see Brevard S. Childs, *Introduction to the Old Testament as Scripture* (London: SCM, 1979), pp. 526-44.

regarding its authenticity are found in the Jewish Talmudic material that frequently relies on pre-Christian oral sources.[5] We will say more about this history below. But first, it must be recognized that Job has several characteristics that set it apart from other Old Testament books, including the Wisdom literature:

- Remarkably, none of the characters is Hebrew. The story takes place east of Israel, in a land called Uz, apparently somewhere between Edom (southern Jordan) and Babylon (south-central Iraq).

- The vocabulary of the book is heavily influenced by Aramaic.

- On the surface Job makes only oblique references to other biblical books and characters.

As with other Old Testament books, we find stories comparable to Job in ancient Near Eastern and Greek literature.[6] Clines helpfully notes that "the Hebrew tale of Job . . . may be indebted to such texts . . . but the Book of Job itself seems to be a fresh and independent creation. The other Near Eastern texts do, however, remind us that the issues raised by the book of Job were not unique to Israel."[7] And, despite the absence of what seem to be clear allusions to the Old Testament, a closer reading reveals many intertextual links with Old Testament wisdom and other Old Testament material.[8] Thus, despite its unusual characteristics, most current scholarship rightly believes Job to be Israelite literature. The non-Hebrew elements seem to us to be a deliberate device to stress the universality of wisdom.

As for its dating, some have argued that the book predates the story of Abraham recorded in Genesis. Others have argued for a date as late as the third or fourth century B.C.[9] Both of these extremes have their

---

[5]In particular, *Baba Batra* 15a-16b.
[6]See Thomas Krüger et al., eds., *Das Buch Hiob und seine Interpretationen: Beiträge zum Hiob-Symposium af dem Monte Verita von 14.-19. August 2005* (Zurich: TVZ, 2007), pp. 1-163.
[7]Clines, *Job 1–20*, p. lx.
[8]See, e.g., Michael Fishbane, "The Book of Job and Inner-Biblical Discourse," in *The Voice From the Whirlwind*, ed. Leo G. Perdue and W. Clark Gilpin (Nashville: Abingdon, 1992), pp. 86-98; Konrad Schmid, "Innerbiblische Schriftdiskussion im Hiobbuch," in *Das Buch Hiob und seine Interpretationen*, pp. 241-61.
[9]See John Day, "Foreign Semitic Influence on the Wisdom of Israel," in *Wisdom in Ancient Israel*, ed. John Day, Robert P. Gordon and H. G. M. Williamson (Cambridge: Cambridge University Press, 1995), pp. 56-57.

share of problems. As far as we can tell, Job was never used in ancient
Hebrew or Jewish ritual, as were Ecclesiastes, Psalms and Deuteronomy. A few verses made it into the first rabbinical Jewish collections of
ritual prayer and worship, but that was well after the fall of the Roman
Empire. There does seem to be evidence of an oral tradition commenting on Job, but no secondary references to or ancient Jewish commentaries on it, as we have with some other Old Testament books. The
earliest evidence we have of Job is the fragments of Aramaic translations that were found among the Qumran Scrolls.[10] The next oldest
reference to Job is in the ancient manuscripts of the epistle of James (Jas
5:11). Job was also included in the Greek Septuagint (LXX). While existing manuscripts of the LXX postdate both Qumran and the earliest
manuscripts of James, they accurately reflect textual and canonical history from the same period as the Qumran texts, or perhaps a bit earlier.
It therefore seems safe to assume that the book of Job achieved a canonical[11] status at about the same time that the Psalms reached its fullest form—around 400 B.C. Just how this moving chronicle of the miseries of a God-fearing non-Jew, living outside the borders of Israel, and
apparently having no Jewish contacts, came to that point is currently
beyond our knowing. We are extremely grateful that it did.

**STRUCTURE AND OUTLINE**

In terms of its genre Job is clearly a lengthy *narrative:*[12] it tells a story
with all the normal features of a narrative: introduction, conflict, climax, resolution, protagonist, antagonists and so on. Yet in every other
case, the Old Testament uses prose to communicate a story of this sort.
As a book composed mostly of poetry, some have sought parallels to Job

---

[10]Job is briefly mentioned in Ezekiel 14:14 alongside Noah and Daniel as an example of a righteous man.
[11]The term "canonical" is used to describe the collection of religious books controlled by the
Jewish religious authorities of the time. We do not imply here that this collection was yet explicitly defined by those authorities.
[12]Of course it contains a variety of genres. Samuel Terrien, *The Elusive Presence: Toward a New
Biblical Theology* (New York: Harper & Row, 1978), p. 361, argues that "this unique document
escapes classification, for it presents a bewildering diversity of literary genres: folktale, proverbial sayings, lament, hymn, invective, prophetic confession, legal controversy, juridical oath,
*onomastica,* and theophany."

in Greek tragedies.[13] Harold Fisch's study of Job, for example, illustrates the many features Job has in common with classical Greek drama or tragedy, especially the way we feel drawn to sympathize with Job's misery, confusion and innocence.[14] As we will see below and especially in the next chapter, the extremes achieved in the poetic images and language evoke empathy for Job in his suffering. Yet, while Job shares some of the rhetorical pathos of Greek poetry, he is not a typical Greek hero.[15] Not only is Job's suffering turned around in the end; but also neither the story nor Job stand alone in their literary context. As Fisch explains, "instead of fable rounded upon itself, we have the undetermined movement of historical time, a witnessing to purposes still to be disclosed and by no means confined to the fate of the hero."[16] Job's suffering has not been fully explained by the end; instead, we are confronted with a powerful picture of Yahweh, which leads us back into the Old Testament and God's work with Israel in her own suffering, sin and future hope.

The second notable characteristic of Job is the "frame narrative" (Job 1:1–3:1 and Job 42:7-17), which surrounds the poetic dialogue, the bulk of the book (Job 3:2–42:6).[17]

I.   Prose Narrative Opening (1:1–3:1)

II.  Poetic Dialogues (3:2–42:6)

III. Prose Narrative Closing (42:7-17)

This feature is clear enough in English but even more striking in the Hebrew. Not only does the form between the sections change from prose to poetry but the vocabulary also elevates from a simple to a complex register. It is like moving from English at eighth-grade level to the

---

[13]See, e.g., Katherine Dell, "Job: Sceptics, Philosophers and Tragedians," in *Das Buch Hiob und seine Interpretationen*, pp. 1-19.

[14]Harold Fisch, "Job: Tragedy Is Not Enough," in *Poetry with a Purpose: Biblical Poetics and Interpretation* (Bloomington: Indiana University Press, 1988), pp. 26-42.

[15]See also Norman C. Habel, *The Book of Job*, OTL (Philadelphia: Westminster Press, 1985), pp. 44-45.

[16]Ibid., p. 42.

[17]See Ryan O'Dowd, "Frame Narrative," in *Dictionary of the Old Testament: Wisdom, Poetry and Writings*, ed. Tremper Longman III and Peter Enns (Downers Grove, Ill.: InterVarsity Press, 2008), pp. 241-45.

English of Shakespeare and back again. This has raised speculation as to how the text was edited and put together, the possibility of divergent sources and so on. Interestingly, however, the two parts are unintelligible without one another. Whatever intrinsic literary merits each section may have, they belong together. The details revealed in the prose give the context within which the poetic dialogue finds profound and universal meaning. It tells why Job is suffering, who is causing his suffering, the means of his suffering and why his suffering will not stop. It also validates Job's claim of righteousness. At the same time, the intense drama of the poetry lends credibility, depth and a human face to an otherwise one-dimensional moral story that justifies God.

As a final point of introduction, the three ways the author(s) refer to God should be noted. Throughout the prologue and epilogue God is referred to both as Elohim (God) and as Yahweh (God's covenant name). Throughout the poetry all the references to God are to Elohim or Shaddai (the Almighty) with only two exceptions: Job mentions Yahweh in Job 12:9, where he assigns his suffering to "the hand of Yahweh";[18] and the very rare use of Adonai (Lord) in Job 28:28. Below, we will suggest how these uses might be deliberately drawing on different aspects of the theology of the creation account in Genesis 1–3 and of Proverbs.

The structure of Job can be outlined as follows:

I. Frame-Narrative Opening (1:1–3:1)

    A. Description of Job and His Family (1:1-5)

    B. First Heavenly Assembly (1:6-12)

    C. First Attack on Job: Loss of Donkeys, Sheep, Camels, Servants and Children (1:13-19)

    D. Job's Response to His Loss (1:20-22)

    E. Second Heavenly Assembly (2:1-6)

    F. Second Attack on Job: Loss of Health; Wife Discourages Him (2:7-10)

---

[18]Though some scholars argue that this is the author's or else a redactor's mistake.

G.  Arrival of Job's Friends, Eliphaz, Bildad and Zophar (2:11-13)

H.  Introduction to the Poetic Discourses (3:1)

II.  Poetic Dialogue with Eliphaz, Bildad and Zophar (3:2–31:40)

  A.  Job's Complaint (3:2-26)

  B.  First Set of Rebukes and Responses (4:1–14:22)

    1.  Eliphaz and Job (4:1–7:21)

    2.  Bildad and Job (8:1–10:22)

    3.  Zophar and Job (11:1–14:22)

  C.  Second Set of Rebukes and Responses (15:1–21:34)

    1.  Eliphaz and Job (15:1–17:16)

    2.  Bildad and Job (18:1–19:29)

    3.  Zophar and Job (20:1–21:34)

  D.  Third Set of Rebukes and Responses (22:1–31:40)

    1.  Eliphaz and Job (22:1–24:25)

    2.  Bildad and Job (25:1–31:40)

III.  Narrative Introduction to Elihu and Elihu's Speech (32:1–37:24)

IV.  The Divine Speeches: Yahweh Answers Job (38:1–42:6)

  A.  First Half of God's Speech (38:1–40:2)

  B.  Job's First Response (40:3-5)

  C.  Second Half of God's Speech (40:6–41:34)

  D.  Job's Second Response (42:1-6)

V.  Frame-Narrative Closing (42:7-17)

  A.  God's Rebuke of the Friends and His Declaration That Job Is Right (42:7-9)

  B.  God's Restoration of Job; His Prosperity and Then Death (42:10-17)

In what follows we will discuss the major sections of Job and then conclude with theological reflection on the book as a whole.

## SETTING THE STAGE: JOB 1:1–3:1

> In the land of Uz there lived a man whose name was Job. This man was blameless and upright; he feared God and shunned evil. (Job 1:1)

The narrative, true to the book's peculiar style, begins by describing an incomparably wise and righteous man who fears Israel's God but who lives in the East, apart from Israel's known habitations and wanderings.

> He had seven sons and three daughters, and he owned seven thousand sheep, three thousand camels, five hundred yoke of oxen and five hundred donkeys, and had a large number of servants. He was the greatest man among all the people of the East. (Job 1:2-3)

In his story *The Man Who Was Thursday,* G. K. Chesterton creates a London suburb called Saffron Park. This suburb is meant in many ways to resemble Job's life in these early chapters. He says of the suburb, "The place was not only pleasant, but perfect."[19] Indeed, these verses stretch the limits of belief; not only does Job appear morally perfect, but the numbers of his children and belongings are typical Old Testament symbols of wholeness and perfection (threes, sevens and tens). The final claim—that Job was the greatest man of the East—completes the image. Such a picture of perfection leads us to expect that there may be more to this story than we are being told: things are just too good to be true.

In the next two chapters, the narrator ushers us rapidly back and forth from Job's life to the heavenly courts—a full three times. Apart from Job's knowledge, a heavenly assembly has convened with "the sons of God" and a nameless accuser (the *satan*) in attendance. The satan is not one of the members of this court (Job 1:6) but rather comes there from "roaming through the earth and going back and forth in it" (Job

---

[19]From G. K. Chesterton, *The Man Who Was Thursday: A Nightmare* (New York: Modern Library, 2001), p. 7. Chesterton's book, based largely on the book of Job, is a wonderful aid for reading Job for theological and cultural insights.

1:7). We are often quick to associate this character with Satan or the devil, named later in Scripture, and then to assign him a character of malice and hatred. But in Job the satan is more of an ambiguous character, a wandering skeptic. That is not to say that the satan does not seek to oppose the Creator and his creatures—even violently—but rather that his main purpose in this book is to sow the seeds of doubt.[20] Skepticism and the fear of the unknown are major temptations for Job and his friends.

Thus the accuser's main interest is to prove that when humans are faced with the reality of a fallen and broken world, faith (fear) in God will not stand up.

> Does Job fear God for nothing?" [the] Satan replied. (Job 1:9)

As we have seen in previous chapters, the "fear of the LORD" is the chief characteristic of the wise person. The satan's accusation is that Job fears God only at the surface level and has never been forced to reckon seriously with wisdom in a fallen and often dark world. Accepting the challenge, God grants the accuser permission, first, to destroy Job's family and his wealthy property (Job 1:13-22) and then, second, to strike Job's body with unbearable boils (Job 2:6-7).

As we would expect from a blameless God-fearer, Job remains faithful throughout these ordeals and does not "sin in what he said" (Job 2:10). But here there is a strange scene with Job's wife who, appearing to have been tempted by the accuser's doubts, advises Job to "curse God and die!"—perhaps an encouragement to commit suicide. The wife's advice seems to be an echo of Eve's counsel to Adam in the garden to eat from the tree of the knowledge of good and evil. In both stories, the women's advice follows the accuser and leads toward a path to death. The parallel may be faint at this point, but images of creation in Genesis 1–3 continue to emerge throughout Job.

News of Job's calamity then reaches his friends:

> When Job's three friends, Eliphaz the Temanite, Bildad the Shuhite and Zophar the Naamathite, heard about all the troubles that had come

---

[20]See Habel, *Book of Job*, p. 89.

upon him, they set out from their homes and met together by agreement to go and sympathize with him and comfort him. When they saw him from a distance they could hardly recognize him; they began to weep aloud, and they tore their robes and sprinkled dust on their heads. Then they sat on the ground with him for seven days and seven nights. No one said a word to him because they saw how great his suffering was. (Job 2:11-13)

The seven-day cycle of mourning, as in Genesis 50:10 and Ezekiel 3:15, symbolizes a complete mourning rite. Job's friends honor Job with their own silence. But such is Job's suffering that seven days simply cannot contain his mourning, rage and grief. Resolution will only come in chapter 42.

After this, Job opened his mouth and cursed the day of his birth. (Job 3:1)

This verse ends the narrative introduction to the book, followed by almost forty chapters of poetic dialogues. The change from simple to complex vocabulary and form parallels the shift in content from Job's silence to his strident demand for understanding and for justice. At the same time, however, the structure of the speeches by Job and his friends—as outlined below—provides the reader with an outsider's perspective that a sophisticated storyteller is at work, teaching us something about the nature of human life in this world: while life for Job on the inside is hell, life viewed from above seems to have some kind of structure and purpose (see figure 6.1 on p. 136).[21]

## THE DIALOGUES WITH THE FRIENDS

Job's provocative curse in Job 3:1 begins a wild series of poetic conversations. It is, in effect, an explosion out of his silence that comes right up to the limit of cursing God. In the first speech, Job curses the day of his birth, the "day," the "light" and the night, strategically reversing the orderliness in God's creative works in Genesis 1. Michael Fishbane provides an enlightening comparison, shown in table 6.1 (on p. 137).[22]

---

[21]Figure 6.1 is adapted from Francis I. Andersen, *Job: An Introduction and Commentary*, TOTC (Leicester, U.K.: Inter-Varsity Press, 1976), p. 20.
[22]Michael Fishbane, "Jeremiah 4:23-26 and Job 3:3-13: A Recovered Use of the Creation Pattern," *Vetus Testamentum* 21 (1971): 151-67. See also Robert S. Fyall, *Now My Eyes Have Seen*

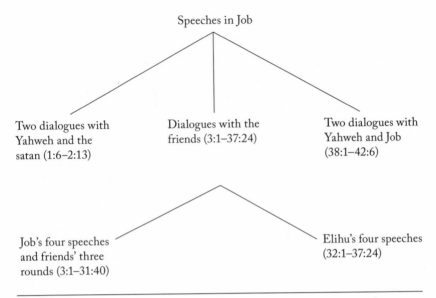

**Figure 6.1**

Job's first speech thus places his sense of suffering and injustice in the context of the order and goodness of creation. Essentially, his accusation is that something is wrong with the way God has made the world or perhaps that God has failed to uphold its order against the forces of chaos. This may not be an obvious complaint to modern readers, but "cosmogonic" poems and myths were a common way for ancient Near Eastern societies to understand and counter these situations; the appeal for justice is an appeal about the world order.

Job selectively uses three names for God. In the prose sections he uses Yahweh, and in the poetic speeches he appeals only to Eloah, Elohim, Adonai and Shaddai. The contrast is easy to see, but it is much more difficult to know what it means for interpretation.

The parallels with Genesis may shed some light on this. In the first creation account, in Genesis 1:1–2:3, a text well recognized for the cosmic allusions to life coming out of chaos and darkness, only Elohim is used to refer to God. In the second creation account, in Genesis 2:4–3:24, the narrative depicts the civilized imagery of the garden

---

*You: Images of Creation and Evil in the Book of Job* (Downers Grove, Ill.: InterVarsity Press, 2002), pp. 102-5.

and personal relationships between people, God and animals. Here God is mentioned nineteen times, but only in the form Yahweh-Elohim (the LORD God)—a term that combines the creator Elohim with the covenant name Yahweh. It is possible that the poetry in Job is pressing a distinction—maybe a false or ironic one—between these two names, though this is a subject that requires much closer consideration. What can be said for sure is that for Job, the very identity of God is at stake.

We can also clearly see that Job would rather have death than life and darkness than light. As we discovered during our study of Proverbs in chapter four, the ancient Near Eastern worldview sees justice, order, creation and wisdom as interconnected. Job's claim that "his *way* is hidden" essentially calls into question the assurance of Proverbs 3:5-7 that

**Table 6.1**

| Job 3 | Genesis 1 |
|---|---|
| 4a That day . . . | 5 The first day . . .<br>3 Let there be light<br>7 . . . the water under the expanse from |
| may it turn to darkness | the water above it. |
| 4b let not God regard it from above<br>5a Let gloom and deep darkness claim it | 2 darkness was over the surface of the deep<br>4 and he separated the light from the darkness |
| 6 That night<br>may thick darkness seize it;<br>may it not be included among the days of the year nor be entered in any of the months.<br>8 May those who curse days curse that day,<br>those who are ready to rouse Leviathan<br>9 May its morning stars become dark;<br>may it wait for daylight in vain and not see the first days of the dawn | 14 Let there be lights in the expanse of the sky to separate the day from the night, and let them serve as signs to mark seasons and days and years.<br><br>21 So God created the great creatures of the sea<br><br>15 And let them be lights in the expanse of the sky to give light on the earth. |

God will guide the way of those who trust in him. This first poem ends with a perplexing surprise.

> What I feared has come upon me;
> what I dreaded has happened to me. (Job 3:25)

Few commentators make much of this powerful parallelism at the end of the first speech. Deep down, Job lived with fear and dread of the future. This perhaps explains Job's motive for offering excessive sacrifices for his sons (Job 1:5): he was afraid of what could happen.[23] This does not mean that Job did not fear God in the sense of having no faith—we are given good reasons to believe that Job is a man of humility and belief—but it does suggest that Job was human after all, as plagued by fear as anyone living in a fallen, corrupt and often dangerous world. Like us, he harbors the lurking fear that the future might rob him of the things he most cherishes. The valiant woman, we remember, laughed at the future (Prov 31:25), but Job's life suggests that this is easier said than done.

In Chesterton's introduction to *The Man Who Was Thursday*—a book, as we have noted, with distinct parallels to Job—there is a poem that connects the fear in the story to the book's intended purpose:

> This is a tale of those old fears,
>     Even of those emptied hells,
> And none but you shall understand
>     The true thing that it tells—
>
> The doubts that drove us through the night
>     As we two walked amain,
> And day had broken on the streets
>     Ere it broke upon the brain.

One can be wise and yet still fearful. One of the main lessons in Job and Ecclesiastes is that the wisdom of Proverbs is not a simple path; human wisdom must be combined with faith and endurance. Faith and hope do not eliminate mystery; they assume and embrace it.[24]

---

[23]Gerald Wilson, *Job*, NIBC (Peabody, Mass.: Hendrickson, 2007), pp. 41-42, suspects that Job might in fact have been plagued by fear all along.
[24]In the final chapter we propose just how wisdom and Job's story might help us do this.

Job's friends speak after having been provoked by what they see as a blasphemous view of God and creation. One by one, they urge Job to be completely honest about the sin in his life that must be the cause of his miseries. A pattern of three rebukes and responses continues until Job 31, each rebuke and response taking a slightly different angle than the last.

Eliphaz
> Is not your wickedness great?
>> Are not your sins endless? (Job 22:5)

Bildad
> How can a man be righteous before God?
>> How can one born of a woman be pure? (Job 25:4)

Zophar
> Such is the fate God allots the wicked,
>> the heritage appointed for them by God. (Job 20:29)

The growing distance between Job and his friends exists on several levels and creates a profound tension throughout the dialogues. Robert Alter shows how the very texture and form of their poetry mimics their differing theologies. In Job 15:9-10, Eliphaz says,

> What do you know that we do not know?
> What insights do you have that we do not have?
> The gray-haired and the aged are on our side,
>> men even older than your father.

"Eliphaz" says Alter, "speaks smugly without suspecting that there might be a chasm between divine knowledge and the conventional knowledge of accepted wisdom."[25] But compare his naive and simple poetry, quoted above, to Job's answers:

> He moves mountains without their knowing it
>> and overturns them in his anger.
> He shakes the earth from its place
>> and makes its pillars tremble.
> He speaks to the sun and it does not shine;
>> he seals off the light of the stars.

---

[25]Robert Alter, *The Art of Biblical Poetry* (New York: Basic, 1985), p. 89.

He alone stretches out the heavens
  and treads on the waves of the sea. (Job 9:5-8)

He deprives the leaders of the earth of their reason;
  he sends them wandering through a trackless waste.
They grope in darkness with no light;
  he makes them stagger like drunkards. (Job 12:24-25)

Job is not afraid to protest. Alter concludes: "Job's cosmic poetry, unlike that of the Friends, has a certain energy of vision, as though it proceeded from some immediate perception of the great things it reports."[26]

The poetry illumines the stark disagreement of the two parties about the nature of God and his justice. The friends assume that God, being wholly good and all powerful, would never bring suffering to a righteous man. But we know that in this point they are totally deceived. Because the three are wrong about their friend Job, they are also wrong about God. A typical statement from Bildad in Job 8:20 presses the contrast between Job and his friends even further: "God will not reject a *blameless* man" (emphasis added), implying that Job is not blameless *(tām)*. But God and the narrator have already made clear that Job *is tām* (Job 1:1, 8; 2:3). As Édouard Dhorme says, "His friends seek to apply normal solutions to the exceptional case."[27] Yet, as Alter suggests, they also seem to lack a fresh experience of the Creator that motivates Job's poetry and aligns it so much more closely to the forms in the divine speeches in Job 38–41.

Alvin Plantinga points out that Job's problem can be understood in two different ways.[28] The first, common interpretation is the intellectual one: Job protests because he cannot understand why God would allow an innocent person to suffer. As Martin Buber perceptively notes, "Job cannot forego either his own truth or God."[29] But there is a second possibility too: Job is angry and disagrees with what God is doing. He may have good reasons, but Job in effect says, "I don't give a fig for

---

[26]Ibid., p. 90.
[27]Édouard Dhorme, *A Commentary on the Book of Job* (Nashville: Thomas Nelson, 1984 [original 1926]), p. cxxxv.
[28]Alvin Plantinga, *Warranted Christian Belief* (New York: Oxford University Press, 2000), pp. 496-98.
[29]Quoted by Harold Bloom, ed., *The Book of Job* (New York: Chelsea House, 1988), p. 2.

those reasons, and I detest what he is doing!"[30] Of course, these two responses are not antithetical, and in our view both are present in Job's response.

The complexity in Job's response provides an important insight into the kind of wisdom we have in the book of Job—much like Ecclesiastes. As is inevitable in profound suffering, intellect *and* experience combine to protest the agony of the situation. The experience exceeds understanding; even if Job knew exactly what God was up to, it would not automatically resolve his suffering.

After the friends' three cycles have run their course, Job turns to his longest and final response (Job 26–31). Job 28 stands out as the peak of his experience and perhaps the major turn in the book's plot.

## Job 28

Although the next chapter presents a close reading of Job 28, we should point out a few important items here. The cosmic power of the poetry in this chapter often leads scholars to regard it as a later addition or perhaps a passage moved from its original place somewhere nearer the divine speeches (Job 38–41). Nevertheless, there are good literary reasons to see its role here as purposeful and strategic in the overall flow of the book.

The uniqueness of the speech is very clearly marked by Job's turn away from addressing his friends to a self-contained parable on wisdom. While many of the themes from the dialogues emerge throughout the poem, the metallurgic and mining vocabulary is new. The gist of the poem is that, although God has very carefully hidden all the precious jewels and metals of the world, humanity has been able to find them out. Not so with wisdom. Wisdom remains elusive despite all the developments and ingenuity of the human race. Thus the conflict in the poem is summarized by the question in Job 28:12 and repeated in Job 28:20:

> But where can wisdom be found?
> Where does understanding dwell?

---

[30]Ibid., p. 497.

This pairing of "wisdom" and "understanding" is common throughout Proverbs (Prov 1:2; 4:5, 7; 9:10; 16:16) and reminds us that wisdom
is a God-given means for us to understand life in this world. Job answers his own question with the long section at the end of the poem,
which begins,

> God understands the way to it,
> and he alone knows where it dwells. (Job 28:23)

It ends:

> And he said to man, "The fear of the Lord—that is wisdom,
> and to shun evil is understanding." (Job 28:28)

The poem thus ends with both positive and negative emotions. Job
affirms that God knows the way to wisdom and grants it to those who
fear him. Yet the fact remains that Job has not yet been granted the wisdom and understanding he needs to resolve his dilemma; why does a
righteous man suffer in God's good and ordered world? Some aspects of
this question will be answered in the book's conclusion; others will not.

The dialogue between Job and his friends closes in Job 31, with the
friends confused and Job as miserable as ever. The narrator's interrup-
tion in Job 32:1-5 introduces a fourth, previously unmentioned friend.
Elihu ("he is my God") is younger than the other friends and the only
character with a remotely Hebrew name. He seems to have been showing deference to his elders by quietly waiting for them to counsel Job;
but now, furious that the other four have failed to come to a resolution,
Elihu rebukes Job and justifies God for the better part of six chapters.

Because Elihu is only introduced in Job 32, and because God does not
address him with the three friends in the epilogue (Job 42:7-17), it is often
argued that this is another later insertion into the story. While it is certainly
possible that the Elihu speeches have been added to the other poems, the
final effect is that of a sophisticated and suspenseful narrative.

Elihu's poetry is more powerful and sophisticated than the friends,
though it does not, as Alter says, "soar like the Voice from the
Whirlwind"[31] in Job 38–41. So while Elihu claims to answer for God,

---

[31] Alter, *Art of Biblical Poetry*, p. 92.

the form of his poetry suggests that he falls short. Where God and the narrator declare Job "upright" *(yōšer)*, Elihu claims to speak from an "upright" heart (Job 33:3) and claims that God could send an angel (perhaps Elihu?) to teach Job what is "upright" (Job 33:23) so that Job might in turn repent and confess that he perverted what was "upright" (Job 33:27). Later he counsels Job that it is right to "fear" God and that God does not regard those who are wise in their own mind (Job 37:24). Some scholars argue that Elihu's is a prophetic voice and that he rightly rebukes Job and his friends for their folly, preparing the way for God's speeches. In our opinion, however, there is an irony in Elihu's speeches in that, while they all sound orthodox, they continually contradict the threefold affirmation in the prologue (Job 1:1, 8; 2:3) and God's confirmation of Job in Job 42:7 that Job is an upright God-fearer. Alter calls Elihu "an irascible, presumptuous blowhard."[32]

Gerald Wilson too notes that "Elihu rejects the very idea of a divine appearance because, in his understanding, God has already rendered his judgment in Job's suffering (34:23) and does not bother to respond to the pleas of the wicked for mercy (35:12-15)."[33] Elihu's long speech fails, not only adding suspense to the story but also "[preparing] the way for God's appearance—even while denying it."[34] The problem exceeds the wisdom of Job's friends.

After a long wait, God finally answers Job in Job 38–41. It is worth pausing to reflect on the amazingly long section of dialogues in Job 3–37. We suggest that at the least they are an important representation of human nature, religion and (limited) experience amid profound suffering. The speeches reflect the ways in which we often mix truth and error. There is much to commend in the words of Job's friends; some of them are nearly verbatim maxims from the book of Proverbs. In the final analysis, though, their positions are misguided—*the right words at the wrong time.* Each of the friends is also palpably human, displaying strong reactions and contradictions in his answers. This too display's

---

[32]Ibid., p. 91.
[33]Gerald Wilson, "Preknowledge, Anticipation, and the Poetics of Job," *JSOT* 30, no. 2 (2005): 243-56 (249).
[34]Ibid., p. 250.

the book's literary brilliance: it reflects the inconsistencies in our own dialogue with others and the odd process of discovering, changing and sometimes clarifying our own opinions in the midst of life's messiness. Perhaps most significantly, we emerge from the seemingly endless dialogues more sympathetic with Job's recurrent appeals to stand before *God*—to have his own judicial hearing in the divine courts (Job 13:15-19; 16:19-21; 19:25-27; 31:5-6, 35). Job is reduced to *looking to* and *hoping only in God*.

## THE DIVINE SPEECHES

> If the poetry of Job . . . looms above all other biblical poetry in virtuosity and sheer expressive power, the culminating poem that God speaks out of the storm soars beyond everything that has preceded it in the book, the poet having wrought a poetic idiom even richer and more awesome than the one he gave Job.[35]

In Job 38:1 the narrator reintroduces God but now refers to him almost exclusively as Yahweh, "the LORD."[36] If we look back to the beginning of Job's speeches in Job 3–9, we find images of power, chaos and mystery paired with the divine title El (Eloah or Elohim). Here we have similar images, but now paired with the covenant name, Yahweh. In this way the reader's perspective is prepared for a rhetorical reconfiguration of Job's language and thus his perspective.

Somewhat ironically, God's *answer* is in fact a series of more than eighty rhetorical *questions*. The second half of God's speech includes extended, mysterious descriptions of Behemoth and Leviathan, which we will discuss below. The two lists of questions are divided by Job's short reply in Job 40:3-5. Looking at God's first words we find a significant literary change of pace:

> Then the LORD answered Job out of the storm. He said:
> "Who is this that darkens my counsel
>     with words without knowledge?

---

[35]Alter, *Art of Biblical Poetry*, p. 87.
[36]See Job 38:7 which could be translated "God" or "angels." Cf. the NIV note on this verse.

> Gird up your loins like a man;[37]
>> I will question you,
>> and you shall declare to me." (Job 38:1-3)

God has held his silence for a long time, and the reader almost flinches at the entrance of the confident and determined divine voice. The word "storm" *(sĕ'ārâ)* appears here for the first time in Job.[38] It is used again in Job 40:6, after Job's brief answer, though its significance here seems uncertain; but that is probably the point. As Wilson suggests, the "storm cloaks the fierce otherness of the presence of God in his fullness in the midst of the world of human experience."[39]

> Have you ever given orders to the morning,
>> or shown the dawn its place,
> that it might take the earth by the edges
>> and shake the wicked out of it? (Job 38:12-13)
> Do you know when the mountain goats give birth?
>> Do you watch when the doe bears her fawn?
> Do you count the months till they bear?
> Do you know the time they give birth? (Job 39:1-2)

God's words are not only imbued with a commanding force; but they also engage the complaints Job has made throughout his speeches. As Alter notes:

> When God finally answers Job out of the whirlwind, he responds with an order of poetry formally allied to Job's own remarkable poetry, but larger in scope and greater in power. . . . That is, God picks up many of Job's key images, especially from the death-wish poem with which Job began (Chapter 3) and his discourse is shaped by a powerful movement of intensification, coupled with an implicitly narrative sweep from the creation to the play of natural forces to the teeming world of animal life.[40]

---

[37]Author's translation. Cf. "prepare to defend yourself" in the NIV.

[38]But compare the similar word *śĕ'ārâ* in Job 9:17, which begins with the letter *śin* rather than *sāmek*. There Job expects the "tempest" to crush him. The storm appears in Elihu's speech also (Job 37:2-5).

[39]Wilson, *Job*, p. 424.

[40]Robert Alter, *The World of Biblical Literature* (London: SPCK, 1992), pp. 188-89.

As we said earlier, the speeches are composed almost entirely of questions. Michael Fox's analysis of these questions reveals a whole range of techniques at work in God's reply to Job.[41] The questions are of three types: (1) *who* questions, which point back to God's power (e.g., "Who fathers the drops of dew?" [Job 38:28]) (2) *what* questions, which emphasize Job's utter inability (e.g., "Does the eagle soar at your command and build its nest on high?" [Job 39:27]), and (3) *have you ever* or *can you* questions, which reinforce the limits of human power and knowledge (e.g., "Can you bring forth the constellations in their seasons or lead out the bear with its cubs?" [Job 38:32]).

Clearly God's power is overwhelming, but so too are his presence and his willingness to invite Job into dialogue. Understandably Job seems to have lost the litigating passion he had earlier in the book. In the middle of God's speeches, Job 40:3-5, Job responds briefly to make two points. First, he acknowledges the power of God's evidence and his own human finitude: "I am unworthy" (NIV), or more literally, "I am humbled" (Job 40:4a). This is probably not a confession of guilt, since Job is aware of his innocence as far as his suffering is concerned. Second, Job realizes that although he has been given space to speak, the speeches teach him that it is better to remain silent. He senses that he has already said enough: "I put my hand over my mouth" (Job 40:4b).

After Job's short confession, God returns to his questions and to two peculiar descriptions of the Behemoth (Job 40:15-24) and the Leviathan (Job 41:1-34).

Look at the behemoth,
    which I made along with you
    and which feeds on grass like an ox.
What strength he has in his loins,
    what power in the muscles of his belly! (Job 40:15-16)

Can you pull in the leviathan with a fishhook
    or tie down his tongue with a rope?
Can you put a cord through his nose
    or pierce his jaw with a hook? (Job 41:1-2)

---

[41]Michael V. Fox, "Job 38 and God's Rhetoric," *Semeia* 19 (1981): 53-61.

Behemoth is the plural word for beast *(bĕhēmâ)*—the same term used for the first creatures on the land in Genesis 1:24, typically considered cattle. It is common nowadays to interpret this as a reference to the crocodile or the hippopotamus; the fact that it "eats grass like an ox" (Job 40:15) makes it more likely that it refers to the latter. The Leviathan, referred to by Job in Job 3:8 and in other Old Testament passages, symbolizes the mysterious nature of creation and justice (cf. Ps 74:14; 104:26; Is 27:1). As in Psalms 74 and Psalm 104 the use of Leviathan here in Job could refer to the whale as the great creature of the deep. The reference in Isaiah 27, however, pictures a "coiling" or "twisting" serpent creature. The mythical connections with water, chaos and the deep cannot be ruled out, nor can the personification of death.[42] Together these two creatures reinforce the overall message of the divine speeches: God's creation is vast, diverse and mysterious, way beyond human control and yet easily within *his* control. But the strength of God's answers to Job is accentuated by the poetry of the questions:

> But whereas Job's intensities are centripetal and necessarily egocentric, God's intensities carry us back and forth through the pulsating vital movements of the whole created world. The culmination of the poem God speaks is . . . the climactic manifestation of a splendidly providential creation that merely anthropomorphic notions cannot grasp.[43]

Many interpreters take these speeches as God's rebuke to Job. While this may have some truth to it, it misses the main thrust of the book's end. That is, God's explicit affirmation of Job in Job 42:1-7 reminds us that guilt and repentance are not in focus but rather deeper lessons about wisdom in a broken world. We point out two such lessons here.

First, there is a lesson of human finitude. Isaiah quotes the LORD saying:

> For my thoughts are not your thoughts,
>     neither are your ways my ways. (Is 55:8)

---

[42]See Fyall, *Now My Eyes Have Seen You*, pp. 127-74, who uses ANE Canaanite mythology to argue that Behemoth and Leviathan sustain the presence of death, evil and the satan figure from Job 1–2.

[43]Alter, *The World of Biblical Literature*, p. 189.

Fox perceptively notes that

> Yahweh does not justify or rationalize his treatment of Job, certainly not
> in terms of retribution. . . . Some suffering, as he can deduce from his
> own experience and the absence of divine self-exculpation, is not a pun-
> ishment and has nothing to do with retribution. One may find solace in
> knowing that misfortune is not a mark of guilt.[44]

But second, we learn that God's powerful and often mysterious rule
of the universe has a maternal hand. God satisfies the land with rain
(Job 38:27); he feeds the lion (Job 38:39) and the raven (Job 38:41); he
gives the wild donkey a home and food (Job 39:5-8). He also provides
freedom and the "wisdom" for horses, ostriches, oxen, locusts, eagles
and hawks to achieve their created purpose in the world. There is a
fearful part to this mystery, but there is also a calming, assuring dimension.[45]

So, while the divine speeches make Job's finitude clear, their focus is
on Yahweh's power and wisdom in creating and ruling his world. Job is
as much rebuked as, together with the characters and the audience,
called to a new wisdom of trust and even wonder—a discipline of humility and faith in the midst of mystery and suffering that returns again
and again to God's ability to rule his world justly and lovingly.

## THE EPILOGUE

At the end of the divine questions, Job answers in Job 42:2-6, followed
by a narrator's conclusion. Each of these sections revisits a major theme
in Old Testament wisdom, bringing the book to its final but still mysterious end.

> I know that you can do all things;
> > no plan of yours can be thwarted.
> *You asked,* "Who is this that obscures my counsel without knowledge?"
> > Surely I spoke of things I did not understand,
> > things too wonderful for me to know. (Job 42:2-3)

[44]Michael V. Fox, "Job the Pious," *ZAW* 117 (2005): 351-66.
[45]Eleonore Stump's *Wandering in Darkness: Narrative and the Problem of Suffering* (Oxford: Clarendon, 2010), pp. 177-226, provides a profound reading of Job through the lens of second-
person narrative which foregrounds God's care for Job and all creation.

As Norman Habel points out, Job's first response in Job 42:2-3 returns to the problem of what it means to know something—the same problem raised in Yahweh's question in Job 38:2, "Who is this that obscures my counsel?"[46] Job's admission is simply that he "knows" God's exceedingly wonder-full ability to surpass our human knowledge. His complaints aired the pain, confusion and loneliness that pressed the limits of his faith. But now, the overwhelming experience of God's presence brings Job to a point of surrender.

His second stanza (Job 42:3) makes this clearer still: Job has indeed spoken from a lack of knowledge or as one without knowledge. As we will explain below, it is important to recognize that the new level of knowledge that Job rises to here is one of submitting to the *mysteries* of God's world—a timely critique of the modern belief that simply increasing our knowledge will solve our problems. Like us, Job does not need to know more; rather, he needs to learn a humble and yet intimate relationship with God that enables him to embrace his creatureliness.

The second part of Job's answer also quotes Yahweh, this time from Job 38:3, playing on the familiar ideas of "seeing" and "hearing."

*You said,* "Listen now, and I will speak;
   I will question you,
   and you shall answer me."
My ears had heard of you
   but now my eyes have seen you. (Job 42:4-5)

In a way, Job 42:4 brings the plot of the book to its climax; Job is finally invited to address God and have the personal meeting he has been longing for (e.g., Job 13:22). The meat of this passage is, however, in the next two verses. Job 42:5 plays on the difference between Job's experience of *hearing* and *seeing* God. These words are stock wisdom vocabulary, which we address in the epistemology section below. The interplay between knowing and not knowing in Job 42:3 is repeated in the form of seeing and hearing in Job 42:5. Human autonomy often manifests itself in a kind of bucket approach to knowledge—the mind is a bottomless receptacle into which we drop endless facts and then

---

[46]Habel, *Job*, pp. 578-79.

seek to arrange them logically. Job's growth in wisdom here is better
understood in terms of the searchlight approach—what we see and
know is always in relation to the light shone on the situation.[47] Through
his encounter with God, Job's torchlight has been illuminated so as to
bring a new perspective on creaturely life. Somehow, in God's immense
and wonderful design, injustice is allowed to play a role in God's making things right again, and even better. *Job does not know how,* but spiritually he is in a position to accept that God can make even this situation work for his good purposes.

We come finally to Job's last words:

Therefore I despise myself
   and repent in dust and ashes. (Job 42:6)

Habel rightly calls this passage "deliberately ambiguous."[48] The most
common interpretation depicts Job repenting, but the Hebrew poetry is
far too nuanced to leave it at that. In the first phrase, the Hebrew verb
*mā'as* could mean "refuse," "reject" or even "loathe," as many translations render the verb in Job's other use of this phrase, in Job 9:21.[49]
However we translate it, it is not entirely clear what Job means. The
second phrase is equally troubling. Habel translates it "I leave my ashes,"
alerting us to the significance of the word "ashes" in this context. We
believe Francis Andersen and others are correct in connecting this
clause to the "dust and ashes" that Abraham speaks of in Genesis 18:27
as an allusion to our created nature—our humanity.[50] We are, after all,
just animated earth or breathing clay. Adam and Eve were made from
the dust (Gen 2:7) and were destined to return to dust upon their death
(Gen 3:19). Assuming Job has these contexts in mind, which we think
is likely, we can see how this verse brings us to a summary statement for
the book: humans are gifted with wisdom, but it is, nevertheless, the
wisdom of *creatures* and not of the infinite divine. In a world of suffer-

---

[47]The image of the bucket and searchlight comes from Karl Popper, "The Bucket and the
Searchlight: Two Theories of Knowledge," in *Objective Knowledge: An Evolutionary Approach*
(Oxford: Clarendon, 1972), pp. 341-61. See further comments on Popper's epistemology and
its relation to OT wisdom in chapter eleven.
[48]Habel, *Job*, p. 579.
[49]Job also uses this verb in Job 31:13, where he claims to not have "rejected" his servants.
[50]Andersen, *Job*, p. 292.

ing, we are profoundly limited in our understanding, and we lament our fallen and distorted creatureliness.

This turn back to prose may also signal the existential conclusion of the mourning rite that began in Job 2:8. Job now rises from his mourning to renewed life before God.[51] The prose in Job 42:7-17 confirms this turn in Job's life. Whereas the long poetic section (Job 3:3–42:6) is marked by a combination of unusual vocabulary and wild dialogues, the opening prose and this closure are composed of fairly simple vocabulary and symbolic completeness. This is like the scenes in the prologue where the narrator relays the events from a perspective unknown to the characters; gone are the intense debates and confrontations of the poetic section.

First, the narrator tells us that Yahweh declares Job's words "right":

> After the LORD had said these things to Job, he said to Eliphaz the Temanite, "I am angry with you and your two friends, because you have not spoken of me what is right *(nĕkônâ)*, as my servant Job has." (Job 42:7)

Here it seems that Job's speech about God is affirmed but not necessarily his claim to being righteous.[52] It is also debated whether the affirmation refers only to the last speech (Job 42:2-6) or to all of Job's words. In our view, God's words affirm both Job's words and actions as righteous. We have already argued that the quality of the poetry sets Job off clearly from his friends. Furthermore, while Job's attitude of submission surfaces throughout the book and not only in Job 42:2-6, it never occurs to Job's friends to think they might be wrong. What's more, the role of the frame narrator is to give us information that Job and the friends do not have—information that has allowed us to sympathize with Job's complaint, but clearly not with the friends. And finally, Job is the only one who prays or seeks counsel with God. The friends merely assume that their accumulated wisdom is sufficient to interpret Job's anomalous situation. It is possible, in fact, to interpret the last phrase in Job 42:7-8 as, "You have not spoken *unto me* as my

---

[51]Heath Thomas, "The Meaning of Mourning in the Book of Job," unpublished paper.
[52]See Wilson, *Job*, p. 472.

servant Job has."[53] Though it is somewhat rare for commentators to follow this translation, it makes good sense given Job's lone appeal to prayer, God's affirmation of his *speech* and his responsibility to *pray again* for his friend's to be forgiven (Job 42:8).

God then rebukes the friends and prepares them for restoration, though Elihu is never mentioned. This scene offers room for rich theological reflection. God requires the three friends to offer seven bulls and seven rams for their sin. Not only is this a symbolic number; but it is also a very demanding request. What have they done to deserve this punishment? Though it is not entirely clear, the main point seems to be a misuse of wisdom that misrepresented God and injured their friend. Words are costly things. Here the friends' task ends. Then, in a striking parallel to Jesus, Job as the suffering one intercedes for his unrighteous friends in order to restore them to God. His role as intercessor in the poetic dialogues is carefully reinforced and affirmed here.

Finally, the narrator tells us that God gave Job ten children to replace the ones he lost, restored Job's possessions to double of what he had before and gave Job a long life of 140 years—possibly double the normal life span (Job 42:16-17).[54] It seems fair to agree with the many interpreters who say that the doubling of possessions is a sign of God's grace. But does this really make up for Job's loss?

The complex resolution to this story continues into Job 42:11. In the prologue Job used to go far away to feast with his children, but now Job's children, family and friends come to him for feasting and *consolation*, bringing him gifts of money and gold for all the "evil *(rāʿâ)* that Yahweh had brought upon Job." Edwin Good suggests in this context that there is a solution to the problem of evil, but one that has been overlooked:

> Now his relatives and friends succeed in what the three failed in, for
> their consoling and comforting is narrated in finite verb forms . . .
> whereas the three friends' consoling and comforting is detailed in in-
> finitives. . . . The comfort of the close human community, not debate

---

[53]Kathryn Schifferdecker, *Out of the Whirlwind: Creation Theology in the Book of Job* (Cambridge, Mass.: Harvard Theological Studies, 2008), p. 107.
[54]See Habel, *Job*, p. 585.

and doctrinal instruction, solves the problem of "all the evil that Yahweh has brought upon him." The problem of evil that has a solution is not the abstract problem of the relation between power and goodness but is Job's own problem of suffering and alienation.[55]

There is truth in this, but we are not sure it adequately resolves the problem of what Job has been subjected to. The legal allusion referred to above and the direct description of what God allowed Job to be put through as "evil" suggest that something went terribly wrong and God is to blame! Even Job's beautiful new daughters (Job 42:14-15) sit somewhat uncomfortably with what has happened to Job's previous children—as if beauty makes up for the loss of a child, let alone ten. We feel as if we're coming to the end of a story with the plot unresolved. There is no explanation or any apology from God for the evil he has brought on a righteous man. However, this lack of apology and the description of Job's suffering as evil force us to reflect more deeply on what has taken place in Job.

We know from the prologue that God gave the satan permission to attack Job but did not execute the damage himself. The key lies in the very different Job that emerges by the end of the story. To a degree, the satan had been correct; Job, to a very real extent, did only serve God because he was protected from evil. But, as is always the case, evil overreaches itself. It would not have occurred to the satan that, by obtaining permission to attack Job, he would instigate a profound formation of Job into the genuinely wise man who serves God simply because God is worthy of such service. Job emerges scarred, but transformed. We will explore this spirituality of suffering in more detail in chapter twelve.

## A THEOLOGY OF JOB

As we have seen, Job is a complex narrative dealing with profound issues. In the process, it illumines multiple themes, and its meaning cannot be reduced to one issue. At the outset it should be noted just what an important book Job is *pastorally*. Christians, especially in North

---

[55]Edwin M. Good, "The Problem of Evil in the Book of Job," in Perdue and Gilpin, *The Voice in the Whirlwind*, pp. 50-69, 69.

America, have not been exempt from the temptation to believe that suffering is always the result of (personal) sin and that if we only obey God then prosperity will result. It is true that sin can, and does, cause suffering. Substance abuse is an example, often resulting in addiction or worse. But by no means is all suffering related to sin. Bad things do happen to good people, and Job is *the* Old Testament reminder of that truth. In such situations the lengthy speeches of the friends are a reminder of how debilitating and shameful it is to equate all sin to suffering. Indeed, the counsel of Job's friends is itself condemned by God as sinful (cf. Job 42:7).

Thus Job has important lessons for those of us who suffer and for those of us who counsel those who suffer. For those who suffer profoundly Job is a reminder that in our darkest hours God is present and at work, even though we have no idea what he is up to and it feels as though the world, and God, has gone mad. For those who counsel, Job calls us to discernment as to when repentance is required and when God is deeply at work in ways we do not understand. In the latter context the worst thing a counselor can do is to offer quick solutions; rather, one needs to provide what support one can and wait with the sufferer to see what God will bring to pass.

Job offers us many other theological paths for exploration. We will take just a few of these here.

***Epistemology.*** Job has long been recognized as a book about the limits of human knowledge. Knowledge, in fact, permeates every turn and fold of the narrative, starting with the scene at the divine courts. We could paraphrase the satan's question in Job 1 as follows: "Is it right for Job to fear you without complete knowledge of your world and how it works?" That is, the satan resents the possibility of people following God without understanding the true complexity of God's rule. We don't even know how the satan achieved this higher knowledge, but he seems to have it.

Added to that, the all-knowing narrator of the story keeps us focused on the gap between what we know and what is known by Job and his friends. These levels of knowledge give the narrative its palpating tension, making us yearn to correct the friends and help Job understand

his situation. As we read along, we find that in Job the insights of the
narrator are our unique privilege; in reality we are characters in the
world much like Job and his friends. We live at ground level and are
never able to peer into the mysterious working of God's divine courts.

But in the story, we live somehow above reality, getting a privileged
view of these strange circumstances that lead to Job's testing. The major
wisdom motifs of seeing and hearing are used in various ways throughout the Bible—in Deuteronomy, Ecclesiastes and Mark in particular.[56]
Job's frequent appeal to stand in the divine courts and see or face his
accuser is really an expression for Job's desire *to understand*. Job's next-
to-last statement returns to this driving ambition:

> My ears had heard of you
>> but now my eyes have seen you. (Job 42:5)

Only now, seeing God did not bring the knowledge he had so
desired. This same human reliance on reason and the senses is critiqued in Ecclesiastes in particular. Such epistemological implications are, among other things, what make Job such a powerful and
memorable book.

We are forced to live with a gap between our experience of suffering
and God's ability to redeem it in the end. Fox aptly states, "The reader
discovers something that Job does not, namely the *significance* of human
ignorance of the rationale for their fate. It is a precondition of piety and
crucial to man's role in the divine order."[57] God is indeed good, and his
purposes will be accomplished in the end; but this journey must be
lived by embracing the mystery and wonder of human life in this world.
This is the great contribution of a book like Job; it places us in a dilemma to teach us about our own limitations. In his book *The God I
Don't Understand*, Christopher Wright articulates this lesson: "Faith
*seeks* understanding, and faith *builds* on understanding where it is
granted, but faith does not finally *depend* on understanding. This is not
to say, of course, that faith is intrinsically irrational (quite the contrary),

---

[56]See chapter 9 below as well as Stephen A. Geller, "Fiery Wisdom: The Deuteronomic Tradition," in *Sacred Enigmas: Literary Religion in the Hebrew Bible* (London: Routledge, 1996); and
Joel Marcus, "Mark 4:10-12 and Marcan Epistemology," *JBL* 103, no. 4 (1984): 557-74.
[57]Fox, "Job the Pious," p. 362.

but that faith takes us into realms where explanation fails us—for the present."[58] Wright illumines some of the great depths in the book of Job. We do not meet a God who is irrational and capricious. On the contrary, God is a wise creator, able to restore perfect order as he wishes. Until that time, we live in a world where we must daily acknowledge that we serve a God whose understanding greatly exceeds our own.

In terms of epistemology, Job not only alerts us to the limits of our understanding but also to the fact that logic and rationality are only *one way of knowing*. Plantinga rightly observes that

> when God does come to Job in the whirlwind, it is not to convince him that God really does have reasons (although it may, in fact, do this); it is instead to still the tempest in his soul, to quiet him, to restore his trust for God. The Lord gives Job a glimpse of his greatness, his beauty, his splendid goodness; the doubts and turmoil disappear and are replaced, once more, by love and trust.[59]

Through his encounter with God, Job is addressed in the deepest part of his being, in what Old Testament wisdom calls *the heart*. Such heart knowledge exceeds logical understanding but is no less real and, at least according to Job, more fundamental and more important.

The depth of knowledge that Job acquires through his encounter with God is important since it alerts us to the faith dimension of a biblical theodicy. Why is it that for some Job is an extraordinary book of comfort amid suffering while for others it is a cop-out that never provides any answers? In his *Repetition*, Søren Kierkegaard provides a moving example of the former:

> If I did not have Job! It is impossible to describe all the shades of meaning and how manifold the meaning is that he has for me. I do not read him as one reads another book, with the eyes, but I lay the book, as it were, on my heart and read it with the eyes of the heart, in a clairvoyance interpreting the specifics in the most diverse ways. Just as the child puts his schoolbook under his pillow to make sure he has not forgotten his lesson when he wakes up in the morning, so I take the book to bed

[58]Christopher J. H. Wright, *The God I Don't Understand: Reflections on Tough Questions of Faith* (Grand Rapids: Zondervan, 2009), p. 22.
[59]Plantinga, *Warranted Christian Belief,* pp. 497-98.

with me at night. Every word by him is food and clothing and healing for my wretched soul. Now a word by him arouses me from my lethargy and awakens new restlessness; now it calms the sterile raging within me, stops the dreadfulness in the mute nausea of my passion. Have you really read Job?[60]

And yet, for others, Job is a pious avoidance of the problem of evil. Eleonore Stump helpfully points out that the problem of suffering and evil presents itself differently to believers and unbelievers. Believers come to Job with some history of relationship with God in the course of which there is a second-person experience that makes a difference to how they approach suffering and thus Job:

> Believers need not and should not think about the problem of evil in the same way unbelievers do, and a believer's resolution of the problem may be successful even if it isn't persuasive to non-believers. This is, in my view, one of the lessons of the book of Job, which we learn when we are sensitive to the nested second-person accounts which make up much of the book. And it helps to explain why contemporary academic accounts of the book take the form that we find in the Anchor Bible commentary, which sees the book as raising a charge against God that is never answered, while a committed believer such as Thomas Aquinas reads the same texts as constituting a good explanation of the way in which loving providence operates to govern the world.[61]

***Job and Christ.*** To Job's question, "Where shall wisdom be found?" the New Testament answers unequivocally, "in Christ." We will see in our discussion of wisdom in the New Testament that Lady Wisdom of Proverbs is a type of Christ. Can the same be said of Job? The most extensive christological reading of Job in modern times is that of Karl Barth, who devotes one hundred pages to Job.[62] Barth argues that Job is a type of Christ as the true witness and his encounter with the falsehood of humanity. The New Testament does not identify Job as a major

---

[60]Søren Kierkegaard, *Fear and Trembling; Repetition,* trans. and ed. Howard V. Hong and Edna H. Hong (Princeton: Princeton University Press, 1983), pp. 204-5.
[61]Eleonore Stump, "Faith and the Problem of Evil," in *Seeking Understanding: The Stob Lectures 1986-1998* (Grand Rapids: Eerdmans, 2001), pp. 528-29.
[62]Karl Barth, *CD* IV/3.1, pp. 368-478.

source for understanding Jesus, but if Jesus is wisdom personified, it is certainly legitimate to make this connection. As with Job, suffering is central to the wisdom Jesus. Hebrews 5:8-9 points out that, like Job, suffering was transformative for Jesus; through it he learned obedience and became perfect. Like Job, Jesus' suffering is hellish; at the Mount of Olives he is in anguish, and his sweat is like great drops of blood (Lk 22:39-46). Neither for Job nor Jesus is suffering undertaken with the calm serenity of Socrates.

Unlike Job, Jesus' protest against the injustice of God is expressed for only two brief moments—in the garden of Gethsemane and on the cross, "My God, my God, why have you forsaken me?" (Mt 27:46; Mk 15:34). Unlike Job, Jesus, in his suffering, takes on himself the burden of the world's guilt and sin. Unlike Job, Jesus dies, crushed by that burden, but rises triumphantly to open the gates of the kingdom to all. Central to the biblical narrative is the slain lamb upon the throne; his death will ultimately remove all suffering, but in the time between his inauguration of the kingdom and its consummation, believers will continue to suffer and continue to need a book like Job. In a far fuller way we know that our Redeemer lives and that we shall yet live to see him.

***Excursus: Theodicy.***[63] Harold Bloom argues that "the Book of Job is not a theodicy, a justification of the ways of God to man, as Milton defines the genre in his sublime theodicy, *Paradise Lost*."[64] The German philosopher Leibniz coined the term *theodicy* in 1710.[65] His aim was to show that the evil in the world is not in conflict with the goodness of God; indeed, this is the best of all possible worlds. The books of Job and Ecclesiastes problematize such a task.[66] But, in our opinion, Job and Ecclesiastes illumine and deepen a biblical theodicy. It is im-

---

[63]Readers may want to read this section after the two chapters on Ecclesiastes (8-9), especially those teaching this book in a class, as theodicy is an issue closely related to both books.

[64]Bloom, *Book of Job*, p. 3. Susannah Ticciati, *Job and the Disruption of Identity: Reading Beyond Barth* (London: T & T Clark, 2005), similarly argues that Job is not about theodicy but personal transformation. In our view this is a false dichotomy.

[65]G. W. F. Leibniz, *Essais de Théodicée sur la bonté de Dieu, la liberté de l'homme et l'origine du mal* (Paris: Garnier-Flammarion, 1969).

[66]See, e.g., Carl Schultz, "The Cohesive Issue of *mišpāṭ* in Job," in *Go to the Land I Will Show You: Studies in Honor of Dwight W. Young*, ed. Joseph E. Coleman and Victor H. Matthews (Winona Lake, Ind.: Eisenbrauns, 1996), pp. 159-75, and chapters 8-9 below.

portant to remember that Job is a believer and that his terrible struggle emerges from the conflict between "his truth" *and* being unable to relinquish God. Indeed, it is the juxtaposition of suffering *and* belief in God that creates the problem of evil.

A sign of emerging Christian attention to theodicy is the widespread popularity of William P. Young's novel *The Shack*. This novel deals with the terrible kidnapping and murder of a father's young daughter and the unexpected journey that ensues. As with Job, it provides no easy answers, but it launches the father on a painful journey of transformation that leads him into a deep encounter with God. *The Shack* is also a reminder of the value of narrative accounts of suffering. Still, we would argue that there are other Christian narratives more useful theologically than *The Shack*.

One thinks, for example, of C. S. Lewis's *A Grief Observed*, the story of the loss of his wife; Nicholas Wolterstorff's *Lament for a Son*, the story of the loss of his son; Jerry Sittser's *A Grace Disguised*, the story of his journey after losing his mother, his wife and a child in an accident caused by a drunken driver; and the many books on suffering by Joni Eareckson Tada. Suffering is terribly unique, but sometimes it helps immeasurably to know that someone else has been in a similar situation and survived.

From a theological and philosophical point of view, theodicy is something of a complex discipline. In what follows we seek to explore some of the major issues involved.

We begin with what most Christians affirm:

1. There is one God—monotheism.

2. God is the creator of the world.

3. God is all powerful.

4. God is personal.

5. God is wholly good.

Evil, both in its natural and moral forms,[67] puts these beliefs in conflict. If God is all powerful he is able to prevent evil, and if God is wholly

---

[67]Evil brought about by human and demonic agents.

good he must be willing to prevent evil.[68] "There is little doubt that the problem of evil is *the* most serious intellectual difficulty for theism."[69] David Hume put his finger on the problem when he wrote, "Is he [God] willing to prevent evil, but not able? Then he is impotent. Is he able, but not willing? Then he is malevolent. Is he both able and willing? Whence then is evil?"[70] In wrestling with this issue Christian philosophers and theologians have come up with the following proposals.

*To deny the omnipotence of God.* The tension between an omnipotent and wholly good God and the evil in the world has led to a recurring temptation to drop either the omnipotence of God or to face up to God not being wholly good. The latter is intolerable—C. S. Lewis's great fear was to discover that God is there but not wholly good. Thus the easier option has been to relinquish the omnipotence of God by coming to the view that he is not all powerful and cannot therefore control evil and consequently cannot be held responsible for it. Harold Kushner's *Why Bad Things Happen to Good People* is a well-known, popular example of this approach. Among philosophers, John Caputo has similarly sought to resurrect a "weakness of God" theodicy, according to which God is powerful but not all powerful. The book of Job never explores such an approach, and it is important to note that resolution for Job comes precisely through an encounter with the omnipotent Creator.

*To question the goodness of God.* Frederick Sontag's theodicy, which he calls anthropodicy, is a good example of this position.[71] For Sontag, we need to start with the problem of evil and then slowly work toward an adequate view of God rather than assuming that we know God is good and omnipotent; for too long, apologies have been made for God. "It is the status of evil in God's nature which forces us to reconceive divinity. Some faults in our world can be explained by claiming that they are not seen as evil in God's sight but only in ours. However, such an event as

---

[68]Stephen T. Davis, introduction to *Encountering Evil: Live Options in Theodicy,* ed. Stephen T. Davis (Atlanta: John Knox Press, 1981), p. 3.

[69]Ibid., p. 2.

[70]David Hume, *Dialogues Concerning Natural Religion* (London: Penguin, 1990), p. 198.

[71]Frederick Sontag, "Anthropodicy and the Return of God," in Davis, *Encountering Evil,* pp. 137-51.

a holocaust surely does not appear 'good' to God in any sense of the word."[72] Sontag thus loosens theism's hold on the perfect goodness of God and invokes mystery at these points. This approach resonates with the tension between "Job's truth" and his experience of God; Job *does* call into question God's justice and goodness, but the narrative overall rejects such a "theodicy."

*The Irenaean theodicy.* The Irenaean theodicy is particularly associated with John Hick,[73] who finds in the thought of Irenaeus the framework for developing a theodicy. According to Hick, God's intention with humankind is to create perfect personal creatures in relationship with him. However, it is logically impossible for God to create humans already in this state because spiritually such a state involves moving freely toward God and freely choosing good over evil. Thus humankind was initially created by means of the evolutionary process as a morally and spiritually immature creature and as part of an ambiguous and ethically demanding world. Unsurprisingly this modern approach is not explicit in Job either, though we can certainly affirm the fact that Job's situation is meant to draw fallen creatures to grow in wisdom and their relationship to God.

*A theodicy of protest, or against theodicy.* This approach has developed particularly since the Holocaust. Christian theology teaches that God cares about history, but John Roth, who advocates a protest theodicy, agrees with Hegel that history is "the slaughter-bench at which the happiness of peoples, the wisdom of states, and the virtue of individuals have been sacrificed."[74] Roth wants evil acknowledged for what it is and God held accountable. The danger in this approach is that one must abandon the notion that God is wholly good.

The Mennonite theologian John Howard Yoder discussed his approach to theodicy in an unfinished 1966 essay titled "Trinity versus Theodicy: Hebraic Realism and the Temptation to Judge God." Yoder is not opposed to theodicy per se; rather he is opposed to the approach often taken to the problem, which he regards as idolatrous. He asks:

---

[72]Ibid., p. 148.
[73]John Hick, "An Irenaean Theodicy," in Davis, *Encountering Evil*, pp. 39-52.
[74]John K. Roth, "A Theodicy of Protest," in Davis, *Encountering Evil*, pp. 7-22, 10.

- Where does one get the criteria by which to judge God?
- Why do we consider ourselves qualified to judge God?
- If we think we are qualified, how does this adjudication proceed?

Yoder thus opposes the narrow sense of theodicy, as articulated by Leibniz, which aims to justify God.[75] In this vein Zachary Braiterman, writing in the context of post-Holocaust theology, coined the phrase "antitheodicy." This means "refusing to justify, explain, or accept [the relationship between] God (or some other form of ultimate reality), evil, and suffering."[76] Yoder also cites two other Jewish post-Holocaust thinkers that Braiterman refers to. Yoder describes their approach as "the Jewish complaint against God, dramatically updated (and philosophically unfolded) since Auschwitz. . . . The faithful under the pogrom proceed with their prayers, after denouncing JHWH / Adonai for what He has let happen."[77] Yoder sees this as a valid form of theology in the *mode* of theodicy, but it is "the opposite of theodicy."[78]

Job certainly is an example of a protest theodicy, and importantly, God at the end of the book affirms his protests. Like Roth, Job wants God held accountable for the evil that has befallen him; but, unlike Roth, he moves beyond such demands through his encounter with God.

*The freewill defense.* From this perspective evil is a consequence of God's giving humans free will. Without the potential to choose evil, humans would be like robots. The freewill defense has an ancient pedigree in Augustine:

---

[75] An important discussion of theodicy in the Yoder tradition is that of Stanley Hauerwas, *Naming the Silences: God, Medicine, and the Problem of Suffering* (Grand Rapids: Eerdmans, 1990). In this work, Hauerwas argues that generally theodicy takes place in the context of Enlightenment presuppositions, which are unacceptable from a Christian perspective. Historically speaking, he argues, "Christians have not had a 'solution' to the problem of evil. Rather, they have had a community of care that has made it possible for them to absorb the destructive terror of evil that constantly threatens to destroy all human relations" (p. 53).

[76] Zachary Braiterman, *(God) After Auschwitz: Tradition and Change in Post-Holocaust Jewish Thought* (Princeton: Princeton University Press, 1998), p. 4.

[77] John Howard Yoder, "Trinity Versus Theodicy: Hebraic Realism and the Temptation to Judge God" (unpublished paper, <http://theology.nd.edu/people/research/yoder-john/documents/TRINITYVERSUSTHEODICY.pdf>).

[78] Ibid.

At bottom, he [Augustine] says, it's that God can create a more perfect universe by permitting evil. A really top-notch universe requires the existence of free, rational, and moral agents; and some of the free creatures He created went wrong. But the universe with the free creatures it contains and the evil they commit is better than it would have been had it contained neither the free creatures nor this evil.[79]

This approach was, however, reformulated and critiqued by J. L. Mackie in an influential article, "Evil and Omnipotence," in 1955. Mackie critiques the claim that evil is a result of human free will. If the will is free, according to Mackie, then logically it is possible for a person to always choose the good. If such a virtuous world is possible, then it is within the power of a good, omnipotent God to create such a world. Thus the claim that God had to choose between a world of robots or one of free agents is a false dilemma.

In response to Mackie, Christian philosopher Alvin Plantinga has presented a robust defense of a freewill theodicy. He argues that evil is consistent with God's existence, because there are some things that even an omnipotent God cannot realize, such as making two plus two equal seven. For Plantinga there are logical truths, what he calls "counterfactuals of freedom," about our choices in various situations. The truths about these choices are necessarily and timelessly true. If, for example, in situation *y,* in which Mike is free either to cheat or not to cheat on an exam, it is either true that if Mike were to be free in *y,* he would cheat on the exam, or if Mike were truly free in *y,* he would not cheat on the exam. If the first proposition is true—Mike would cheat in the exam—then God cannot bring about the possible world in which Mike does not cheat in the exam.

Furthermore, Plantinga argues for the possibility that a person will sin at least once no matter what context God puts her in. Such a person suffers from what Plantinga calls "transworld depravity." Though it is possible that she has the ability to choose to do good in every situation, it remains true that she will choose to sin in at least one of them. And God can do nothing to bring about sinless possible worlds because they

---

[79]Plantinga, "The Free Will Defense," in *The Analytic Theist: An Alvin Plantinga Reader,* ed. J. F. Sennett (Grand Rapids: Eerdmans, 1998), p. 25.

are up to the sinner, and she will choose otherwise. God may be omnipotent, but he cannot alter free decisions. Perhaps all persons suffer
from "transworld depravity" so that the actual world, though not the
best possible world, is the best one God could create if he is to respect
the free will of the human creature. This may account for moral evil, but
what of natural evil? Plantinga appeals to the idea of Satan as the cause
of natural evil; his "luciferous defense."[80] Furthermore, natural evil may
also be the result of powerful, evil moral agents such as demons.

On the surface, the calm logic of the freewill defense seems miles
away from the experience of someone like Job.[81] And yet, there *are* ways
in which Job provides insight as to why he was allowed to suffer. Stump
points out that in God's speeches he stresses not only his power but also
his maternal care for his creation. She asserts:

> If an innocent person suffers, then, it will be because a good God, a lov-
> ing God involved face-to-face with his creatures, produces out of his
> suffering a good meant for that person which in the circumstances
> couldn't have been produced, or produced as well, without the suffering.
> The inference to this explanation about suffering is available to Job. . . .
> In addition, however, Job has another source of information about God's
> reasons for allowing him to suffer. . . . It is the experience of God which
> he has while God is talking to him.[82]

But what good might only have been possible for Job through such
suffering? Susannah Ticciati, drawing on Karl Barth's reading of Job,
argues perceptively that

> we have come to understand Job's obedience as exploration. As we ex-
> pressed it aphoristically above: Job's self is the process of its probing. But
> this means that his obedience, sanctification, or integrity is best under-
> stood, not primarily about being or becoming anything, nor primarily
> about doing anything, but about *being transformed*. Job's integrity is con-
> stituted by his ongoing transformation.[83]

---

[80]Stephen T. Davis, "Free Will and Evil," in Davis, *Encountering Evil*, pp. 69-83, 75.
[81]Plantinga, *Warranted Christian Belief*, pp. 494-98, includes a discussion of Job in his freewill
    defense.
[82]Stump, "Faith and the Problem of Evil," pp. 524-25.
[83]Ticciati, *Job and the Disruption of Identity*, p. 170.

The mystery of suffering will always remain, but suffering as a vehicle used by God for transformation is a major clue to what God is doing in such experiences.

## CONCLUSION

Job is an extraordinary book, and it is remarkable that it is part of the canon of Scripture. The Jewish literary scholar George Steiner once remarked publicly that on a good day at work he could go home and imagine Shakespeare sitting down and writing his plays. But, said Steiner, he could not imagine the same with the speeches of God in Job. There is something quite beyond human insight in them. And ultimately, this is the great gift of Job: God. True wisdom allows God to be God while recognizing that such openness may take one on unexpected journeys and through unexpected suffering. Wisdom is a gift, but, as Proust notes, "We must discover it [wisdom] for ourselves after a journey that no one can take for us or spare us."[84] God, Job assures us, despite his apparent silence, is in it *all* and deeply at work in ways we often cannot imagine or see amid the journey.

## RECOMMENDED READING

### Introductory studies

Alter, Robert. "Truth and Poetry in the Book of Job." Chap. 4 of *The Art of Biblical Poetry*. New York: Basic, 1985.

Wright, Christopher J. H. *The God I Don't Understand: Reflections on Tough Questions of Faith*. Grand Rapids: Zondervan, 2009.

Wright, N. T. *Evil and the Justice of God*. Downers Grove, Ill.: InterVarsity Press, 2006.

### Commentaries

Andersen, Francis I. *Job: An Introduction and Commentary*. TOTC. London: Inter-Varsity Press, 1976.

Habel, Norman C. *The Book of Job*. OTL. Philadelphia: Westminster Press, 1985.

Reitman, James. *Unlocking Wisdom: Forming Agents of God in the House of*

---

[84]Marcel Proust, *Within a Budding Grove* (1919).

*Mourning: A Canonical-Linguistic Exposition of the Books of Job and Ecclesiastes.* Springfield, Mo.: 21st Century Press, 2008.

Wilson, Gerald. *Job.* NIBC. Peabody, Mass.: Hendrickson, 2007.

### Scholarly studies

Barth, Karl. *CD* IV/3.1, §70, pp. 368-478.

Fox, Michael V. "Job 38 and God's Rhetoric." *Semeia* 19 (1981): 53-61.

Plantinga, Alvin. "Suffering and Evil." Chap. 14 of *Warranted Christian Belief.* New York: Oxford University Press, 2000.

Stump, Eleonore. "Faith and the Problem of Evil." In *Seeking Understanding: The Stob Lectures 1986-1998,* pp. 491-550. Grand Rapids: Eerdmans, 2001.

————. *Wandering in Darkness: Narrative and the Problem of Suffering.* Oxford: Clarendon, 2010.

---

## 7

---

# Where Can Wisdom Be Found?

*Human thoughts know many of the world's ways . . . (Job 28:1-11). But*
*they do not know the way to God, . . . for there is no way since every good*
*and every good and perfect gift comes down from above.*

—SØREN KIERKEGAARD, *SPIRITUAL WRITINGS*

OUR EXPLORATION OF JOB REVEALED that uncertainty and mystery
are a difficult but important part of wisdom. Job 28 is a memorable contribution to this lesson. In the last chapter we noted that Job 28 stands
out from its context, with the result that most modern scholarship suspects that it is out of place, written much later or an inappropriate addition to the book. Many of these views fail to take the final, literary shape
of Job seriously. Our aim in this chapter is to read Job 28 as an integral
part of Job while still taking note of critical views on the matter.

## READING JOB 28

Job 28 was never a problem for premodern readers, but it has become
controversial in the last century. There are several reasons for the modern unease: (1) there is a relatively calm, irenic tone when compared
with the anguish and defensiveness in Job 26–27 and Job 29–31,[1] (2) we
find the book's only use of God's name *Adonai* (Lord) in Job 28:28, (3)
it is argued that Job 28 is a premature climax to the narrative, and (4)
there is a possible contradiction in the language of Job 28:28.[2]

---

[1]The anguish underlying Job's questions about where wisdom can be found should not be underestimated.

[2]For more on these problems see Alison Lo's excellent study, *Job 28 as Rhetoric: An Analysis of Job
28 in the Context of Job 22–31*, VTSup 97 (Atlanta: Society of Biblical Literature, 2003).

Commentary in the historical-critical tradition seeks to address these problems by dividing the book into historical traditions and sources. Such work is highly speculative and distracts from the powerful role this poem plays in its surrounding literary context. The proof of the pudding is in the eating, and we hope to show below that Job 28 fits perfectly well in its context and, read as such, makes a rich contribution to the theology of Job.[3]

That context is set up by the speeches in Job 26–27. Job 27 is a typical speech by Job, a protest of his innocence and affirmation of the justice and sovereignty of God. Job 26, however, is a short poem that appeals to the wonders of God's creation and the limits of human wisdom, much like Job 28, the cosmogony in Proverb 8 and many psalms (e.g., Ps 19; 29; 46; 104). Some scholars thus believe that Job 26 and Job 28 are out of character for Job at this point, and others believe that they contradict Job's earlier arguments. Most account for this mismatch of material by concluding that these chapters have been moved from elsewhere in the book or added to an earlier form of the book.[4] Job 29–31, meanwhile, marks the end of Job's speeches, signaled by the shift from the serene tone in Job 28 back to a final protest.

The question interpreters face is how to account for this calm chapter between the two angry and protesting sections of the book. We believe that such changes in tone are more of a problem for historical studies carried out in isolation from literary studies. So, while we do find merit in many of these source and form-critical studies, we still believe that this section of Job should be read in its original literary form.

Alison Lo's use of *character development* is particularly fertile for the way

---

[3]Examples of scholars who also read Job 28 as integral to the book are Lo, *Job 28 as Rhetoric;* Walter Moberly, "Solomon and Job: Divine Wisdom in Human Life?" in *"Where Shall Wisdom be Found?" Wisdom in the Bible, the Church and the Contemporary World*, ed. Stephen C. Barton (Edinburg: T & T Clark, 1999), pp. 3-17; John E. Hartley, *The Book of Job*, NICOT (Grand Rapids: Eerdmans, 1988); Francis I. Andersen, *Job: An Introduction and Commentary*, TOTC (Leicester, U.K.: Inter-Varsity Press, 1976); and Susannah Ticciati, *Job and the Disruption of Identity: Reading Beyond Barth* (London: T & T Clark, 2005), pp. 183-90.

[4]See the important essay by Edward L. Greenstein, "The Poem on Wisdom in Job 28," in *Job 28: Cognition in Context*, ed. Ellen van Wolde (Leiden: Brill, 2003), pp. 253-80, who argues both for linguistic reasons (i.e., the poem starts with the Hebrew particle *ki*, connecting it to something prior) and thematic reasons that the poem in Job 28 is a continuation of Elihu's speech in Job 32–37.

it enables us to appreciate how Job's suffering moves him from lament, to complaint, to a calm affirmation of God's wisdom, and then back again to protest and complaint. These shifts, rather than indicating alternative sources or late additions, resonate with Job's wildly fluctuating experience. Furthermore, the gap between Job's defensive and faithful extremes also creates a tension for us as readers, increasing the sense of crisis and the need for a resolution to the story. Viewed in this way, the appeal to cosmic creation in Job 26 is a window into Job's creation theology, where he knows—but finds hard to trust—that God has indeed made the world with wisdom and justice. Job 28 represents the most heightened expression of Job's creation theology—calm and affirming and yet also, as we will argue below, a powerful caricature of his friends' naive wisdom.

Job's speech in Job 28 is the first literary climax in the book, and it builds to its own climax at its conclusion, where God gives his definitive statement on the place of wisdom: "The fear of the Lord—that is wisdom," and, "to shun evil is understanding." Hearing this, we are drawn back to the threefold affirmation in Job 1–2 of Job fearing God and turning from evil. Here lies the theological dilemma for the chapter: Job fears God, and yet he lacks the wisdom to understand why he suffers. "Job cannot forego either his own truth or God."[5]

This dilemma is reason enough for Job to lapse back in Job 29 to the defensive posture of Job 27. It is not unusual in literature to have such an aside in the midst of a speech. In Job's case, his move from defense to theological contemplation and back to defense is just what we would expect from a believer struggling desperately to come to grips with his experience. Job is not a one-dimensional character, nor is this story a flat, moral fable. Whether Job was an historical person or not, the depiction of his struggle as he spirals up and down between faith and protest fits with what we would expect from a believer amid such terrible suffering.

## OUTLINE

Job 28 consists of three distinct stages (Job 28:1-11, 12-19, 20-28) set

---

[5]Martin Buber, quoted by Harold Bloom, ed., *The Book of Job* (New York: Chelsea House, 1988), p. 2.

apart by the refrain repeated in verses 12 and 20. Norman Habel's analysis of the chapter suggests that Job's speech focuses our attention on three major aspects of wisdom: its "place," its "way" and its "process of discovery," which is displayed in the outline in table 7.1. All three of these themes appear in an intricate design in the poem's final section (Job 28:23-27).[6]

These poetic images of wisdom's place, way and process of discovery are found throughout Proverbs 1–9 and Proverbs 31. Our reading below makes use of these themes and the way they encourage us to hear Job's story in the context of wisdom in Proverbs.

This poem is probably new to many readers. But in an oral culture like Israel's it is likely that this story was heard again and again. This is significant because, as Gerald Wilson suggests, the real power of a poem is revealed in the second, third, fourth readings and beyond. This is true of much great literature, storytelling and movie-watching in the way we come back to familiar scenes and see and hear more than we did before. Wilson also suggests that rereadings create "preknowledge" that in further readings or hearings can make the story more suspenseful. In Job, these rereadings are especially strong as they compound the intense rhetoric and poetry in the book.[7] We can feel and hear the surprises just around the corner. It may help to imagine them as we point out Job's very precise use of language to make his points.

There[8] is a mine for silver
    and a place where gold is refined. (Job 28:1)

Ellen van Wolde emphasizes the striking visual nature of this chapter, as the narrator moves us from one highly descriptive scene to the next.[9] But, as John Elwolde warns, many get so caught up in the visual mining imagery that they miss the poetic metaphor that holds it all together:

---

[6]Norman C. Habel, *The Book of Job*, OTL (Philadelphia: Westminster Press, 1985), pp. 394-95.

[7]Gerald Wilson, "Preknowledge, Anticipation, and the Poetics of Job," *JSOT* 30, no. 2 (2005): 243-56.

[8]The Hebrew particle *ki* is left out of the NIV but translated "surely" by other versions. The reader should be aware that the poem continues a previous thought.

[9]Ellen van Wolde, "Wisdom, Who Can Find It? A Cognitive and Non-Cognitive Study of Job 1-11," in *Job 28: Cognition in Context*, ed. Ellen van Wolde (Leiden: Brill, 2003), pp. 1-35.

**Table 7.1**

| | | | |
|---|---|---|---|
| I. Place | | 28:1-2 | A source *(môṣā²)*[a] for silver and a location *(māqôm)* of precious metals |
| | Discovery | 3-4 | mortals search *(ḥôqēr)* for metals |
| II. Place | | 5-6 | Earth has a place *(māqôm)* for stones |
| | Way | 7-8 | way *(derek)* not known by birds or beasts |
| | Discovery | 9-11 | mortal eyes see *(r²h)* precious things that are hidden *(ʿlm)* |
| III. Place | | 12 | Refrain: But what is wisdom's place *(māqôm)*? |
| | Way/discovery | 13-14 | Mortals do not know *(yādaʿ)* its worth [or way][b] and cannot find *(mṣ²)* it; it is not in the deep or the sea |
| | Discovery | 15-19 | Wisdom's value is greater than all precious treasures, nor can they be given in exchange for it |
| IV. Place | | 20-22 | Refrain: "But wisdom, where can it be found *(mṣ²)* and what is the place *(māqôm)* of understanding?". . . It is hidden *(ʿlm)* from human eyes |
| V. Place | Way/discovery | 23-27 | God knows its way *(derek)* and place *(māqôm)*, he saw *(r²h)* and searched *(ḥqr)* for it |
| The secret revealed | | 28 | God says: Fearing the Lord *(ʾădōnay)* is wisdom, turning from evil is understanding |

[a]This word looks and sounds like the verb *mṣ²* ("to find"), which appears several times in this poem. The origin of the word is not certain. See Marvin H. Pope, *Job*, AB (Garden City, N.Y.: Doubleday, 1965), pp. 177-83, for lexical analysis on the poem.

[b]Note that Habel and Stephen A. Geller prefer the BHS reading "way" *(darkāh)* in place of "worth" *(ʿerkāh)*, following the LXX. The text-critical evidence is not strong, but Geller's arguments on the basis of context are very persuasive, "'Where Is Wisdom?' A Literary Study of Job 28 in Its Settings," in *Judaic Perspectives on Ancient Israel*, ed. Jacob Neusner, Baruch A. Levine and Ernest S. Frerichs, with Caroline McCracken-Flesher (Philadelphia: Fortress, 1986), pp. 166-68.

My feeling is that commentators have been so fixated by the possibility of a metallurgical or mining background to vv. 2-11 that they have missed the structural and semantic relationship, at the same time obvious and delicate, between v. 1 and vv. 12 and 20, where the primary metaphor is that of wisdom as silver and gold. . . . This figurative relationship has been distorted, so that the search for wisdom and understanding is *preceded* by a search for silver and gold, without realizing that the silver spoken of *is* wisdom, the gold *is* understanding, an identification hardly unknown from elsewhere in the Bible (e.g. Prov. 16:16; Eccl. 7:12).[10]

Stephen Geller also attempts to explain this metaphorical imagery by pointing to a deeper, more nuanced meaning behind it. He says that the images from nature and mining, which he calls "realistic," extend through their metaphorical associations and contrast their "real" meaning in the poem (access to wisdom). The result of the contrast is the premise that human skill in mining is not the same as human skill in understanding God's purposes. What he describes as an "impressionistic"[11] form of writing alerts us to the literary sophistication of Job 28.

Man puts an end to the darkness;
> he searches the farthest recesses for ore in the blackest darkness.
>     (Job 28:3)

On first appearance this verse speaks of the human capacity to mine deep into the darkness of the earth. But we know already that these terms are highly metaphorical. Greenstein helpfully points out that in ancient Near Eastern cosmology, there are likely two conceptual models for the location and origin of wisdom.[12] The more dominant model in Babylonian cosmology is that wisdom is in the heavens, while the model in Ugaritic and most Semitic cosmologies is that wisdom is in the deeps of the earth. We find both models in the Bible, though the depth model seems to dominate Job 28.

---

[10]John Elwolde, "Non-Contiguous Parallelism," in van Wolde, *Job 28*, p. 111.
[11]Stephen A. Geller, "Where Is Wisdom," in *Sacred Enigmas: Literary Religion in the Hebrew Bible* (London: Routledge, 1996), p. 158.
[12]Greenstein, "Poem on Wisdom," pp. 254-63.

Consider that, up to now, Job's suffering has consistently been linked to the cosmic chaos of "darkness" *(hōšek)* and "the deep" *(tĕhôm* and *salmāwet)*. All three of these terms evoke the mysterious intersection of creation, chaos and suffering. In Genesis, *hōšek* is a common word used in the early chaotic sections of the creation account (Gen 1:2, 4-5, 18); it appears a remarkable twenty-eight times in Job, both in Job's speeches (Job 3:4-5, 9; 28:3) and in the divine speeches (Job 38:2, 19). *Tĕhôm* ("the deep"), also familiar in the creation texts in Genesis (Gen 1:2; 7:11; 8:2; 49:25), is applied to Job's suffering in Job 28:14, 38:16, 38:30 and Job 41:24. Finally, *salmāwet* is used ten times in Job and occurs several times in the Psalms to refer to this same intersection of cosmic darkness and suffering (see especially Ps 23:4; 107:10, 14). Zophar uses similar language of the "mysteries" and "limits" of God's wisdom and the "depths of the grave" to describe this cosmic darkness as the impenetrable realms of God's wisdom (Job 11:7-8).

This set of symbols functions in two ways in the poem. On the one hand, humanity has been able to delve into deep underwater caves, trenches and mines. Even today, electron microscopes and robotic spacecraft have afforded us precise knowledge of dark and dangerous places, giving us increased confidence in our ingenuity. On the other hand, in Job 28:3, as well as in Job 28:11, 14, the darkness and chaos language also works metaphorically to critique the *darkness* of the friends' wisdom. In fact, the implication is that the friends have trapped themselves without admitting it. They continually defer to God's cosmic wisdom above human knowledge, but all the while, they all accuse Job of guilt, thus implying that they have the wisdom to interpret Job's mysterious suffering. They demand that Job admit the limits of his wisdom, but they refuse to live by these limits themselves. How do they know that they are right and Job is wrong? Job now responds poetically as if to say that in all their sophisticated words of wisdom (searching for gold and silver) his friends have found nothing but cosmic darkness.

The accusation builds throughout the following verses.

The earth, from it food comes;
but is overturned below as by fire.

> sapphires come from its rocks,[13]
>   and its dust has gold. (Job 28:5-6)

We provide our own translation for these verses to help retain the original vocabulary and to emphasize the antithetical relationship between the poetic lines (as in the ESV and NRSV). At the surface the earth gives food, *but* below is "overturned" (*hāpak*) with fire. (The original audience would have suspected a hot earthen core based on their knowledge of volcanoes.) While the animals are sustained by the earth's most basic production at the surface (Job 28:7-8), only humans have the ability to journey deep into the earth's hot storehouse of rare and precious treasures (cf. Job 28:9-11). In these dangerous, powerful deeps, humans have been able to extract sapphires and gold. Francis Andersen may be right to hear a rebuke of Bildad's final argument here: humans are only maggots or worms (Job 25:6)—useless, senseless animals.[14] But, Job rightly replies, our inability to understand suffering, or to have infinite wisdom, does not make us mere animals. We are image bearers of the Creator and among all created life second only to God. We are able to extract extraordinary treasures from the dangerous lower world. But neither does that make us gods! Rather, we are something in between and that is what leads to the problem of knowing.

Looking more closely at the mining imagery in Job 28:3-8, we can see Job making two symbolic or rhetorical moves in his dialogue with his friends. First, the path in Job 28:3-8 moves from horizontal images across the land's surface to vertical places of birds and depths of the mines. These spatial dimensions—breadth, height and depth—reflect the exhaustive effort humans make in the search for wisdom.[15] Second, these dimensions also evoke the symbolic places of chaos: vast skies, dark deeps and vast deserts. Job thus seems to call into question the whole range of ancient Near Eastern conceptual models for wisdom, showing that none of them can answer this case.

Geller is among a few who see yet another biblical pattern at work in

---

[13]This passage is known to have difficulties in translation, and there are countless suggestions for amending it.
[14]Andersen, *Job*, p. 224.
[15]Geller, "Where Is Wisdom," pp. 160-64.

the way the imagery of deserts and destruction point to God's judgment at Sodom and Gomorrah (cf. Jer 51:43; 50:12-13; Is 13:20-21; Ezek 35:7-15). Job 28:5 describes the earth as "overturned" *(hāpak)* by fire, a term used specifically in the Old Testament for the overturn of the wicked city of Sodom (e.g., Gen 19:25; Deut 29:22; Amos 4:11; Isa. 13:19).[16] Taken this way, Job's highly symbolic language implies that his friends' verbose search for wisdom, like Sodom, will be overturned with God's judgment. In what feels like the most measured poetry of Job's speeches, Job's symbolism reveals that he has taken the proverbial boxing gloves off!

The desert/destruction imagery is then opposed to the images of paradise and Eden in Job 28:6, with its jewels and dust of gold (cf. Gen 2:11-12; Is 54:12; Ezek 28:14). Geller explains how these poetic images and words serve Job's purpose:

> In an inhospitable desert region man, laboring with almost divine skill, finds a netherworld Eden of preternatural wealth. But the rapid succession of complementary (Underworld-desert-Sodom), partially conflicting (desert-paradise) motifs also intimates meanings that prose could never achieve with such startling simultaneity. . . . Even to find riches, digging into Sheol must bear a dark meaning.[17]

Surely the friends have pursued their wisdom too confidently and arrived at their conclusions too soon. The full thrust of this rhetoric is reached in Job 28:11.

> He searches the sources of the rivers
> and brings hidden things to light.

This verse is the first climactic statement in the poem, drawing together all the images used thus far: humans go into the "dark" places of the earth (Job 28:3) and bring things to "light" (*'ôr*, Job 28:11). Several interpretations of this imagery are possible. The friends suppose they have wisdom, and it could be that Job, having seen more darkness (suffering) than his friends, is suggesting that he is the only one who can truly bring riches (wisdom) to light. Like animals, his

---

[16]See also Greenstein, "Poem on Wisdom," pp. 268-69.
[17]Geller, "Where Is Wisdom," p. 163.

friends have remained on the surface of this story.

Geller suggests another, more intriguing possibility: the friends' approach to wisdom implies an understanding of humanity that surpasses our created design: "Man's mining activities thus mimic divine creation, splitting, crushing, overturning (cf. v. 5) and so on. . . . So powerful are the divine creation motifs in vv. 9-11 that they totally submerge the narrative, 'realistic' plane of meaning. In obtaining jewels man mimics, and perhaps mocks the creator."[18] We think Geller may go too far here in suggesting that divine imitation is mockery. Divine imitation, as we find throughout the Bible and the Gospels especially, is our highest calling.

But surely the friends have gone to great lengths to reprove Job and thus put themselves in the place of God. For them, the accusation surely fits. What initially sounds like praise of humanity is in fact subtle irony and implicit judgment. To claim to be able to explain all mysteries, as the friends have, is to act presumptuously in the place of God.

But how exactly have these friends gone wrong? The answer may not be far from our own backyard. So much of modern Christian theology has lost sight of the created order, particularly its wild and dangerous nature, and reduced the Christian life to spiritual salvation alone. Job's friends are caught in something of a similar kind of problem; they are only able to see this event of suffering in relation to sin, justification and human fault. But we know from the prologue that this is not the way to interpret Job's situation, and the imagery here pushes us to have more than just a two-dimensional view of sin and suffering in the world and thus of the way God chooses to rule it. Human rebellion will always result in suffering, but suffering and chaos also have other purposes in his world.

Furthermore, the fact that Job and his friends find themselves distanced from God's wisdom leads many scholars to assume that the book of Job points to two kinds of wisdom: (1) cosmic and divine and (2) human and practical. There is a certain truth to the gap between human and divine knowledge of the world; God's wisdom is above ours

---

[18]Ibid., p. 164.

(Is 55:8-9). But the same spiritualizing risk emerges here as we tend to push spiritual salvation apart from wisdom. In the process, human wisdom gets reduced to mere technique, good behavior and practical skill, having no rooting in God's own wisdom and his cosmic designs for the world. Chapters four and five of this book argued the exact opposite; our work to build houses, careers, cities, businesses and more are all acts in keeping with God's wise work in creating the world and setting it on its way. So, rather than taking Job 28 as a basis for two types of wisdom, we should see it as staking out the limits of our wisdom, both in knowing and doing. As Susannah Ticciati perceptively notes,

> When the hymn claims of wisdom, "God discerns the way to it, and he knows its place" (v. 23), its purpose, by designating wisdom as something of God, is not to oppose it to the activity of vv. 1-11, but to set this activity in relation to God. Just as Job's activity of searching was not in conflict with God's, but took place in intimate relation with it, so in this hymn are human and divine activity understood in their relation to one another. In sum, wisdom may not be attainable by humans in the way that other goods are, but it may inform their endeavours when carried out in the greater context of God.[19]

Thus, like God's wisdom, our wisdom has a cosmic foundation that gives way to practical application. But unlike God's wisdom, our wisdom comes to a limit where we must embrace the mysterious—to learn the discipline of wonder.

## REFRAIN

The first of two refrains (Job 28:12, 20) marks the middle of this poem and signals a gradual turn to completing the total picture.

> But where can wisdom be found?
>> Where does understanding dwell? (Job 28:12)

The NIV obscures the original Hebrew, in which wisdom is a personal figure, emphasized by her position at the beginning of the sentence: "but wisdom, where shall she be found?" Understanding sits in

---

[19]Ticciati, *Job and the Disruption of Identity*, p. 187.

parallel as a virtual synonym for wisdom, and "dwell" evokes wisdom's personified home. Job seems to say that the friends have leaned on memorized formulas and truisms to answer Job's case. But wisdom, as Wilson observes, is not a commodity to be found under rocks;[20] nor does it come from memorized theology or catchy slogans. She is far more like a person with a home, sought out in relationship, not craft.

Job will come back to this refrain again, for he is not yet done with his response. The friends have been far too confident in their conclusions. In Job 28:13-14 he continues with the motif of wisdom's unique place while adding comments about her unique value.

> Man does not know her worth;
>    she cannot be found in the land of the living.
> The deep says "she is not in me";
>    The sea says "she is not in me."

We have again altered the NIV and kept the ambiguous feminine references in the translation to retain the personal tone in these verses. Not only is wisdom not found under rocks or in mines; but also, neither do the two greatest cosmic powers of the ancient world—the deep and the sea—hold her. One of the implications we should draw from this point is that God has prepared wisdom's home, and he alone can guide us to it. But the whole of this chapter also shows a subtler side of Job's response to his friends: they have never taken the cosmic poems and images of creation, which they have used in their arguments to convict Job, as a warning to apply the mystery of wisdom and its limits to themselves.

Job 28:15-19 continues to build on the mystery of wisdom's place and her priceless value, using several verbs and adjectives in an intensifying sequence. Wisdom cannot be "bought," "valued," "equaled" or "had" (exchanged for). Its price is "beyond rubies [pearls]"; it cannot "compare with topaz" or be "bought with gold." Altogether, Job 28:15-19 lists seven rare gems in addition to gold and silver, also treasured objects of

---

[20]Gerald Wilson, *Job*, NIBC (Peabody, Mass.: Hendrickson, 2007), p. 306. Wilson also seems to suggest a contradiction between this verse and passages like Prov 2:1-5; 3:13-15, which do encourage us to seek wisdom like a miner. If this is his intention, we disagree. The rhetorical and theological use of this metaphor in these two wisdom texts is clearly different.

the search in Job 28:1-11. Thus both parts of the poem so far (Job 28:1-11, 12-20) come together to affirm that nothing humans have or do in the natural world assures them access to wisdom.

Job 28:20 repeats the refrain from Job 28:12, but with a slight change: "Where can wisdom be found?" (Job 28:12) to "Where does wisdom come from?" (Job 28:20). The change in the Hebrew is only one word, and the point seems basically the same. However, the change from "finding" to "coming" may be an indicator that the only hope is for wisdom to come from outside the creation.[21] Job 28:20 opens the third and final section of the poem (Job 28:21-28), where the location of and way to wisdom will gradually be revealed. The verses in Job 28:21-23 are the last in the poem's negative theme of the inaccessibility of wisdom. Lo here identifies a symbolic parallel between Job 28:13-14 and Job 28:21-22:

> "land of the living" (Job 28:13) / "eyes of every living thing" (Job 28:21)
> "the deep" and "the sea" (Job 28:14) / "abaddon" and "death" (Job 28:22)

These two oft-repeated extremes of high/low and living/dead together represent the fullest limits of God's created world (cf. Job 28:3-6 and Gen 1:2). The cosmic imagery is likely a means to critique other forms of ancient Near Eastern wisdom that encouraged humans to seek wisdom *in* the creation.[22] Hebrew wisdom *operates* in these places, but it does not *dwell* there. Abaddon and death have only "heard" of it, but they don't have it. Wisdom dwells with the one true God, who "sees" it, as the poem and the book aim to make clear.

Geller rightly picks up on the intentional juxtaposition of "seeing" and "hearing" in this section, which we have also commented on in previous chapters. Humans have gone *looking* for wisdom, or understanding, but have emerged empty-handed. The book is gradually leading us with Job to *see* God as the means to *see* wisdom. Job's final words in Job 42:4-5

---

[21]But see the more intricate comparison made by Elwolde "Non-Contiguous Parallelism," pp. 104-8.

[22]"Death" in Job 28:22 may be a play on the Canaanite deity, who—in this passage—does not have wisdom.

reinforce the point that to see, or know, God is to find wisdom.[23]

Job finally turns to his conclusion in Job 28:23-28.

> God understands the way to it;
>> and he alone knows *its place*. (Job 28:23)

Here the NIV unfortunately fails to translate the final word literally, obscuring the continuity of this verse with the poem so far. God, and only God, knows the *way* to and the *place* of wisdom.

The next four verses (Job 28:24-27) accomplish at least three related tasks in the poem. First, they confirm that wisdom is indeed integrally tied to the creation; God saw it (Job 28:27) when he was purveying all the works of his hands. Second, these verses tie wisdom specifically to the limits and order of the creation. Job gives four examples of places where God has set such boundaries in the world:

- The *force* or weight of the wind

- The waters by its *measurement*

- The *decree* for the rain

- The *way* for the thunderbolt

Most of these images also appear in Job 26, Psalm 104 and the wisdom poem in Proverbs 8 where, as we discussed in chapter four above, Woman Wisdom observed the carved or grooved nature of all creation (Prov 8:27-31). These verses in Job 28 affirm that all things, including the way to wisdom, have a place in God's created designs.

Third, these verses set up an unexpected play on the language of *place*. The surprise here is that wisdom is not literally *there* to find or get. The place turns out to be a metaphor for the *how* of a life that pursues Yahweh in faith and obedience.[24] The final verse in the poem makes this clear.

> And he said to man,
>> "The fear of the Lord—that is wisdom
>> and to shun evil is understanding." (Job 28:28)

---

[23]See our comments on these verses in chapter 6 above.

[24]Geller, "Where Is Wisdom," p. 166, and Greenstein, "Poem on Wisdom," p. 274, both believe that the lack of a "place" for wisdom transitions into the "when" of wisdom, that is, the primordial act of creation.

This verse stands outside the meter and in opposition to the content in Job 28:1-11, leading some to regard it as out of place.[25] Others like Habel and Lo argue that it is a fitting end to the poem, and we believe they do so for good reason. Listening to it in context, we encounter the powerful and perhaps unexpected way this verse brings the whole chapter into line with the traditional wisdom in Proverbs. Proverbs began with the fear of the LORD and the accessibility of wisdom in Proverbs 1–9. Then, as we noted above, Proverbs 10–30, especially Proverbs 30, raises many contradictions and questions regarding the inaccessibility of wisdom. Job 28 mimics this material in the opposite direction, moving from the accessibility of created treasures (Job 28:1-11) to the inaccessibility of wisdom (Job 28:12-27) to the accessibility of wisdom through the fear of the LORD (Job 28:28).[26]

Not only does Job 28:28 stand out of meter and in tension with the rest of poem; but there is also a sense in which this whole chapter is held together by sets of such tensions.[27] Consider the tension between saying and knowing:

- The deep says *(ʾāmar)*, "it *is not* in me." (Job 28:14)
- And he [God] says *(ʾāmar)* to man, "The fear of Adonai, that *is* wisdom." (Job 28:28)

- Man *does not know (yādaʿ)* its worth. (Job 28:13)
- God understands and *knows (yādaʿ)* its place. (Job 28:23)

Furthermore, beasts stand in contrast to humanity, humanity to God, and wisdom to earthly treasures. The main lesson is explicit in Job 28:28: the path to wisdom is not via human achievement, nor even through the creation, but by fearing God and obeying his commands.

That point is clear in Proverbs already. The more subtle points of Job 28 emerge in the intricacy of the poetry and cosmic imagery, which make the fear of God all the more specific and demanding. This world

---

[25]See Habel, *Job*, pp. 400-401.
[26]See Lo, *Job 28 as Rhetoric*, p. 213.
[27]See Habel, *Job*, p. 393, and Lo, *Job 28 as Rhetoric*, p. 213.

is a dangerous, often trying place, and humans must embrace the limits of wisdom and the discipline of wonder. We learned that through the contradictions in Proverbs, and we learn it again more emphatically now.

It is remarkable to see how the poetic language and structure facilitate such profound insights. Poetry, as we saw in chapter three, teaches us that apparent opposites do not lead to absurdity but rather to greater understanding. An apparent sense of inexplicable injustice, therefore, does not end in a rejection of traditional wisdom; rather, it illumes it more deeply.

It is relevant to ask at this point whether it is too early in the book for Job to express such optimism. We do not think so. All of us have likely been in the midst of some kind of suffering and then, for a moment or two, have come to a relative peace about God's rule and care for us in our present circumstances. The whole Pentateuch and the Old Testament historical books, in fact, are stories moving between times of Israel's faithfulness and success and rebellion and anguish. So we recognize the possibility of faith and clarity in suffering, but we also all recognize that it is nearly impossible to maintain this mindset permanently. That is why wisdom, wonder and humility are disciplines that we have to learn and practice. Nor should the anguish in the question of Job 28:12, 20 be ignored. For Job, finding an answer to the whereabouts of wisdom is a matter of life and death.

## THEOLOGICAL REFLECTIONS

Read in its context in Job and of the Old Testament wisdom literature, Job 28 provides rich resources for theological reflection. In this section we reflect on some of its major theological themes.

***Back to the beginning.*** Proverbs starts with the fear of the Lord as the beginning of wisdom; Job 28 ends with it. In an intriguing way this mirrors Job's development. His sufferings have confronted him unequivocally with the limitations of his understanding, and his journey must be one back to that foundation of wisdom; but he hasn't the slightest idea how to find his way to that place. His return to that starting point, now to know it more deeply, will only be made possible when wisdom comes to him from outside the creation.

In this way this remarkable poem leads us back to that basic insight of wisdom: it always begins with and returns to the fear of the Lord. The *archē*, the origin from which biblical faith seeks to understand the world, is never *immanent* within creation but outside of it.[28] For Job and the Old Testament, God exists before and outside of nature. God is not the sun, the waters, the heavens or even a human king. He is *the origin* of all those things. Both the ancient and modern worlds are full of pagan worldviews central to which is the idea that the *archē* is immanent in nature. Contemporary Darwinism and much popular naturalism deifies nature in this way, but Job reinforces the Hebrew teaching that nature's purpose is to testify to God's glory in, before and beyond nature (Ps 19:1-6; 24:1-2; 104:1-35). Like Job 38–41, Job 28 reinforces that natural laws, while highly regular, are governed by something beyond our intellectual grasp. And Job 28 reminds us that the *archē* is far more than a reference point; it is the living God, who is, as C. S. Lewis noted, no tame lion, but the hunter, the warrior, the king, the God who approaches at infinite speed.

In a negative way, Job 28 also reinforces this wild, uncontrollable God's generous desire to share his wisdom with humanity and the immense possibilities of a wisdom journey based on the fear of the Lord. Such faith is never restricted to the "sacred" parts of life but explores the whole of life as God has made it, including mining, technology, mineralogy, underwater exploration and the exploration of space. Sadly God's very generosity allows humans to make themselves the measure of all things, and often it takes a journey like that of Job to realize that all wisdom comes from the living and true God.

***Embracing our creatureliness.*** In his book *Original Sin*, Alan Jacobs traces the role the doctrine of Adam's sin has played throughout Western culture.[29] Despite the relentless increase of war, terrorism, genocide, mass shootings, crime, hatred, fraud, deadbolts, passwords, security systems, security guards, surveillance cameras and the gen-

---

[28]For the philosophical significance of this, see L. Kalsbeek, *Contours of a Christian Philosophy: An Introduction to Herman Dooyeweerd's Thought* (Lewiston, N.Y.: Edwin Mellen, 2002).

[29]Alan Jacobs, *Original Sin: A Cultural History* (New York: HarperOne, 2008).

eral societal fear that pervades our modern culture, popular opinion is, ironically, uncomfortable with the idea of sin, much less original sin. What could be more apparent today? One could argue, in fact, that the root of much modern sin is *pride* in our achievements in human knowledge.

Roughly up until the Enlightenment, pride was regarded as the first of the seven deadly sins. But since then times have changed. Cornelius Plantinga says,

> What has changed is that, in much of contemporary American culture, aggressive self-regard is no longer viewed with alarm. Instead, people praise and promote it. This is a culture in which schoolchildren outrank Asian schoolchildren not in math ability but in self-confidence about their math ability. . . . In this culture, avant-garde literary critics teach "imperial readers" that what they bring to a Milton text is more important than what the text brings to them, and trendy preachers imply that the main problem with savings and loan embezzlers is that they do not love themselves unconditionally.[30]

Job 28 is insightful in this respect in portraying the amazing abilities of humans while also stressing our limits as creatures and positioning all our knowledge within the fear of the Lord.

Job's friends, however, speak from confidence in their theological expertise and are quick to defend their own sense of right.[31] This expertise arises in three patterns: their repeated, explicit claims to have knowledge (Job 4:8, 12-16; 5:3, 27; 8:8-10; 12:2-3; 15:17-19; 18:2; 20:3-4; 32:6-10); the detailed content of their wisdom and knowledge; and Job's rebukes for their claims to be wiser than him (Job 12:2-3; 13:2). The poem in Job 28 is positioned in the middle of this drama, seeming at first to be a celebration of human wisdom but then catching us unawares with a critique of human self-confidence. Indirectly the poem thus rebukes the friends for their naiveté: issuing rebukes and proverbial truisms is akin to digging deep into the earth's core for gold. It is remarkable work and a testament to humanity, but it is not

---

[30]Cornelius Plantinga, *Not the Way It's Supposed to Be: A Breviary of Sin* (Grand Rapids: Eerdmans, 1995), pp. 82-83.
[31]See Lo, *Job 28 as Rhetoric*, p. 67.

all there is to wisdom. Wisdom begins and grows only with humility before the Lord.

Our modern world embodies a story that resembles this attitude in Job's friends, only our age is worse for its shameless secularity.[32] The secular turn of recent centuries has replaced religion with new idols like progress, education, technology and imperialism. The hope has been that in place of religion these new techniques will finally deliver us from suffering and give us a new utopia.[33] Certainly our education, progress and technology have given us many benefits in sanitation, medicine, safety, comfort and convenience. But they have also given us whole new generations of weapons and sophisticated means to defraud, cheat, steal and torture. The secular humanist project has not succeeded as hoped, yet our culture bids us to press on, trusting that we just need to tinker with our knowledge and technology until we are finally happy with ourselves.

Modern education, even Christian education, typically mimics this modern self-image of progress. Schools and universities are constructed and administered to maximize the transfer of knowledge from one social group to another. Marilynne Robinson laments the "gradegetting" culture of the modern university, which has lost its original humanist love of learning and its appreciation for the whole life of the student.[34] We now conduct a rapid push to graduation, with little or no time built in for reflection and spiritual development. We might have a claim to something meaningful if—for every ten classes focused on content—we had one focused on inner spirituality, virtues like humility or the limits of knowledge. But we are far from that; those subjects do not fit the needs of jobs in our technology-driven world.

Thus, Job's story, which began with the objections of a mysterious accuser—heavily reminiscent of Genesis 3—turns out to be much less about Satan than about the way we deal with temptation, evil, sin and

---

[32]See, for example, Henri de Lubac, *The Drama of Atheist Humanism* (San Francisco: Ignatius, 1983).

[33]See Richard Bauckham, *Bible and Mission: Christian Witness in a Postmodern World* (Grand Rapids: Baker Academic, 2003), p. 5. We consider the book an essential read.

[34]See Marilynne Robinson, introduction to *The Death of Adam: Essays on Modern Thought* (New York: Picador, 2005), pp. 7-10.

wisdom in day-to-day human life. The greatest temptation for all of the characters is to claim, or even to desire, to know too much. Comparable biblical examples are Adam and Eve's desire for knowledge and wisdom in Genesis 3:6 and the church at Corinth, with their prideful attachment to knowledge (1 Cor 8:1-3). The search for knowledge, these texts all remind us, must always be informed by our faith in God and a sense of our creaturely limits.

*Poetry, wisdom and knowledge.* The poetry of Job 28 is a reminder that the human quest for wisdom and our ability to live the inexplicable suffering of this world require us to embrace the power of metaphor and poetry. As Robert Alter notes:

> Job's poetry was an instrument for probing, against the stream of the Friends' platitudes, the depths of his own understandable sense of outrage over what befell him. God's poetry enables Job to glimpse beyond his human plight an immense world of power and beauty and awesome warring forces. This world is permeated with God's ordering concern, but as the vividness of the verse makes clear, it presents to the human eye a welter of contradictions, dizzying variety, energies and entities that man cannot take in.[35]

Clearly this does not mean that the quest for wisdom ends irrationally. On the contrary, truth, knowledge and the metaphorical power of poetry should never be separated, as they have been in the recent centuries of "scientific" Western culture. In the poetry of this poem we find a creative combination of prayer, theology and a highly subversive critique of Job's friends. The book of Lamentations and many of the psalms are like this too, not to mention the many places in the New Testament where poetry is used to speak to the deepest truths about Christ (e.g., Phil 2:6-11; Col 1:15-20).[36]

The point of course is that Job's situation is a not a matter just for abstract theology. It is part of a debate both with God and with a community that calls on the most creative linguistic expressions of experience, nature and theology to address a painful impasse. As Holy Scrip-

---

[35]Robert Alter, *The Art of Biblical Poetry* (New York: Basic, 1985), p. 110.

[36]Thanks to Dan Reid for reminding us of this. We take these passages up in more detail in chapter ten below.

ture, Job is a word from God to us, providing us with the language of protest and prayer needed to *live* suffering before God.

## RECOMMENDED READING

### Introductory studies
Kugel, James L. "Job 28." Chap. 6 of *The Great Poems of the Bible: A Reader's Companion with New Translations.* New York: Free Press, 1999.

### Scholarly studies
Geller, Stephen. A. "Where Is Wisdom?" Chap. 5 of *Sacred Enigmas: Sacred Religion in the Hebrew Bible.* London: Routledge, 1996.

Lo, Alison. *Job 28 as Rhetoric: An Analysis of Job 28 in the Context of Job 22–31.* VTSup 97. Atlanta: Society of Biblical Literature, 2003.

Wolde, Ellen van, ed., *Job 28: Cognition in Context.* Biblical Interpretation 64. Leiden: Brill, 2003.

# 8

# Ecclesiastes

*I was trying to find the origin of evil,*
*but I was quite blind to the evil in my own method of research.*

—AUGUSTINE *CONFESSIONS* 7.5

ECCLESIASTES IS A BOOK THAT RESONATES deeply with many people today. It is endlessly quoted, often out of context, and provides a great reservoir of metaphors and images for people to draw on. In one of their tours, U2 had Bono, decked out in his devil horns, pick up a young woman from the crowds and slow dance with her through the song. In the Welsh concert he picked up a fundamentalist Christian who used the opportunity to berate him for his horns! As they danced he explained to her that the horns were ironic, just like Ecclesiastes.

Ecclesiastes may resonate with readers today, but it is not an easy book to understand in Hebrew or in English. In Craig's commentary on Ecclesiasts he notes in the preface that Ecclesiastes is a lot like an octopus: just when you think you have all the tentacles under control—that is, you have understood the book—there is one waving about in the air! In this way Ecclesiastes mirrors life and the journey of its main character, Qohelet; life is complex and perplexing, and finding a wise way to understand and live this perplexity is no easy task.

## INTRODUCTION

Ecclesiastes is part of the Old Testament *Writings* and with Proverbs and Job is one of three undisputed wisdom writings. Contemporary scholars remain deeply divided as to whether Ecclesiastes is a deeply pessimistic book or one that affirms life and joy. The dominant view nowadays is that Ecclesiastes is pessimistic and that with Job it represents a *crisis* in the mechanical view of wisdom set out by Proverbs. However, as we have seen, the view of wisdom in Proverbs is far more nuanced than it is often given credit for; and, in our view, Ecclesiastes ultimately affirms life and joy, as do Proverbs and Job, but only as the end result of a ferocious struggle with the brokenness of life.

## OUTLINE OF ECCLESIASTES

There has been a great deal of debate among scholars as to whether or not Ecclesiastes is a literary unity. In the latter half of the twentieth century the consensus moved toward affirming its unity, although the great exception remains the epilogue, Ecclesiastes 12:9-14, which has generally been seen as the addition of a later editor or editors. In the Hebrew Old Testament Ecclesiastes is named after its central character, *Qohelet* (translated as "the Teacher" in the NRSV). In Ecclesiastes Qohelet's deeply existential quest for meaning in life is set before us by a narrator. The nature of Qohelet's roller-coaster journey resists a tight, logical structure. At times Ecclesiastes seems to be all over the place, precisely because that is how the journey was for Qohelet! This does not mean, however, that Ecclesiastes lacks unity but that it is not the sort of *logical* unity we would find much easier to analyze. Qohelet's journey challenged him to the core of his being, and Ecclesiastes is *performative* in this respect; just as Qohelet found it exceedingly difficult to see how the jigsaw pieces of life fit together, so the reader finds it hard to see how Ecclesiastes fits together.

But fit together it does, and in recent years major progress in the reading of Ecclesiastes was made when Michael Fox proposed that we attend to Ecclesiastes as a literary whole,[1] identify the main voices in it and explore their interrelationship. Such an approach enables us to see that Qohelet's is the main—but not the *only*—voice in Ecclesiastes. Qohelet's voice is framed by that of a narrator, who introduces Qohelet

[1]Michael V. Fox, "Frame-Narrative and Composition in the Book of Qohelet," *Hebrew Union College Annual* 48 (1977): 83-106.

in Ecclesiastes 1:1-11 and concludes the presentation of Qohelet in Ecclesiastes 12:8-14. The only other place in which the narrator's voice is heard is in Ecclesiastes 7:27. The main characters in Ecclesiastes are thus the narrator, who presents Qohelet's journey for our instruction, and Qohelet himself, who undertakes the journey. We simply do not know the prehistory of the book, and Fox's approach encourages us to take the book seriously as a literary whole, including the epilogue. One would need compelling reasons not to do so, and in our opinion the reasons generally given do not hold up to scrutiny. This approach to interpreting Ecclesiastes is represented in figure 8.1.

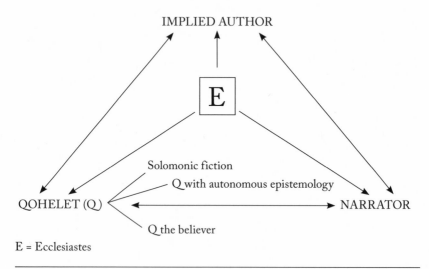

**Figure 8.1**

According to this approach the way to discover the message of Ec-clesiastes is to inquire after the implied author (IA)—that is, where the text itself implies that the author stands in relation to the content of Ecclesiastes and thus what its message is, taken as a whole. Thus Trem-per Longman, for example, argues that the implied author agrees with the narrator in strongly distancing himself from Qohelet's teaching.[2] One inquires after the IA by first exploring the characters in the text and their interrelationship, namely, the narrator and Qohelet. As we

---

[2]Tremper Longman III, *The Book of Ecclesiastes*, NICOT (Grand Rapids: Eerdmans, 1998), pp. 37-39.

will see below, Qohelet himself is represented in a number of ways: as king in Jerusalem (the Solomonic fiction), as an explorer in the grip of an autonomous (Greek) epistemology and as a believing Israelite who affirms the meaning of life in the carpe diem passages and other sections such as Ecclesiastes 5:1-7. The tension between these two latter "Qohelets" is central to the book and accounts for its dynamic and dialogical nature. Second, to discern the message of the text it is important also to ask how the IA relates to the narrator and to Qohelet. Meir Sternberg maintains that in biblical narrative the IA and the narrator are the same.[3] Fox and Norbert Lohfink suggest that in Ecclesiastes they are not.[4] Our conclusion, as will be argued below, is that the voices of the narrator and the IA are one and the same.

Such an approach yields the following sort of outline for Ecclesiastes:[5]

I.   Frame Narrative (1:1-11)

    A.   Title (1:1)

    B.   Statement of the Theme of the Book (1:2)

    C.   The Programmatic Question (1:3)

    D.   A Poem About the Enigma of Life (1:4-11)

II.  Qohelet's Exploration of the Meaning of Life (1:12–12:7)

    A.   Qohelet's Description of His Journey of Exploration (1:12-18)

    B.   Testing Pleasure and the Good Life (2:1-11)

    C.   The Problem of Death and One's Legacy (2:12-23)

    D.   Eating, Drinking and Enjoying One's Labor! (2:24-26)

    E.   The Mystery of Time (3:1-15)

    F.   The Problem of Injustice (3:16-22)

---

[3]Meir Sternberg, *The Poetics of Biblical Narrative: Ideological Literature and the Drama of Reading* (Bloomington: Indiana University Press, 1985), pp. 74-75.

[4]Craig learned this in a discussion with Lohfink. Such an approach means that the author might not agree entirely either with the narrator or Qohelet.

[5]See Craig G. Bartholomew, *Ecclesiastes*, BCOTWP (Grand Rapids: Baker Academic, 2009), pp. 83-84.

## ECCLESIASTES 1:1: QOHELET AND SOLOMON

The words of Qohelet, the son of David, king in Jerusalem.

Qohelet is presented by the narrator as a king in Jerusalem with great wisdom (Eccles 1:1, 12). Our minds run to Solomon, of course, but he is never actually named. This way of pointing to Solomon, sometimes called the "Solomonic guise," is a part of the royal fiction that gives the book both an allusive and ambiguous character.[6] The Solomonic royal fiction moves into the background through the course of the book, although it surfaces again at points. We know from Ecclesiastes 12:9-10 that Qohelet was a wisdom teacher, and Ecclesiastes was most likely written in the postexilic period, probably in the fourth century B.C. However, that Qohelet's identification with Solomon is *fictional* does not mean for a moment that it is "untrue" or that we can disregard it. It is crucial to understanding Ecclesiastes that we imagine Qohelet as a Solomon-like figure with great resources and special gifts of wisdom, as 1 Kings tells us. By adopting the persona of Solomon, Qohelet is not just conducting his search as a wise man but as the wisest king.[7] We are to think of Qohelet as someone who knows the worldview of Israel intimately and who has all the power and resources for the quest he embarks on. Ecclesiastes 1:1 also leads us to *expect* Qohelet to embody and proclaim the sort of view of wisdom we find in Proverbs.

## ECCLESIASTES 1:2-18: QOHELET'S QUEST

"Utterly enigmatic," says Qohelet, "Utterly enigmatic, everything is enigmatic."

Nothing prepares us for the shock of this summary of Qohelet's teaching! In Ecclesiastes 1:1 the narrator introduces us to *Qohelet*, who we

---

[6]Solomonic authorship is sometimes seen as a conservative litmus test for a high view of Scripture. However, many Christians throughout history have doubted Solomon's authorship including some of the church fathers and Protestant Reformers. Today, most scholars accept that Solomon did not write Ecclesiastes. The evidence is internal and external. An example of the internal evidence is that, even if Qohelet was Solomon, his speeches are cast in a third-person framework and we do not know who the narrator is. In terms of external evidence scholars are agreed that the Hebrew of Ecclesiastes is late. See Bartholomew, *Ecclesiastes*, pp. 43-54, for a detailed discussion of the authorship of Ecclesiastes. Eric Christianson, *A Time to Tell: Narrative Strategies in Ecclesiastes* (Sheffield, U.K.: Sheffield Academic Press, 1998), pp. 128-72, rightly argues that the "Solomonic guise" influences more of Ecclesiastes than is often recognized, and he notes on p. 148 that it "continually reasserts itself."
[7]Ibid., p. 131.

are to imagine as a Solomon-like figure; a believing Israelite who is gifted with exceptional wisdom. Nothing, therefore, prepares us for this summary in Ecclesiastes 1:2 of the conclusion that Qohelet comes to again and again throughout the book—namely, that everything is "vanity" or, as we prefer to translate the Hebrew word *hebel*, "enigmatic." There is a great deal of discussion about how best to translate *hebel*, ranging from "vanity" (KJV), "useless" (GNB), "absurd" (Fox), "transience" (Fredericks), to "meaningless" (NIV).[8] Literally *hebel* means something like "vapor," but clearly in Ecclesiastes it is used metaphorically. The difficulty is to know whether there is a central core to its use in Ecclesiastes, and if so, what it is. Clearly *hebel* has negative connotations, but in our opinion its core meaning is particularly foregrounded by the phrase that regularly accompanies it, namely "striving for the wind." It is not that the wind is unreal but that one cannot get ahold of it; hence our preference for translating *hebel* as, "enigma/enigmatic." Qohelet is not claiming that life is meaningless but that for all his effort he cannot locate the meaning of life amid what he observes and experiences; life is thoroughly enigmatic.

Life may be meaningful, but if so that meaning is utterly elusive; it cannot be discovered. Having "Solomon" express such a view is akin to the shock the reader feels in Jonah, who, upon receiving divine revelation—"And the word of the LORD came to Jonah"—immediately sets off in the *opposite* direction to Nineveh. How, we are led to ask, is it possible that someone like Solomon could come to this kind of view?

Ecclesiastes' enigmatic nature forces the reader to stop and reflect, just as Qohelet was being made to stop and struggle with what he was dealing with. Already we experience this with the narrator's association of Qohelet with Solomon. The surprise of Ecclesiastes 1:2 pushes us to reflect on how it could be possible that someone like *Solomon*—so gifted with wisdom—could come to such a view. And if we take the canon of Scripture seriously, this pushes us to reflect more deeply—just what Ecclesiastes is designed to do—on Solomon. Was he really so wise, or was he more complex than we had thought? What is the true nature of

---

[8]See Bartholomew, *Ecclesiastes*, pp. 93-96, 104-7.

wisdom? Because historical-critical scholars generally separate Old Testament wisdom from Old Testament narrative, this question is rarely pursued. However, once we note that Old Testament wisdom is much more integrated with the other genres of Old Testament literature, we can start to see the power and nuance of Qohelet's association with Solomon.

Our major source for the story of Solomon is 1 Kings 1–11.[9] In this narrative, wisdom and law are central themes, as are intertextual connections with Genesis.[10] Solomon is indeed granted great wisdom by God, and his major achievements are to build the temple and to extend the borders and fame of Israel. However, this image of Solomon is not all there is to him. Even from the outset his character is depicted as ambiguous in terms of his devotion to the LORD; Solomon's consolidation of his throne is brutal (1 Kings 2); contrary to Deuteronomy, he takes Pharaoh's daughter as his wife (1 Kings 3:1);[11] and he worships at the high places (1 Kings 3: 2-3). By the end of 1 Kings 1–11 Solomon has wandered far from God's ways and has become enmeshed in idolatry. As Leithart notes,

> Solomon reaches the heights of political and cultural attainments, develops creativity in all spheres of endeavor, yet his cultivation and energy are ultimately directed toward finding new ways to violate the Yahweh's covenant with Israel. . . . Solomon's life . . . shows a wise man who fails precisely at the height of his wisdom, precisely at the moment when everyone acknowledges his wisdom, indeed, precisely in his exercise of wisdom.[12]

---

[9]Solomon's story is also told in 2 Chronicles 1–9. The relationship between the two stories is disputed. See, inter alia, Raymond B. Dillard, *2 Chronicles*, WBC 15 (Waco, Tex.: Word, 1987); Sara Japhet, *I & II Chronicles: A Commentary*, OTL (Louisville: Westminster John Knox, 1993). The different contexts for which 1 and 2 Kings were written as well as their different aims go a long way to explain the differences. Chronicles focuses in particular on Solomon as the builder of the temple, but even in its very positive narration 2 Chron 8:11 is alert to the idolatry involved in Solomon's marriage to Pharaoh's daughter.

[10]See Peter Leithart, *1 & 2 Kings* (Grand Rapids: Brazos, 2006); K. I. Parker, "Solomon as Philosopher King? The Nexus of Law and Wisdom in 1 Kings 1–11," *JSOT* 53 (1992): 75-91.

[11]In our opinion Iain Provan, *1 and 2 Kings*, NIBC (Peabody, Mass.: Hendrickson, 1995), p. 44, is right in interpreting Solomon's marriage this way, as opposed to Leithart, *1 & 2 Kings*, p. 43, who argues that, "Solomon's marriage to Pharaoh's daughter fulfills the Abrahamic promise to bless the nations."

[12]Leithart, *1 & 2 Kings*, p. 82.

R. N. Whybray perceptively notes of the Deuteronomistic historian, whom he believes wrote 1 Kings 1–11, that "the author was well aware, as were the authors of Proverbs, that not everything which passes for wisdom should be accepted at its face value, and also that wickedness can assume the character of wisdom for its own purposes."[13]

Solomon is paradigmatic of the truth that being gifted with great wisdom and power and wealth is not enough to guarantee wisdom. Solomon asks God for a hearing heart (*lēb šōmēaʿ*; 1 Kings 3:9). Listening to God and the advice of the wise is central to Old Testament wisdom. Solomon builds the temple and, intriguingly, as we will see, at the heart of Ecclesiastes is Qohelet's instruction that we should approach the temple reverently to listen/to hear (Eccles 5:1-6)—the same verb is used— for God's instruction.[14] But, is this what Solomon and Qohelet do? Through Qohelet's association with Solomon, immediately followed by this thoroughly unorthodox statement in Ecclesiastes 1:2, we are thus compelled to stop and reflect on the true nature of wisdom. Wisdom is not always what it seems, and we need to be careful about claims to be wise that may in fact turn out to be folly. As we will see, this is emblematic of Qohelet's turbulent journey. He too will claim to be searching by wisdom, but is it really wisdom that is guiding him?

> What is the benefit for humankind in all one's labor
>     at which one labors under the sun? (Eccles 1:3)

We do not have to wait to find out the answer to our question above. Ecclesiastes 1:3 is a rhetorical question that recurs in Ecclesiastes and sums up Qohelet's quest and that the entire book seeks to answer: what do people gain from all their toil under the sun? Humans labor at so much, but how does this ultimately benefit them? In Ecclesiastes 1:4-11 the narrator makes use of a poem to give us an initial idea of why Qohelet is so tempted to conclude that "everything is wearisome" (Eccles 1:8):[15] both history and nature, characterized by a circular repeti-

---

[13]R. N. Whybray, *The Intellectual Tradition in the Old Testament*, BZAW 135 (Berlin: de Gruyter, 1974), p. 90.

[14]As Eccles 5:1-6 demonstrates, for Ecclesiastes, as for 1 Kings 1–11, wisdom and law are correlates and inseparable.

[15]The poem has a chiastic structure (A B C B' A'), the center of which is Eccles 1:7-8. See Bar-

tiveness that never seems to arrive anywhere, seem to confirm that nothing is ever settled.

In Ecclesiastes 1:12-18 Qohelet himself comes onto the stage and tells us about his quest:

> I, Qohelet, was king over Israel in Jerusalem.
>
> I set my heart to seek and to explore by[16] wisdom all that is done under the heavens. It is an evil task which God has given to human beings with which to be afflicted.
>
> I have seen all the works which are done under the sun, and see, everything is enigmatic and a striving after the wind.
>
> What is crooked cannot be made straight and what is lacking cannot be counted.
>
> I dialogued with my heart, saying, "I have demonstrated greatness and added to wisdom more than all who were over Jerusalem before me." And my heart observed much wisdom and knowledge.
>
> And I set my heart to know wisdom, and to know madness and folly. I know that this also is a striving after wind,
>
> for in much wisdom is much vexation and the one who increases knowledge increases pain.

As Qohelet is introduced and as he describes his quest, it becomes clear that the very real question about *work* and labor in Ecclesiastes 1:3, which recurs throughout the book, backs into the deeper question of the *very meaning of life*, which in turn backs into the deeper epistemological[17] question still of *how we know* if life is meaningful, given all the confusing data. Thus Qohelet's quest is multilayered as the following diagram indicates:

What is the point of work?

What is the meaning of life?

How do we know if life is meaningful?

---

tholomew, *Ecclesiastes*, pp. 109-12.

[16]*Bĕ* here expresses means or instrument. "By wisdom" is a preferable translation to Longman's adverbial translation, "to explore wisely" (*Ecclesiastes*, p. 77) because Qohelet here sets out not only his program but also his methodology.

[17]Craig's definition of "epistemology" is how to go about knowing something so that we can trust the results of the knowing process.

In terms of the Old Testament context it is particularly important to read Ecclesiastes against the background of Proverbs, which, as we have seen, articulates a *character-consequence* theology rooted in creation. This theology assumes the rich meaningfulness of life and teaches that the fear of the Lord will in general lead to blessing and prosperity. Living in the postexilic period, the evidence seemed to indicate that Yahweh's purposes had run aground, and for an Israelite like Qohelet this raised acute questions about the meaning of life. Hence his description of his task in Ecclesiastes 1:12-18. He tells us that

> I set my heart to seek and to explore by wisdom all that is done under the heavens. (Eccles 1:13)

There are no limits to Qohelet's quest; his aim is nothing less than to explore all that is done in the creation! Not surprisingly, therefore, we find Qohelet attending to many different areas of life to see if meaning can be found in them.

## QOHELET'S METHODOLOGY

Intriguingly Qohelet is clear in Ecclesiastes 1:13 (cf. Eccles 2:9) that the method he is using to conduct his search is "wisdom," *hokmâ*, the key word in Proverbs and the Old Testament for that wisdom whose starting point is the fear of the LORD. In Ecclesiastes 1:16 he describes himself as acquiring great "wisdom"—again the same word. And yet shockingly we find in Ecclesiastes 1:13 what we find throughout Ecclesiastes, namely, that this "wisdom" keeps leading Qohelet to very negative conclusions:

> I set my heart to seek and to explore by wisdom all that is done under the heavens. *It is an evil task which God has given to human beings with which to be afflicted.*

Against the background of Proverbs, the reader is thus forced to look very closely at this "wisdom" that is leading Qohelet to such disturbing conclusions. Is it really the wisdom of Proverbs? A close examination of Qohelet's method—what we should call his *epistemology*, how he goes about answering his question such that he can trust the results—reveals that it is quite different from what Proverbs calls wisdom. As Qohelet describes his quest and as it unfolds throughout the book, we find Qohelet's quest informed by an epistemology dependent on reason, observation and experience *alone*. He does not begin, as Proverbs insists we must, with the fear of the LORD! By contrast, the great characteristic of Ecclesiastes is Qohelet's continual use of the first-person pronoun "I," which indicates his dependence on *himself* rather than the LORD for an answer to the perplexing meaning of life. Clearly this is a very different "wisdom" to that in Proverbs, which makes its starting point the fear of the LORD, and as Ecclesiastes develops it will become more and more apparent that what he here calls "wisdom" is in fact what Proverbs calls "folly." Irony—saying one thing but meaning the opposite—is a central feature of Ecclesiastes, and already in Ecclesiastes 1 we get a feel for things to come.

Close attention to Qohelet's method, his epistemology, which he himself foregrounds as "wisdom," is thus essential if we are to understand Ecclesiastes as a whole. As the book develops it becomes poignantly apparent that the major problem is his method.[18] In this respect there is a striking parallel between Qohelet's search for meaning and Augustine's search for wisdom. Exposure to the writings of the Roman rhetorician Cicero awakened Augustine's desire for wisdom. Thus began the search that would eventually lead him to Christ. But as with Qohelet, Augustine's journey took many twists and turns before he found Christ. As he perceptively notes of his narrative of his journey to faith in the *Confessions*, "I was trying to find the origin of evil, but I was quite blind to the evil in my own method of research."[19] The church historian Henry Chadwick has noted that Augustine was probably the greatest intellect of his day in the Roman Empire. Clearly Qohelet is a powerful intellect, but a major lesson of Ecclesiastes is that a high IQ is not the same as wisdom.

The fourth-century-B.C. context is helpful in understanding Ecclesi-

---

[18]This is an important difference between Qohelet and Solomon as he is portrayed in 1 Kings 1–11. Both ultimately suffer from idolatry, but Qohelet's is intellectual in a way that Solomon's is not.

[19]See the citation to the epigraph in this chapter.

astes in this respect. Greek philosophy was in the air, and Qohelet draws from Greek thought an *autonomous* epistemology dependent on reason, observation and experience *alone,* which he uses to explore the question of life's meaning(lessness). As becomes clear in Ecclesiastes such an epistemology is antithetical to that of Proverbs and biblical wisdom so that, in this way, the deeper question Ecclesiastes poses is *how* you determine if life is meaningful amid circumstances in which nothing seems to make sense.

### ECCLESIASTES 1:12–12:7: QOHELET'S JOURNEY

Ecclesiastes *is* a carefully crafted whole, but as befits Qohelet's excruciating search for meaning the book tracks back and forth as Qohelet explores area after area of life. The tension between his analysis of life through the grid of his autonomous epistemology, which leads him again and again to the conclusion that life is "enigmatic," and the positive affirmation of life he knows from his upbringing as a believing Israelite exemplified in the carpe diem passages (e.g., Eccles 2:24-26), combined with the growing sense of irony drive the book forward to its denouement in Ecclesiastes 11:6–12:14.

A favorite phrase of Qohelet's is life "under the sun," by which he refers to all of life as God has made it. And in his quest for solving life's riddle, Qohelet ranges across a dizzying variety of areas of life. In Ecclesiastes 2:1-11 he explores pleasure and the good life, including wine, architecture, horticulture, music and sex. But none yield the answer he seeks.

In Ecclesiastes 2:12-23 he explores the problem of death and one's legacy. The enigma of death and the shadow it casts over the question of life surfaces repeatedly in Ecclesiastes (see Eccles 9:1-12). In Ecclesiastes 3:1-15 by means of a poem he investigates the problem of time; God has created us such that we need an overarching story of life, but where is it to be found? In Ecclesiastes 3:16-22 Qohelet focuses on injustice; in the law courts where one would expect to find justice he finds injustice! In Ecclesiastes 4 he examines the agonizing problem of oppression (see also Eccles 5:8-17), the problem of rivalry in work, the problem of individual isolation and lack of supportive community, as well as the problem of bad government (see Eccles 8:1-9).

The location of meaning in wealth and its pursuit is a major theme in Ecclesiastes;[20] it is connected with oppression in Ecclesiastes 5:8-17, where the vulnerability of wealth is explored, as well as in Ecclesiastes 6:1-9; and Ecclesiastes 10:1-20 culminates in the ironic statement that "money meets every need" (Eccles 10:19). Ecclesiastes 11:1-6 is about doing everything one can to secure one's wealth, but as Qohelet concludes in Ecclesiastes 11:6, this can never be guaranteed.

Each succeeding area that Qohelet explores with his epistemology of experience, observation and reason gets him nowhere; again and again he concludes that all is "enigmatic." In Ecclesiastes 7:13-22 the stress this results in surfaces strongly. If God has made life crooked (Eccles 7:13) and if the character-consequence theology of Proverbs simply doesn't work (Eccles 7:15), then perhaps the answer is to be moderately wise and righteous and moderately wicked (Eccles 7:16-17)! This leads in Ecclesiastes 7:23-29 into a reflective section in which Qohelet looks back on his journey.

> [23]All this I tested by wisdom. I said, "I will be wise," but it was far from me.
> [24]That which is, is far off, and extraordinarily deep. Who can find it?
> [25]I turned my heart to know and to explore and to seek wisdom and an explanation, and to know wickedness, stupidity, folly and madness.
> [26]And I am finding more bitter than death the woman who is a snare, and whose heart is a trap and whose hands are chains. The one who pleases God escapes her, but the sinner is seized by her.
> [27]Observe: "This is what I have found," says Qohelet, "adding one thing to another to find an explanation,
> [28]which my soul still seeks but I have not found. One person among a thousand I have found but a woman among all these I have not found."
> [29]Only observe this: I have found that God made the human person straight but they have sought out many schemes.

The recurrence of the voice of the narrator in Ecclesiastes 7:27—this is the only place in Ecclesiastes where this happens—alerts us to the importance of this passage for understanding Qohelet's journey. Against the background of Proverbs we should understand the two women re-

---

[20]This, of course, has a major background in the narrative of Solomon, who accumulated great wealth. A motif at work in Ecclesiastes may well be a critique of misdirected kingship.

ferred to as Lady Wisdom and Dame Folly. Qohelet has apparently conducted his investigation by "wisdom," but it has led him right into the arms of Dame Folly (Eccles 7:26). And although he is an excellent sleuth, he cannot find Lady Wisdom (Eccles 7:28). The irony of his journey comes into full view at this point. In Ecclesiastes 7:13 he relates what is wrong with the world, saying that God has made it crooked, but by Ecclesiastes 7:29 the problem is revealed to be not God but humankind! It is no wonder the narrator draws our attention to this passage. Qohelet has claimed to be examining all of life under the sun by "wisdom," but we can now see that his epistemology bears all the marks of "folly." Like Augustine, Qohelet has been trying to find the origin of evil—what is wrong with the world?—while being blind to the evil in his own method of research.

In the course of Qohelet's journey we find not only his negative *hebel* conclusions but also startlingly positive statements. These are commonly known as his carpe diem ("seize the day") sayings and are found in Ecclesiastes 2:24-26; 3:10-15; 3:16-22; 8:10-15; 9:7-10; 11:7-12:7. "Carpe diem" might suggest that they embody a form of hedonism by affirming pleasure in response to his despair over discovering life's meaning, but in our opinion this is quite the wrong way to read them. The Israelites, and Old Testament wisdom in particular, strongly affirmed life in all its dimensions as God made it and, rather than promoting a nihilistic hedonism, these passages celebrate the gift of life. They speak of eating and drinking, enjoying one's work, enjoying marriage and taking pleasure in life as God's gift, and they get stronger as the book progresses.

*The* challenge for the interpreter of Ecclesiastes is how they relate to the decidedly negative *hebel* conclusions. The answer, in our opinion, is that they are deliberately set in *contradictory juxtaposition* to the *hebel* conclusions. As a believer brought up in Israel Qohelet knows these things to be true, but how are they to be reconciled with what he observes and his analysis through his autonomous epistemology? This is *the* problem that Qohelet is struggling with, and the juxtaposition of these contradictory views compels the reader to enter into the same struggle.

On the one hand, as a believer Qohelet knows that life is meaningful and good, but on the other, he observes everywhere the terrible brokenness of life, and analyzed through his epistemology, this leads him to conclude that life is utterly enigmatic. This excruciating tension lies at the heart of Ecclesiastes; indeed, by the time we reach Ecclesiastes 9:7-10 the juxtaposition is threatening to collapse under its irresolvable tension. How does one resolve this problem? Is there a way to resolve it?

## RESOLUTION

The path to resolution comes from two directions. First, as we have seen, as Qohelet's journey progresses it becomes increasingly apparent that his epistemology is not that of wisdom but of folly. Ecclesiastes 5:1-7 and Ecclesiastes 7:23-29 are key passages in this respect. Ecclesiastes 5:1-7, which some scholars regard as the center of Ecclesiastes,[21] urges the reader to approach the temple cautiously in order to *listen to God's instruction,* and it concludes with the similar exhortation to *fear God.* The theology of this section is comparable to the insistence in Proverbs that the fear of the LORD is the beginning of wisdom. And as we noted above, Ecclesiastes 7:23-29 foregrounds in dramatic fashion that Qohelet's autonomous epistemology has led him right into the arms of Dame Folly! Thus the one way in which resolution comes is in the growing recognition that an autonomous epistemology, which depends on observation, experience and reason alone and which does not start with the fear of the Lord, will only get one deeper and deeper into despair when faced with the enigmas of life.

Second, resolution comes through the indication of a better epistemological foundation in Ecclesiastes 11:7–12:7. The proverb of Ecclesiastes 11:7 shines out like a firefly, indicating that hope and resolution are possibilities:

Truly, light is sweet,
    And it is good for the eyes to observe the sun.

The two dominating exhortations of this section are "rejoice" and "remember." "Remember your creator" in Ecclesiastes 12:1 is the sec-

---

[21]Norbert Lohfink, *Qoheleth: A Continental Commentary* (Minneapolis: Fortress, 2003), p. 8.

ond major clue to resolving Qohelet's struggle. The verb *zākar* ("to remember") occurs earlier in the book in Ecclesiastes but in a negative
context about what not to remember or what won't be remembered
(Eccles 5:20; 9:5, 15). But the two injunctions to remember here (Eccles 11:8; 12:1) show us a different side of Qohelet's view of memory.
Isaiah is another book that uses the verb *zākar* in this twofold way.[22]

Deuteronomy is perhaps an even more important place where *zākar*
is used in this way.[23] If Israel is to enter the land and enjoy God's blessing there, then it is crucial that she remember the journey God has
brought her on, and her tradition, established above all else at Mount
Sinai.[24] As in Deuteronomy, remembrance in Ecclesiastes 12:1 is far
more than a casual reminder; it means let your whole perspective on life
be informed by the view that God is creator of everything. This is precisely what has been missing in Qohelet's epistemology; it has all been
rooted *in himself*—one of the great characteristics of Ecclesiastes, as we
have seen, is the endless use of the first-person pronoun "I." The answer to the perplexities of life is to find a way back to that starting point
in God as the creator of everything. This does not take one away from
the struggles of life—Ecclesiastes 12:1 is followed by some of the darkest verses in Ecclesiastes, as Qohelet describes death and cosmic judgment to come—but it puts one in a position to affirm life and its meaning amid the very real struggles of life.

## ECCLESIASTES 12:8-14: THE EPILOGUE

In Ecclesiastes 12:8-14 we hear the voice of the narrator once again.
Intriguingly he tells us that Qohelet was one of the wise men in Israel,
an affirmation reminiscent of God's remarkable affirmation of Job's
journey in Job 42:7. Further affirmation of Qohelet's journey is found
in what is referred to as the canonical motif in Ecclesiastes 12:12. There
are many books available on wisdom but, whereas Ecclesiastes is trust-

---

[22]See Choon-Leong Seow, *Ecclesiastes*, AB (New York: Doubleday, 1997), p. 370.

[23]This is one of several striking connections between Ecclesiastes and Deuteronomy. See Bartholomew, *Ecclesiastes*, p. 368n45 and Ryan O'Dowd, *The Wisdom of Torah: Epistemology in
Deuteronomy and the Wisdom Literature*, FRLANT (Göttingen: Vandenhoeck & Ruprecht,
2009), pp. 49-51.

[24]See O'Dowd, *Wisdom of Torah*, pp. 25-52.

worthy, one must be wary of the multitude of others. But perhaps the most remarkable affirmation of Qohelet's journey is found in Ecclesiastes 12:11, in which Qohelet's words are associated with the words of the wise "given by one shepherd." In our view this "one shepherd" is God, so that we are encouraged by the author to hear God's address, *his* instruction, through the words of Qohelet![25]

Ecclesiastes 12:9 tells us that Qohelet "pondered and sought out and arranged many proverbs." In recent decades scholars such as Robert Alter and Meir Sternberg have demonstrated a sophisticated poetics in the Old Testament literature. Ecclesiastes 12:9 alerts us to expect similar sophistication in Ecclesiastes. Qohelet carefully crafted and edited his teachings. This confirms our point at the outset that, while Ecclesiastes is not a simple logical unity, it is a remarkable literary unity that befits the painful struggle of Qohelet.

Ecclesiastes 12:13-14 sums up the entire book: all has been heard, and the conclusion is, fear God and keep his instructions, for this is the "whole person"; this is what human life is really about. We have noted throughout this chapter that epistemology is central to this book. Ecclesiastes 12:13-14 reminds us that our epistemology will always flow from our view of what it means to be human, that is, from anthropology. And in the narrator's conclusion we are provided with a profound insight into what it means to be human, namely, to embrace our creatureliness; to live reverently *coram Deo*, before the face of God, in grateful obedience. The fear of the LORD truly is the beginning of wisdom, and, as Karl Barth perceptively notes, "Basically, and comprehensively, therefore, to be a man is to be with God."[26]

In terms of our diagrammatic representation of how to read Qohelet above, it is worth noting that at the end of his journey Qohelet arrives at the same point as the narrator. Thus, in our view, *ultimately* the narrator, the implied author and Qohelet hold the same view. The crucial challenge of Ecclesiastes is not the radical differences between the

---

[25]Eccles 12:11 is illuminating in terms of the inspiration of the Bible, alerting us, as it does, to the full humanity and inspiration of Scripture. It is also helpful in indicating the journey Scripture sometimes requires us to go on in order to hear God's address.

[26]Karl Barth, *CD* III/2, p. 131.

voices, but how, once you find yourself in a situation like that of Qohelet, you find your way home again.

## ECCLESIASTES TODAY

Ecclesiastes 12:11 associates the book with the words of the wise; like the
other sayings of the wise they goad us into the right way and provide a
firm place to stand amid the challenges of life. Eugene Peterson has rightly
described Ecclesiastes as a "smooth stone" for pastoral work.[27] Ecclesiastes
*is* a book of great pastoral relevance today when so many people struggle
with the meaninglessness of life. Ecclesiastes affirms that struggle and
vividly shows how tough it can be. It is also important to remember that
Qohelet was a believer—Christians are *not* exempt from this kind of
struggle, as though Ecclesiastes is "only" an evangelistic tract.

Proverbs alerts us to the exceptions to the character-consequence
motif, but what do such exceptions look like in real life? In different
ways Job and Ecclesiastes embody such exceptions. We know what
happened to trigger Job's crisis of faith, but we are never told what led
to Qohelet's. Job's crisis manifests itself through events that any of us
would find unbearable, but Qohelet's crisis manifests itself as an intellectual struggle. Both are excruciating, and both Job and Qohelet find
their very existence at stake.

In our day, in which so much popular Christianity is what has been
called Christianity-lite,[28] these types of struggles may seem out of
place. But in the history of Christian spirituality they are commonplace, as is apparent from the title of Saint John of the Cross's classic,
*The Dark Night of the Soul,* in which he argues that any Christian who
enters deeply into relationship with God will sooner or later face dark
nights that are utterly perplexing and in which God seems absent.

The narrator's surprising affirmation of Qohelet's wisdom is a wonderful affirmation of Qohelet's struggle to find a way through the excruciating loss of meaning and back to the starting point of the fear of
the LORD. Pastorally, Qohelet thus encourages us to take such struggles

---

[27]Eugene Peterson, *Five Smooth Stones for Pastoral Work* (Grand Rapids: Eerdmans, 1990).
[28]Dick Staub, *The Culturally Savvy Christian: A Manifesto for Deepening Faith and Enriching
Popular Culture in an Age of Christianity-Lite* (San Francisco: Jossey-Bass, 2007).

seriously when they come upon us and to be aware that wise Christians *do* go through such experiences. We do not know how Qohelet got into this situation, and often in practice we find that such a crisis descends on us unawares, and, before we know it we, like Qohelet, are fighting for our lives. There is a sense in which, as Ecclesiastes reminds us, it is less important how we got into this state than being willing to let the struggle unfold, trusting that resolution will come.

But what, we might ask, is the purpose of these "exceptions" to the character-consequence theme? Saint John of the Cross believed that God is so deeply at work in these experiences and his light shining so brightly that we experience his light as utter darkness. We think this is true, and it alerts us to the fact that in the bigger picture "exceptions" may be quite the wrong word. For what Job and Ecclesiastes alert us to is that wisdom is *far more* than knowing how to live or knowing a lot of doctrine and facts from the Bible. Wisdom has to become embodied in particular humans so that they truly start to image God in their lives; because of our brokenness, suffering is inevitably one of the ways in which God forms us to be like him.

Qohelet had a very high IQ—Ecclesiastes is the most philosophical book in the Bible. He was very powerful and wealthy, and he really thought he was wise, but his crisis revealed his wisdom for what it actually was, namely, folly. Like so many modern Christians, Qohelet equated wisdom with *head* knowledge and *his* ability to discern meaning in life. His journey shows us that to *truly* become a whole person for whom the fear of the LORD is the beginning of wisdom is no easy process. C. S. Lewis likens this process to having a delightful, small cottage. We are overjoyed when God comes to live there, but when he starts to knock walls down and reconstruct the house we are far less happy about his presence.[29] The "exceptions" are not a lapse in God's love but, paradoxically, are a sign of the extent of his love for us and his determination to pursue what is the very best for us. Such a process— part of what is traditionally called sanctification—will inevitably involve suffering, and sometimes it will be excruciating.

---

[29]C. S. Lewis, *Mere Christianity* (Glasgow: Fount Paperbacks, 1977), p. 172.

Ecclesiastes and Job thus play an important role in evoking for us the richness and depth of real wisdom. They also offer hope amid the toughest struggles. Resolution does not come easily in a profoundly broken world, but it can be found—or can find one—as one lives with the struggle and works one's way back to a starting point in the recognition of God as the creator and redeemer of the world. The references to God's commandments in Ecclesiastes 12:13 and to the temple in Ecclesiastes 5:1-7 remind us that God is not only the creator but also the redeemer, who made the Israelites his people and whose redemptive work culminates in Jesus Christ, the full embodiment of wisdom. Christ suffered terribly, but his suffering was the key to his incarnation. Our suffering is never atoning like that of Christ, but if we surrender to it and wait, it can become truly redemptive, making us more and more like Christ. When this terrific struggle opened up in Qohelet's life, he never ran from it; he faced it head on, and this authentic embrace of the struggle laid the basis for ultimate resolution. In this respect Qohelet is reminiscent of Socrates, who refused to be cowed in asking difficult questions. This is one reason why the Danish philosopher Søren Kierkegaard liked Socrates so much; he was *authentic*. We urgently need authentic Christians today, and Qohelet shows that such authenticity is not easily won, but the journey is worth it, and it is full of meaning.

The journey toward authentic faith relates to all of life. In his writings, Kierkegaard introduces interesting characters such as the knight of infinite resignation and the knight of faith: the former faces up to the realities of life, but in a spirit of resignation. The latter moves beyond resignation to authentic faith; he relinquishes all hold on life but wonderfully receives it *all* back, but now as pure gift. Qohelet alerts us to the same reality; he realizes that if life is meaningless this affects every area of life, which is why his search is so relentless and all encompassing. What is not always noticed is that if, as we think, he finds resolution, this has implications for all those aspects of life he explored. As Gordon Spykman perceptively comments, "Nothing matters but the kingdom, but because of the kingdom everything matters."[30] Through

---

[30]Gordon J. Spykman, *Reformational Theology: A New Paradigm for Doing Dogmatics* (Grand Rapids: Eerdmans, 1992), p. 478.

suffering, which seems to threaten our very lives, we find that life in all its wonderful ordinariness is given back to us, but now as pure gift. And thus, as Ecclesiastes 11:7 evokes, amid the troubles of life, we find a way to waken in the morning to the sheer mysterious wonder of a new day "under the sun."

## RECOMMENDED READING

### *Introductory studies*
Bartholomew, Craig G. "Ecclesiastes." In *Dictionary for Theological Interpretation of the Bible,* ed. Kevin J. Vanhoozer, Craig G. Bartholomew, Daniel J. Treier and N. T. Wright, pp. 182-85. Grand Rapids: Baker Academic, 2005.

———. "Ecclesiastes." In *Theological Bible Commentary,* ed. Gail R. O'Day and David L. Petersen. Louisville: Westminster John Knox, 2009.

———. "Qoheleth in the Canon?! Current Trends in the Interpretation of Ecclesiastes." *Themelios* 24 (1999): 4-20.

### *Commentaries*
Bartholomew, Craig G. *Ecclesiastes.* BCOTWP. Grand Rapids: Baker Academic, 2009.

Ellul, Jacques. *The Reason for Being: A Meditation on Ecclesiastes.* Translated by J. M. Hanks. Grand Rapids: Eerdmans, 1990.

Krüger, Thomas. *Qoheleth: A Commentary,* trans. O. C. Dean Jr. Hermeneia. Minneapolis: Fortress, 2004.

Murphy, Roland E. *Ecclesiastes.* WBC 23A. Dallas: Word, 1992.

Seow, Choon-Leong. *Ecclesiastes.* AB. New York: Doubleday, 1997.

### *Scholarly resources*
Bartholomew, Craig G. *Reading Ecclesiastes: Old Testament Exegesis and Hermeneutical Theory.* AnBib 139. Rome: Editrice Pontificio Istituto Biblico, 1998.

Boda, Mark, and Tremper Longman III, eds. *Ecclesiastes.* Winona Lake, Ind.: Eisenbrauns, forthcoming.

Fox, Michael V. *A Time to Tear Down and a Time to Build Up: A Rereading of Ecclesiastes.* Grand Rapids: Eerdmans, 1999.

# 9

# For Everything
## There Is a Season

*What then, is time? I know well enough what it is,*
*provided that nobody asks me; but if I am asked*
*what it is and try to explain, I am baffled.*

—AUGUSTINE, *CONFESSIONS*, XI, 14

Sᴄʜᴏʟᴀʀs ᴅɪꜰꜰᴇʀ ᴀʙᴏᴜᴛ ʜᴏᴡ ᴍᴜᴄʜ of Ecclesiastes is poetry.[1]
In fact, Ecclesiastes is a wonderful example of the difficulty of distinguishing prose from poetry. The NIV considers 60 percent of Ecclesiastes to be poetry, the NRSV 25 percent, and the Good News Bible/Today's English Version and the Revised English Bible regard Ecclesiastes 3:2-8 as the only poetic passage in the book![2]

In selecting a poetic passage from Ecclesiastes clearly we are on good ground in opting for Qohelet's poem about time in Ecclesiastes 3:1-8. Not only is this passage clearly poetic; but it is also one of the most well-known and oft-quoted passages in the book. The poem is about the wonderful rhythm of God's order for his creation. It evokes the same sense of order in time that we find expressed in prose in Genesis 1:1–2:3.

---

[1]Readers should note that we have used substantial material from Craig G. Bartholomew, *Ecclesiastes*, BCOTWP (Grand Rapids: Baker Academic, 2009), pp. 158-74, in this chapter.
[2]See W. Sibley Towner, "Ecclesiastes," in *The New Interpreter's Bible*, ed. Leander Keck (Nashville: Abingdon, 1997), 5:270. Percentages are based on the layout of the text in the different versions.

How to think about time *is* complex. As Augustine says in the *Confessions*, he knows what time is until he is asked to explain it! With Qohelet's wide-ranging exploration of wisdom and life, it is not surprising that sooner or later his attention would come to rest on time. In Ecclesiastes 3 Qohelet uses a poem to express wisdom's view that time is subject to God's good order for creation, but then, as is so typical of Qohelet, he proceeds to problematize this view. Thus we have included Qohelet's response to this poem in our discussion below.

## ECCLESIASTES 3:1-15

> For everything[3] there is a season,
>    and for every matter a time under the heavens.
> A time to give birth and a time to die,
>    a time to plant and a time to uproot what has been planted.
> A time to kill and a time to heal,
>    a time to break down and a time to build.
> A time to weep and a time to laugh,
>    a time to mourn and a time to dance.
> A time to throw stones and a time to gather stones,
>    a time to embrace and a time to refrain from embracing.
> A time to seek and a time to do away with,
>    a time to keep and a time to throw out.
> A time to tear and a time to repair,
>    a time to be silent and a time to speak.
> A time to love and a time to hate,[4]
>    a time for war and a time for peace.

Ecclesiastes 3:1, which is more general in content, is the heading of the poem and summarizes its content. It also has a terse chiastic form (a b b' a'), which is not clear in the English translation: everything—a season : a time—every matter. This internal parallelism is used here to

---

[3]*Lakkōl* ("for everything") could be translated as "for everyone," i.e., for every person. So James L. Kugel, *The Great Poems: A Reader's Companion with New Translations* (New York: Free Press, 1999), pp. 310-11. However, the generalized and comprehensive list of activities makes "everything" the better translation.

[4]For the translation see Bartholomew, *Ecclesiastes*, pp. 158-59.

open the segment of poetry.[5] The style of the poem as a whole is clear from the repetition of the infinitive construct form,[6] a consequent recurrence of the long $\bar{o}$ sound, the repetition of the word "time" ($\overline{\,}et$), the intricate chiasmus and the way in which the verses set out twenty-eight contrasting activities. This poem has the longest set of lines—fifteen in a row—with internal (half-line) parallelism in the Old Testament.[7] Also significant is the antithetic nature of the internal parallelism, since the preferred type of internal parallelism is synonymous.[8] J. A. Loader notes that in Ecclesiastes 3:2-8 "we have the most intricate chiastic composition in the Old Testament."[9]

Loader has analyzed the poem in detail.[10] He notes that each of the verses in Ecclesiastes 3:2-8 consists of two poetic lines, and each of these lines consists of two halves, the one half stating the opposite of the other (e.g. birth vs. death, plant vs. uproot). The two lines in each verse run parallel to one another. Each statement, according to Loader, refers to a favorable and an unfavorable matter, and in each verse these are parallel to each other. Thus Ecclesiastes 3:2, for example, can be depicted as follows:

| Favorable (F) | (birth) | Unfavorable (U) | (die) |
|---|---|---|---|
| F | (plant) | U | (uproot) |

However, in verse 3 the order is reversed to:

U  F
U  F

It should be noted that "favorable" versus "unfavorable" is an inappropriate designation for the opposites described in the poem. Some of the opposites fit this pattern, but not all. Mourning (Eccles 3:4) is certainly less favorable than dancing, and making war (Eccles 3:8) less

---

[5]Wilfred G. E. Watson, *Traditional Techniques in Classical Hebrew Verse*, JSOTSup 170 (Sheffield, U.K.: Sheffield Academic Press, 1994), p. 162.

[6]Except in Eccles 3:8b.

[7]On internal parallelism see Watson, *Traditional Techniques*, pp. 104-91.

[8]Ibid., p. 157.

[9]J. A. Loader, *Polar Structures in the Book of Qohelet*, BZAW 152 (Berlin: Walter de Gruyter, 1979), p. 11.

[10]For Loader's detailed analysis see his "Qoheleth 3:2-8—A 'Sonnet' in the Old Testament," *ZAW* 81, no. 2 (1969): 240-42.

favorable than peace. But in most of the other antonyms, such a judgment is not clear. Giving birth (Eccles 3:2) may be a tough experience,
as may be dying. The work of planting (Eccles 3:2) may be just as hard
as clearing a field. Thus, although Qohelet describes opposites, he is
not necessarily describing favorable and unfavorable activities. His concern is that for all these different activities and events there would appear to be a right time. In depicting the structure of the poem it is
preferable to use "+" and "-" to indicate the opposite activities, as does
Wilfred Watson.[11]

Thus one finds the following chiastic pattern in the poem:

| 2 | + | – | A |
|---|---|---|---|
|   | + | – |   |
| 3 | – | + | B |
|   | – | + |   |
| 4 | – | + |   |
|   | – | + |   |
| 5 | + | – | B' |
|   | + | – |   |
| 6 | + | – |   |
|   | + | – |   |
| 7 | – | + | A' |
|   | – | + |   |
| 8 | + | – | C |
|   | – | + |   |

Clearly chiasm dominates the structure of the poem; however, much
will depend on how we read the individual verses. Awareness of the
structures must not detract from a close reading of the poem as an individual, unique creation.

> For everything there is a season,
>     and for every matter a time under the heavens. (Eccles 3:1)

We do not know whether the poem is a composition by Qohelet or a
poem he quotes. Either way, it expresses his thought at this point and
is marshaled as part of his argument. The poem deals with a major

---

[11]Watson, *Traditional Techniques*, 366.

concern of biblical wisdom, namely, what is fitting or appropriate at a particular time.[12] Proverbs 26:1-12 is an excellent example of this— there is an appropriate time to answer a fool and a time not to answer a fool. Wisdom involves knowing the fitting time. Ecclesiastes 3:1 states the general principle, which is then fleshed out in the rest of the poem: there is an appropriate season and time for every activity in the creation.[13] This principle rests, as Old Testament wisdom does, on the belief in creation and its orderliness. As Genesis 1 makes clear, part of God's shaping of the creation as a wonderful home for humans is the seasons and rhythms he builds into the creation, which humans are called to respond to as they manifest God's image in the creation.

Some, however, argue that the poem depicts a *deterministic* world, in which humans have no choice. Loader argues that in the poem Qohelet only describes but does not prescribe. He is not saying what people should do but merely describing situations and events people find themselves in. "When the occasion arrives, the event that fits it occurs. This is a deterministic view according to which fate has fixed all things in advance and there is nothing anyone can do about it."[14] Similarly Roland Murphy says of the poem that "its purpose is to underscore that all events are determined by God and are beyond human control."[15] The view that this poem teaches a strong doctrine of determinism seems to us clearly wrong.[16] There are two activities in Ecclesiastes 3:2-8 that are completely out of human control, namely, giving birth and dying. However, every other activity is one in which humans can respond at the right time or choose not to. The second line in Ecclesiastes 3:2, for

---

[12]As Gerhard von Rad, *Wisdom in Israel*, trans. James D. Martin (London: SCM, 1970), pp. 138-43, notes.

[13]John R. Wilch, *Time and Event: An Exegetical Study of the Use of ʿeth in the Old Testament in Comparison to Other Temporary Expressions in Clarification of the Concept of Time* (Leiden: E. J. Brill, 1969), p. 120, emphasizes the number of pairs; there are seven double pairs, which "represent all the possibilities that may take place within the range of human activity and experience."

[14]J. A. Loader, *Ecclesiastes: A Practical Commentary* (Grand Rapids: Eerdmans, 1986), p. 35.

[15]Roland Murphy, *Ecclesiastes*, WBC 23A (Dallas: Word, 1992), p. 33.

[16]This view is argued for most extensively in Dominic Rudman, *Determinism in the Book of Ecclesiastes*, JSOTSup 316 (Sheffield, U.K.: Sheffield Academic Press, 2001), in which he argues that "Qoheleth's statement in 3:1 . . . and the catalogue of items in 3:2-8 outline a deterministic worldview in which all human actions and emotions are controlled by the deity" (p. 177).

examples, has agriculture in mind. It has its own order—there is a time to plant and a time to uproot, with a view to replanting. A good farmer knows the right time but has the freedom to ignore the rhythms of nature and plant in the wrong season and uproot in the wrong season, to his own detriment, of course. The background to Qohelet's thought at this point is to be found in traditional wisdom and Old Testament teaching, according to which God has ordered his creation in a fixed way, but humans are free to respond to that order as they choose.[17] The creation order that holds for agriculture is fixed, but the human response is not. The same is true of the other activities described in the poem. Thus the poem does not articulate the sort of determinism Loader and Murphy refer to but, as with Proverbs, speaks of the propitious time that correlates with how God has made the world.

Two words are used for time in Ecclesiastes 3:1, but it is difficult to discern much difference in meaning between them. The second word for time, ʿēt, is the one that recurs throughout the poem and some eleven times after Ecclesiastes 3:1-8. Qohelet's point is that the order in creation extends across the whole of it, and hence he enumerates the gamut of human life and activities. Ecclesiastes 3:2-8 lists fourteen pairs of opposites and thereby evokes completeness. Qohelet is concerned with life "under the sun."

> A time to give birth and a time to die,
> > a time to plant and a time to uproot what has been planted.
> A time to kill and a time to heal,
> > a time to break down and a time to build. (Eccles 3:2-3)

As is normal with poetry, the reference is often open-ended, and we cannot always be sure precisely what activities Qohelet is referring to or even if he intended a single meaning.

Ecclesiastes 3:2-3, the first strophe, deals with beginnings and endings. Ecclesiastes 3:2a refers to human life and its limits—a time to give birth and thus a time of new life, and a time to die. Ecclesiastes 3:2b refers to plant life—in agriculture there is a time to plant and a

---

[17]Passages like Ps 1:3; Gen 8:22; and the emphasis on creation order in Prov 1:1–9:18 are obvious examples.

time to pull up what was planted. Planting and uprooting may also
have a wider metaphorical reference, as the intertextual parallels to Jeremiah 1:10 indicate: "See, I have appointed you this day over the nations and over the kingdoms, to pluck up and to pull down, to destroy
and to overthrow, to build and to plant."[18]

Ecclesiastes 3:3 starts with the endings and is thus in a chiastic relationship to Ecclesiastes 3:2. There is a time to kill and a time to heal.
Killing could refer to legitimate capital punishment or holy war, and
healing to the cultic restoration of a person or medical treatment.
Breaking down could refer to destruction of buildings in war, and
building to the consequent reconstruction or to the normal processes of
knowing when to tear down a building and when to rebuild.

> A time to weep and a time to laugh,
>> a time to mourn and a time to dance.
> A time to throw stones and a time to gather stones,
>> a time to embrace and a time to refrain from embracing. (Eccles
>> 3:4-5)

Ecclesiastes 3:4 deals with emotions—there is a time for grief and a
time to celebrate. This is given a more concrete expression in the second half of the verse—grief manifest as mourning and celebration
manifest as dancing. It is unclear precisely what Ecclesiastes 3:5 refers
to; Murphy asserts that "the peculiar nature of the metaphor remains
unexplained."[19] *Qohelet Rabbah* interprets the gathering of stones as a
reference to sexual intercourse and the throwing out of stones as sexual
restraint.[20] This would fit well as a parallel to the second line in Ecclesiastes 3:5; however, the biblical support for this reading of stones is
weak. R. N. Whybray takes the gathering of stones to refer to clearing
a field for construction and the throwing of stones to refer to ruining a
neighbor's field by throwing stones into it.[21] The problem with this
view is that it makes deliberate ruin of a neighbor's field the only activ-

[18]Watson, *Traditional Techniques*, p. 156, notes that Jer 1:10 "evokes Qoh. 3:2-8."
[19]Murphy, *Ecclesiastes*, 33.
[20]Robert Gordis, *Koheleth—The Man and His World: A Study of Ecclesiastes*, 3rd ed. (New York: Schocken, 1968), follows this reading.
[21]R. N. Whybray, *Ecclesiastes*, NCB (Grand Rapids: Eerdmans, 1989), pp. 71-72.

ity that is clearly sinful in the list of twenty-eight, and from a wisdom perspective there would not be a right time for such an activity. It is better to take this verse to refer to clearing a field of stones (to throw stones) and to gathering stones for building. In parallel to the second line in Ecclesiastes 3:5, this could mean that the land is cleared for the building of a house, a home, in the context of which embracing and refraining from embracing take place. Embracing can refer to sexual intercourse or the more general showing of affection.

> A time to seek and a time to do away with,
>> a time to keep and a time to throw out.
> A time to tear and a time to repair,
>> a time to be silent and a time to speak. (Eccles 3:6-7)

Ecclesiastes 3:6 probably has to do with possessions. There is a time to seek new ones and a time to let them go, a time to hold onto possessions and a time to get rid of them. The context of Ecclesiastes 3:7 may be that of mourning—"a time to tear" could refer to the tearing of a garment that signified grief (Cf. Gen 37:29; 2 Sam 13:31). "A time to repair" would then refer to the repairing of the garments at the end of the mourning period. Similarly, being silent and speaking might also refer to fitting responses to those in mourning—the book of Job provides a good example of how hard it is to know when to keep silent and when to speak.

> A time to love and a time to hate,
>> a time for war and a time for peace. (Eccles 3:8)

Ecclesiastes 3:8 deals with personal emotions (love and hate) and with public correlates to those emotions (war and peace). Hate need not imply something wrong and sinful—in Deuteronomy 12:31, for example, God is referred to as "hating" the ways in which the Canaanites worshiped their gods, and the example is given of child sacrifice.

Today we find our experience of time ambivalent to say the least. We recall hearing the suggestion that the "www" in internet addresses should be changed because it takes too long to say www! In Western culture we are constantly torn between being too busy—"time waits for no man"—and trying to fill our leisure time so that we don't have to face up to the emptiness of our lives.

Ecclesiastes 3:1-8 *is* in touch with the fallenness of the world. It recognizes that we live in a world in which, tragically, there is a time for war and a time to kill. In this respect Qohelet's poem differs from Genesis 1, which envisages a world without which such "times." Nevertheless, the poem insists that God's good order for the creation continues to hold so that time is a gift, and if we are wise there is sufficient and appropriate time for all elements of a full human life. Far from depicting time as a threat and another stress factor, this poem extends time and its accompanying rhythms as an invitation to the wise to discern the appropriate time so that they might live life to the full amid God's good but fallen creation. Amid our speed-driven and stressed-out world, Ecclesiastes 3:1-8 offers us a "vision to enter into, a door to walk through, a place from which to see and feel things differently."[22]

Qohelet, however, strongly resists this invitation.

The structure of Ecclesiastes 3:1-15 as a whole is as follows:

| | |
|---|---|
| 3:1-8 | a poem on time |
| 3:9 | a rhetorical question about the benefit of work in such a timed world |
| 3:10-11 | observational response to the question |
| 3:12-13 | first confessional ("I know") response to the question |
| 3:14-15 | second confessional ("I know") response to the question |

## ECCLESIASTES 3:9-15

What profit is there for the worker in all that in which he labors?

I have seen the task which God has given humankind to be preoccupied with.

He has made everything fitting in its time. Furthermore, he has placed eternity in their heart, but still one is unable to discern what God has done from the beginning to the end.

I know that there is nothing better for them than to rejoice and to do good in one's days.

---

[22]P. Elbow, foreword to M. R. O'Reilley, *The Peaceable Classroom* (Portsmouth, N.H.: Heinemann, 1993), p. x.

> And also everyone who eats and drinks and enjoys the fruits of his labor—it is God's gift.
>
> I know that everything which God does will last forever; nothing can be added to it and nothing can be taken from it. God has done this so that they should fear him.
>
> What is has already been. What will be has already been. And God will seek out what has been pursued. (Eccles 3:9-15)

Ecclesiastes 3:9 poses again the programmatic question (cf. Eccles 1:3; 2:22) that Qohelet is seeking to answer. Now it is asked in relation to time and discerning what is fitting or appropriate in a particular situation. Qohelet recognizes that there is an order to creation (Eccles 3:11a), but does this help with his quest? Clearly not—as Qohelet says in Ecclesiastes 3:11. "I have seen" in Ecclesiastes 3:10 is a constituent part of Qohelet's response to the apparent order in time. It evokes his epistemology, or searchlight, that he brings to the data of life. Empirically one cannot discern the order in creation and thus cannot determine the right time for an activity. The reason for this, according to Qohelet, is that God has put eternity in human hearts, but one cannot discern what God has done from the beginning to the end.

There are a number of difficult issues in Ecclesiastes 3:10-15: First, how is "eternity" *(hā ʿōlām)* to be understood? Is it "world" (LXX), "a sense of past and future" (NRSV), "a sense of duration,"[23] "ignorance,"[24] "distant time"[25] or "a consciousness of the eternal"?[26]

Second, should "but still one is unable" in Ecclesiastes 3:11b be understood as introducing a purpose clause, thus indicating that the presence of *hā ʿōlām* ensures that humans will not understand what God is up to, or should it be understood in the sense of "but still," that is, as introducing a result clause and thereby referring to the limitations of human knowledge?

Third, how should the last part of Ecclesiastes 3:14, "they should

---

[23]Murphy, *Ecclesiastes*, p. 34.
[24]Whybray, *Ecclesiastes*, p. 73-74.
[25]Thomas Krüger, *Qoheleth: A Commentary*, trans. O. C. Dean Jr., Hermeneia (Minneapolis: Fortress, 2004), p. 87.
[26]Graham Ogden, *Qoheleth* (Sheffield, U.K.: JSOT Press, 1987), p. 55.

fear him," be understood? Should it to be understood to refer to fearing/ standing in awe (Murphy) or seeing (Ogden)? Ogden translates Ecclesiastes 3:14b, "God has done (this) so that they might see (what proceeds) from him."[27] And finally, how should *yĕbaqqēš ʾet-nirdap* ("he will seek out what has been pursued") in Ecclesiastes 3:15b be translated? Murphy translates it, "And God seeks out what has been pursued,"[28] suggesting that the reference is to the past or events of the past. On the basis of parallels between Ecclesiastes 3:14b and Ecclesiastes 3:15b, Ogden suggests that Ecclesiastes 3:15b should be translated, "God requests that it be pursued," with "it" referring to the enjoyment of Ecclesiastes 3:12-13.[29]

The question of time is central to Ecclesiastes 3:10-15. In Ecclesiastes 3:1-8 time signifies the right occasion for things to take place in a creation ordered by God. This provides the background for the rhetorical question in Ecclesiastes 3:9: in such a timed world what is the value and purpose of human labor and toil?

The first response in Ecclesiastes 3:10-11 is a negative one. Everything may have its divine time, but the human cannot discover it. Two contextual clues help in knowing how to translate *hāʿōlām*. First, as Murphy notes, the contrast between "time" and *hāʿōlām* suggests a temporal meaning, something along the lines of "duration."[30] Similarly Thomas Krüger takes *hāʿōlām* to refer to a distant time "that extends far beyond the life of an individual human being in the direction of either the past or future or both."[31] Second, it seems to us that we should not ignore the recurrence of *ʿōlām* ("forever") in Ecclesiastes 3:14, where it characterizes God's activity. These clues suggest that we should think of *hāʿōlām* as something to do with the way God has made the human person and the world. In a timed world humans recognize that "there is a time and a place" *and* that in order to discern this they need a sense of the larger picture, what philosophers might call origin and telos, or a metanarrative, a grand story or worldview.

---

[27]Ibid., p. 57.
[28]Murphy, *Ecclesiastes*, pp. 29, 36.
[29]Ogden, *Qoheleth*, p. 58.
[30]Ibid., p. 30.
[31]Krüger, *Qoheleth*, p. 87.

However, Qohelet's problem is that they cannot get access to this larger sense of "duration."[32]

If our understanding of *hāʿōlām* is correct, then "but still" should be understood as introducing a result clause. It is the limitation of human knowledge that Qohelet sees as making the human's toil enigmatic in Ecclesiastes 3:10-11. The "gift" of "eternity" is a terrible burden from this angle.

The second and third responses to the question of Ecclesiastes 3:9 are introduced by "I know" *(yādaʿtî)*, whereas Qohelet's observation that the human person cannot discern God's works is introduced by "I have seen." These two "I know" responses are very different in content to the first "I have seen" response. Here the opportunity that God's order of creation presents for eating, drinking and working is seen as a positive gift, in line with Ecclesiastes 2:24-26. What we have here is a juxtaposition of different responses rather than Ecclesiastes 3:12-15 being a compensation for the negative conclusion of Ecclesiastes 3:10-11.

The tension between Ecclesiastes 3:9-11 and Ecclesiastes 3:12-15 is made even stronger if one follows Ogden in translating the last part of Ecclesiastes 3:14 as, "God has done (this) so that they might see[33] (what proceeds) from him,"[34] since this stands in stark contrast to "yet they cannot find out" in Ecclesiastes 3:11. The juxtaposition of being unable to find out and yet knowing would strengthen the contrast in this section. However, even if one translates Ecclesiastes 3:14b along the lines of "stand in awe before him,"[35] this still forms a strong contrast with the

---

[32]Robert Davidson, *The Courage to Doubt: Exploring an Old Testament Theme* (London: SCM, 1989), p. 198-99, intriguingly suggests that Qohelet is playing on the different meanings of *hāʿōlām*: "It may well be that Qoheleth is deliberately playing upon different meanings of this word, particularly the time, past, present and future theme and the idea of hiddenness." A suggestion is that *hāʿōlām* comes from a root *ʿlm* meaning to hide. R. B. Y. Scott, *Proverbs, Ecclesiastes*, AB (Garden City, N.Y.: Doubleday, 1965), pp. 220-21, thus translates *hāʿōlām* as "enigma."

[33]*Šeyyirʾû* could be the *qal* imperfect of "to see" or of "to fear."

[34]Ogden, *Qoheleth*, p. 57.

[35]It should be noted that we understand this sense of fearing God in a far more positive, mainstream OT way than Roland E. Murphy, "Qohelet's 'Quarrel' With the Fathers," in *From Faith to Faith: Essays in Honor of Donald G. Miller on His Seventieth Birthday*, ed. D. Y. Hadidian (Pittsburgh: Pickwick, 1979), p. 241, who agrees with Zimmerli that such fear involves living under a closed heaven. Contra James L. Crenshaw, "The Eternal Gospel (Eccl 3:11)," in *Essays in Old Testament Ethics: J Philip Hyatt, in Memoriam*, ed. J. L. Crenshaw and J. T. Willis

frustrated enigmatic response of Ecclesiastes 3:10-11. The recurrence of the opening rhetorical question in Ecclesiastes 3:9 (cf. Eccles 1:3), with its implied negative answer, plus the reference to the harsh task that God has given the human person in Ecclesiastes 3:10, strengthen the enigmatic focus of Ecclesiastes 3:9-11.

Ecclesiastes 3:15, and especially Ecclesiastes 3:15b, is not easy to interpret. On all accounts it expresses God's sovereignty but should not be interpreted as a negative expression of this, as Whybray, for example, does.[36] The language of Ecclesiastes 3:15a is akin to that where Qohelet reflects negatively on the repetitiveness of history. However, as Krüger perceptively notes, Ecclesiastes 3:15a "takes up the concept of a constant repetition of similar things from 1:4-11 and interprets it theologically (cf. Gen. 8:22)."[37] God's seeking out what has been pursued then refers to God's making sure that what happened once happens again, so that Ecclesiastes 3:15 "summarizes and combines the statements about God's work in both verse 11a and verse 14a."[38] In other words, God sustains the order he puts into creation so that there is always a fitting time and a place for things and activities. Whether or not Ogden is right in reading the last part of Ecclesiastes 3:15 as a reference to God's calling humans to joy, Ecclesiastes 3:15 is a development of Ecclesiastes 3:14, and both should thus be seen as a positive expression of God's sovereignty. Ecclesiastes 3:12-15 is therefore an answer to Ecclesiastes 3:9, but an answer that is juxtaposed next to a very different and negative answer in Ecclesiastes 3:10-11.

## QOHELET AND THE THEOLOGY OF TIME

As happens throughout Ecclesiastes, this section thus presents us with two contradictory approaches to the mystery of time. The one despairs of being able to discern the time and the place, whereas the other celebrates time as the context in which to rejoice, do good, eat and drink, and enjoy one's labor. The contrast is stark and opens up a

---

(New York: Ktav, 1974), p. 48, as well. We do not think that Qohelet here articulates a pessimistic determinism.

[36]Whybray, *Ecclesiastes*, p. 75.

[37]Krüger, *Qoheleth*, p. 90.

[38]Ibid.

gap in the reading—how is the tension between these two approaches to be resolved?

The key is to note the different *epistemologies* that inform the two approaches—when he depends on reason and observation alone, Qohelet despairs over ever being able to discern the appropriate time for anything. However, as a believer, Qohelet knows that time is a gift and provides the possibility of eating and drinking, working, and enjoying the fruit of one's labor. Qohelet's problem is that, committed as he is to his autonomous epistemology, he cannot solve the tension between these views.

Epistemology is at stake once again.[39] To know this order, human beings require a sense of the origin and telos of creation, but from Qohelet's autonomous perspective it is precisely this they lack. God has constituted them with this need, but they lack such a sense of the duration of time—the result is that they cannot discern God's order and everything is rendered enigmatic. Qohelet's problem is that, in the context of his epistemology of reason, experience and observation, he cannot access the larger *story* that will make sense of the order he observes in time. Humans need a metanarrative from which to make sense of life, but they are limited and thus live in the terrible epistemological tension between what they need and the realities of life.

In chapter eight we noted how resolution comes to Qohelet through a return to a starting point in God as creator rather than in himself and his reason. Another way of putting this would be to say that Qohelet finds resolution by returning to the biblical metanarrative, of which creation is the indispensable foundation. As regards time and history Robert Herrera perceptively notes that

The foundational charter of the philosophy of history is found in one

---

[39]Kugel, *Great Poems*, pp. 315-16, perceptively notes that "he [Qohelet] is out to speak the truth; but he is limited to what he happens to be able to see, and say, at any one time. Koheleth's position might be compared to that of a man in a room walking around some object in the center—say, a globe—at a distance of five or ten feet. At any given moment he is able to describe *part* of the globe in great detail. . . . But as he moves around everything changes. Where once in the middle of the picture there was water there is now dry land. So in order to describe the globe he ends up presenting a series of snapshots, each one slightly different from the one before it and the one after it; in fact, from opposite points of the room they have absolutely nothing in common."

biblical verse: "God, at the beginning of time, created heaven and earth."
. . . This text, as traditionally interpreted, shattered the pagan conception of an eternal universe parceled out in an infinity of cycles. That
view was voiced by Berossus, the Babylonian astrologer, who maintained
that the universe passes through a number of Great Years with each
cosmic cycle reproducing that which had preceded it. The doctrine of
creation entailing linear time opened a vast horizon of novel events that
took history beyond the limits of the ancient chroniclers. Even Herodo-
tus . . . was imprisoned in a circle.[40]

Similarly Meijer Smit stresses the importance of creation in his articulation of a Christian philosophy of history:

> When I maintain that *God is the meaning of history* I mean to say that
> history has meaning in that it is totally, in all its elements and phenom-
> ena, in all its subjects and objects, *related to, oriented to* God. He has
> created the world in relation to himself. . . . That means for history not
> only fullness of meaning but also freedom, since for its meaning it is not
> dependent on the historical process, nor on the autonomous person.[41]

This implication of the opening salvo of the biblical story is even
clearer when the whole canon of Scripture is taken into account. Oscar
Cullmann rightly asserts that "the New Testament writings for the first
time give to all revelation an essential anchorage in time; here for the
first time the line is consistently carried through in its central significance for salvation and faith. Thus it is not as if we had to do with a
Jewish survival; rather, that which is intimated in Judaism is here completely carried out."[42] Qohelet had only the intimations, although these
are ignored in his discussion of time. But we have the full revelation in
Christ, and this provides the grand story within which it is possible to
live and to discern what is fitting and wise.[43] As Al Wolters notes, "An

---

[40]Robert A. Herrera, *Reasons for Our Rhymes: An Inquiry into the Philosophy of History* (Grand
Rapids: Eerdmans, 2001), p. 13.

[41]Meijer C. Smit, *Toward a Christian Conception of History*, ed. and trans. H. D. Morton and H.
Van Dyke, Christian Studies Today (Lanham, Md.: University Press of America, 2002), p.
325.

[42]Oscar Cullmann, *Christ and Time: The Primitive Christian Conception of Time and History*, rev.
ed., trans. F. V. Filson (Philadelphia: Westminster Press, 1957), p. 38.

[43]See Craig G. Bartholomew and Michael Goheen, *The Drama of Scripture: Finding Our Place in
the Biblical Story* (Grand Rapids: Baker Academic, 2004).

implication of the revelation of God in creation is that the creation order is *knowable*. That is also the significance of the *call* of Wisdom to all—she appeals to everyone to pay attention and learn from her, for insight and understanding are genuinely available to them if they heed her. This fundamental knowability of the creation order is the basis of all human understanding, both in science and everyday life."[44]

One of the major theological reflections on time is that of Karl Barth.[45] Barth rightly notes that time "is the form of our existence. To be man is to live in time."[46] In terms strongly reminiscent of Qohelet, Barth acknowledges how time can confront us as a monstrous enigma:[47] "Infinite, also, is the impossibility of escaping its enigma as the enigma of man himself, man who is, and who would like to be in time and have time, who is in point of fact temporal, and whose being in time is of this nature."[48] Time is a "given"; it is part of our *creaturely* condition, and for Barth it becomes a monstrous enigma because of our alienation from God, and thus from ourselves. Time confronts us with the boundaries and limits of human existence. For Barth we can only come to terms with time when we recognize God as Creator:

> What emerges . . . is that man is not God, but a needy creature of God. . . . To say "man" or "time" is first and basically, even if unwillingly and unwittingly, to say "God." For God is for man as He has time for him. It is God who gives him his time. . . . Time as the form of human existence is always in itself and as such a silent but persistent song of praise to God.[49]

The secret of time is, for Barth, "the will and act of God."[50] In Qo-

---

[44]Albert M. Wolters, *Creation Regained: Biblical Basics for a Reformational Worldview* (Grand Rapids: Eerdmans, 1985), p. 29. See the whole of chapter 2.

[45]Karl Barth, *CD* III/2, §47, titled "Man in His Time," pp. 437-640. This section is over two hundred pages long. We cannot discuss it in any detail here, but it is a deeply insightful examination of the theology of time. Particularly relevant for Ecclesiastes is section 2, "Given Time."

[46]Ibid., p. 521.

[47]Ibid., pp. 511-17.

[48]Ibid., p. 515.

[49]Ibid., p. 525.

[50]Ibid., p. 527. The indispensability of relating time to God as Creator is underscored in Barth's emphatic statement (ibid., p. 551) that "we understood time and our being in time as real by considering it as the form of human existence willed and created by God. We thus purged the

helet's language it is, "Remember your creator before . . . before . . . before . . ." (Eccles 12:1-2, 6).

As Anthony Thiselton notes, "In theism, God may be said to give the gift of time as opportunity; as an interval for promise, hope and faithfulness; as a resource for which humankind is accountable; or as sheer gift for enjoyment."[51] How do we receive this gift in our culture, in which time has become an enemy to be conquered through time management courses and careful planning, so we can do more in less time?

Intriguingly this is precisely the question Dorothy Bass addresses in her book *Receiving the Day: Christian Practices for Opening the Gift of Time*. As Bass notes,

> At the heart of this practice is praise of the One who created the earth and separated the light from darkness. This One is still active in earth and all creatures, including ourselves. Every day, this One offers gifts— life, light, and hours in which to work and eat and love and rest—and invites humankind to join in the ongoing work of caring for creation and all who dwell therein.[52]

Receiving the day is rooted in a view of our world as creation, and Bass suggests the following practices for receiving the day.

***Honoring the body, day by day.*** Humans are embodied creatures, and rhythms of eating, drinking and washing are an important part of human identity. People who lose their homes report that the loss of this rhythm is one of the hardest aspects of such loss.[53] Kathleen Norris, in *The Quotidian Mysteries*, notes that

> our culture's ideal self, especially the accomplished, professional self, rises above necessity, the humble, everyday, ordinary tasks that are best left to unskilled labor. The comfortable lies we tell ourselves regarding these "little things"—that they don't matter, and that daily and personal and household chores are of no significance to us spiritually—are ex-

---

concept of time from all the abstractions by which it is inevitably confused and darkened when the divine will and action are left out of account and time is not understood as His creation."

[51]Anthony C. Thiselton, *A Concise Encyclopedia of the Philosophy of Religion* (Oxford: Oneworld, 2002), p. 309.

[52]Dorothy C. Bass, *Receiving the Day: Christian Practices for Opening the Gift of Time* (San Francisco: Jossey-Bass, 2001), p. 18.

[53]Ibid., p. 32.

posed as falsehoods when we consider that reluctance to care for the body is one of the first symptoms of extreme melancholia. Shampooing the hair, washing the body, brushing the teeth, drinking enough water, taking a daily vitamin, going for a walk, as simple as they seem, are acts of self-respect. They enhance one's ability to take pleasure in oneself and in the world.[54]

*The offering of attention.* Qohelet encourages us to enter into life attentively. The opposite of attention is distraction, and in today's busyness, attentiveness suffers. Annie Dillard has made it her task as a writer to attend to the creation. Eugene Peterson describes Annie as an exegete of the creation, just as Calvin is an exegete of Scripture. The doctrine of creation calls us to attention because "matter is real. Flesh is good. Without a firm rooting in creation, religion is always drifting off into some kind of pious sentimentalism or sophisticated intellectualism. . . . The physical is holy."[55] Dillard spent a year attending to a creek and its surroundings and published her experiences in *Pilgrim at Tinker Creek*. Her explorations are rigorous and in turns puzzling and mysterious. But she "ends up on her feet applauding."[56]

> Emerson saw it. "I dreamed that I floated at will in the great Ether, and I saw this world floating also not far off, but diminished to the size of an apple. Then an angel took it in his hand and brought it to me and said, 'This must thou eat.' And I ate the world." All of it. All of it intricate, speckled, gnawed, fringed, and free. Israel's priests offered the wave breast and the heave shoulder together, freely, in full knowledge, for thanksgiving. They waved, they heaved, and neither gesture was whole without the other, and both meant a wide-eyed and keen-eyed thanks. Go your way, eat the fat, and drink the sweet, said the bell. A sixteenth-century alchemist wrote of the philosopher's stone, "One finds it in the open country, in the village and in the town. It is in everything which God created. Maids throw it on the street. Children play with it." The giant water bug ate the world. And like Billy Bray I

[54]Kathleen Norris, *The Quotidian Mysteries: Laundry, Liturgy, and "Women's Work"* (New York: Paulist, 1998), p. 40.
[55]Eugene Peterson, *The Contemplative Pastor: Returning to the Art of Spiritual Direction* (Grand Rapids: Eerdmans, 1989), p. 68.
[56]Ibid., p. 69.

go my way, and my left foot says, "Glory," and my right foot says, "Amen": in and out of Shadow Creek, upstream and down, exultant, in a daze, dancing, to the twin silver trumpets of praise.[57]

***Attending to God.*** Bass's third practice involves making times for God regularly each day: "The Christian practice of receiving the day begins with setting aside a part of each day for attention to God. This piece of time leans deliberately into the wind, grounding us to resist the forces that hurry us on to distraction. . . . Putting down an anchor or two amidst the swells of each day is essential if we are to avoid bobbing on its surface or being washed away by its demands."[58] This is a topic that Qohelet addresses in particular in Ecclesiastes 5:1-7, where he exhorts us to approach God and *listen*.

***Saying no to say yes.*** Receiving the day, especially in our frenetic consumer culture, involves choosing what not to do as well as what to do. Qohelet's exhortations to embrace the ordinary is much harder nowadays than it was in his day, with TV, the Internet and all the things that constitute our speed-driven culture. Recovering the ordinary will mean dispensing with the clutter that fills our lives.

***Unmastering the day.*** Bass's final step involves a recognition that there is much about our days that we cannot control, and we need to relinquish control at these points. "Saint Francis is reported to have said, 'In baptism we have died the only death that matters.' It is, finally, in this kind of confidence, this kind of trust, that we are free to receive this day as a gift—and also to receive it as a day that bears gifts, including the gift we become when we lose ourselves in faithful living."[59]

It is no easy thing to receive the gift of this day, this time, for at times our days will be difficult, if not excruciating. But then there is a time too for dying, for breaking down, for mourning. Belden Lane describes the difficult years when his mother was dying from cancer. Reflecting later on the pain of that time he found that in Laura Gilpin's poem "The Two-Headed Calf," he recognized his experience. This

[57]Annie Dillard, *Pilgrim at Tinker Creek*, in *The Annie Dillard Reader* (San Francisco: Harper-Perennial, 1994), p. 424.
[58]Bass, *Receiving the Day*, pp. 36-37.
[59]Ibid., p. 43.

searing poem captures the challenge and reality of receiving the gift of time when it is very hard to discern the gift in the present:

> Tomorrow when the farm boys find this
> Freak of nature, they will wrap his body
> In newspaper and carry him to the museum.
>
> But tonight he is alive and in the north
> field with his mother. It is a perfect
> summer evening: the moon rising over
> the orchard, the wind in the grass. And
> as he stares into the sky, there are
> twice as many stars as usual.[60]

## RECOMMENDED READING

### Commentaries

See the relevant sections in the commentaries listed at the end of chapter eight.

### Scholarly resources

Cullmann, Oscar. *Christ and Time: The Primitive Christian Conception of Time and History.* Rev. Ed. Translated by F. V. Filson. Philadelphia: Westminster Press, 1957.

Fox, Michael V. "Time in Qohelet's 'Catalogue of Times.'" *Journal of Northwest Semitic Languages* 24, no. 1 (1998): 25-39.

Schultz, Richard L. "A Sense of Timing: A Neglected Aspect of Qoheleth's Wisdom." In *Seeking Out the Wisdom of the Ancients: Essays Offered to Honor Michael V Fox on the Occasion of his Sixty-Fifth Birthday,* edited by R. L. Troxel, K. G. Friebel and D. R. Magary, pp. 257-67. Winona Lake, Ind.: Eisenbrauns, 2005.

### Theological and philosophical resources

*Introductory*

Spykman, Gordon J. *Reformational Theology: A New Paradigm for Doing Dogmatics,* pp. 151-57, 163-66, 268-70. Grand Rapids: Eerdmans, 1992.

Thiselton, Anthony C. "Time." In *A Concise Encyclopedia of the Philosophy of Religion.* Oxford: Oneworld, 2002.

---

[60]Laura Gilpin, *The Hocus-Pocus of the Universe* (Garden City, N.Y.: Doubleday, 1977), p. 59, quoted in Belden C. Lane, *The Solace of Fierce Landscapes: Exploring Desert and Mountain Spirituality* (New York: Oxford University Press, 1998), pp. 35-36.

*Advanced*

Barth, Karl. *CD* III/2, § 47, "Man in His Time."

Ricoeur, Paul. "Biblical Time." In *Figuring the Sacred: Religion, Narrative, and Imagination,* ed. M. I. Wallace, trans. D. Pellauer, pp. 167-80. Minneapolis: Fortress, 1995.

———. *Time and Narrative.* 3 vols. Chicago: Chicago University Press, 1984-1988.

Turetzky, Philip. *Time.* New York: Routledge, 1998.

*Practical*

Bass, Dorothy C. *Receiving the Day: Christian Practices for Opening the Gift of Time.* San Francisco: Jossey-Bass, 2001.

Stookey, Laurence H. *Calendar: Christ's Time for the Church.* Nashville: Abingdon, 1996.

---
**10**
---

# Jesus, the Wisdom of God

*My purpose is that they may be encouraged in heart and united in love,*
*so that they may have the full riches of complete understanding, in*
*order that they may know the mystery of God, namely,*
*Christ, in whom are hidden all the treasures*
*of wisdom and knowledge.*

COLOSSIANS 2:2-3

OUR PRIMARY FOCUS IN THIS BOOK has been on the Old Testament Wisdom literature. On its own terms Old Testament wisdom is exhilarating, but can you imagine what might happen if Lady Wisdom herself appeared to us? According to the New Testament, this is one way of understanding what happened in the incarnation. Thus, no examination of Old Testament wisdom is complete without exploring its fulfillment and embodiment in Jesus. The next three chapters flow out of our work in the Old Testament in order to explore wisdom in the New Testament and a Christian theology of wisdom for today.

## SECOND TEMPLE JUDAISM

So where, how and why did the New Testament writers appeal to Old Testament wisdom? Recent scholarship suggests that to answer this question we must first explore the religious and intellectual culture at the time of Jesus' earthly ministry. This intertestamental period, or what is often called Second Temple Judaism, is where we begin.

*Greek wisdom.* It is first necessary to recognize how Greek wisdom was expanding throughout the Greek and Roman empires in the centuries surrounding the writing of the New Testament. Because this wisdom shared so many ideas with Hebrew wisdom, it was readily adapted into Jewish thinking (and has been in Jewish and Christian thought to this day). It is into this world of merging Jewish and Greek ideas that the New Testament was written.

Given so many centuries of development, Greek wisdom and philosophy had branched out into a diverse variety of schools. Nevertheless, important similarities between Greek and Hebrew wisdom allowed the New Testament writers to make use of it.[1] Most importantly, ancient Greek and Jewish thought both viewed wisdom as an aspect of the human relationship with the creation and created or natural order. Furthermore, although Greek philosophy generally divided theory from practice, Greek wisdom was concerned with both. This is particularly true of Aristotle's notion of wisdom and *phronēsis.* To be wise is not just intellectual but includes relating well to the world ethically, skillfully, politically and economically.[2]

There are also important divergences. Greek wisdom was highly dualistic, meaning that it tended to privilege *ideas* over *matter* and the *spiritual* over the *physical.* Although Greek wisdom encouraged the pursuit of wisdom *in* the world, to be truly wise meant pursuing the immaterial divinity within each human. Colin Gunton says, "Accordingly, divine wisdom could be attained by thought. . . . Wisdom for this strain of Hellenism was thus a focus of the essential *continuity* between the human and the divine"; and Greek wisdom was "at least potentially written into the human soul."[3]

But Hebrew (and Christian) wisdom begins with the fear of the Lord (Prov 1:7; 9:10). To be wise is to acknowledge our nature *as creation* and God as the one and only *Creator.* Wisdom is not innate but a

---

[1]For a brief but illuminating study of these ancient forms of wisdom, see Colin Gunton, "Christ, the Wisdom of God: A Study in Divine and Human Action," in *Where Shall Wisdom Be Found? Wisdom in the Bible, the Church and the Contemporary World,* ed. Stephen C. Barton (Edinburgh: T & T Clark, 1999), pp. 249-61.

[2]Aristotle *Nichomachean Ethics* 6.

[3]Gunton, "Christ, the Wisdom of God," pp. 252-53, emphasis added.

gift from God to his creatures. The strong warning from Proverbs 26:12, "Do you see a man wise in his own eyes? / There is more hope for a fool than for him," stands in direct opposition to this Greek wisdom of upward mobility and innateness. Furthermore, Hebrew wisdom, like all Hebrew theology, rejects the form-versus-matter dualism of Greek thought. The heavens and the earth are united in the end (Col 1:20), and the spiritual realm is not privileged over earthly realities, as in Greek philosophy. So while Greek wisdom probably encouraged the growth of a wisdom movement in ancient Israel, as we will see below, books like 1 Corinthians and John encouraged the church to make a definitive break from its philosophical and theological leanings.

***Kingdom and messiah.*** Second, Israel's return from Assyrian and Babylonian exile in the sixth and fifth centuries B.C. gave new impetus for the hope of a Messiah, or indeed of many messiahs, who would establish the kingdom in their midst. These two expectations—a king and his kingdom—were inseparably linked together in Israel's story throughout the Old Testament,[4] a story that combined three interdependent hopes: (1) the promise of a future king to arise from Israel, bringing redemption, justice, righteousness and peace (Gen 49:10; Deut 33:5; Is 9:1-7); (2) inheritance of a land or place (Gen 12:1; Deut 12; Jer 33:12-13; Is 49:8; Amos 9:13-15); and (3) judgment and gathering of the nations (Gen 12:3; Is 49:6; Amos 9:12).

In this context wisdom was just one of many characteristics of the messiah ruler who would usher in the kingdom. As has been observed by many scholars, messianic hopes were not programmatic, as if all Old Testament prophecies and Jewish traditions imagined a single individual with a list of traits who would come at a particular point in time. Rather, messianism was a complex set of cultural beliefs and hopes that developed in many directions in the years surrounding Jesus' earthly ministry. Jewish expectations were high, and terms and figures like Wisdom, Adam, Spirit, Word, Son of God, Elijah, the Prophet, Son of David, king and Torah were a few of the many ways used to speak of the coming figure and his coming kingdom. A few

---

[4]See Richard Bauckham, *Jesus and the God of Israel: God Crucified and Other Studies on the New Testament's Christology of Divine Identity* (Grand Rapids: Eerdmans, 2008), p. 8.

points must be made about this expectant time before we can discuss
its relation to wisdom.

Historians differ as to how Second Temple Judaism and early Christianity related to these messianic hopes.[5] N. T. Wright helpfully draws
our attention to the overwhelming presence of messianic themes in the
Second Temple era.[6] In the Old Testament alone we find themes of a
prophet like Moses (Deut 18:15), the son of God and a Davidic king
(Ps 2; 8; 89), the Son of Man (Dan 7), and the many familiar Advent
passages on the coming one in Isaiah (Is 9; 11; 42; 61). Wright also
identifies four types of prominent Second Temple sources that point to
a coming leader: the Qumran scrolls (4Q174; 1QSa 2:11-21; 1QSb
5:23-9), the *Psalms of Solomon* 17:21-32, Josephus's *Jewish War* (6.312-
15) and finally *4 Ezra*'s vision of a coming apocalyptic creature in chapters 11 and 12. The parallels between *4 Ezra* and Daniel 7 here are
unmistakable. And throughout Second Temple messianism, allusions
to and quotations from Old Testament texts are everywhere. Clearly
messianism was vibrant in Jesus' day.

Wright then draws six important conclusions about Jewish messianic
expectation: (1) it was focused on the nation and *its* restoration, not
individual salvation; (2) the focus of the Messiah could "under certain
circumstances" be put on a particular individual; (3) when this focus
occurred, it could be constructed in any number of ways—one messiah
or two, Davidic descent or not; (4) "the main task of the Messiah, over
and again, is the liberation of Israel, and her reinstatement as the true
people of God"; (5) he would be the agent of Israel's God; and (6) he
was not necessarily expected to suffer.[7] In sum, messianic hopes were
strong throughout the Jewish world, but they were not as neat and uni-
form as we might imagine.

Perhaps most importantly, the Messiah was imagined as a human
figure. The king or prophet or lawgiver would be like Moses, Elijah
and David. This is where the New Testament departs from the themes

---

[5]Some believe the early Christians downplayed the Messiah to distance themselves from Jewish
  religion.
[6]See N. T. Wright, *The New Testament and the People of God* (Minneapolis: Fortress, 1992), pp.
  307-20.
[7]Ibid., pp. 319-20.

and content of the Second Temple literature and develops them around the historical Jesus, as will see below.

A final point should be made about messianic expectations. One way of thinking about the identity of the Messiah was through a theology of Adam. Wright again helps us understand the historical and theological significance of this identity. The stories in Genesis make it clear that Israel had become God's "true humanity" after Adam. But they had failed to renew the life of Eden for themselves, much less for the whole world, as they were intended to do. The coming Messiah would be a *new Adam*, a representative figure who would lead Israel back into their inheritance as God's covenant people—back into kingdom life for the whole of humanity.[8] As we will see, wisdom is a way New Testament writers make this connection.

***Hebrew wisdom.*** A third point to consider is that in the Second Temple period, after Israel had returned from captivity—with its long and intense exposure to ancient Near Eastern and emerging forms of Greek wisdom—their view of wisdom had developed in significant ways. Not only had it absorbed wisdom ideas from surrounding cultures; but it had also become a major feature of new messianic/kingdom expectations.

Prior to the exile, wisdom could safely be characterized as embodying two things—God's design for the creation and, as a result, the way humans were meant to participate in that world. Thus, wisdom was secular, not as in atheistic or nonreligious, but as something chiefly aimed at practical and moral human behavior in the "created order of things."[9] While flowing out of Israel's experience of salvation (as indicated by the constant reference to Yahweh), wisdom was not a category for explaining salvation in the future.[10] Wisdom in the Old Testament is fully aware of sin but does not seek to provide a solution.

When we come to the postexilic and Qumran texts, the genres have changed, and wisdom has taken on a more central role in Israel's world-

---

[8]N. T. Wright, *Climax of the Covenant: Christ and the Law in Pauline Theology* (Minneapolis: Fortress, 1992), pp. 24-25.

[9]Gunton, "Christ, the Wisdom of God," p. 250.

[10]Though Deut 4; 32 and Job and perhaps Isaiah make it possible, it is only so indirectly.

view. In this way, there is probably no pure "Wisdom literature" in the Second Temple era and Qumran communities.[11] Instead, we find wisdom in several books from the Second Temple era whose concerns are focused on the issues of kingdom, prophecy, messiah and Torah.[12] The most well-known texts from Sirach (Ben Sira), Baruch and the Wisdom of Solomon in this respect are the following:[13]

**Sirach 17:1, 7**

The Lord created human beings out of earth,
    and makes them return to it again.

He filled them with knowledge and understanding
    and showed them good and evil.

**Sirach 24:1, 9, 22-23**

Wisdom praises herself,
    and tells of her glory in the midst of her people.

Before the ages, in the beginning, he created me,
    and for all the ages I shall not cease to be.

"Whoever obeys me will not be put to shame,
    and those who work with me will not sin."
All this is the book of the covenant of the most high God,
    the law that Moses commanded us
    as an inheritance for the congregations of Jacob."

**Baruch 3:9**

Hear the commandments of life, O Israel;
    give ear and learn wisdom!

These texts demonstrate how the integration of the Old Testament traditions of Torah, wisdom, prophecy and history—an integration often more implicit than explicit in the Old Testament—was being made explicit to speak to a new time and place. Much like Proverbs 8,

---

[11]Excluding of course the possibility that Job, Ecclesiastes and/or Proverbs 31 could all have been written then.

[12]The major texts are Sirach (Ben Sira); Baruch; *1 Enoch;* the *Psalms of Solomon;* the *Letter of Aristeas;* the third *Sibylline Oracle;* the Wisdom of Solomon; *4 Maccabees; 4 Ezra;* the Apocalypse of Baruch; and several texts from the Qumran scrolls.

[13]The following texts are taken from the NRSV.

and Proverbs 1–9 in general, wisdom here is personified, usually as a woman created by God in the beginning and now calling Israel back to Torah and to God's ways. Gerald Sheppard notes that in this period

> wisdom became a theological category associated with an understanding of canon which formed a perspective from which to interpret Torah and prophetic traditions. In this sense wisdom became a hermeneutical construct for interpreting sacred Scripture. . . . One can easily see how the role of Wisdom as Torah (Sir. 24:23), which is here assigned to Israel and Jacob (Sir. 24:8) and flourishes in Jerusalem (vv. 13-17), parallels the constitutional ordinances of Deuteronomy, which are likewise to be enforced upon realization sof the promised territory. . . . Once again, historical narrative from the Torah, originally not concerned with Wisdom, provides the principal content of a Wisdom Song like one finds in Proverbs.[14]

Sheppard goes on to say, "Quite naturally the NT writers could do the same for Jesus, the Word and Wisdom of God 'through whom also he created the world.'"[15] In other words, as the early church wrestled with understanding Jesus' deity and redemptive work, wisdom provided a natural resource for interpreting the Jesus event.

Developments in the understanding of wisdom are crucial in this respect. There are three basic approaches. The first is that Woman Wisdom is a literary personification of the wisdom God uses to make the world.[16] Second, other scholars describe her as a hypostasis, having some existence "between a person and personification."[17] Roland Murphy correctly observes, however, that wisdom "cannot remain focused,

---

[14]Gerald T. Sheppard, *Wisdom as a Hermeneutical Construct*, BZAW 151 (Berlin: Walter de Gruyter, 1980), pp. 12, 42. We would nuance Sheppard's view by noting that historical narrative does often manifest an awareness of and concern with wisdom. A prime example is 1 Kings 1–11. Cf. also Wright, *Climax of the Covenant*, p. 26: "Since those who fear the Lord, who walk in his ways, are the children of Israel who observe the Torah, wisdom becomes closely identified with Torah itself (e.g. Ben-Sira 17.11; 19.20; 24.1-34; 38.34, 39.1-11, 2 Baruch 3.9-4.4); together they form the charter for Israel's national life *precisely* as the way of life of God's true humanity."

[15]Sheppard, *Wisdom as a Hermeneutical Construct*, p. 45, citing col. 1.

[16]Of course, the issue gets far more complex when one begins to address the different figures of wisdom in the OT. See Michael V. Fox, *Proverbs 1–9*, AB (New York: Doubleday, 2000), pp. 352-59, for helpful discussion and arguments on why personification fits best with Proverbs 1–9.

[17]James D. G. Dunn, *The Theology of Paul the Apostle* (Grand Rapids: Eerdmans, 1998), p. 271.

or at least adequately defined, at any one point along this path from Proverbs to Sirach and beyond."[18] In other words, the idea of Woman Wisdom develops throughout these texts, and by the time of the Second Temple wisdom, her role is much stronger.[19] James D. G. Dunn thus chooses to describe her as an "extended metaphor,"[20] which we find helpful for the way it reinforces the picture of a world calling on the wisdom tradition in order to discern God's ways in his world. However, Richard Bauckham, on the basis of passages like Wisdom 7:22–8:1, believes that wisdom is more than just a literary device. Second Temple Judaism's "perfectly clear distinction between God and all other reality is made in other terms, which in this case place God's Wisdom unequivocally within the unique divine identity."[21] Clearly, the degree to which Second Temple Judaism saw wisdom as part of the divine nature is disputed among Old Testament and New Testament scholars. What is nevertheless clear is that by the time we come to Jesus' earthly ministry, wisdom has taken on a divine uniqueness that provides the New Testament writers with a powerful way to understand and respond to the Messiah.

## THE CHURCH AND THE NEW TESTAMENT

We need to remember that the New Testament writers were drawing on the *whole* Old Testament tradition to interpret the life and events of Jesus of Nazareth. Wisdom is not the thematic umbrella for this effort but rather one of many concepts that aided them in their work. In the language of traditional Christology, Jesus is depicted as prophet, priest, king *and* as wise man par excellence.

How then does wisdom fit within this larger context? The way Lady Wisdom grew to communicate God's work in the world becomes clear when we think of some of the questions the early church struggled

---

[18]Roland E. Murphy, *Proverbs*, WBC 22 (Nashville: Thomas Nelson, 1998), p. 281.

[19]See Roland E. Murphy, "The Personification of Wisdom," in *Wisdom in Ancient Israel*, ed. J. Day, Robert P. Gordon and H. G. M. Williamson (Cambridge: Cambridge University Press, 1995), pp. 222-33.

[20]Dunn, *Theology of Paul the Apostle*, p. 272. Technically personification is a type of metaphor, or too closely linked for Dunn's point to be helpful. We do admire his desire to go beyond mere personification and identify wisdom with the divine.

[21]Bauckham, *Jesus and the God of Israel*, p. 17.

with: If the kingdom has indeed arrived, who is this Jesus and in what way has he ushered in the kingdom? If Jesus is Yahweh, how can he be human? If God died and rose again, how are we meant to live? Wisdom—with its Old Testament associations with king, Torah and creation—provided a powerful way to answer these questions. It allowed, for example, the church to explain Jesus' unique identity as the Christ who is Yahweh.[22] In the New Testament, wisdom is used to identify Jesus as the preexistent Creator, the ethical governor and exemplar, the agent of reconciliation and the *clue* or *key* to understanding the nature of redemption and world order. In this way Christ *is* wisdom.[23]

Needless to say, this approach is not uncontroversial. Early form criticism, for example, generally sought to separate New Testament texts into two groups: Jewish Christianity based on Israel, torah and kingdom, and Hellenic Christianity founded on Gnosticism and forms of Greek wisdom.[24] Such an approach remains popular today. But we believe that the early Christians held to a resolutely Jewish, monotheistic expectation of the Messiah and the kingdom, making use of Torah and wisdom to engage and even resist their increasingly Greek culture.[25] In this context, wisdom was used to demonstrate Jesus' deity, his oneness with the Father and Spirit, his role in the creation, and his fulfillment of the standards and hopes of the Torah. We will explore these connections as we traverse the books of the New Testament below.

## THE GOSPELS AND ACTS

While the Synoptic Gospels are clearly written within the Jewish tradition of king, Torah, Word, kingdom, Son of God and so on, they appear to lack explicit references to Hebrew wisdom. Closer analysis reveals, however, that each of these Gospels (and Acts) is aware of the wisdom tradition and makes use of it in the context of its larger aim.

---

[22]Ibid., pp. 194-95.

[23]See Larry Hurtado, *Lord Jesus Christ: Devotion to Jesus in Earliest Christianity* (Grand Rapids: Eerdmans, 2003), p. 125.

[24]Wright, *New Testament*, pp. 418-27.

[25]Ibid., pp. 427-35. Though they say less about wisdom, Hurtado, *Lord Jesus Christ*, and Bauckham, *Jesus and the God of Israel*, both interpret the historical record in a similar way.

***Matthew.*** Like Luke and John, Matthew begins his Gospel with an
allusion to creation. The first two words—*biblos geneseōs*—lay the
foundation for his project. The crux of this foundation is Matthew's use
of the Greek *geneseōs* ("birth, lineage, beginning"). Echoing the first
words of Genesis, Matthew begins the story of Jesus as one of new
creation.[26] As W. D. Davies notes,

> Matthew is concerned to assert in the prologue that the coming of Jesus
> was a new creation. The significance of the prologue is to suggest that
> the birth can be compared adequately only with the creation of the uni-
> verse itself. The first phrase of Matthew is not a title for the genealogy
> only but for the whole Gospel of the new creation or the new Genesis.[27]

The references to wisdom in Matthew must be understood in this
context. For example, the visit from the Gentile "wise men" (*magoi*) in
Matthew 2:1 is a subtle way of using wisdom to illumine this Jesus, who
is beginning a new work for the world.[28] Like the queen of Sheba who
was drawn to Israel because of Solomon's wisdom, the wise men from
the east are led to the source of wisdom, Jesus (cf. Mt 12:42).

Among other things, Matthew portrays Jesus as the new Moses,
who provides the new Israel with her new law (especially in Mt 5–7).[29]
The strongest evocations of wisdom come in the conclusion to the Sermon on the Mount (Mt 7:24-27). This parable of the two houses is a
clear allusion to the two houses of Proverbs 9.[30] Like Lady Wisdom,
Jesus' teaching calls to its hearers and, as in Old Testament wisdom,
there are two possible responses: the wisdom of obedience and the neglect of folly. The person who hears and acts on Jesus' words is like a
wise person who builds his or her house on a rock so that it can with-
stand the worst weather (cf. Job and Ecclesiastes). Implicit in this con-

---

[26]W. D. Davies and D. C. Allison, *Matthew 1–7*, ICC (London: T & T Clark, 1988), pp. 149-56.

[27]W. D. Davies, *The Sermon on the Mount* (Cambridge: Cambridge University Press, 1966), p. 13.

[28]See Stephen C. Barton, "Gospel Wisdom," in Barton, *Where Shall Wisdom Be Found*, pp. 94-95.

[29]See Davies, *Sermon on the Mount*, pp. 10-18.

[30]A point not often made in commentaries but noted by Ben Witherington III, *Jesus the Sage: The Pilgrimage of Wisdom* (Minneapolis: Fortress, 1994), pp. 356-57.

clusion is that Jesus is himself Lady Wisdom; he is wisdom incarnate so that the wise person builds his or her house on *his* teaching. It is not surprising, therefore, that Matthew would say "one greater than Solomon is here" (Mt 12:42).

Matthew also portrays Jesus as a new Moses. But, as Davis rightly notes, he is far more than that: "The purely Mosaic or didactic function of Jesus is transcended. True, Christians are disciples of Christ but they are such within the larger context of incorporation in Jesus and worship him as their Lord."[31] In this respect it is intriguing to note that his new "law" differs significantly from Mosaic law in its form and focus. A new act in the drama of Scripture—indeed, the central act—has now dawned, and while Jesus affirms and fulfills the law of Moses, he teaches with the new situation in mind. Intriguingly his new style of "law" has many resemblances to wisdom.

Ben Witherington's extensive work on wisdom sayings and aphorisms in the New Testament is helpful in this respect. He argues that Jesus intentionally avoids traditional wisdom ideas like hard work, seeking wisdom or the fear of the Lord. Instead, he says, Jesus uses aphorisms to engage in a countercultural debate with the abuses of traditional wisdom. For example, the aphorism in Matthew 6:24, "You cannot serve God and Money [Mammon]," works counter to the overriding act-consequence scheme of the typical wisdom sage in Jesus' day.[32] Jesus also uses wisdom sayings to teach his eschatological hope for the future—one that will go through the cross to glory.

Wisdom is also a valuable resource for Jesus' teachings about kingdom life. As we will see in the following chapter, the early church also drew on the wisdom tradition to explain the new ethical demands of the kingdom.

Matthew's use of wisdom theology is also clear in Matthew 11–12. This narrative sits between the second and third discourses and is memorable for the prayer in Matthew 11:25-30:

At that time Jesus said, "I praise you, Father, Lord of heaven and earth,

---

[31]Ibid., p. 28.
[32]Ibid., pp. 161-83.

because you have hidden these things from the wise and learned, and revealed them to little children. Yes, Father, for this was your good pleasure. All things have been committed to me by my Father. No one knows the Son except the Father, and no one knows the Father except the Son and those to whom the Son chooses to reveal him. Come to me, all you who are weary and burdened, and I will give you rest. Take my yoke upon you and learn from me, for I am gentle and humble in heart, and you will find rest for your souls. For my yoke is easy and my burden is light.

Stephen Barton discerns three wisdom lessons from this passage.[33] First, the prayer resembles other wisdom prayers that give thanks for revealing wisdom to "infants" (Wis 10:21; Sir 3:19; 1 Cor 1:19-31), "contradicting" Daniel's prayer of thanks for revealing wisdom to the wise (Dan 2:19-23). Second, the prayer illustrates that wisdom comes in relationship with the Son, who shares the authority of the Father. Third, the clear goal of this wisdom is the Son's "rest"—a promise ripe with Old Testament allusions to the exodus rest (Mt 1:23; 28:20) but also pointing to the Messiah's eschatological rest. As Barton says: "Jesus the wisdom of God teaches the way of wisdom, authorises the way of wisdom, and gives access to it both by his invitation to the 'weary and heavy ladened' and by exemplifying it in the humble servanthood of his own way of life (cf. 12:15-21)."[34]

*Mark.* In contrast to Matthew's Gospel of Jesus the teacher of wisdom, Mark uses wisdom ideas to portray the identity of Jesus as hidden in a *mystery*. In this respect Mark's approach is reminiscent of Job 28; wisdom is real, but who will reveal it? And how will it be found? Indeed, the word "mystery" (Mk 4:11), which occurs nowhere else in the Synoptic Gospels, probably has a partial background in Wisdom 2:22, which refers to the secret purposes of God. Mark's preference for emphasizing the complexity of "seeing," "meeting" and "comprehending" Jesus as the Messiah almost certainly makes use of similar themes to those found in Second Temple literature.[35] The secret of Jesus' identity

---

[33]See Barton, "Gospel Wisdom," pp. 96-98.
[34]Ibid., p. 98.
[35]See Joel Marcus, "Mark 4:10-12 and Marcan Epistemology," *JBL* 103, no. 4 (1984): 557-74.

and mission can only come as a gift of God, who "reveals" him.[36]

Here, Barton points to the familiar passage in Mark 6:1-5, where Jesus' own family and community in Nazareth fail to understand Jesus' identity and authority:

> Jesus left there and went to his hometown, accompanied by his disciples. When the Sabbath came, he began to teach in the synagogue, and many who heard him were amazed. "Where did this man get these things?" they asked. "What's this *wisdom* that has been given him, that he even does miracles!"

A "mutual distancing" develops here: the people of his hometown take "offense" at Jesus (Mk 6:4), while he is "amazed at their unbelief" (Mk 6:6).[37] Ironically the people recognize the wisdom of his teaching and yet respond in unbelief. The *wisdom* required to see and follow Jesus must be revealed by the Father. The strongest Old Testament wisdom parallel to this is found in Job. Like the people of Jesus' hometown, Job is faced with a situation he cannot understand. Like Job, Jesus' hearers must learn that only the Father knows the way to the source of wisdom.

*Luke-Acts.* Most scholars agree that Luke has the greatest interest in the Spirit among the Synoptic Gospels. In fact, as Max Turner says, "The Spirit is the uniting motif and the driving force within the Lukan salvation history and legitimizes the mission to which this leads."[38] The Spirit is the agent that reveals to people God's work of ushering in the kingdom of Jesus and then enables them to respond to that kingdom in obedient living. Luke's approach to wisdom is tied not only to this revealing and enabling work of the Spirit but also to Jesus' teachings and example of prayer for his followers.

Luke's Gospel records a memorable scene during Jesus' childhood where he captivates the teachers in the temple with his answers to their questions (Lk 2:41-51), an event that marks him as a "messianic figure

---

[36]Ibid.

[37]Barton, "Gospel Wisdom," p. 101.

[38]Max Turner, "Luke and the Spirit: Renewing Theological Interpretation of Biblical Pneumatology," in *Reading Luke: Interpretation, Reflection, Formation,* ed. Craig Bartholomew, Joel B. Green and Anthony C. Thiselton (Grand Rapids: Zondervan, 2005), p. 268.

endowed with divine wisdom and certif[ies] Jesus' heroic character in a way appreciated by the Greco-Roman world."[39] This passage is enclosed by two references to Jesus' being "filled with wisdom" (Lk 1:40) and growing "in wisdom and stature" (Lk 2:52). Luke thus tells us that the Spirit provides for Jesus' ministry and self-understanding. And, like Jesus, Luke intends for us to receive the spirit of wisdom to pursue our own ministry.

As Joel Green and others also notice, prayer and the anointing of the Spirit are major links between Luke and Acts.[40] The story of Stephen in Acts 6–7 makes the connection to wisdom a central part of this linkage.[41] Stephen is selected among six others to assist the disciples by serving the widows (Acts 6:1-2). These men were all "full of the Spirit and of wisdom" (Acts 6:3), and Stephen in particular is singled out for being "full of God's grace and power," doing "great wonders and miraculous signs among the people" (Acts 6:8). When the Jewish leaders opposed Stephen, "they could not stand up against his wisdom or the Spirit by whom he spoke" (Acts 6:10). Stephen's long testimony in Acts 7:1-53 provokes the leaders to murder him. In the death scene Stephen is found "full of the Holy Spirit" and praying, "Lord Jesus, Receive my spirit" (Acts 7:55, 59). The fact that Paul watched and approved of this killing (Acts 7:58-8:1) and yet later writes about the radical nature of wisdom in Jesus is by no means coincidental. (See more on wisdom in Paul's letters below.)

Thus prayer and wisdom in Luke-Acts are not primarily hermeneutical or epistemological concepts, though they are certainly rich in both of dimensions; they are, rather, more an invitation for followers to *comprehend* and *participate* in God's redemptive work in Jesus, just as John, Stephen, Paul and others did. Prayer seeks the wisdom to understand God's redemptive work and our role in that unfolding drama. Prayer, together with the Spirit, also provides the way for us to grow in our

---

[39]Joel Green, *The Gospel of Luke*, NICNT (Grand Rapids: Eerdmans, 1997), p. 155.

[40]Ibid., pp. 71-73. Cf. Craig Bartholomew and Robby Holt, "Prayer in/and the Drama of Redemption in Luke: Prayer and Exegetical Performance," in *Reading Luke: Interpretation, Reflection, Formation*, ed. Craig Bartholomew, Joel B. Green and Anthony C. Thiselton (Grand Rapids: Zondervan, 2005), pp. 360-61.

[41]See Barton, "Gospel Wisdom," pp. 102-3.

spiritual transformation and in our understanding of God and Scripture, which reveals him.[42]

**John.** Although the Greek word *sophia* is absent from John's Gospel, an abundance of wisdom theology and themes is not.[43] Other prominent themes in the epistles and Gospels such as the kingdom of God and the resurrection are also largely omitted from John's highly symbolic book. Instead, John's Gospel has been particularly crafted to make symbolic use of Jewish theology to point to the uniqueness of Jesus as the God-man who brings God's glory and salvation. Wisdom theology appears in several ways.[44]

John's prologue (Jn 1:1-18; cf. Heb 1:1-3) presents the strongest blend of Greek and Hebrew wisdom in the New Testament. John writes to introduce the arrival of the *logos,* who was "in the beginning," "with God," equal to God and the one through whom "all things were made" (Jn 1:1-3). The *logos* was a dominant idea in ancient Greek philosophy, especially among the Stoics, and referred to the rational principle of the universe. But the term had also been used in Jewish circles by Philo of Alexandria to speak specifically about wisdom and God's creative word in Genesis 1:1-3. Thus John appropriates Greek ideas and language but fills them with Judeo-Christian theology to explain the Jesus event.

Not only is Genesis 1 evident in John's prologue, so too is the passage in Proverbs 8:22-31, where we read that Woman Wisdom was created by God in the beginning and became an agent in his original creation of the world. But if this is was John's intention, why did he choose the word *logos* to describe Jesus "in the beginning" rather than *nomos* ("law") or *sophia* ("wisdom"), which might seem more in line with John's Old Testament allusions? Among many probable reasons, a few stand out. First, the book of John is about the *man* Jesus the son of Joseph (Jn 1:45). The masculine *logos* is thus preferred to the feminine word *sophia.*

---

[42]Cf. Bartholomew and Holt, "Prayer," pp. 361-69.

[43]Barton, "Gospel Wisdom," p. 104.

[44]In what follows we draw on Peder Borgen, "The Gospel of John and Philo of Alexandria," pp. 46-76, and especially James H. Charlesworth, "Lady Wisdom and Johannine Christology," pp. 92-133, both in *Light in a Spotless Mirror: Reflections on Wisdom Traditions in Judaism and Early Christianity,* ed. James H. Charlesworth and Michael A. Daise (Harrisburg, Penn.: Trinity Press International, 2003).

Second, wisdom was the first work of God's creation, but still created (Prov 8:22-24), whereas the eternal idea of a Greek *logos* allows John to express Jesus' existence from the beginning with God. Third, *logos* is a larger concept than *nomos*, both philosophically and theologically; this allows John to assign much greater significance to Jesus' identity.

Fourth, the idea of wisdom incarnate or personified was nothing new to Jewish theology, but in John's Greek world *logos* was always seen as an immaterial idea. It was unimaginable to Greeks that the *logos* should become flesh. And yet this is precisely what John claims has happened in Jesus. John highlights Jesus' incarnation (Jn 1:14) and follows him all the way to Golgotha, carrying his own cross to die a fully human death (Jn 19:17). The Greek esteem for the perfect mind, the ascent of reason and the search for a perfect philosophy of the *logos* are blown apart here. We don't ascend to God on our own, as the Greeks would have it; rather, the eternal ordering power of the universe came down to be personally present to us. In the process he is humbly and willingly murdered and then powerfully raised again to establish eternal life here and now. Thus the point of the prologue is not "just" that Jesus was present at creation, or even that Jesus created with the Father, but that the same divine author of the first event has come in the flesh to begin his new creation.

Wisdom is also evident in John's emphasis on Jesus' "living" *(eskēnōsen)* among us (Jn 1:14). This is drawn from similar pictures of wisdom dwelling with humanity in both the Qumran scrolls (Ps 154:5-6) and Sirach 24:8.[45] Lady Wisdom, too, dwells with humanity, having been sent by God to bring his revelation and glory (Prov 8:30-31; Wis 7:25; 9:10). Jesus' own being sent and then sending his disciples pervades the whole gospel of John (Jn 1:6; 5:23; 12:45; 17:18).

Wisdom language informs John's Gospel in many other ways, including the "way," life and eternal life (cf. Prov 8:35); the bread from heaven (Jn 6:31-58); the vine (Jn 15:1-8; Sir 24:17); love; joy; and the picture of ascent and decent to which Jesus refers again and again. All of these were common wisdom themes.

---

[45]Charlesworth, "Lady Wisdom," pp. 102, 117.

More than any of the other Gospel writers, John has a sophisticated way of drawing on Greek and Hebrew wisdom theology in order to reshape it and thus present Jesus as the key to our salvation and flourishing in this world for all eternity.

## PAULINE EPISTLES

While the Gospels usually only make implicit use of wisdom to understand Jesus, the Pauline epistles[46] make explicit use of wisdom theology. Two overlapping wisdom themes appear in Paul's theology: (1) he uses wisdom ironically to expose the false wisdom of the surrounding cultures—Jewish and Greek—and (2) he portrays the unfolding wisdom of the Old Testament story, which now points to the identity of the Christ, his work in redemption and our lives in the newly begun creation. We will look at three Pauline texts to examine Paul's theology of wisdom more closely.

*First Corinthians 1–4.* While the two passages surveyed below demonstrate Paul's positive use of wisdom, an equivalent concern for Paul is to critique the rationalist and elitist patterns of wisdom in the Greco-Roman world of the early church.[47] First Corinthians and Romans contain the strongest expressions of Paul's counterwisdom rhetoric. The words "wisdom" (*sophia*) and "wise" (*sophos*) occur forty-four times in the thirteen Pauline letters; however, twenty-eight of these appear in 1 Corinthians—twenty-six in the first three chapters alone.

This is because, as Richard Hays rightly notes, Paul is speaking into a context where Greek wisdom had become so deeply infused in the Corinthian culture that it was manifesting itself adversely in boasting and pride in knowledge and speech.[48] Paul's solution, it must be said, is highly rhetorical speech itself, but in an ironic way. His opening

---

[46]We are aware of a general scholarly consensus that Paul did not write all the letters. In our opinion the evidence is not conclusive, and in the absence of clear alternatives, the convention of labeling the books as Pauline is convenient.

[47]There is nothing new about this aspect of Scripture. From Proverbs and Ecclesiastes to John and Paul, the Bible constantly affirms the shared content with wisdom in other cultures for the very purpose of emphasizing the uniqueness of wisdom, which comes only from the triune God.

[48]Richard B. Hays, "Wisdom According to Paul," in Barton, *Where Shall Wisdom Be Found*, pp. 111-23.

salutation gives thanks that God has given grace and blessed them in all "speech" and "knowledge" (1 Cor 1:5)—highly cherished virtues in Greek wisdom. Yet this is a set up, a friendly affirmation that will turn to rebuke and exhortation. In 1 Corinthians 1:20 Paul paraphrases several Old Testament texts to get to the heart of the Corinthian spirit: "Where is the wise man? Where is the scholar? Where is the philosopher [debater] of this age? Has not God made foolish the wisdom of the world?"

The Corinthians had used their expertise in rhetoric and knowledge to form elitist divisions in the church. Paul intends to use speech and knowledge as a means to present another form of wisdom. Though most scholars rightly recognize the foolishness of the cross of Christ as Paul's central critique of this culture, it is more accurate to say that he is using a fully trinitarian theology of wisdom[49] to make at least three points about the wisdom of God.

First, Paul contrasts their boasting about wisdom with his preaching, or "word" *(logos)*, of the cross. The "logos," we will see, is a different form of knowledge, resulting in a different form of speaking. The content of this new wisdom, centered on the cross, is foolishness to the Greek world—crucifixion was the basest form of criminal punishment of the Roman world. And yet it is the very "foundation" of the Christian gospel. Paul explains that since the world "in its wisdom did not know" God (1 Cor 1:21), God sent the apostles to "preach" Christ to Jews and Greeks as "the power of God and wisdom of God" (1 Cor 1:24). The content of this preaching is laid out in the next two points.

Second, this wisdom is apocalyptic and prophetic. There is a tendency in some conceptions of Jewish wisdom to think it is only about living successful, happy lives in the present. But wisdom is always oriented to creation, always grounded in God's original design for the world and its future flourishing in his care forever. In the cross of Christ, we encounter the glory and power of God's eternal kingdom

---

[49]E. Elizabeth Johnson, "Wisdom and Apocalyptic in Paul," in *In Search of Wisdom: Essays in Memory of John G. Gammie* (Louisville: Westminster John Knox, 1993), p. 276, argues that christocentric interpretations fall short of the full theocentric context. We agree and would go further to point to the intricate trinitarianism that flavors Paul's argument.

breaking into this world and initiating dramatic transformation and renewal. Notably, it is the "Spirit of wisdom" and "power" who anoints the church against the wisdom "of this age," which, in its ignorance, crucified the Lord of Glory (1 Cor 2:4, 10-11, 15). Wisdom knows how to recognize the *time* of redemption in the present.

Third, this wisdom extinguishes all boasting and imagines a new way. The Corinthians in their human boasting and divisions had been living out of the flesh and this age (1 Cor 1:11-13; 3:1-4; cf. Rom 1:18-23). But the foolishness of the cross lays the foundation for a new way of wisdom.

> But God chose the foolish things of the world to shame the wise; God chose the weak things of the world to shame the strong. He chose the lowly things of this world and the despised things—and the things that are not—to nullify the things that are, so that no one may boast before him. (1 Cor 1:27-29)

Thus, the cross here moves from a critique of self-seeking wisdom to provide a radically alternative way of life. Human boasting is eliminated on the one hand, but on the other hand, in its place Christ offers us "love rather than jealousy and quarreling. Authentic wisdom is thus characterized by unity and humility rather than by special knowledge or rhetorical skill."[50]

While many scholars take 1 Corinthians 4 as beginning a new section in the letter, it is nevertheless an extension of the argument in the first three chapters. In it Paul demonstrates how his and Apollos's lives are an outworking of the wisdom of the cross on display for the church in Corinth so that they might learn to end their pride and boasting (1 Cor 4:6-7). In contrast to the Corinthian habits of pridefully seeking wisdom, Paul and Apollos have become "fools for the sake of Christ" (1 Cor 4:10), enduring sacrifices and suffering (1 Cor 4:11-13) so that the Corinthians may learn to "imitate" them (1 Cor 4:16). This is cruciform living—an embodiment of the radical self-denial, love and suffering of the cross as the means to redemption and life. Speaking of 1 Corinthians 1:30, Hays captures this teaching wonderfully: "There is no such

---

[50]Hays, "Wisdom According to Paul," p. 120.

thing as 'wisdom' apart from covenant relationship with God ('right-eousness') that leads to holy living ('sanctification') made possible by God's act of delivering us from slavery ('redemption') through the cross. Those who are in Christ participate in this covenant reality."[51]

Paul uses a rhetoric of the cross to unmask the "wisdom" of the Corinthians. In the process what they considered wisdom is revealed to be folly! True wisdom is found in Christ alone, Lady Wisdom incarnate. This exposure of a false claim to "wisdom" has a striking parallel in Ecclesiastes. Qohelet thought he was exploring the world by "wisdom," but it turned out that he was blind to the folly of his autonomous way of knowing. "Wisdom" is not always what it claims to be.

Paul's preaching against false wisdom in 1 Corinthians and his similar writing in Colossians 2:8 have been used to argue that Christians should have nothing to do with philosophy and the wisdom of the world. The primary example of this view is found in chapter seven of Tertullian's work *Prescriptions Against Heretics*, where he says, "What does Jerusalem have to do with Athens?" It is important to note that this is a dangerous misrepresentation of Paul. He is not against philosophy but against wisdom and knowledge that is not rooted in Christ and used for Christ's purposes. Like Proverbs, Paul insists that if we go wrong at the start we will never attain true knowledge of the world. But, in Christ, we have the clue to all creation and are to pursue that clue in all areas of life.

***Colossians 1:15-20: Creation Christology.*** Colossians, like the other prison epistles (Ephesians, Philippians and Philemon), is a letter of exhortation seasoned by pastoral concern and prayers.[52] In almost all of these prayers, Paul asks God to give the churches "wisdom" and "understanding" (Eph 1:8, 17; 3:10; Col 1:9, 28; 2:3, 23; 3:16), which will help them to comprehend Jesus' cosmic work to redeem the world and also empower them with the appropriate response to their new membership in Christ and his kingdom. Although Philippians and Philemon lack the word "wisdom" *(sophia)*, their prayers still point to the same purposes—"that your love may abound more and more in knowl-

---

[51]Ibid., p. 117.
[52]Eph 1:15-22; 3:14-21; 6:18-20; Phil 1:3-11; Col 1:3-14; 4:2-4; Philem 4-6.

edge and depth of insight" (Phil 1:9) and that you may have a "full understanding *[epignōsei pantos]* of the good things we have in Christ" (Philem 6).

It is important to recognize the way the prayers shape the teachings in these texts; Paul is embodying the very theology he teaches. For us to grasp who God is, what he has done and what we must do in response is a matter of prayerful living—walking before the face of God, *coram Deo*. In the Father's presence we receive the wisdom and knowledge that orients our new life with God in Christ.

Thus, as we look briefly at the wisdom text in Colossians 1:15-23, we do so recognizing that Paul's doctrinal exposition flows out of his prayers: "Asking God to fill you with the knowledge of his will through all spiritual wisdom and understanding . . . that you may live a life worthy of the Lord and may please him in every way: bearing fruit in every good work, growing in the knowledge of God" (Col 1:9-10). At the height of the prayer, Paul then says of the Son:

> He is the image of the invisible God, the firstborn of all creation. For by him all things were created, in heaven and on earth, visible and invisible, whether thrones or dominions or rulers or authorities—all things were created through him and for him. And he is before all things, and in him all things hold together. And he is the head of the body, the church. He is the beginning, the firstborn from the dead, that in everything he might be preeminent. For in him all the fullness of God was pleased to dwell, and through him to reconcile to himself all things, whether on earth or in heaven, making peace by the blood of his cross. (Col 1:15-20 ESV)

This short passage embodies all the major hopes and expectation of the Second Temple period—the Messiah, we now see, is the preexistent king, coequal with the Father, the creator of the world and redeemer, through whom everything will be made new. It is also noteworthy how Paul is able to use wisdom to orient our epistemology (knowing and believing), ethics (behaving), redemption (salvation and transformation) and sense of community (human flourishing) in a prayer for wisdom.

Bauckham points out that this text has been used in Christian theology for three major purposes: (1) in seeking to establish the pre-existence of the Christ as Creator, (2) in developing a theology of the Son's dominion in overcoming both cosmic and worldly powers, and (3) in renewing a theology of creation, especially in response to the recent ecological crises.[53] While these are all fruitful lines of study, Bauckham suggests that it is better to say that the text moves from one extraordinary central reality in a thousand related directions all at once:

> It is God's wisdom that *orders* creation for its well-being, God's wisdom that *can be perceived* in the good order of the natural creation, God's wisdom that *ordains* good ways of human living in the world, and God's wisdom that, beyond the disruption of creation's good by evil, *purposes* the ultimate well-being, the shalom, the peace of the whole creation. . . . Where is [this] wisdom to be found? Wisdom is found in the whole creation and it is found in the crucified and risen Jesus and somehow these two are the same.[54]

***Ephesians 1:3-14: Spiritual Wisdom.*** Whereas Colossians places more emphasis on a theology of new creation in Christ, Ephesians has a stronger sense of the *spirituality of wisdom* in the Christian life—our mysterious union with the trinitarian God in Christ. Three things contribute to this spiritual tone of the letter.

First, this spiritual wisdom is visible above all by the prevalence of prayer. The first prayer or blessing to God (Eph 1:3-14), consisting of twelve verses, is an unbroken sentence in the Greek. The first two verses summarize the running list of praises that unfold there: "Praise be to the God and Father of our Lord Jesus Christ, who has blessed us in the heavenly realms with every spiritual blessing in Christ. For he chose us in him before the creation of the world to be holy and blameless in his sight."

A prayer of thanksgiving picks up again in Ephesians 1:16-23 and then again in Ephesians 3:14-19, with a final flourish of praise in Ephe-

[53]Richard Bauckham, "Where Is Wisdom to be Found? Colossians 1.15-20 (2)," in *Reading Texts, Seeking Wisdom: Scripture and Theology*, ed. David Ford and Graham Stanton (Grand Rapids: Eerdmans, 2003), pp. 129-38.
[54]Ibid., p. 132, italics added.

sians 3:20-21, thus encompassing and filling the first three chapters in and with prayer.

Second, these prayers rejoice that God the Father has "blessed us in the heavenly realms with every spiritual blessing in Christ" (Eph 1:3). Thomas Yoder Neufeld says that many of these terms of spiritual encounter are unique to Ephesians and lack precise definition. Paul is speaking of mysterious realities that surpass common understandings of time, place and human nature.[55] Somehow, it appears, realities from a future heavenly place are being realized here and now by virtue of our being "in Christ."

Third, the church, as Paul says in Ephesians 1, has been predestined for these blessings from all eternity, blessings we have *in Christ:* "In him we have redemption through his blood, the forgiveness of sins, in accordance with the riches of God's grace" (Eph 1:7). This group of phrases, "in him" and "in Christ," is unique to Paul's writings. Ephesians uses the phrase at double the rate of the other Pauline books; it appears eleven times just in this first twelve-verse prayer!

"In Christ" also dominates the other "cosmic wisdom" epistles, where we also find Paul writing in the midst of prayer. But just what does this phrase mean? Dunn suggests that to be "in Christ" is to be born into a mysterious union and participation with him both in his death and resurrection (cf. Eph 1:7; Col 1:15-20).[56] Many, however, are inclined to limit this phrase only to symbolic or spiritual levels. In our opinion this misses the full power of the realities Paul so emphatically declares. Our membership in Christ is a mysterious union that is spiritual, physical and ontological (at the level of our very being). *Only a creation theology is able to capture the benefits we have in him.*

As we saw in Luke-Acts above, this new relationship with God is connected to prayer, the Spirit and wisdom. The same is true here, as Paul combines being in Christ with wisdom and salvation:

> In him we have redemption through his blood, the forgiveness of sins,
> in accordance with the riches of God's grace that he lavished on us with

---

[55]Thomas R. Yoder Neufeld, *Ephesians,* BCBS (Scottdale, Penn.: Herald, 2002), pp. 40-43.
[56]Dunn, *Theology of Paul the Apostle,* pp. 410-11.

all wisdom and understanding. And he made known to us the mystery of his will according to his good pleasure, which he purposed in Christ, to be put into effect when the times will have reached their fulfillment—to bring all things in heaven and on earth together under one head, even Christ. (Eph 1:7-10)

Paul describes nothing less than a new event of creation, which brings about God's eternal plans for the world. Now, in Christ, we have been given not just the intellectual comprehension of these events; but we have also actually died and been re-created into the new cosmic world that is being reconciled in Christ. Consider how Paul combines the terms "wisdom" (*sophia*) and "insight" (*phronēsis*) (Eph 1:8), a word pair that occurs throughout Proverbs 1–9, but most notably in Proverbs 8:1, during Woman Wisdom's longest speech. Neufeld rightly argues that we cannot ignore the Old Testament idea of the personification of Woman Wisdom being applied to Christ: "In *Wisdom* we come face to face with the immeasurable. . . . It is difficult if not impossible to set limits to the allusive and evocative power of Ephesians."[57] The call to love and embrace Woman Wisdom is now expanded beyond its previous limits as we are beckoned to awake to the new life we have in Eternal Wisdom himself.

*James.* James is well known for his call to anyone who lacks wisdom to "ask God, who gives generously to all without finding fault" (Jas 1:5). Unlike Paul, or the Synoptic writers, James does not aim to equate Jesus with personified wisdom or messianic wisdom. Instead, James's book aims more broadly to "move his readers towards 'perfection' (1:4; 3:2) through fulfillment of the 'law of freedom' (1:25; 2:8, 10, 12) and through the wisdom God gives (1:5; 3:17)."[58] In this way, James is most like the Hebrew wisdom sayings in Proverbs and Sirach, but also close to Jesus' wisdom sayings, which we discussed above. Rather than delivering an argument or constructing a theological perspective, James writes to a Jewish audience to continue seeking wisdom and lawfulness, which they learned as Jews, but now as followers of "the Lord Jesus Christ" (Jas 1:1).

---

[57]Neufeld, *Ephesians*, p. 49.
[58]Richard Bauckham, *James: Wisdom of James, Disciple of Jesus the Sage* (New York: Routledge, 1999), p. 35.

In his excellent study of James, Bauckham outlines fives types of sayings in James:[59]

## 1. Aphorism

In the same way, faith by itself, if it is not accompanied by action, is dead. (Jas 2:17)

## 2. Similitude and parable

As the body without the spirit is dead, so faith without deeds is dead. (Jas 2:26)

## 3. Example or model

Elijah was a man just like us. He prayed earnestly that it would not rain, and it did not rain on the land for three and a half years. Again he prayed, and the heavens gave rain, and the earth produced its crops. (Jas 5:17-18)

## 4. Prophetic judgment oracle

Now listen, you rich people, weep and wail because of the misery that is coming upon you. Your wealth has rotted, and moths have eaten your clothes. Your gold and silver are corroded. Their corrosion will testify against you and eat your flesh like fire. You have hoarded wealth in the last days. Look! The wages you failed to pay the workmen who mowed your fields are crying out against you. The cries of the harvesters have reached the ears of the Lord Almighty. You have lived on earth in luxury and self-indulgence. You have fattened yourselves in the day of slaughter. You have condemned and murdered innocent men, who were not opposing you. (Jas 5:1-6)

## 5. Diatribe

But someone will say, "You have faith; I have deeds."

Show me your faith without deeds, and I will show you my faith by what I do. You believe that there is one God. Good! Even the demons believe that—and shudder.

You foolish man, do you want evidence that faith without deeds is

---

[59]Ibid., pp. 35-60.

useless? Was not our ancestor Abraham considered righteous for what he did when he offered his son Isaac on the altar? You see that his faith and his actions were working together, and his faith was made complete by what he did. And the scripture was fulfilled that says, "Abraham believed God, and it was credited to him as righteousness," and he was called God's friend. (Jas 2:18-23)

To us, James's epistle is most intriguing for the way it brings us back to the Old Testament themes of wisdom, torah and living well in God's created order. The exalted Lord Christ (e.g., Jas 1:1; 2:1) takes the place of the fear of the LORD, giving wisdom a more eschatological flavor. The Creator has redeemed his creation from within and will return again soon in judgment. With his victory and the model of his earthly life, our pursuit of wisdom and Torah are intensified, not eliminated.

This comes to expression in the overarching theme of James, which encompasses all the other concerns, namely *wholeness*.[60] This theme is introduced in 1:2-4; trials are to be embraced because they produce endurance and the result is that the readers may be *teleioi kai holoklēroi* (mature and complete). *Teleios* with its cognate verb *teleioun* forms a favorite word group of James and his use of this word group is a major way in which he articulates the theme of completeness or integrality (1:4, 17; 2:8, 22; 3:2). Significantly, the two words occur seven times— seven symbolizing completeness—just as God's wisdom is character- ized in 3:17 by seven qualities.

Bauckham helpfully analyzes James's treatment of wholeness and in- tegrality in terms of five aspects. First, integration is concerned with the wholeness of the individual and the community. The whole person is whole*heartedly* devoted to God; the heart being as in Old Testament wisdom literature the source of words and deeds (1:26; 3:12, 14). The person in James is viewed holistically as embodied and constituted of

---

[60]On the importance of the theme of wholeness in James see also Raymond A. Martin, *James* (Nashville: Thomas Nelson, 1988); Elsa Tamez, *The Scandalous Message of James: Faith without Works is Dead* (New York: Crossroad, 1992); and J. H. Elliot, "The Epistle of James in Rhe- torical and Social Scientific Perspective—Wholeness and Patterns of Replication" *BTB* 23 (1993): 71-81. Perfection is also a major theme in Hebrews. See David L. Petersen, *Hebrews and Perfection: An Examination of the Concept of Perfection in the "Epistle to the Hebrews"* SNTSMS 47 (Cambridge: Cambridge University Press, 1982). Petersen, however, lacks the new creation eschatological insight grasped so clearly by Bauckham.

heart, speech, and the hands or the whole body. "Thus the whole life of an individual is integrated or included in the total dedication of the person to the service of God."[61] Similarly the community is called to be whole (2:13; 3:13, 17; 4:11-12; 5:16, 19). Remarkably, 1:18 extends the idea of wholeness to the whole creation! Second, wholeness is related to the *exclusion* of that which militates against it. As 4:4 states one cannot be friends with "the world" and with God. James's dualism is not one of earth versus heaven but one of life lived in obedience to God in opposition to life lived in disobedience to God.[62] Third, in James wholeness is achieved by adding one thing to another (cf. 3:17). The law is a whole and must be fulfilled as such (2:8-13). Suffering and patience in suffering (1:2-4; 5:7-11) must be endured since they are part of the journey to wholeness. Fourth, wholeness involves consistency. Wholeness requires that what one does is consistent with what one says, with one's hearing, knowing, saying and believing. "In other words, wholeness is about the consistent devotion of the whole person, the whole of life, the whole community and ultimately the whole cosmos to God."[63] Fifth, in James it is God who ultimately embodies wholeness. As Bauckham notes, "At stake is the belief that the wholeness of human life is possible only in relation to a specific centre outside of the self: God."[64]

Two more points bear drawing out in relation to James's emphasis on Torah and wisdom. First, James demands law-keeping (righteousness) as a necessary part of true faith (Jas 1:22-25; 2:8-26). This teaching, once a major stumbling block for Luther and other Reformers fixed on justification by faith alone, has in recent decades been shown to be far closer to Paul's teaching on faith and works than was originally conceived. For Paul and James, mere assent to Christ's lordship is inadequate, because it only involves our rational capacity. With the whole creation redeemed, James's goal is to bring his readers to full "perfection" or "wholeness" (Jas 1:4). Our journey through the Old Testament wisdom books in previous chapters of this book helps us understand

---

[61]Bauckham, *James*, p. 178.
[62]See Bauckham's helpful comments in this respect (ibid., pp. 179-80).
[63]Ibid., p. 181.
[64]Ibid., p. 183.

how wisdom, grounded in God's eternal design for creation, always aimed at making us fully human in what we believe, who we are and what we do. Thus, for James, salvation is both forgiveness from sins (Jas 5:16) and completion or perfection of human life on earth in our relation to God, ourselves, our neighbor, our speech and our work—themes that run throughout the Old Testament Wisdom literature. In the New Testament, wisdom and law still point the way to this whole and ordered life, as does the exalted Christ, who models for us the humility, endurance and obedience in death and victory in resurrection.

Second, James creatively uses Old Testament law and wisdom to draw us into a moral life radically transformed by Jesus' life and death.[65] Bauckham again notes that James's letter only formally cites two Old Testament texts, both carefully selected to stand as summaries of the law and wisdom: Leviticus 19:18 in James 2:8 and Proverbs 3:34 in James 4:6.[66] The context for the Proverbs passage in James is an extended discussion on wisdom from above and wisdom from below (Jas 3:17–4:10): "But he gives us more grace. That is why Scripture says: 'God opposes the proud but gives grace to the humble'" (Jas 4:6). The message here complements the section that quotes the Leviticus passage: "Love your neighbor as yourself" (Jas 2:8). In its extended context (Jas 2:1-13), this passage from Old Testament Torah focuses our attention on remembering the poor and avoiding the temptation to favoritism. The lengthy passage on wisdom from above (Jas 3:17–4:10) similarly encourages self-humiliation, meekness and lowliness, leaving God to exalt us in the end (Jas 4:10).

Jesus' own teachings continually draw our eyes to the needs of the poor, and James adopts this pattern applying it to the church as a way of life for us to embody.[67] As Bauckham explains: "Now, in the messianic renewal of God's people through the Messiah Jesus, God has again chosen the poor to be the paradigmatic members of this renewed Israel ... in some sense the model to which all other members must conform."[68]

---

[65]See the helpful book by David E. Holwerda, *Jesus and Israel: One Covenant or Two?* (Grand Rapids: Eerdmans, 1995).
[66]Bauckham, *James*, pp. 142-55.
[67]See Peter H. Davids, *The Epistle of James*, NIGCT (Grand Rapids: Eerdmans, 1982), p. 45.
[68]Bauckham, *James*, pp. 192-93.

Thus wisdom and law in James remind us of the character-consequence teaching that dominates so much of Proverbs and Job. Not only are we to be wary of riches and sympathetic to the poor as emphasized throughout the law and Proverbs; but also now, transformed by our faith, we follow Christ into our own simplicity and poverty as the means for God to powerfully establish his kingdom among us.

## CONCLUSION

Wisdom is not *the* key to interpreting the New Testament, but one cannot understand Jesus, his kingdom or his redemption without it. The neglect of Old Testament wisdom has led to a neglect of the wisdom dimension of the New Testament. In this chapter we have only been able to scratch the surface of the myriad ways in which Old Testament wisdom informs the New Testament, but it should be clear that taking wisdom seriously leads us to a bigger view of Jesus and a greater sense of his relevance for all of life. Jesus is Lady Wisdom incarnate; he is the one in whom, by whom, through whom and for whom this world was made.

The incarnation signals a dramatic shift in the storyline of the Bible. Wisdom in the Old Testament focuses on the created order, what can be called God's structure for the world. But it does not give attention to the overarching direction of the creation—how the world will move from creation to fall and back to a redeemed new creation again. Wisdom in the New Testament affirms the creation order of the Old Testament, but it focuses it historically in the mystery of God's purposes bound up in Jesus, the agent who saves creation and leads it to the destiny God always intended for it. In Christ, God himself has taken on the human role of redemption and blessing previously assigned to Israel and then given it back not just to Israel but also to all the nations and peoples of the world. Wisdom then embodies the new, radical way for us to live in God's world and play our role in proclaiming and conforming to his kingship.

## RECOMMENDED READING

Barton, Stephen C., ed. *Where Shall Wisdom Be Found? Wisdom in the Bible, the*

*Church and the Contemporary World.* Edinburgh: T & T Clark, 1999.

Bauckham, Richard. *James: Wisdom of James, Disciple of Jesus the Sage.* New York: Routledge, 1999.

Charlesworth, James. H., and Michael A. Daise, eds. *Light in a Spotless Mirror: Reflections on Wisdom Traditions in Judaism and Early Christianity.* New York: Trinity Press International, 2003.

Sheppard, Gerald T. *Wisdom as a Hermeneutical Construct: A Study in the Sapientializing of the Old Testament.* BZAW 151. Berlin: Walter de Gruyter, 1980.

# 11

# The Theology of
# Old Testament Wisdom

*The wise man is the one who sees reality as it is,*
*and who sees into the depths of things. That is why only*
*that man is wise who sees reality in God.*

—DIETRICH BONHOEFFER, *ETHICS*

In OUR OPINION A BIBLICAL HERMENEUTIC is incomplete if it does not culminate in reflecting on God's address to us today. In these final two chapters we move in that direction. In this chapter we draw together the threads of the previous chapters and ask what a coherent theology of Old Testament wisdom looks like. In the final section we explore the relationship between Old Testament wisdom and other parts of the Old Testament. In the concluding chapter we will examine examples of the ways in which Old Testament wisdom helps us to hear God's address today.

## THE WISDOM OF CREATION
We noted in chapter two that Old Testament wisdom shares with wisdom in the ancient Near East an understanding of the whole of life as ordered by the divine. Wisdom's notion of creation order is akin to that of Ma'at in Egypt and the concept of wisdom and law in the literature of Mesopotamia. Thus Old Testament wisdom is distinctive not in its sense of an order to creation but because of its understanding of the

single divine source of that order: "Over against the polytheistic naturalism of Babylonia and the confused 'consubstantial' ideas of the
Egyptian pantheon, Israel affirmed, 'The Lord our God, the Lord is
one.'"[1] This ethical monotheism is one of the most astonishing "achievements" of Israel:

> With some entail of that danger always implicit in superlatives one may
> raise the question whether any other single contribution from whatever
> source since human culture emerged from the stone ages has had the
> far-reaching effect upon history that Israel in this regard has exerted
> both through the mediums of Christianity and Islam and directly
> through the world of Jewish thinkers themselves.[2]

Israel's monotheism is now granted so readily that we easily overlook
the radicality of this belief in the context of the ancient Near East. In
Egypt, Ma'at was the goddess of creation. Thus in some way all the
gods are said to live by Ma'at's ordering of the world. Yet neither Ma'at
nor the divine pharaoh, who was most responsible for her, created the
world. In other words, we find a conspicuous lack of the centering of
creation order in the one God, Yahweh, of the Bible. Egypt is like most
other polytheistic religions in this way with the absence of a center that
transcends the creation and speaks authoritatively from the outside.
Lacking such authority, these ancient cultures produced countless wisdom documents and mythological stories without great concern for
their consistency.

Proverbs, however, presupposes and teaches ethical monotheism—
there is one God and one source of wisdom. The interlude in Proverbs
3:13-20 is a long praise of wisdom's great worth. The last and most
important of her many praises is that Yahweh used her to create the
world. The power of this claim is its uniqueness in the ancient Near
East. There is only one God and creator, and wisdom is the key to getting in touch with him and his purposes for us. Proverbs 3:19 is clear

---

[1]William Irwin, "God," in Henri Frankfort et al., *The Intellectual Adventure of Ancient Man: An Essay on Speculative Thought in the Ancient Near East* (Chicago: University of Chicago Press, 1946), p. 224.
[2]Ibid. Cf. also Rodney Stark, *Discovering God: The Origins of the Great Religions and the Evolution of Belief* (New York: HarperOne, 2007), pp. 156-209, 393-99.

and emphatic[3] that *Yahweh* by wisdom founded the earth; he *alone* by understanding established the heavens. Furthermore, the earth, the heavens, the deeps and the clouds are his creations and not divine in any sense. Israel's unique conjunction of ethical monotheism with wisdom points to four major implications for Israel's worldview.

### Wonder.

Wonder is the first of all the passions.[4]

My main concern at that time was to assign a place to the act of adoration in a world which seemed more and more determined to banish it.[5]

Contrary to the nations that surrounded her, Israel's religion positioned its people before a single source of authority, wisdom and power; any questions that arose in the course of daily experience ultimately lead back to Yahweh, the single source of creation and the sovereign ruler over it. More than anything else, this meant that Israel lived with an overwhelming sense of wonder—what Gerhard von Rad calls remaining open in a serious way to the mysterious.[6] Oliver O'Donovan says that "wonder and incomprehension are not the first aspect of Wisdom that is usually spoken of; yet they are, it seems to me, fundamental to the wisdom project. . . . The fear of the Lord begins in comprehending wonder."[7] Proverbs 30:18-19 is a good example of the sense of wonder that pervades Proverbs:

> Three things are too wonderful for me;
>     four I do not understand:
> the way of an eagle in the sky,
>     the way of a snake on a rock,
> the way of a ship on the high seas,
>     and the way of a man with a girl. (NRSV)

---

[3]Indicated by the fact that "Yahweh" occurs first in the sentence contrary to the normal order of verb-subject-object.

[4]René Descartes, *The Passions of the Soul*, trans. Stephen H. Voss (Indianapolis: Hackett, 1989), p. 52.

[5]Gabriel Marcel, *Tragic Wisdom and Beyond*, trans. Stephen Jolin and Peter McCormick (Evanston, Ill.: Northwestern University Press, 1973), pp. 193-94.

[6]Gerhard von Rad, *Wisdom in Israel*, trans. James D. Martin (London: SCM, 1970), pp. 72-73.

[7]Oliver O'Donovan, "Response to Craig Bartholomew," in *A Royal Priesthood: The Use of the Bible Ethically and Politically* (Carlisle, U.K.: Paternoster, 2002), p. 113.

Proverbs 30:1-4 speaks of the limits of our knowledge of God, whereas these verses speak of the limits of our knowledge even of his creation. As Raymond van Leeuwen rightly notes, "These verses portray simple wonder at marvelous phenomena in God's creation."[8] O'Donovan is right to say that, whatever its confidence in wisdom and God's ordering of the world, the text of Proverbs "remains poised at the point of wonder."[9]

Thus it is appropriate for wisdom in the New Testament to be oriented to God's appearance in the flesh as the ultimate source of wonder and mystery. Paul's blessing in Ephesians 1 declares that in wisdom and understanding God has "made known to us the mystery of his will according to his good pleasure, which he purposed in Christ" (Eph 1:9). In Colossians Paul describes Jesus' work of redemption as a mystery, which Jews now share with Gentiles as "Christ in you, the hope of glory" (Col 1:27). For Paul (Rom 11:33-36) and for Peter (1 Pet 1:10-12), the "depths" and "glory" of God's work are present by way of our union with Christ. The marital love that accompanies our search for wisdom in Proverbs is attached to Jesus, the bridegroom of the church. We attend to this mystery not in some analytical, detached way, but as the very object of our adoration, righteousness, salvation, glory and eternal hope.

*Comprehensive scope.*

All the colors of this most beautiful world grow pale once you extinguish its light, the firstborn of creation.[10]

But if we look for the world's explanation beyond itself and find it in a God who is infinite and self-existent love, bliss and splendour, then we can look back and see it bathed in his beauty and reflecting it from its myriads of facets.[11]

---

[8]Raymond van Leeuwen, "Proverbs," in *The New Interpreter's Bible,* ed. Leander Keck (Nashville: Abingdon, 1997), 5:254.
[9]O'Donovan, "Response," p. 114.
[10]Johann G. Hamann, *Writings on Philosophy and Language,* ed. and trans. Kenneth Haynes (Cambridge: Cambridge University Press, 2007), p. 78.
[11]Eric Lionel Mascall, *The Christian Universe* (Wilton, Conn.: Morehouse-Barlow, 1966), pp. 64-65.

Jesus' incarnation and his bodily resurrection are the strongest affirmations of the goodness of creation. Sadly, this is not a truth that the church has always grasped. Rodney Stark notes that in the axial period, the period of the emergence of the great monotheistic religions, polytheism became increasingly embarrassing, providing a weak basis for philosophical reasoning and public life.[12] In search of truth, justice, and right and wrong, an increasing need was felt for more than wandering myths and the "immoral" nonsense carried out by the gods that had satisfied earlier generations.[13]

As Greek philosophy began its rise to dominance in the fifth century B.C., it was strengthened by a singular though ambiguous god as the source of truth and justice. But as this philosophy developed, the major paradigm was that of Plato's dualism, where God, the mind, and the Good all existed as forms and ideas, separated from the physical world below. With truth and justice above and the creation below, a new view of creation took hold as chaotic, imperfect and evil. A similarly negative approach to the material world was embodied in ancient Gnosticism.

Gnostic dualism quickly took root in pagan, Jewish and Christian thinking. The primary sources for Christian Gnosticism were the Gnostic Gospels, often attributed to Peter, James, Pilate, Judas and Mary Magdalene. Until the last century these were only known through Irenaeus's strong critique in his *Against Heresies* (A.D. 180). As Stark explains:

> It has long been charged by scholars that Irenaeus greatly misrepresented these "heretics," the better to discredit them, which seemed a reasonable judgment when one read the absurd views he attributed to each author. Then, in the late nineteenth century, several of these "lost Gospels" were discovered. . . . Guess what? The good bishop had followed the original texts essentially word for word, distorting nothing, perhaps thinking that they "were so contorted and ludicrous that the heretics were best condemned out of their own mouths."[14]

---

[12]Stark, *Discovering God*, pp. 202-3.

[13]Ibid., p. 323.

[14]Ibid., p. 325. Additional quotation from Philip Jenkins, *Hidden Gospels: How the Search for Jesus Lost Its Way* (Oxford: Oxford University Press, 2001), p. 29.

But, as Stark perceptively observes, "Remarkably enough, these 'lost' scriptures enjoy much greater credibility today than they ever did back when they were written."[15] As we will note in chapter twelve, we live amid a resurgent Gnosticism, presenting comparable challenges to those Irenaeus faced.

Here we note, contra Gnosticism, wisdom's welcome embrace of the creation and the goodness of its created order. This is extremely important today, just as it was in Israel's ancient context. Not only is the divine source of creation order unitary in the Old Testament but also, unlike the gods of Egypt and Mesopotamia, Yahweh is not indifferent to his creation and humankind. Rather, he longs that his people might find his wisdom built into his creation and live life to the full in accordance with it. In Proverbs 8:22-31 Yahweh's wisdom is personified as a master worker (Prov 8:30) and integrally part of his marvelous work of creation. His wisdom in creation is described as "daily his delight" (Prov 8:30), and in comparison with ancient Near Eastern creation stories Proverbs 8:31 is significant: wisdom rejoices in Yahweh's inhabited world and delights in the human race! Nothing could be further removed from the indifference of the ancient Near Eastern gods than Yahweh's exhilarating engagement with the creation. It is a picture of a master craftsman fully engaged and taking pure joy in his skilled work. Indeed, "Israel's great attainment was the vision that we may walk this earth with the confident tread of a son in his father's house."[16]

This section in Proverbs 8 makes it clear that the whole of the creation is a result of Yahweh's wise craftsmanship: it includes the earth; the depths; the shaping of the mountains, fields and soil; the heavens; the skies; the sea; and the inhabited world—that is, nature, humankind *and* culture. God's creation *by his wisdom* is utterly comprehensive, and we should not be at all surprised that the wisdom offered to and needed by humans is therefore also comprehensive. Creation and wisdom thus thoroughly subvert the Christian dualism that has become so commonplace in too much contemporary Christianity in which the "soul" and the church—the sacred—are all that matter while the rest of the cre-

---

[15]Ibid.
[16]Irwin, "God," p. 230.

ation—the secular—is left to go its own way. Theologian Gordon Spykman captures the utter comprehensiveness of wisdom succinctly: "Nothing matters but the kingdom, but because of the kingdom everything matters."[17] Craig often uses the popular chorus, "Turn your eyes upon Jesus, look full in his wonderful face, and the things of the earth will grow strangely dim, in the light of his glory and grace," as an example of the incipient gnosticism in contemporary Christianity. While we understand the positive sentiment in this chorus, we suggest that a wise, more biblical version would be: "Turn your eyes upon Jesus, look full in his wonderful face, and the things of the earth will receive their true perspective, in the light of his glory and grace."

It is instructive to see the comprehensive areas that wisdom addresses in Proverbs 1–9. Proverbs 1:8-19 warns against resorting to violence against the innocent in order to accrue wealth. In many countries of the world, such as South Africa, in which Craig grew up, such teaching has a powerful contemporary and literal relevance. But in the United States, where Ryan grew up, corporations and businesses are far from immune to corruption and practices that oppress workers, often based in poorer countries. In Proverbs 1:20-32 Lady Wisdom calls out in the public areas of Israel's life: the squares, where business and public life were conducted, and in the city gates, where the courts would sit to administer justice. Similarly Proverb 8:2-3 goes out of its way to stress that the call of wisdom (cf. Prov 8:1) is heard everywhere in daily life: on the heights, beside the way, at the crossroads, beside the gates and at the entrance of the portals!

Because God created the world by wisdom, there is no area of created life to which wisdom does not apply. J. B. Phillips wrote a famous book titled *Your God Is Too Small*. This remains true of far too many Christians today. As John Stott once noted, if you listen to our prayers in church, you would think we worshiped the local deity! Old Testament wisdom demolishes such a small, restricted view of a God who is confined to church life and our private lives. Biblical wisdom is foundational for both private *and* public life, for practical *and* theoretical

---

[17]Gordon J. Spykman, *Reformational Theology: A New Paradigm for Doing Dogmatics* (Grand Rapids: Eerdmans, 1992), p. 478.

knowledge, for church *and* culture. Little wonder, therefore, that the author of Proverbs describes the fear of the LORD as the *beginning* of wisdom. God's wisdom is enormous, and the fear of the LORD is the place from which to begin a journey of exploration that is as vast as the cosmos itself.

*Individual.* Western culture is deeply individualistic, and much Western Christianity has followed suit. It is thus helpful to note how Proverbs 1–9 addresses the civic life of Israel *as well as* the individual. If Western Christianity is vulnerable to a sacred/secular dichotomy, it is also guilty of an individualistic Christianity that reduces faith to a personal matter with no or little public responsibility. We have noted above how Lady Wisdom addresses all of Israelite life but also how the one valiant woman in Proverbs 31 literally applies her "hands" to everything from baking, crafts and agriculture to public works of mercy and trading in the marketplace. This alerts us to the appeal to the individual Israelite in Proverbs 1–9. The most common form of address in this section is to "my son," singular (cf. Prov 1:8; 2:1; 3:1, 21; 5:1; 6:1; 7:1). In Proverbs 4:1, 5:7 and 7:24 the plural "sons" is used. Intriguingly in the conclusion to Proverbs 8 (Prov 8:34), "Blessed is the person [literally "man"]," is used to sum up the advantages of wisdom.

As we noted in our discussion of Proverbs, "my son" should not be taken to mean that the teaching is relevant only to young boys; Proverbs 1:1-6 makes this clear, as does the use of "person" in Proverbs 8:34. The reference to "my son" is part of the awareness in Proverbs that finding wisdom at the liminal points of life is of great consequence to what follows. "My son" is part of the liminal rhetoric of Proverbs. For our purposes, what is relevant is that Proverbs clearly stresses the importance of *the individual's* pursuing wisdom. In this way Proverbs 1–9 is akin to Psalms 1–2—the introduction to the Psalter. Psalm 2 deals with the nations, thereby reminding us that the instruction (Torah) of Yahweh has international and creation-wide implications. But Psalm 1 begins with the individual person and only moves to the plural when it deals with the wicked. Wisdom *must* be personally and individually pursued and appropriated, but it can never be confined to one's personal life alone.

William Irwin highlights an important contrast between Israel's wisdom and wisdom in the rest of the ancient Near East. In relation to Proverbs 3:13-15, in which finding wisdom and understanding is better than obtaining silver, gold and rubies, he notes that

> the striking feature of this is the repudiation of precisely those good things which earlier sages had accepted as the ends of life: gold, silver, rubies, things of desire. Since the days of the Egyptian sage Ptahhotep these had been prized as the mark and content of life's worth. But here some Hebrew thinker—rather, it appears, the entire late school of Hebrew sages—asserts boldly that there is something else in life which far transcends them, or through which at most these can best be enjoyed.[18]

Proverbs celebrates all of life as God has made it. But, in line with the overall message of the Old Testament, Proverbs insists that the gifts must never be placed above the giver. Indeed, because all of life was created by God in his wisdom, "the ultimate reality in the physical world is the wisdom of God!"[19] And even among the people of God—Israel—the sages recognized that wisdom must be *personally* appropriated and pursued.

***Imaging God.*** With its roots in the doctrine of creation, Old Testament wisdom, unsurprisingly, has myriad connections with Genesis 1–3. Genesis 1:26-28 describes humankind as made in the image of God. This *imago Dei* is dynamic in the sense that, as humans live under God's reign, they manifest his likeness in the creation. Wisdom gets at the same point. As we noted above, in Proverbs 8 Yahweh's wisdom is personified: "He took, we might say, this attribute and built it into the nature of things as they are, most of all into the being of man."[20] And it is precisely *this* wisdom that the Old Testament wisdom books say is available to us: "For Yahweh gives wisdom" (Prov 2:6). Life, as we know, is a complex business; Proverbs 10–31 and especially Job and Ecclesiastes make this crystal clear. How inestimably valuable, therefore, to have access to the very wisdom by which the world has been made and by which it is sustained! And it follows that the wiser we become, the more we become like God; we image him in his good creation.

---

[18]Irwin, "Man," in Frankfort et al., *Intellectual Adventure*, p. 288.
[19]Ibid., p. 290.
[20]Ibid., pp. 289-90.

In Egypt, Pharaoh's mouth was regarded as the temple of Ma'at. Pharaoh was himself regarded as one of the gods. In such a context it is easy to see the premium on wisdom that would be granted to one man. Intriguingly, in Israel wisdom is thoroughly democratized; it is available to all who will attend to its call and seek it earnestly. The striking image of the valiant woman of wisdom in Proverbs 31 undermines the male and regal associations of wisdom in most ancient cultures. Because wisdom's source is Yahweh, it is freely available to all of his people, male and female, rich and poor. As we noted, Proverbs 1–9 addresses "my son" in particular, but Proverbs as a whole ends with an incarnate embodiment of wisdom in a wealthy Israelite *woman*.

And here is the notable supremacy of Hebrew thought over its apparent parallel in Plato. He envisioned a republic led by elite philosopher kings; but for the Hebrew thinker the appeal of wisdom was to all people, wherever and whatever they might be; in particular it called to the simple and foolish, for whom Plato would have had only a place of menial service.[21]

## The Character-Consequence Motif of Wisdom

Not surprisingly Proverbs goes out of its way to evoke the benefits of attaining wisdom:

> Her income is better than silver,
>     and her revenue better than gold. (Prov 3:14 nrsv)

Contrary to Egyptian thought, wisdom offers something *better* than silver and gold, but does it offer anything less than prosperity and wealth?

In the past, Proverbs has often been taken to present a naive view of retribution in which obedience and virtue leads automatically to blessing—both material and spiritual—and disobedience leads to a curse. Job is then said to challenge this in a major way—aside from its problematic epilogue, which reinstates retribution. Ecclesiastes is said to trash the idea of retribution altogether. Now it *is* true that Proverbs 1–9 clearly teaches the character-consequence structure of life through the

[21]Ibid., p. 292. See Plato *The Republic*, book III, 414-17.

vision of the world it evokes: choosing wisely, choosing the way of wisdom rather than folly, eating at Lady Wisdom's house, is the path to blessing.[22] This result is clearly taught in Proverbs 1–9: folly will lead to calamity (Prov 1:26), whereas wisdom will lead to security and preservation (Prov 1:33). Wisdom will lead to abiding in the land (Prov 2:2) and to length of days, years of life and abundant welfare. However, it is all too common to overlook the fact that the overall picture in Proverbs is more complex than this.

The first Solomonic collection of the book following Proverbs 1–9 consists of two sections: Proverbs 10–15 and Proverbs 16–22. The first section is largely made up of antithetical proverbs, in which the first line is answered by a contrasting second line. Proverbs 10–15 stresses the contrast between the righteous and the wicked and the consequences of their lifestyles. The character-consequence structure is persistent in this section (see, e.g., Prov 11:3, 5-6, 8, 21). The righteous are protected, rescued from evil and established in the land.

These are the sort of places, as we noted earlier, from which prosperity theology is derived, but is it right in its reading of these verses? The answer is found by attending closely to the development of the theme of retribution in Proverbs *as a whole*. Taken as a whole, Proverbs by no means presents a mechanical, automatic character-consequence understanding of retribution. This has been clearly demonstrated in an excellent article on wealth and poverty in Proverbs by Raymond van Leeuwen.[23] Van Leeuwen points out that there are large groups of sayings in Proverbs that assert a simple cause-and-effect relationship whereby righteousness leads to wealth and wickedness to poverty, such as we have observed in Proverbs 1–9 and Proverbs 10–15. These are examples of the character-consequence theme. However, they do not concern concrete, individual acts and their consequences: "It is the long-term character and direction of a person or group (as 'righteous' or 'wicked')

---

[22]The *character*-consequence structure is more commonly referred to as the *act*-consequence structure. *Character* is better, in our opinion, because in Proverbs wisdom is about the life of a person as a whole and not just individual deeds.

[23]Raymond van Leeuwen, "Wealth and Poverty: System and Contradiction in Proverbs," *Hebrew Studies* 33 (1992): 25-36. Cf. also J. A. Gladson, "Retributive Paradoxes in Proverbs 10–29" (Ph.D. diss., Vanderbilt University, 1978). See above, chapter four, pp. 96-97.

which determines life consequences and 'destiny.'"[24] It is a failure to recognize this long-term character that leads scholars to the mechanical view of retribution in Proverbs:

> These proverbs, when taken by themselves, are the basis for the view of some scholars that the tidy dogmatism of Proverbs does not correspond to reality and is doomed to collapse under the weight of reality, as happened in Job and Qoheleth. Since the foregoing sayings are not always exemplified in human experience, their falsification presumably led to a crisis of faith in Yahweh's maintenance of a just world order.[25]

However, proverbs are by their very nature partial utterances, and this type of mechanical approach does not do justice to the many sayings in Proverbs that manifest a more complex understanding of the way God works in creation. Because wisdom is based on the fear of the LORD, there is an awareness of the limits of human wisdom and an openness to wonder, or the "imponderable."[26] Particularly noteworthy in this respect are the "better-than" sayings in Proverbs, which acknowledge the reality that wisdom and prosperity *often do not* accompany one another (see, e.g., Prov 15:16-17; 16:16, 19). The overall picture is a far more complex one, which van Leeuwen sums up as follows:

> In general, the sages clearly believed that wise and righteous behaviour did make life better and richer, though virtue did not guarantee those consequences. Conversely, injustice, sloth, and the like generally have bad consequences. The editor-sages who structured Proverbs sought first to teach these basic 'rules of life,' thus the heavy emphasis on character-consequence patterns in both Proverbs 1–9 and 10–15. We must first learn the basic rules; the exceptions can come later. Though very aware of exceptions to the character-consequence rule, the sages insisted that righteousness is better than wickedness. The most fundamental and profound reason for this is that they believed that God loves the one and hates the other. For Israel's sages that sometimes seems the only

---

[24]Van Leeuwen, "Wealth and Poverty," p. 27.
[25]Ibid., pp. 28-29.
[26]The latter phrase is von Rad's. See his excellent chapter, the "Limits of Wisdom," in *Wisdom in Israel.*

answer. . . . The sages knew that there are limits to human wisdom. General patterns may be discerned, but many particular events may be unjust, irrational, and ultimately inscrutable.[27]

Van Leeuwen has focused his analysis on the issue of wealth and poverty, but it applies to many other areas discussed in proverbs as well. Take politics, for example. Proverbs 8:15-16 might be taken to imply that all kings rule by wisdom, just as some have taken Romans 13:1-7 to validate unjust regimes as appointed by God and therefore deserving unconditional support. However, verses like Proverbs 16:12 provide nuance to the total picture: "It is an abomination to kings to do evil" (NRSV). Similarly Proverbs 31:1-9 recognizes that rulers can become indulgent and forget to attend to justice for the poor.

It is in Proverbs 16–22, the second half of the first Solomonic collection, that most of the exceptions occur. In this way the sequence of Proverbs 10–15 to Proverbs 16–22 (and following, see Prov 28:6) embodies a "developmental pedagogy."[28] Readers need first to be instructed in the basic rules, and then they can be taught about the exceptions. Indeed, the mature, wise individual will learn through instruction from the book of Proverbs *when* to use which proverb. We stressed earlier that the fear of the LORD does not close down the mind but engages it fully. This is surely the lesson of the fascinating juxtaposition of the two antithetical proverbs in Proverbs 26:4-5. There are situations in which the character-consequence theme is fitting, and there are situations in which the better-than proverbs are more appropriate. The wise person will know which is which.

Character-consequence is a far better description of wisdom's theology than the more common "act-consequence" description because it alerts us to the *depth* at stake in wisdom. This depth dimension is implicit throughout Proverbs; note the better-than motif in reference to silver and gold at the start of this section. What is implicit in Proverbs is explicit in Job and Ecclesiastes, which not only focus on "exceptions" to the character-consequence motif but also nuance it by alerting us

---

[27]Van Leeuwen, "Wealth and Poverty," pp. 32-33.
[28]Raymond C. van Leeuwen, "Proverbs," in *A Complete Literary Guide to the Bible,* ed. Leland Ryken and Tremper Longman III (Grand Rapids: Zondervan, 1993), p. 261.

unequivocally to the fact that wisdom involves more than acting wisely; it is about being transformed in the depths of our being. In chapter twelve we will discuss the theology of suffering in Old Testament wisdom, but suffice it to say here that, after the extraordinary journey Job went through, he himself declares that "I had heard of you by the hearing of the ear, but now my eyes see you" (Job 42:5 ESV). Thus the suffering Job endured formed his *character* in a way that would never have happened but for his suffering. Similarly Qohelet's profound intellectual struggle leads him ultimately back to remembering his creator; he arrives at the beginning but this time to understand it far more fully. As T. S. Eliot says toward the end of his famous poem the *Four Quartets*,

> We shall not cease from exploration
> And the end of all our exploring
> Will be to arrive where we started
> And know the place for the first time.[29]

Thus one reason why we get into trouble about the relationship between Proverbs and Job and Ecclesiastes is that we have a superficial view of wisdom. This is exemplified and caricatured in the health, wealth and prosperity doctrine that originated in America and has been exported to some of the poorest countries in Africa. Such doctrine reduces wisdom to an Egyptian sort, according to which the goals of wisdom are silver, gold and rubies. In general, wisdom *will* lead to a healthy, biblical prosperity,[30] but central to that will be a deep encounter with God, which will involve radical purification and probably intense suffering. Especially in the consumer West we are so immersed in the toxins of our culture that we have no idea how profoundly egocentric we are. "The human ego has an immense gravitational pull. Left unchecked, it asserts its sovereignty by drawing everything into itself. . . . Rather than being created in the image of God, I create God in *my* image. I make a God who serves *me*. I, in effect, take the place of God

---

[29]For an excellent reading of the *Four Quartets* see Thomas Howard, *Dove Descending: A Journey into T. S. Eliot's* Four Quartets (San Francisco: Ignatius, 2006).

[30]John R. W. Stott, *Ephesians* (Leicester, U.K.: Inter-Varsity Press, 1969), pp. 34-35, is incorrect in our view to understand "spiritual blessing" in Eph 1:3-14 as marking a shift from the material nature of blessings in the OT to "spiritual" blessings in the New.

as the one who is the source of goodness, truth, and beauty."[31]

Wisdom involves detachment from things in the sense that "we detach ourselves from them as a way of recognizing that we are not their source and they are not our destiny. . . . And this allows us to let God be what *God* is, for in doing this, '*God forms himself for the man out of all things.*'"[32] This involves profound formation and alerts us to the depth dimension of wisdom. Little wonder that Proverbs places such emphasis on seeking wisdom. The urgent pleas in Proverbs for us to seek wisdom are akin and not unrelated to Sister Wendy's comments on prayer: Jesus' "insistence on faith and perseverance are surely other ways of saying the same thing: you must really want it, it must engross you."[33]

As early as Proverbs 3:11-12, we discover that seeking wisdom will involve exposing ourselves to Yahweh's discipline and reproof, which we are urged to welcome. Hebrews 12 counters any superficial reading of these verses, placing them as it rightly does in the context of heroic faith amid terrible trials requiring extraordinary resilience. And Proverbs contains verses like Proverbs 17:3:

> The crucible is for silver, and the furnace is for gold,
> but the LORD tests the heart. (NRSV)

Job and Ecclesiastes provide us with examples of what such testing may involve.

The benefits of wisdom are great; indeed, they are far greater than we imagine. Wisdom is about *God* first and foremost, and its attainment requires depth formation of our character by the living God, the hunter, the warrior, the king, the God who approaches at infinite speed.

### KNOWLEDGE AND WISDOM

Proverbs 1:1-6 makes it clear that wisdom has to do not least with the acquisition of knowledge. Wisdom extends to "discipline," "understanding" and a "prudent life." It leads to justice, righteousness, fairness and interpretation. Wisdom is thus more comprehensive than knowl-

---

[31]Frederick Bauerschmidt, *Why the Mystics Matter Now* (Notre Dame: Sorin, 2003), p. 62.
[32]Ibid., p. 68.
[33]Sister Wendy Beckett, *Sister Wendy on Prayer* (New York: Random House, 2007), p. 2.

edge but part of being wise is being able to understand the order Yahweh has built into his world. It is this emphasis that causes Irwin to note that "in the Wisdom Literature the appeal of learning and the life of the mind is clearly and forcefully presented."[34] Irwin finds this objective order to the world clearly expressed in Proverbs 1–9, Ecclesiasticus and the Wisdom of Solomon. He refers to it as a concept of "natural law" and notes that it is Israel's own achievement; its relation to Greek notions of natural law must be sought apart from Israelite dependence on Greece.[35]

Old Testament wisdom clearly teaches a doctrine of creation order to which all are subject but is it rightly described as natural law? In the history of Christian thought, natural law is particularly associated with Thomas Aquinas and his followers, who taught that to a significant extent the order of creation could be discovered by reason alone apart from revelation. Some have argued that Old Testament wisdom's epistemology is empirical, and if this is the case then it would appear that Irwin's appellation is correct—that wisdom is observing laws or patterns in nature and applying them to life.

However, contrary to a widespread assumption, wisdom's epistemology is not autonomous or empirical in the strict sense.[36] Many of the sages' teachings undoubtedly derive from the observations of generations of wise men but were *always* shaped in accordance with prior ethical-religious principles. Whatever the actual source of their teaching, the sages do not, according to Michael V. Fox, offer their experience as the source of new knowledge, and they rarely invoke experiential arguments. The rare appeal to what is seen is a rhetorical strategy and not a fundamental methodological procedure. Fox refers to Proverbs 24:30-34, 7:6-20 and 6:6-8 as examples. The first two passages contain references to what the teacher "saw," in the one case with respect to what happened to a lazy man's field, and in the other he "saw" a woman enticing a youth to fornication. As Fox points out, in Proverbs

---

[34]Irwin, "Man," in Frankfort et al., *Intellectual Adventure*, p. 267.

[35]William Irwin, "Man in the World," in Frankfort et al., *Intellectual Adventure*, p. 295.

[36]Michael V. Fox, *Qohelet and His Contradictions*, JSOTSupp 71 (Sheffield: Sheffield Academic Press, 1989), p. 90.

24:30-34 the observation is followed by a lesson, but the observation calls the truth to mind rather than the truth being discovered or inferred from the observation. "The sage does not say that he saw a field gone wild, looked for the cause, and found that its owner was lazy, nor does he claim to have looked at lazy farmers and observed what happens to their fields. Rather he came across a field gone wild, and this sparked a meditation on its causes."[37]

In Proverbs 7 the teacher reports observing the seduction but makes no claim to have observed the consequences; these he knows already! Similarly when the wise man exhorts the pupil in Proverbs 6:6-8 to "Go to the ant . . . consider its ways, and be wise," the ant is being used as an illustration of diligence. The observation of the ant is used to make the wise man's point emphatic, but not to prove the point in the first place.

Personal experience, Fox points out, is cited more commonly in theodicy.[38] See Psalm 37:25 for example:

I have been young, and now am old,
  yet I have not seen the righteous forsaken
  or their children begging for bread. (NRSV)

Psalm 73:3 is another example:

I was envious of the arrogant;
  I saw the prosperity of the wicked. (NRSV)

However, as Fox perceptively points out, "Observation in theodicy testifies to old truths; it does not uncover or argue for new ones."[39]

---

[37]Ibid., p. 91. Crenshaw, "Qoheleth's Understanding of Intellectual Inquiry," in *Qohelet in the Context of Wisdom*, ed. Anton Schoors, BETL 136 (Leuven: Leuven University Press, 1998), p. 206, insists contra Fox that Prov 7:6-27; 24:30-34 *are* examples of an observer, like Qohelet, interposing "his subjective consciousness between experience and audience." T. Frydrych, *Living Under the Sun: Examination of Proverbs and Qoheleth*, VTSup 90 (Leiden: Brill, 2001), pp. 54-56, argues along the same lines. However, this is to fail to note that observation is never neutral; one always gathers data in the perspective of some "torchlight." Observation is theory-laden. This is particularly true of Prov 7:6-27, in which observation clearly operates within a value-laden framework of adultery and prostitution as wrong and dangerous. Proverbs's approach to the world never claims to be autonomous, whereas Qohelet's does.

[38]Fox, *Qohelet*, pp. 91-92.

[39]Very little work has been done in this area. Crenshaw, "Wisdom and Authority: Sapiential Rhetoric and its Warrants," in *Congress Volume: Vienna 1980*, ed. J. A. Emerton, VT Sup 32

It may be that Fox overstates his case, for proverbial wisdom has its *Sitz im Leben* in life and is the sort of experiential knowledge that takes hold in a culture and becomes part of common wisdom as it is found again and again to fit the world. Thus there is an experiential and observational dimension to wisdom *but* never from a neutral, autonomous viewpoint. Indeed, in our opinion—and we think this is the view of Old Testament wisdom too—a neutral, value-free approach to the world is simply not possible. The philosopher Karl Popper evokes this in his images of the bucket and the searchlight.[40] An autonomous approach to knowledge thinks of our mind as resembling a bucket; we simply accumulate perceptions and knowledge in it. The searchlight theory, by comparison, recognizes that we always search within a framework, a horizon of expectations. Observations can, under certain circumstances, act like a bomb and destroy the framework, but "theory" always precedes observation. This is very helpful because it alerts us to the fact that it is a particular searchlight, a particular framework that is always operating in Old Testament wisdom even as it draws on observation and experience.

Proverbs 7:6-23 is a good example of the searchlight approach. The author witnesses a young man going off with a prostitute. For the author this is like a bird rushing headlong into a snare, oblivious of the terrible consequences. There is nothing in the "facts" of the situation to provide the author's decidedly negative assessment of this situation, so, from where does he derive his reading of it? One only has to think how

---

(Leiden: Brill, 1981), pp. 10-29, explores the rhetoric of wisdom along the lines of threefold warrant: ethos, pathos and logos. Fox, *Qoheleth and His Contradictions*, p. 90, perceptively notes that rhetoric is an expression of an underlying epistemology. Ethos, pathos and logos will be present in any rhetoric, but as Fox notes, the question is how they are realized in specific texts. Fox notes that Crenshaw mentions arguments from consensus as the form of logos characteristic in Wisdom literature and thus suggests that "the seemingly empirical arguments in Wisdom Literature are primarily ways of strengthening ethos by creating consensus." Much work remains to be done in this area. Ryan O'Dowd, *The Wisdom of Torah: Epistemology in Deuteronomy and the Wisdom Literature*, FRLANT (Göttingen: Vandenhoeck & Ruprecht, 2009), makes an important contribution in this direction. Annette Schellenberg, *Erkenntnis als Problem. Qohelet und die alttestamentliche Diskussion um das menschliche Erkennen*, OBO 188 (Göttingen: Vandenhoeck & Ruprecht, 2002), is also an important investigation of Qohelet and OT epistemology.

[40]Karl Popper, "The Bucket and the Searchlight: Two Theories of Knowledge," in *Objective Knowledge: An Evolutionary Approach* (Oxford: Clarendon, 1972), pp. 341-61.

a (post)modern person might describe such a situation as a celebration of youthful sexuality to realize how value-laden the description is. In our opinion the author's perspective is that of an orthodox Israelite who knows that adultery is sinful and destructive, as the Ten Commandments make clear. This raises of course the relationship between wisdom and law, which we will discuss below. But what is clear is that Old Testament wisdom is not a type of natural law, if by that is meant that one can access God's order for creation independently of the fear of the LORD. As von Rad notes, the genius of the Israelite perspective on knowledge is the recognition that you can go wrong right at the beginning. Or, as Paul Ricoeur puts it,

> Nothing is further from the spirit of the sages than the idea of an autonomy of thinking, a humanism of the good life; in short of a wisdom in the Stoic or Epicurean mode founded on the self-sufficiency of thought. This is why wisdom is held to be a gift of God in distinction to the "knowledge of good and evil" promised by the Serpent.[41]

Where we *do* find an autonomous epistemology is in Ecclesiastes, as discussed in chapter eight, above. However, Ecclesiastes is crafted in the postexilic context by a wisdom teacher as an ironic exposure of such an autonomous epistemology, which seeks wisdom through personal experience and analysis without the "glasses" of the fear of God. As such, Ecclesiastes is an example of contextualization of biblical faith or what Norbert Lohfink calls "a model of enculturation."[42] Qohelet puts himself into the shoes, as it were, of the autonomous "Greek" worldview and applies it to the world he observes and experiences, but only in order to show that it leads again and again to enigma rather than truth. His autonomous epistemology keeps running up against the enigma of life when pursued from this direction, and it appears impossible to find a bridge between this enigma and the good that he experiences and that the biblical tradition alerts one to. The resolution of this

---

[41]Paul Ricoeur, *Essays on Biblical Interpretation*, trans. Lewis Seymour Mudge (Philadelphia: Fortress, 1980), p. 88.

[42]Norbert Lohfink, *Qoheleth: A Continental Commentary* (Minneapolis: Fortress, 2003), p. 6. However, we are less optimistic than Lohfink about Qohelet's attempt to draw as much as possible from the Greek worldview without abandoning Israel's wisdom.

paradox is found in the fear of God (rejoicing and remembrance), which enables one to rejoice and apply oneself positively to life in the midst of all that one does not understand, including especially death. Thus, Ecclesiastes is far from supporting the view that Old Testament wisdom is a form of natural law; rather, it does precisely the opposite. Starting with reason, observation and experience alone without the fear of the LORD is like trying to shepherd the wind. It gets you nowhere.

As we saw in our discussion of Job, it too embodies an epistemology alert to the limits of human understanding. From an Old Testament wisdom—and in our opinion, a Christian—perspective, the postulate of neutrality assumed by autonomy is impossible; in our quest for knowledge there will always be some form of faith informing our quest, and the way forward is to reject the many attempts at autonomous knowledge and to embrace *faith seeking understanding* while remaining aware of the limits of human understanding.[43]

It is important to note that this is as true of practical knowledge as it is of scientific knowledge. An unfortunate divide between practical knowledge and scientific knowledge emerged in the post-Enlightenment period, a divide that continues to dominate academic study today. In general, this approach distrusts everyday, lived experience and insists that true *truth* about the world is attained through scientific analysis rooted in the human ego. A contemporary example of this is Brian Greene's *The Fabric of the Cosmos: Space, Time and the Texture of Reality:* "*The* overarching lesson that has emerged from scientific inquiry over the last century is that human experience is often a misleading guide to the true nature of reality."[44]

Although this trust in autonomous scientific reason remains dominant, fortunately a number of scholars have addressed this problem. Astute philosophical analyses of it are found, for example, in the works of Johann Georg Hamann, Nikolai Berdyaev, Gabriel Marcel, Martin Buber, Michael Polanyi, Alfred North Whitehead, Alvin Plantinga,

---

[43]For a philosophical defense of this view, see Roy Clouser, *The Myth of Religious Neutrality* (Notre Dame: University of Notre Dame Press, 1991).

[44]Brian Greene, *The Fabric of the Cosmos: Space, Time and the Texture of Reality* (New York: Vintage, 2004), p. 5.

Nicholas Wolterstorff, and the Dutch philosophical tradition of Herman Dooyeweerd and Dirk Hendrik Theodoor Vollenhoven.[45] All of these thinkers have in common a critique of post-Enlightenment epistemology in so far as it creates a bifurcation,[46] a cleavage[47] between lived experience and scientific analysis. "We have just now seen that theoreticians, because they habitually remain imprisoned by abstractions, are always liable to substitute what is often only a grotesque caricature for a reality which is living and, like everything which lives, is threatened."[48] Marcel rejects the "antiseptic objectivity"[49] of scientism and seeks a recovery of a science rooted in wisdom, communion, intersubjectivity and wonder. "With the eclipse of mystery goes the atrophy of the sense of wonder."[50]

Old Testament wisdom literature, as we have seen, has much to say about an epistemology rooted in the fear of the LORD, and Ecclesiastes in particular exposes the problems one gets into when one tries to discern the meaning of the world apart from remembering one's Creator. In terms of knowledge acquisition, it is crucial to note that Old Testament wisdom resists the post-Enlightenment cleavage between practical and scientific knowledge. *Both* need to be sought in the context of wisdom, of the fear of the LORD. Wisdom has as much to do with fractals and quantum physics as it does with marriage and family life.

---

[45]Nicolas Berdyaev, *The Destiny of Man* (New York: Harper & Row, 1960), pp. 1-22. For a useful introduction to Marcel's thought, see Sam Keen, *Gabriel Marcel* (Richmond, Va.: John Knox Press, 1967). Michael Polanyi, *Personal Knowledge: Towards a Post-Critical Philosophy* (New York: Harper & Row, 1964). Polanyi notes that "man stands rooted in his calling under a firmament of truth and greatness. Its teachings are the idiom of his thought: the voice by which he commands himself to satisfy his intellectual standards. . . . He is strong, noble and wonderful so long as he fears the voices of this firmament; but he dissolves their power over himself and his own powers gained through obeying them, if he turns back and examines what he respects in a detached manner. . . . Then man dominates a world in which he himself does not exist. For with his obligations he has lost his voice and his hope, and been left behind meaningless to himself" (p. 380). Alfred North Whitehead, *Concept of Nature* (Cambridge: Cambridge University Press, 1920). Nicholas Wolterstorff, *On Universals: An Essay in Ontology* (Chicago: University of Chicago Press, 1970).

[46]Whitehead's term.

[47]Berdyaev, *The Destiny of Man*, p. 2. "A cleavage takes place in reality, and in knowledge it expresses itself as objectivization."

[48]Marcel, *Tragic Wisdom and Beyond*, p. 101.

[49]Keen, *Gabriel Marcel*, p. 1.

[50]Ibid., p. 10.

Not surprisingly, an effect of modernity's emphasis on autonomy and universal scientific knowledge has been to marginalize the traditional—and often local—knowledge encapsulated in proverbs. The result is that proverbial wisdom is not taken very seriously in the West, although it continues to thrive in many other cultures. And in the history of Christian thought, there have been times when proverbs were highly valued. The early publication that made Erasmus famous was his *Adages,* a collection of proverbs. Pascal's famous seventeenth-century *Pensées* are in the form of proverbs. And much of the content of the twentieth-century Christian philosopher Simone Weil's *Gravity and Grace* is in aphoristic, proverbial form.

Many proverbs encapsulate local, practical knowledge, often handed down from generation to generation, as well as universal truths, and they remain indispensable for human life, which is always lived in a particular place and at a particular time. "Proverbs are potent truths embodied in a grain of sand."[51] Craig, when on holiday in South Africa, enjoys baking, and he has discovered that a local recipe is often superior to an "international" one, because baking is inevitably affected by local ingredients, air pressure and so on. Proverbs offer this kind of local, particular knowledge for ordinary people, thereby encouraging us to seek wisdom in our particular contexts and to be open to learning from those around us. Proverbs also encapsulate universal truths; "The fear of the LORD is the beginning of wisdom" is a great example. The difference between such universal truths and scientific abstractions is that they are in a memorable form, available to the ordinary person. Post-Enlightenment science replaces Plato's philosopher kings with science kings, whereas in the Old Testament, wisdom is democratized and available to all who will attend to her voice. The pithy, poetic form of proverbs makes them memorable, and in cultures like Israel they enabled ordinary folk to store up a reservoir of wisdom to be called on in challenging situations.

This is not to deny for a moment the value of science but to insist that lived, everyday experience is primary and that wise science will deepen our experience of everyday life rather than distrusting it and

---

[51]Jewell Parker Rhodes, foreword to *Proverbs for the People,* ed. Tracy Price-Thompson and Ta-Ressa Stovall (New York: Dafina, 2003), p. ix.

providing in its place an abstract alternative, which is then declared to be the true *truth* about the world. As Wolterstorff rightly says of the "ontologist":

> Yet the task of the ontologist is not to postulate new and astonishing entities, not to take us aback with his surmises, not to reveal secrets never suspected. His task is to describe that *rich reality* in the midst of which we live and act, believe and disbelieve, hope and despair. If he is successful, and if we are at all perceptive, we will not find him describing a terrain which, by his description, is astonishingly different from that in which we thought we lived. We will find him describing that terrain which has all the features of the familiar.[52]

We need to recover the proverbial tradition in the Old Testament and to nurture a living tradition of proverbs in our cultures today. African cultures in particular retain a vibrant tradition of proverbs,[53] and, as Jewell Parker Rhodes notes, "Africans and descendants of Africans could always wrap pain in humor, speak universal truths in a handful of words, and shout out sayings that could lift your spirit high. Each proverb becomes a moment of revelation, a meditative moment for readers to consider their heritage and the health of their spirit."[54] It is easy, for example, to see how the proverb from Mozambique, "Walking in two is medicine," is deeply African while connecting integrally with Qohelet's reflections in Ecclesiastes 4:9-12. Wisdom, it has been noted, dwells in places, and if in the West we want to recover wisdom it will, among other things, involve a recovery of the sort of wisdom encapsulated in proverbs.

## THE RELATIONSHIP OF OLD TESTAMENT WISDOM TO COVENANT, LAW AND PROPHETS

Early in the twentieth century, wisdom was neglected because it was thought to be secular and marginal to Israel's faith. The discovery of the similarity of Old Testament wisdom to ancient Near Eastern (Egyptian and Mesopotamian) wisdom and Old Testament wisdom's theology of

---

[52]Wolterstorff, *On Universals*, p. xiii. Italics added.
[53]See the short stories centered on a proverb in Price-Thompson and Stovall, *Proverbs for the People*.
[54]Rhodes, foreword to *Proverbs for the People*, p. ix.

creation led to a renewed interest in it. However, some scholars continue to argue that wisdom is marginal to Old Testament theology. H. D. Preuss is an extreme example of such a position.[55] In his view:

1. Wisdom is marginal to Israel's faith.

2. The God of wisdom is not Yahweh.

3. Wisdom concentrates on the orders in reality.

4. Retribution is one of these orders. The sages sought to discover this mechanical correspondence between action and consequence, as reflected in Proverbs.

5. A deed-consequence viewpoint is the basic dogma of early wisdom.

On the basis of such an approach, Job and Ecclesiastes are taken to represent a crisis in Old Testament wisdom.[56] Frank Crüsemann says of Ecclesiastes that "this difference between Koheleth and his predecessors must be taken as the starting point for understanding Koheleth,"[57] and suggests that Ecclesiastes brings Job to its logical conclusion.[58]

A critical question is whether or not early wisdom was of this non-Yahwistic sort. Ancient Near Eastern comparisons would suggest otherwise, since invariably ancient Near Eastern wisdom is profoundly religious, as we have seen. Roland Murphy points out that, although this notion of a wisdom crisis looms almost as large in scholarly discussion as does the exile of 587 B.C., the earliest tradition clearly interpreted Qohelet as working within the wisdom tradition.[59] As he tersely puts it, "There is no record that the book of Ecclesiastes was received with consternation."[60]

---

[55]H. D. Preuss, *Einführing in die alttestamentliche Weisheitsliteratur* (Stuttgart: Kohlhammer, 1987), pp. 114-36.

[56]See Hartmut Gese, "The Crisis of Wisdom in Koheleth," in *Theodicy in the Old Testament*, ed. James L. Crenshaw (Philadelphia: Fortress, 1983), and Hans Schmid, *Wesen und Geschichte der Weisheit: eine Untersuchung zur altorientalischen und israelitischen Weisheitsliteratur* (Berlin: A Töpelmann, 1966), on the crisis of wisdom.

[57]Frank Crüsemann, "The Unchangeable World: The 'Crisis of Wisdom' in Qoheleth," in *God of the Lowly: Socio-Historical Interpretations of the Bible* (Maryknoll, N.Y.: Orbis, 1984), p. 61.

[58]Ibid.; F. Crüsemann, "Hiob und Kohelet," in *Werden und Wirken des Alten Testaments: Festschrift für Claus Westermann zum 70 Geburtstag*, ed. R. Albertz (Göttingen: Vandenhoeck & Ruprecht, 1980), p. 381.

[59]Roland Murphy, *Ecclesiastes*, WBC 23A (Dallas: Word, 1992), p. lxi.

[60]Ibid. For Murphy's understanding of Qohelet's relationship to traditional wisdom see pp. lxii-lxiv.

The subject of the origin and development of Wisdom literature in Israel is a complex one that we cannot pursue in detail here. However, in their canonical forms there are good reasons for rejecting the sort of understanding of the Job-Ecclesiastes-Proverbs relationship that Preuss advocates. As we have noted, for example, in its canonical form Proverbs is clear that the fear of *Yahweh* is the beginning of wisdom.

Furthermore, once one recognizes that the understanding of retribution in Proverbs is more complex than a mechanical deed-consequence notion, then Job's and Ecclesiastes' relationship to Proverbs and traditional wisdom has to be reevaluated. Rather than contradicting Proverbs, Ecclesiastes and Job focus on profound experiences of *apparent* contradictions to the character-consequence theme of Proverbs and thereby, far from destroying it, deepen our understanding of what wisdom and character formation in this tradition involves.

In Old Testament theology the relationship between law and wisdom remains contested.[61] Murphy has helpfully suggested that "the problem of the relationship between wisdom literature and other portions of the Old Testament needs to be reformulated in terms of a shared approach to reality."[62] And similarly Henning Graf Reventlow seems to us on the right track in his recovery of Hans Schmid's[63] comprehensive notion of righteousness as order of the world. "The starting point for his deliberations is the remarkable breadth of the term 'justice': it comprises, beyond the juridical scope and wisdom, also nature/fertility, war/victory, cult/offering and kingdom. Behind these special fields a comprehensive world-order becomes visible, which as a whole can be characterized by the term 'righteousness.'"[64]

---

[61]For a useful discussion of the relationship of these two traditions, which both seek to order the lives of God's people, see Joseph Blenkinsopp, *Wisdom and Law in The Old Testament: The Ordering of Life in Israel and Early Judaism*, rev. ed. (New York: Oxford University Press, 1995).

[62]Roland Murphy, "Wisdom—Theses and Hypotheses," in *Israelite Wisdom: Theological and Literary Essays in Honor of Samuel Terrien* (Missoula, Mont.: Scholars Press, 1978), p. 38.

[63]Schmid, *Gerechtigkeit als Weltordnung*.

[64]Henning Graf Reventlow, "Righteousness as Order of the World: Some Remarks Towards a Programme," in *Justice and Righteousness: Biblical Themes and Their Influence*, ed. Henning Graf Reventlow and Yair Hoffman, JSOTSup 137 (Sheffield, U.K.: Sheffield Academic Press, 1992), p. 165.

It needs to be remembered that the strong distinction between law and wisdom is a modern construct; historical-critical scholars still assume that it is only with Ecclesiasticus and the Wisdom of Solomon that the two were conceptually related. In our opinion there is ample evidence in the Old Testament Wisdom literature of an awareness of Old Testament law such that an understanding of their relationship goes back much earlier. Ecclesiastes has much more to say about law than in its epilogue, and in Proverbs and Job the predominance of the name Yahweh for God indicates an awareness of him as the covenant lawgiver.[65] How then might these two approaches have been understood to relate to each other?

Both Old Testament law and wisdom have in common the ordering of the life of God's people.[66] Van Leeuwen has analyzed the root metaphors of Proverbs 1–9 and argues persuasively that

> underlying the bipolar metaphorical system of positive and negative youths, invitations/calls, "ways," "women," and "houses" in Proverbs 1–9, is a yet more fundamental reality which these images together portray. These chapters depict the world as the arena of human existence. This world possesses two fundamental characteristics. First is its structure of boundaries or limits. Second is the bi-polar human eros for the beauty of Wisdom, who prescribes life within limits, or for the seeming beauty of Folly, who offers bogus delights in defiance of created limits.[67]

Van Leeuwen argues that the worldview that Proverbs exhibits is a "carved" one in that "cultural and personal exhortation is grounded in the reality of the created world with its inbuilt normativity."[68] Justice

---

[65]See Raymond van Leeuwen, "Liminality and Worldview in Proverbs 1–9," *Semeia* 50 (1990): 122, for some of the links between Proverbs and Job and the Pentateuch. Van Leeuwen argues that certain texts in Proverbs and Job presuppose the historical tradition of the gift of the land.

[66]Murphy, "Wisdom—Theses and Hypotheses," is critical of the close association of wisdom with the search for order, arguing that this question is a modern one, which focuses on the presupposition of Israel's wisdom approach. However, see van Leeuwen, "Liminality and Worldview," for a powerful defense of taking the tacit presupposition of cosmic order seriously in Wisdom literature.

[67]Ibid., p. 116.

[68]Ibid., p. 118.

and righteousness are built into the world, but we will only read their order rightly as we are deeply rooted in the LORD.

This link of wisdom with creation has long been recognized. What is often not noted, though, is that the order that Proverbs finds in the "carved" creation is not and cannot be simply read out of the creation. This is the point that Fox makes about Israelite wisdom; it is not empirical but assumes ethical principles which it uses observation to support.[69] This is the sort of position exemplified in Genesis 1–3. The ordering of creation is not antithetical to instruction from Elohim/ Yahweh Elohim. Order and instruction/Torah go hand in hand, and obedience requires both a good creation and instruction. The point is that Wisdom literature assumes certain ethical principles that are not just read off creation but are very similar to the principles found in the law. Van Leeuwen, for example, argues that Proverbs 1–9 indicates that it is in "the liquid abandonment of married love" that healthy *communitas* takes place. As van Leeuwen notes, "This reality has its parallel at Sinai."[70]

Thus it can be argued that while wisdom is most closely related to creation, it presupposes instruction, or Torah. Similarly, when the narrative frame within which law always occurs in the final form of the Old Testament is foregrounded, it becomes apparent that the law of Yahweh the redeemer God is also the law of the Creator God. This link between Yahweh as Creator and redeemer is central to covenant in the Old Testament[71] and alerts us to the link between law and creation. Our suggestion, therefore, is that law and wisdom share an underlying and often tacit presupposition of a "carved" creation order. This is their shared reality. Instruction from Yahweh would therefore not be seen to conflict with the way he ordered his creation but would provide the ethical principles for discovery of that order.

The relationship of wisdom to the prophets—and of the prophets

---

[69]Fox refers to Qohelet's epistemology as empirical, but we prefer the term *autonomous*. Classically, empiricism is the view that true knowledge is derived exclusively from sense perception, whereas Qohelet depends on reason, experience and observation.

[70]Ibid., p. 132.

[71]See Craig G. Bartholomew, "Covenant and Creation: Covenant Overload or Covenantal Deconstruction," *Calvin Theological Journal* 30 (1995): 11-33.

to Old Testament covenant and law—is also controversial among biblical scholars. Once again the data indicates a closer relationship than might be apparent at first glance. In Ecclesiastes 12 Qohelet is clearly aware of prophetic eschatology and in our opinion holds a view much the same as that of many of the prophets. Furthermore, a strong doctrine of creation (and covenant) is invariably manifest in the prophetic books. As Irwin notes, the ethical monotheism of Israel is clearly present in the prophetic oracles against other nations.[72] The prophets warn Israel of coming judgment on the basis of her covenant relationship with Yahweh; but aside from passages that clearly articulate a theology of creation, the oracles against the nations presuppose an understanding of Yahweh as the only God whose sovereignty extends over all nations. Thus once again the doctrine of creation serves to illuminate the link between wisdom, law/covenant *and* prophets.

## CONCLUSION

Old Testament wisdom embodies a powerful, coherent theology. And as such it complements rather than contradicts the theology of the rest of the Old Testament. In an earlier chapter we have already noted the way in which the wisdom tradition carries through into the New Testament and is fulfilled in Christ. At the start of the next chapter we will examine the relationship between Old Testament wisdom and the kingdom of God, the main theme of Jesus' teaching, before going on to explore the relevance for today of Old Testament wisdom in Christian life and thought.

## RECOMMENDED READING

Frankfort, Henri, H. A. Frankfort, John A. Wilson, Thorkild Jacobsen and
    William Irwin. *The Intellectual Adventure of Ancient Man.* Chicago: University of Chicago Press, 1946.
Knierim, Rolf. *The Task of Old Testament Theology: Substance, Method, and Cases.* Grand Rapids: Eerdmans, 1995.
O'Dowd, Ryan. *The Wisdom of Torah: Epistemology in Deuteronomy and the*

---

[72]Irwin, "God," in Frankfort et al., *Intellectual Adventure,* pp. 224-38.

*Wisdom Literature.* FRLANT. Göttingen: Vandenhoeck & Ruprecht, 2009.

Rad, Gerhard von. *Wisdom in Israel,* trans. James D. Martin. London: SCM Press, 1970.

Schmid, H. H. *Gerechtigkeit als Weltordnung.* Tübingen: Mohr, 1968.

# 12

# The Theology
# of Wisdom Today

*A Theology of the Old Testament will have to be rewritten in each
generation, for each has different needs and each will interpret the past
in its characteristic way. But it will have its inevitable poles around
which all else turns. Over against each other are God and man,
and all that lies between can be conceived as belonging to
the Kingdom, the active kingly rule, of God.*

—H. WHEELER ROBINSON,
*INSPIRATION AND REVELATION
IN THE OLD TESTAMENT*

IT HAS NOT BEEN HARD FOR OLD TESTAMENT scholars to
see how the historical books, covenant and the prophets relate to the
active kingly rule of God, but in modern times they have struggled to
see how Old Testament wisdom fits under such a rubric. Since the
emergence of historical criticism in the late nineteenth century, Old
Testament Wisdom literature has struggled to recover from a Cinder-
ella status of not being invited to the ball! The second half of the twentieth century witnessed a resurgence of interest in Old Testament wisdom, but scholars still struggle to relate its theology to that of the rest
of the Old Testament.

In our opinion everything depends on how one understands *God's
kingly rule*. If this is understood only as the *history of salvation* and the

*great events of redemption,* then indeed it is hard to see the place of wisdom. But once one acknowledges that Yahweh the royal redeemer is also the Creator, a new and richer way of understanding wisdom becomes possible.

This should make good sense to us. Genesis 1–3, with its shift in God's name from "Elohim" (Gen 1:1–2:3) to "Yahweh Elohim" (2:4–3:24), goes out of its way to tie the Creator to the redeemer and thus creation to redemption.[1] God the redeemer is the creator of all, and his great works of redemption are an integral part of his overarching sustaining and ordering of creation. Intriguingly the Old Testament Wisdom literature consciously draws our attention to this connection by insisting that the fear of *Yahweh* is the beginning of wisdom. In Ecclesiastes, Qohelet moves toward resolution of his desperate struggle for meaning with the exhortation to "Remember your creator," and although Job is not an Israelite, *Yahweh*—not least as the Creator God—is the central character in the book of Job.

At the heart of Old Testament wisdom is the belief that wisdom can only be attained by starting with holy reverence for and trust in Yahweh, the redeemer God who had acted powerfully in the exodus to bring Israel to himself (cf. Ex 3:1-22; 6:1-30; 19:3-6). So while wisdom is a matter of negotiating the challenges of life successfully through God's dynamic order for *creation,* we do so with the warning that starting anywhere but with the fear of Yahweh will destine us for failure.[2] It is only as we are deeply rooted in the LORD and instructed by him that we are able to read the creation order correctly.[3]

Among New Testament scholars there has been an unhelpful tendency to stress that the kingdom of God in the Synoptic Gospels is about God's king*ship* rather than his king*dom*. In our opinion this is a false and unhelpful dichotomy. Kingdom is as much about *the domain*—or place—over which God exercises his reign as about the fact that *he*

---

[1]See Craig G. Bartholomew and Michael Goheen, *The Drama of Scripture: Finding Our Place in the Biblical Story* (Grand Rapids: Baker Academic, 2004), p. 30.

[2]See Gerhard von Rad, *Wisdom in Israel*, trans. James D. Martin (London: SCM, 1970), pp. 60-65.

[3]For the best statement of this kind of epistemology see Oliver O'Donovan, *Resurrection and Moral Order: An Outline for Evangelical Ethics* (Grand Rapids: Eerdmans, 1986), pp. 76-97.

*reigns* over this domain.[4] The kingdom of God is about the recovery in and through Jesus of God's purposes for the whole creation; as Oliver O'Donovan helpfully explains in *Resurrection and Moral Order,* the resurrection of Jesus is the reaffirmation of creation so that we must not set kingdom ethics against creation ethics. Indeed, a problem with the quote from Wheeler Robinson in the epigraph above is its anthropocentrism, its human-centeredness. God's rule is not just about humankind but also about his purposes with all of creation.

Kingdom is a dynamic concept, and it reminds us that we live in a different act of the biblical drama than that of the Israelites, so we cannot just lift Old Testament wisdom out of the Bible and always apply it directly to today. But if, as O'Donovan suggests, Christ's kingdom affirms the creation, we should expect to find myriad clues in Old Testament wisdom to how to live wisely today. The fear of the LORD, now climactically revealed in Jesus, remains the beginning of wisdom. Little wonder that Jesus concludes the longest summary of his teaching, the Sermon on the Mount, with a parable about a wise person and a foolish person. The wise person is one who by obeying Jesus' words builds his or her house on the rock, and it withstands the winds and the floods. The foolish person does not. This is classic wisdom teaching updated in the light of Jesus' incarnation and teaching.

O'Donovan notes that an important contribution of wisdom is that it provides the resources to deal with novel situations in the light of what we already know, and in this respect Markus Bockmuehl's argument that the early church frequently resorted to the wisdom tradition as they worked out how to live for Christ in their pluralistic situation is instructive.[5] The church found itself in a new act in the drama of Scripture and was thus faced with many novel situations requiring wisdom. Bockmuehl shows how the Gospels, Acts and Paul utilized a variety of observations from the created order in this respect:

In other words, the New Testament authors' description of the created

---

[4]See Craig G. Bartholomew, *Placemaking: A Christian View of Place Today* (Grand Rapids: Baker Academic, forthcoming).

[5]Markus Bockmuehl, *Jewish Law in Gentile Churches* (Grand Rapids: Baker Academic, 2000), pp. 113-43.

order is invariably underwritten by the incarnation and resurrection of Christ; it can never be considered other than *ex post facto.* . . . And yet, from this vantage point, it is all the more remarkable that the early Christian focus of attention still always remains the created *universe* and all its citizens. The moral theatre of redemption is nothing less than the *world* that God has loved. Creational givens are at once relativized, embraced and redeemed in the light of Christ's resurrection, and of the renewal of creation that he promises and we await.[6]

Old Testament wisdom, like the kingdom of God, relates to all of life, and in the rest of this chapter we will explore *some* of the many implications of wisdom for Christian life and thinking today.[7]

## WISDOM AND EDUCATION

T. S. Eliot perceptively notes that

the values which we most ignore, the recognition of which we most seldom find in writings on education, are those of Wisdom and Holiness, the values of the sage and the saint. . . . Our tendency has been to identify wisdom with knowledge, saintliness with natural goodness, to minimize not only the operation of grace but self-training, to divorce holiness from education. Education has come to mean education of the mind only; and an education which is only of the mind . . . can lead to scholarship, to efficiency, to worldly achievement and to power, but not to wisdom.[8]

Israelites were educated in a variety of ways. As the fifth commandment reminds us, a major way of passing on the Israelite traditions was in the home, and this was doubtless one of the primary sources of education. Then there was the cultus, where Israelites would go to have the

---

[6]Ibid., p. 143.

[7]In the history of Christian theology wisdom plays a major role. This engagement has been lost in modern theology, but it is good to see wisdom resurfacing in theologies such as Kevin J. Vanhoozer, *The Drama of Doctrine: A Canonical Linguistic Approach to Christian Theology* (Louisville: Westminster John Knox, 2005). Biblical wisdom opens out onto all areas of creation, and there are many areas we could have added to our discussion below. See, e.g., Warren S. Brown, ed., *Understanding Wisdom: Sources, Science and Society* (Philadelphia: Templeton Foundation Press, 2000).

[8]T. S. Eliot, *The Idea of a Christian Society and Other Writings* (London: Faber and Faber, 1982), p. 142.

rituals enacted that embodied Israel's story as well as to hear the law taught (cf. Eccles 5:1-2). The prophets too would have been a powerful source for formation of the Israelites, calling them back to covenant faithfulness. And in the Wisdom literature, we have the deposit of the teaching of the sages or wise men and women. Qohelet was one such sage; as Ecclesiastes 12:9-10 notes, he taught knowledge to the people, weighing, studying and arranging proverbs.

While a theology of Old Testament education, like Old Testament theology, could be approached from different angles, there is much to be said for wisdom as the overarching, unifying goal of education. In Deuteronomy God's Torah or law is said to provide the Israelites with wisdom:

> You must observe [the laws] diligently, for this will show your *wisdom* and discernment to the peoples, who, when they hear all these statutes, will say, "Surely this great nation is a *wise* and discerning people!" For what other great nation has a god so near to it as the LORD our God is whenever we call to him? And what other great nation has statutes and ordinances as just as this entire law that I am setting before you today? (Deut 4:6-8 NRSV)

As we argued in chapter eleven, the instruction (Torah) provided by law is inseparably related to creation order and thus provides the Israelites with wisdom and discernment. God's creation *by wisdom* is foundational to all that follows in the drama of Scripture so that one can see how all the streams of Old Testament literature—narrative, law, prophecy, psalms—are designed to enable the Israelites to live wisely as God's people.

Many different goals have been proposed for a biblical model of education: responsive discipleship, freedom, responsible action, shalom, commitment and witness.[9] We suggest that wisdom is perhaps even better since, while it embraces all of these models, it evokes the creation- wisdom-education nexus in a way that none of the above do.[10]

---

[9]See Michael Goheen and Craig Bartholomew, *Living at the Crossroads: An Introduction to Christian Worldview* (Grand Rapids: Baker Academic, 2008), pp. 169-71.

[10]An important attempt to use wisdom as the key to education is Doug Blomberg, *Wisdom and Curriculum: Christian Schooling After Postmodernity* (Sioux Center, Iowa: Dordt College Press, 2005).

Psychologist Robert Sternberg is arguably the most prominent voice seeking to include wisdom in educational practices today. One of Sternberg's concerns is that we are witnessing increases in IQs but no corresponding decrease in hate in our Western societies. Sternberg has sought an approach to education that genuinely contributes to *the public good* and in the process has found a major resource in the concept of "wisdom." He has edited at least two major books with wisdom in the title: *A Handbook of Wisdom: Psychological Perspectives* and *Wisdom: Its Nature, Origins and Development* and has personally authored *Wisdom, Intelligence and Creativity Synthesized.*[11] This is to say nothing of his many articles. Sternberg has even written an essay on education called "Foolishness."[12]

In a coauthored essay from 2007, Sternberg defines wisdom as:

The application of intelligence, creativity, and knowledge as mediated by values toward the achievement of a common good through a balance among (a) intrapersonal, (b) interpersonal, and (c) extrapersonal interests, over the (a) short- and (b) long-terms, in order to achieve a balance among (a) adaptation to existing environments, (b) shaping of existing environments, and (c) selection of new environments. [13]

Here is a clarification of Sternberg's terms:

Intrapersonal = self-interests

Interpersonal = interests of others

Extrapersonal = other aspects of the context in which one lives, e.g., one's city or *religion*

We welcome this significant recovery of wisdom in education. Stern-

[11]Robert J. Sternberg and Jennifer Jordan, eds., *A Handbook of Wisdom: Psychological Perspectives* (Cambridge: Cambridge University Press, 2005). Robert J. Sternberg, ed., *Wisdom: Its Nature, Origins and Development* (Cambridge: Cambridge University Press, 1990). Robert J. Sternberg, *Wisdom, Intelligence and Creativity Synthesized* (Cambridge: Cambridge University Press, 2003).

[12]Robert J. Sternberg, "Foolishness," in Sternberg and Jordan, *A Handbook of Wisdom*, pp. 331-52.

[13]Robert Sternberg, Alina Reznitskya and Linda Jarvin, "Teaching for Wisdom: What Matters Is Not Just What Students Know, but How They Use It," *London Review of Education* 5, no. 2 (2007): 145.

berg is right in our opinion that North American education has become woefully *reductionistic* and urgently needs to be opened up to relate to whole, embodied persons in relationship. However, Sternberg's relegation of "religion" to an "extrapersonal" factor on par with the city we live in is in stark contrast to biblical wisdom.

Sternberg himself acknowledges in his introduction to *Wisdom: Its Nature, Origins, and Development* that "to understand wisdom fully and correctly probably requires more wisdom than any of us have."[14] This resonates with Old Testament wisdom. In Job 28 we have a majestic poem that reflects on the inaccessibility of wisdom to humans sounded through the haunting refrain, "But where shall wisdom be found?" Even death and Abaddon have only heard rumors of it! But God knows its place, with the result that "truly the fear of the LORD, that is wisdom" (Job 28:23).

This is precisely the same point made throughout Old Testament wisdom, namely, that the fear of the LORD is the beginning of wisdom. From a biblical perspective the starting point in the quest for wisdom is crucial: you not only teach *for* wisdom, as Sternberg suggests, although Proverbs 1:1-6 makes it crystal clear that you do do this—but, just as much, you also teach *from* wisdom. No one that we know of has articulated this as clearly as the German scholar Gerhard von Rad in his classic *Wisdom in Israel:*

> The thesis that all human knowledge comes back to the question about commitment to God is a statement of penetrating perspicacity. . . . It contains in a nutshell the whole Israelite theory of knowledge. . . . There lies behind the statement an awareness of the fact that the search for knowledge can go wrong . . . because of one single mistake at the beginning. To this extent, Israel attributes to the fear of God, to belief in God, a highly important function in respect of human knowledge. She was, in all seriousness, of the opinion that effective knowledge about God is the only thing that puts a man into a right relationship with the objects of his perception.[15]

---

[14]Robert J. Sternberg, "Understanding Wisdom," in Sternberg, *Wisdom: Its Nature, Origins and Development*, p. 3.
[15]Von Rad, *Wisdom in Israel*, pp. 67-68.

If von Rad is right, as we think he is, this moves the issue of religion from being "extrapersonal" to deeply intrapersonal and interpersonal. Biblical wisdom resists finding a way into religious dialogue through "values" or as an extrapersonal item alongside items such as which city one lives in. Biblical wisdom also resists the notion that religion in general can provide adequate resources for wise education. For Proverbs it is the fear of the LORD that is the starting point of wisdom, certainly not religion in general. The LORD is the very particular Creator God, who rescued Israel from slavery and brought them to himself at Sinai, where he established them in covenant relationship with himself.

We appreciate Sternberg's emphasis on education for *the common good;* it subverts the pervasive individualism and consumerism of so much North American culture. But who is to define what the "common good" looks like? A committed Muslim will have one view, a secular humanist another, an orthodox Jew another and a Christian yet another. We are well aware nowadays that these differences cannot be trivialized. Alasdair MacIntyre, one of the most prominent philosophers of our day, has helpfully alerted us to the fact that knowledge acquisition and thus education is always *traditioned*—it always operates in a particular tradition. For MacIntyre this is unavoidable.[16] Like biblical wisdom, such an approach offers a challenge to the fact-value distinction in Sternberg's model and in so much education theory today. Are facts value-free? Or is not the modern valuing of "facts" over values itself value-laden?

Taking wisdom seriously in the education debate would push education to open out into an acknowledgment of the *plurality* of traditions within which we and our views of wisdom operate so that these each is allowed room to come to fruition in education; then the real debate could begin about a genuinely common good that creates space for as many as is healthily possible. A legacy of the Enlightenment tradition in education is that there is such a thing as neutral public education, in effect privatizing religion and marginalizing wisdom.

A surprising example of the Enlightenment vision of education is

---

[16]Alasdair MacIntyre, *Whose Justice? Which Rationality?* (London: Duckworth, 1988).

clearly articulated by the Catholic historian James Turner in his debate with Mark Noll:

> Faith gives no *epistemological* edge. When I am writing history—even writing about Christianity—faith does not necessarily make me a better historian or give me any clearer insight into the past. Christianity might make me a *worse* historian, if it biased me against weighing evidence in as clear-eyed a manner as possible. Otherwise, faith bears almost no relevance to my scholarship.[17]

As we have seen repeatedly in Proverbs, Job and Ecclesiastes, the one thing that wisdom, and thus faith, does indeed provide *is* an epistemological edge. If von Rad, as quoted above, is right, then this sort of neutral, objective approach to learning and education is a dangerous charade, obscuring the powerful Enlightenment metanarrative that informs it. Taking Old Testament wisdom seriously will alert us, contra Turner, to the urgency of injecting religion into our research and educational practices.[18] The crucial question will be *how* we take wisdom seriously in education, but Old Testament wisdom knows of no third way such as Turner's; either our education will be wise or it will be foolish.

Biblical wisdom orients us toward the world in a particular way, with the LORD *Christ* at the center and us decentered as creatures. In other words, wisdom, read in the context of the biblical story, provides us with a distinctive worldview out of which we can begin this work of fleshing out a biblical vision for education. We are not the first to suggest this move from Scripture to education; indeed, there are a great many resources that will enrich our task.[19] Here are just a few points we believe emerge from such a reading of scripture.

1. Education needs to be infused with a sense of wonder and awe at

[17]Mark A. Noll and James Turner, *The Future of Christian Learning: An Evangelical and Catholic Dialogue*, ed. Thomas Albert Howard (Grand Rapids: Brazos, 2008), p. 106.
[18]See ibid., p. 107.
[19]Some helpful historical and cultural studies of education in the OT are Norman Whybray, *The Intellectual Tradition in the Old Testament* (Berlin: Walter de Gruyter, 1974); James Crenshaw, *Education in Ancient Israel: Across the Deadening Silence* (New York: Doubleday, 1998); Daniel J. Estes, *Hear, My Son: Teaching and Learning in Proverbs 1–9* (Grand Rapids: Eerdmans, 1997); Walter Brueggemann, *The Creative Word: Canon as a Model for Biblical Education* (Philadelphia: Fortress, 1982).

God and his good creation. What better motivation for exploring every aspect of the world God has created!

2. Education needs to start with, to continue with and always to return to the fear of the LORD. Wisdom commits us to a notion of integrally Christian education, with wisdom taken seriously in all subjects, and resists the model of a neutral school with religion as one subject. In Lesslie Newbigin's memorable words, wisdom commits us to taking with the utmost seriousness the fact that "Christ is the clue to all that is."

3. Wisdom alerts us to the fact that there is *more* to wise formation than the school. We have noted the central role of the home and the temple in Old Testament education. Wisdom is about the formation of the whole person and a wise theory of education will be sensitive to the fundamental role of the family and the church in the formation of a person from child to teenager to adult.

4. Wisdom will alert us to the particular contribution of primary school and secondary school as well as the role of the college or university. In Israelite culture education was relatively undifferentiated. Even if there were schools they were for the privileged few, whereas in contemporary Western culture schooling is compulsory, and an increasing number go on to university education.

    Whereas wisdom relates to the whole person, schools and universities focus in particular on intellectual development and the acquisition of knowledge. The more developed our societies have become, the more years of schooling that are required in order to function effectively in them. In our view such a development is a part of God's dynamic creation; intellectual development and growth in knowledge are wonderful gifts, provided they too are rooted in the fear of the LORD.

    Naturally the extent to which education focuses intensively on intellectual development will vary from preschool to elementary school to high school to university. At all stages the holistic nature of the human person will need to be taken seriously, but we should not fear or downplay intellectual development. The intellect is a great gift of

God, and wisdom invites us to explore with rigor every aspect of the creation. Wisdom is as relevant to astrophysics and quantum physics as it is to avoiding the adulterer. Neglect of the intellectual side of wisdom will cause us to fall prey to the scandal of anti-intellectualism.[20] Denton Lotz rightly notes that "the west will never be converted until the college is converted. And the college will never be converted until there is a radical rediscovery of the unity of all truth in Jesus Christ."[21]

5. Wisdom alerts us to the power and complexity of education. It is one thing to gain a vision of wise education; it is quite another to render it incarnate! Christian education has produced examples of education that are anything but wise, and non-Christians are capable as image bearers of being remarkably insightful when it comes to education. In his *Lessons of the Masters*, George Steiner evokes the power of education:

> To teach seriously is to lay hands on what is most vital in a human being. . . . Poor teaching, pedagogic routine, a style of instruction which is, consciously or not, cynical in its mere utilitarian aims, are ruinous. They tear up hope by its roots. Bad teaching is, almost literally, murderous and metaphorically, a sin. It diminishes the student, it reduces to gray inanity the subject being presented. It drips into the child's or the adult's sensibility that most corrosive of acids, boredom, the marsh gas of ennui. Millions have had mathematics, poetry, logical thinking, killed for them by dead teaching, by the perhaps subconsciously vengeful mediocrity of frustrated pedagogues. . . . The majority of those to whom we entrust our children in secondary education . . . are amiable gravediggers. They labour to diminish their students to their own level of indifferent fatigue.[22]

By contrast, Steiner describes his Thursday-morning doctoral seminars in Geneva as "as near as an ordinary, secular spirit can come to Pentecost."[23]

---

[20]See Mark Noll, *The Scandal of the Evangelical Mind* (Grand Rapids: Eerdmans, 1994).

[21]Denton Lotz, "Christian Higher Education and the Conversion of the West," in *Faithful Learning and the Christian Scholarly Vocation*, ed. Douglas V. Henry and Bob R. Agee (Grand Rapids: Eerdmans, 2003), p. 133.

[22]George Steiner, *Lessons of the Masters* (Cambridge, Mass.: Harvard University Press, 2003), p. 18.

[23]Ibid., p. 19.

Wise education will be truly Pentecostal, infused with the Spirit of wisdom. But it will be *education*, that is, deep formation, and not just Bible study or secular education covered with a veneer of superficial Christianity. Such education is not quickly achieved but takes years and lifetimes to develop as it builds on the insights of the Christian tradition and on insights gained from non-Christians, slowly bringing all captive to Christ.

One reason wise education is hard to describe is that, especially at the university level, there are few major examples to refer to. Christians have focused much attention on the family and the school but less on the university. Good Christian schools and competent homeschooling have gone a long way toward wise education, at least in North America. And at the college level there is a plethora of Christian institutions scattered across North America, no mean achievement. But in the West we can think of no single major research university that stands out as overtly Christian. Oxford and Cambridge have the architecture, but no one would argue that their curricula are unified in Jesus. Much work remains to be done in taking wisdom seriously in education.

## WISDOM AND POLITICS

Politics has to do with government and justice in a society. Today, whether at the local or national level, it is not hard to see the need for political wisdom. But how can Old Testament wisdom help us in our modern societies, which are so different politically from Israel and the ancient Near East? If Scripture is God's Word for all of life, then it is essential that we excavate the biblical resources for politics today. As Oliver O'Donovan points out, we have to make the journey from what God said to Abraham to how to respond to Iraq today, but he rightly insists that while at an intuitive level faith may make that journey instantly or the preacher in half an hour, it may take a lifetime of scholarship.[24]

O'Donovan's *Desire of the Nations* is itself an exercise in the theo-

---

[24]Oliver O'Donovan, *The Desire of the Nations: Rediscovering the Roots of Political Theology* (Cambridge: Cambridge University Press, 1996), p. ix.

logical moves required, and clearly the task is complex and much contested. However, as O'Donovan stresses, if politics is to resist the idol of contemporary historicism—the view that we are adrift amid the flux of history with no absolute standards for justice—then the journey must be undertaken.

In *Resurrection and Moral Order* O'Donovan discerns the inner logic of Scripture in Jesus' resurrection as the reaffirmation of creation. In the Old Testament Wisdom literature, as we have seen, we find similarly a strong articulation of creation order: "If we now try to characterise the theological attitude of Wisdom, we must say: Wisdom thinks resolutely within the framework of a theology of creation."[25] And in Old Testament wisdom, as in the ancient Near East, creation order is closely related to justice and political rule: if the translation of *ʾāmôn* as "craftsman" or "artisan" in Proverbs 8:30 is correct,[26] then wisdom is here "personified as the king's architect-adviser, through whom the king puts all things in their proper order and whose decrees of cosmic justice are the standard for human kings and rulers (v. 15)."[27] Indeed, there is a surprising amount of material in Proverbs about kingship and rule. Because wisdom is the means by which Yahweh creates the world, there is no area of life in which wisdom is not required. We might say in the light of Proverbs that theology must be political if it is to be wise!

The major places in which Proverbs deals with rule and kingship are Proverbs 16:10-15; 28:1-28; 29:1-27 and 31:1-9. However, the verses that establish unequivocally the connection between creation, wisdom and politics are Proverbs 8:15-16 (NRSV):

> By me kings reign,
>     And rulers decree what is just;
> by me rulers rule,
>     and nobles, all who govern rightly.

These verses make the closest connection between wisdom and gov-

---

[25] Walther Zimmerli, "The Place and Limit of Wisdom in the Framework of the Old Testament Theology," *Scottish Journal of Theology* 17 (1964): 148.
[26] We agree in this respect with Roland Murphy, *Proverbs*, WBC 22 (Nashville: Thomas Nelson, 1998), p. 48; and Raymond C. van Leeuwen, "Proverbs," in *The New Interpreter's Bible*, ed. Leander Keck (Nashville: Abingdon, 1997), p. 94.
[27] Ibid.

ernment in all of Proverbs, and this not just in Israel but universally.[28] And the practice of government is made possible by, and in response to, Yahweh's creation order. The use of *ḥqq* in this chapter alerts us to the close connection between the ruler and God: "Just as the Lord 'marked out' *(ḥāqaq)* 'the horizon on the face of the deep' and 'gave to the sea its boundary' *(ḥāqaq)*, and as God 'marked out' *(ḥāqaq)* 'the foundations of the earth' (vv. 27, 29), so also do human rulers 'decree' *(ḥāqaq)* 'what is just' (v. 15)."[29]

Several items are worth noting at this point. Government is here viewed as a human activity within history in diverse nations, but it derives its authority from being an ordained activity within creation. Throughout Proverbs, as in the ancient Near East generally, God's kingship is paralleled closely by that of the human ruler. The emphasis in these verses, furthermore, is at least partly on the political *act* as decisive: "Rulers decree what is just," whether exercised by king, rulers or nobles. This may provide biblical support for O'Donovan's view that a political theology should focus first on authority as act rather than as institution: "The political act is the divinely authorised act."[30] The triple terminology of office (kings, rulers, nobles) may suggest flexibility about institution but not about the exercise of judgment.

Clearly Proverbs envisages human rule as subject to that of the LORD. Rulers are not free to do as they wish; as in Romans 13:1-7 they are God's servants with a God-given responsibility to establish *justice for all*. Political rule, we might say, is according to Proverbs a specific way in which the wisdom of God is imaged in his creation. Wisdom in Proverbs implies a myriad of ways of such imaging, but politics is specifically mentioned in Proverbs 8 as a prime example. From this perspective politics is as much a vocation as any other area of life in which we may be called to serve God. A recovery of this vocational dimension and responsibility to God would transform politics in most societies today, in which corruption and personal gain often dominate.

---

[28]The meaning of *rôzĕnîm* ("rulers," Prov 8:15) is unsure, but always refers to foreign officials (cf. Michael V. Fox, *Proverbs 1–9*, AB [New York: Doubleday, 2000], p. 273).

[29]Van Leeuwen, "Proverbs," p. 92.

[30]O'Donovan, *Desire of the Nations*, p. 20.

Even in the Old Testament the forms of government change and develop, the move from prophet leaders to judges to a monarchy being the most obvious example. Politics has to relate to a society amid its changes and developments, and one might wonder if Old Testament wisdom, with its notion of creation order, is up to such challenges. Indeed, a major issue in wisdom studies today is the relationship between wisdom and historical literature in the Old Testament.[31] How does wisdom relate to story and Torah? For the ancients, O'Donovan notes, wisdom was the view that every novelty manifested in some way the permanent creation order so that, however new it was, it was not totally incommensurable with what preceded and could therefore be understood.[32] Some have suggested that Israel did not have the same sense as Greek thinking of stability set against change and history, but O'Donovan disagrees:

> The re-presentation of wisdom as law declares, in fact, the central point of Israel's faith, which is the meeting of life-in-the-world with life-before-God. . . . On the one hand, the understanding of the world-order, so necessary for the life in the world, was known to be the personal and gracious gift of the God who had chosen Israel for himself. On the other, the burning fire of election, that transcendent storm which swept through history as the Lord revealed himself, intended nothing other than the blessing of life upon the earth. Wisdom, with its cool observational detachment and its inherent restriction to the educated, was made available to all in the form of law, and was co-ordinated in the covenant with the summons to worship and rejoice. . . . In *torah* the moral authority of created order and the transcendent authority of the electing God were made one. That was the source of Israel's security, the watch-tower from which her prophets could comprehend the events of the ancient Near East, always threatening dissolution and meaninglessness, and make of them a song of praise and thanksgiving.[33]

O'Donovan's overall position is right in our opinion. Canonically wisdom and story/law complement each other. In Proverbs 28 and

---

[31]See John Goldingay, *Theological Diversity and the Authority of the Old Testament* (Grand Rapids: Eerdmans, 1995), chap. 7, for a useful discussion.
[32]O'Donovan, *Resurrection and Moral Order*, p. 189.
[33]Ibid., pp. 189-90.

Proverbs 29 there is a close association of wisdom, government and Torah. Torah here is both the law of Moses and the teaching of the wise.[34] In these chapters wisdom and law fit comfortably and easily together. Indeed, the foundation of wisdom in the fear of *Yahweh* alerts us to wisdom's relationship to covenant since Yahweh is above all else the name of the God who rescues Israel and brings her to himself and establishes her in covenant relationship with himself. The foundational covenant text in the Old Testament is Genesis 1 as William Dumbrell has shown.[35] Covenant, with its foundation in creation, its strong sense of historical development and as the basis for Old Testament law, provides, in our opinion, a biblical link between creation order and history. Or to state the matter another way, both Genesis and Old Testament wisdom envision a dynamic order of creation and not a static one.

In terms of politics, the complementary nature of law and wisdom is important. Law establishes the principles by which a society is to be run, but in practice politics requires *wisdom* in dealing with specific situations. And as we saw in our earlier examination of Old Testament wisdom, it is about knowing what action is appropriate in a *particular* situation. There is a time to answer a fool and a time to be quiet; the wise person knows the difference. Such particularity is central to politics. Take George W. Bush and Tony Blair's decision to go to war against Iraq in 2003, for example. Was it a wise decision? Undoubtedly Saddam Hussein was a cruel and despotic ruler but was war declared thoughtfully as a last resort in line with the theory of just war? As more information trickles out about the knowledge available to Blair and Bush the importance of wisdom in politics becomes ever clearer.[36]

An intriguing question is whether the rooting of government in creation and covenant affects political theology in any major way. Contrary to the fears of some,[37] it does not detract from, but actually facili-

---

[34]Van Leeuwen, "Proverbs," p. 246.

[35]William J. Dumbrell, *Covenant and Creation: An Old Testament Covenantal Theology* (Exeter: Paternoster, 1984).

[36]See, e.g., Geoffrey Wheatcroft, "NO, Prime Minister," *NYRB* 57, no. 20 (December 23, 2010): 28-32.

[37]These fears are not unfounded. The God-given authority of rulers has been used to legitimate the worst forms of oppression. Apartheid South Africa is a good example, where texts like Romans 13 were used to legitimate racism and oppression. The important point is that this is

tates, the possibility of critique of rulers—Proverbs combines an affirmation of political rule with some devastating critiques of misdirected authority.[38] Ecclesiastes is full of material dealing with misdirected politics; this is one of the things Qohelet struggles with as he desperately seeks meaning in life. Proverbs 31:1-9 is an insightful text in terms of the possibility of oppressive rule:

> The sayings of King Lemuel—an oracle his mother taught him:
> "O my son, O son of my womb,
>    O son of my vows,
>  do not spend your strength on women,
>    your vigor on those who ruin kings.
>
> "It is not for kings, O Lemuel—
>    not for kings to drink wine,
>    not for rulers to crave beer,
>  lest they drink and forget what the law decrees,
>    and deprive all the oppressed of their rights.
>  Give beer to those who are perishing,
>    wine to those who are in anguish;
>  let them drink and forget their poverty
>    and remember their misery no more.
>
> "Speak up for those who cannot speak for themselves,
>    for the rights of all who are destitute.
>  Speak up and judge fairly;
>    defend the rights of the poor and needy."

King Lemuel's mother here instructs her son, the king, not to forget his responsibilities as a ruler. Implicit in this instruction is the view of the ruler as a servant of God whose role is to maintain justice in the nation (cf. Rom 13:1-7) and the potential for rulers to abuse their authority. Particularly notable is the responsibility of the king for the poor and destitute, what some Catholic theology has come to call "the pref-

---

a misreading of Romans 13 and of OT Wisdom literature, to say nothing of the rest of Scripture.

[38]See, e.g., Prov 16:12; 28:3, 15-16; 29:2, 7, 12, 16; 31:1-9. Note too Prov 8:16—"all who govern rightly." If the NRSV translation is right, which we think it is, then this verse already distinguishes appropriate government from misdirected government and associates wisdom only with the former!

erential option for the poor." Our world is awash with the poor and oppressed, and we think our governments could do more to take Proverbs 31:8 seriously today!

Thus, the doctrine of two ways in Proverbs—that of folly and wisdom—applies as much to politics as it does to any other human activity. What it *may* also do is contribute to the Thomist versus Reformed debate about whether politics is a result of the fall or part of God's original intention with creation. Old Testament wisdom links government strongly to creation. Ronald Clements, for example, says that for wisdom, "the holding of political office and the wielding of political power were understood as part of the grand design of the universe."[39] Clements relates this to the needs of Israel in the exilic and postexilic era in which more of an international perspective was required. The rooting of government in creation in Proverbs provides support for a Thomist perspective. Clearly government is deeply affected by the fall and sin, but from a wisdom perspective it does not originate as a result of sin but is a structure built into God's good creation. In our comfortable, Western democracies we tend to take "good" government for granted. Often, it is only when government goes really badly that we realize how essential it is for human flourishing. To live through the Rwandan genocide or in Iraq or Afghanistan today would soon alert us to the vital importance of a healthy government that seeks justice for all citizens.

In a fallen world the issue of politics and the use of force is an important issue. In an unfallen world, government would still be needed, but clearly its role is profoundly affected by the fall and not least in relation to the use of force. A major insight of Old Testament wisdom is that God's order continues to hold for the complexities of situations resulting from folly/sin in the world. Thus Ecclesiastes 3 notes that there *is* a time for war and a time for making peace; the wise ruler knows the difference! Michael V. Fox rightly argues that in Ecclesiastes 3 "the fact that there is a 'time for war' does not mean that God predestined the Congressional declaration of war against Japan on December 8, 1941. Rather, there are conditions right for war, situa-

---

[39]Ronald E. Clements, *Wisdom in Theology* (Grand Rapids: Eerdmans, 1992), p. 96.

tions when war is called for and can be effectively prosecuted."[40]

While war was never God's desire for his creation, the use of force is often necessary, and wisdom alerts us to the fact that the wise person knows when to resort to force and when not to. Old Testament wisdom is clearly not pacifist in its view of the use of force, and neither, in our opinion, is the rest of the Bible.[41] The crucial question arising from Ecclesiastes 3 is *how* we know when it is the right time for war. In this respect wisdom is the same as Newbigin's comment about Jesus: he is *the clue* to all that is. This is insightful because neither Old Testament wisdom nor Jesus provides all the answers; rather, they provide the indispensable clues that must be pursued if answers are to be found. Wisdom alerts us unequivocally to the fact that government is from God, that it is established to facilitate justice and that at times it will be right to resort to the use of force and to war. These are crucial clues, but they hardly tell us whether it was right to go to war against Iraq or not. From these clues we need to develop a theology of politics, justice and the use of force. Such a theology will need to learn all it can from the history and practice of politics in our world and the ways in which Christians have sought to answer these questions in the past.

In our view a good example of such a theology as it relates to war is the *just war theory*. This, O'Donovan tells us, received its classic expression in the early modern period:

> The modern Christian discussion of war and peace (i.e. since the sixteenth century) presupposes the pluralism of the nation-state system, a multitude of 'peoples' becoming aware of themselves and asserting themselves in claims to absolute sovereignty. . . . The heart of the question, both in antiquity, and in modernity, is how these centres of political self-complacency are to be brought to recognize the sovereignty of the reign of God.[42]

---

[40]Michael V. Fox, *A Time to Tear Down and a Time to Build Up: A Rereading of Ecclesiastes* (Grand Rapids: Eerdmans, 1999), p. 198.

[41]Jesus' teaching in Mt 5:38-48 is often taken to teach pacifism. However, Romans 12 and 13 are illuminating in this respect. Romans 12:14-21 contains teaching similar to that we find in the Sermon on the Mount, but it is followed by Rom 13:1-7, which deals with government and its legitimate wielding of the sword. The point is that we are not to take justice into our own hands but that government is God's designated structure for bringing about justice in society.

[42]Oliver O'Donovan, *The Just War Revisited* (Cambridge: Cambridge University Press, 2003), pp. 11-12.

Typical lists of the characteristics of a just war include legitimate authority, just cause, war as a last resort, the prospect of success, and discrimination and proportion in the execution of the war. O'Donovan notes that any account of just war must emerge from the political authority of government and thus be undertaken to establish justice.[43]

We do not have the space here to flesh out a wise account of just war for today. In this respect readers are referred to such fine treatments as O'Donovan's *The Just War Revisited*, which is peppered with contemporary examples. For our purposes it suffices to know that the Bible alerts us to the existence of wisdom in relation to war but that this has to be sought through prayer, study, experience and engagement with the Christian and political traditions. Sadly such wisdom as is embodied in the just war tradition is almost unknown by the public today and hardly ever referred to in media coverage of wars. "Loss of this deliberative perspective in the modern world has helped to empty the citizen's responsibilities of practical significance, reducing us all to the status of amateur journalists and commentators. . . . The opinionated public . . . does the opposite of what citizens of a state at war ought to do, which is to deliberate with their government and army, so providing a sounding-board for the serious exercise of judgment on alternative courses of action."[44] A recovery of the wisdom of politics would go a long way toward helping recover such deliberation in our societies.

## WISDOM AND SPIRITUALITY

People are well aware that Old Testament wisdom has much to say about suffering, which we will deal with below, but it is not always noticed that Old Testament wisdom as a whole articulates a profound spirituality.

Wisdom spirituality is *based on the experience of salvation*. It is not by coincidence that Old Testament wisdom declares the fear of *Yahweh* to be the beginning of wisdom and knowledge. Yahweh, the favorite name for God in the Old Testament, evokes his role as the redeemer who

---

[43]Ibid., p. 14.
[44]Ibid., p. 17.

rescues Israel from slavery and brings them *to himself* (see Ex 3:1-22; 6:1-30; 19:4). Although the theology of Old Testament wisdom is quintessentially one of creation, it is never one of creation apart from redemption.[45] The use of "Yahweh" in Proverbs evokes God's redemption of Israel and the story of his bringing them from slavery to Sinai, where he reveals himself to them and establishes them in a covenant with himself. With the consecration of the tabernacle, Yahweh sets up his residence among his people, and this mobile sanctuary becomes permanent with the building of the temple.

It is *this* narrative that provides the content for "the fear of the LORD." Yahweh is the Creator God who, as part of his purpose for recovering his creation and leading it to fulfillment, chooses Israel to be his people and enters into an intimate relationship with them. As Israel's experiences at the foot of Mt. Sinai make clear, Yahweh is God, and holy, and dangerous to sinners. Little wonder, therefore, that the starting point of wisdom is a holy reverence for Yahweh, a reverence that recognizes and "allows" God to be God.

Such a reverence *decenters* the wise and reorients them to their appropriate place as worshiping *creatures*. At the heart of Old Testament wisdom is the recognition that we are *not* God, a recognition that is also at the heart of Christian spirituality, as discussed in chapter eleven. This will no doubt seem obvious to readers; but while it is one thing to confess it, it is quite another to live it, especially in the modern West. Our culture is heir to the achievements and idolatries of the Enlightenment. Scientific progress and technology have brought very real gains that few of us would want to be without. But accompanying this progress has been a confidence in "man as the measure of all things," a decentering of God.[46]

A good example of this spirit that is so dominant in our culture is found in the nineteenth-century poem "Invictus," by William Ernest Henry.

---

[45]For a fine theology of the relationship between creation and redemption, see Ola Tjørhom, *Embodied Faith: Reflections on a Materialist Spirituality* (Grand Rapids: Eerdmans, 2009).

[46]See James Reitman, *Unlocking Wisdom: Forming Agents of God in the House of Mourning* (Springfield, Mo.: 21st Century Press, 2008), pp. 335-52, for a personal and insightful reading of wisdom's critique of self-sufficiency.

Out of the night that covers me,
Black as the Pit from pole to pole,
I thank whatever gods may be
For my unconquerable soul.

In the fell clutch of circumstance
I have not winced nor cried aloud.
Under the bludgeonings of chance
My head is bloody, but unbowed.

Beyond this place of wrath and tears
Looms but the Horror of the shade,
And yet the menace of the years
Finds, and shall find, me unafraid.

It matters not how strait the gate,
How charged with punishments the scroll.
I am the master of my fate:
I am the captain of my soul.

This poem was understandably a great encouragement to Nelson Mandela in his imprisonment on Robben Island in South Africa, and gives the name to the acclaimed film *Invictus,* about the rugby World Cup in South Africa shortly after the first democratic election there in 1994. One can understand the pathos of the poem, but the last two lines give the game away; from a wisdom perspective we are neither the masters of our fate nor the captains of our souls.

We are far more deeply broken than we realize, and our strategies for remaining captain of our souls are endless. Thomas Merton, Thomas Keating,[47] Cynthia Bourgeault and many others aptly describe these strategies as our false selves. When we are brought to God in Christ, these false selves do not just disappear; they have to be dismantled, the process traditionally called sanctification. Suffering, as we will see below, is a major tool God uses to dismantle these false selves. Note the penetrating insight in the view, central to Old Testament wisdom, that the starting point and foundation of the wise life is holy reverence for God.

---

[47]Thomas Keating, *Foundations for Centering Prayer and the Christian Contemplative Life* (New York: Continuum, 2004).

Wonderfully, the life centered on God does not detract from the earthy, ordinariness of embodied human life but puts it in true perspective and frees us up to participate in its glory. "Earth is so thick with divine possibility that it is a wonder we can walk anywhere without cracking our shins on altars."[48] The importance of the ordinary in Old Testament wisdom and Christian spirituality is such that we will deal with it in a separate section below. Suffice it here to note that, as some authors have rightly sought to recover the holistic dimensions of created life in reaction to the sacred/secular dualism of too much contemporary Christianity, they have unfortunately embraced the new gnosticism that has emerged with the rediscovery of the Gnostic Gospels.[49]

We have both found Cynthia Bourgeault's writings on Christian spirituality very helpful,[50] but in her book *The Wisdom Jesus* she appropriates insights from the Gnostic Gospels in *unwise* ways. Bourgeault rightly seeks a spirituality that is transformative of the whole person but wrongly argues that this requires jettisoning the traditional doctrines of the fall and redemption. She suggests that we

> approach the mystery of the incarnation through a conceptual framework that does not rely on fall and redemption at all but unfolds along an entirely different line of understanding. Instead of a cosmic course-correction, this other approach envisions the steady and increasingly intimate revelation of divine love along a trajectory that was there from the beginning.[51]

In typical Gnostic fashion, Bourgeault argues that, from God's perspective, the "real operational challenge is not sin and evil; it is posed by the vastly unequal energetic frequencies between the realms. . . . How can the divine radiance meet and interpenetrate created life with-

---

[48]Barbara Brown Taylor, *An Altar in the World: A Geography of Faith* (New York: HarperOne, 2010), p. 15.

[49]On the new Gnosticism see Rodney Stark, *Cities of God: The Real Story of How Christianity Became an Urban Movement and Conquered Rome* (New York: HarperCollins, 2006), pp. 141-81.

[50]See Cynthia Bourgeault, *Centering Prayer and Inner Awakening* (Cambridge, Mass.: Cowley, 2004); idem, *Chanting the Psalms: A Practical Guide with Instructional CD* (Boston: New Seeds, 2006).

[51]Cynthia Bourgeault, *The Wisdom Jesus: Transforming Heart and Mind—A New Perspective on Christ and His Message* (Boston: Shambhala, 2008), p. 95.

out incinerating it?"[52] We are at the bottom of "the great chain of being."[53] God's answer is the incarnation but with Jesus no longer viewed as the one who rescues us from sin but as the bridge between the realms. Using insights from the *Gospel of Thomas,* she explains the resurrection in terms of one's temporal being becoming fused with its causal archetype so that one can then put down and pick up one's temporal form when one chooses to do so.[54]

For all the poignant insights in *The Wisdom Jesus,* Bourgeault's theology is a far remove from Christian orthodoxy. Ironically, in reaching for an approach that facilitates full transformation of our embodied personhood, Bourgeault appropriates Gnostic concepts, which work in the opposite direction. This becomes apparent, for example, in her interpretation of the many dwelling places of "my Father's house" in John 14:2 not as "physical places but rather states of consciousness or dimensions of divine energy."[55] Bourgeault's Gnostic framework introduces irresolvable tensions into her work. On the one hand, as we saw above, there is an enormous gulf between our earthly level at the bottom of the chain of being and God's at the top; and yet Bourgeault insists that an implication of Jesus' resurrection is that "the walls between the realms are paper thin."[56] Bourgeault introduces a conceptual framework that is deeply at odds with that of Scripture—a metaphysical gulf derived from a Neo-Platonic/Gnostic set of beliefs. This erases the biblical doctrine of sin and undermines the eschatological sweep of Scripture toward new heavens and a new earth.

Little wonder that Old Testament wisdom itself warns against "wisdom" that is not rooted in biblical wisdom (cf. Prov 30:5-6; Eccles 12:12). But most important of all is that Old Testament wisdom provides us with the resources for a material spirituality that is fully transformative without having to draw on Gnosticism. For Old Testament wisdom the problem we need to be rescued from is not the gulf between God's realm and ours; Old Testament wisdom insists especially

---

[52]Ibid., p. 101.
[53]Ibid., p. 97.
[54]Ibid., p. 133.
[55]Ibid., p. 96.
[56]Ibid., p. 133.

in Proverbs that Lady Wisdom's voice is constantly calling to us *in* God's good creation. The problem, rather, is the human choice for folly rather than wisdom, that is, the problem *is* sin and positioning ourselves as God rather than worshiping God as creatures. In leading us again and again to that starting point of the fear of the LORD, wisdom offers us the way into a journey of transformative renewal, which is what Bourgeault seeks.

## WISDOM AND THE ORDINARY

An enduring characteristic of Old Testament wisdom is its passionate affirmation of life in all the dimensions in which God has made it: adolescence, sexuality, marriage, work, business, agriculture, speech, eating and drinking, politics and justice, and so on. William Irwin rightly notes that "the wholesomeness of Israel's thinking insured that basic in the conception of the good life was a sufficiency of material things. The Hebrews were no starving saints or unwashed sceptics. They accepted the good things of life with zest."[57] The culmination of Proverbs in the hymn to the heroic woman remains a powerful image of the incarnate vitality of wisdom. In Old Testament wisdom this is also clear in the carpe diem passages in Ecclesiastes, which affirm work, eating and drinking, marriage, and sheer joy at being alive.

The celebration of life and the affirmation of feasting in Ecclesiastes resonate deeply with Jesus' ministry, especially as it is described in Luke's Gospel, in which Jesus seems to go from party to party: "Jesus literally ate his way through the Gospels."[58] David Ford notes that

> Jesus went to meals, weddings and parties and had a feast-centred ethic. The images are vivid: water turned into wine; guests jockeying for places at table and being told to aim for the lower places . . . a woman sinner shocking the company by anointing Jesus and being forgiven by him; the reversal of expectations as the poor, handicapped and outsiders of all sorts are welcomed at the feast of the Kingdom of God

---

[57]William Irwin, "Man," in Henri Frankfort et al., *The Intellectual Adventure of Ancient Man: An Essay on Speculative Thought in the Ancient Near East* (Chicago: University of Chicago Press, 1946), p. 264.

[58]Herbert Anderson and Edward Foley, *Mighty Stories, Dangerous Rituals: Weaving Together the Human and the Divine* (San Francisco: Jossey-Bass, 1998), p. 155.

while those who thought themselves sure of a place are left out; advice about not inviting to your banquet those who will invite you back; a master sitting a servant down and serving him; the Prodigal Son welcomed back unconditionally with the best robe, a ring, shoes, the fatted calf and a celebration; Jesus' last supper, which was probably also a celebration of Passover; Jesus washing his disciples' feet; and the mysterious meals of the risen Jesus.[59]

Herbert Anderson and Edward Foley describe Jesus as "A Storyteller with Bread." They remind us

> how much of his ministry is remembered through the food and dining metaphors that provide the vernacular for narrating the Jesus event. His food was the will of the one he called Father, and this divine will, in turn, became the enduring banquet for any who dared to follow him. Jesus' ministry, his evangelizing, his legacy were so intimately linked to the ritual metaphors of dining and food that, in his fascinating book *Six Thousand Years of Bread* (1944), H. E. Jacob could title his chapter on Jesus as "Jesus Christ: The Bread God." . . . And as remembered over and over in the Gospels, they killed him because of the way he ate; that is, because he ate and drank with sinners.[60]

Ecclesiastes, with its particular emphasis on celebration and feasting, offers itself as a major source from which Jesus would have taken his understanding of the kingdom. In Matthew 11:16-19 Jesus specifically relates his eating and drinking to wisdom. The book of Revelation looks forward to the marriage feast of the Lamb, and John, in his final exhortations, encourages all those of us who thirst—and this side of the consummation of the kingdom, we do indeed thirst—to come and drink of the water of life. Commenting on the Mary-Martha story in Luke's Gospel, in which Martha is busy while Mary sits at Jesus' feet, Augustine asks, "What was she doing? I know," he says, "She was eating Christ!"[61] That ultimately is the place to which wisdom must lead us. Only thus, will we be able to love God with our whole hearts as "a

---

[59]David Ford, *Self and Salvation: Being Transformed* (Cambridge: Cambridge University Press, 1999), p. 268.

[60]Ibid., pp. 154-55.

[61]Augustine, Sermon 179.5, quoted in *Luke*, ed. Arthur A. Just, Ancient Christian Commentary on Scripture (Downers Grove, Ill.: IVP Academic, 2003), p. 182.

kind of *cantus firmus* to which the other melodies of life provide the counterpoint. . . . Where the *cantus firmus* is clear and plain, the counterpoint can be developed to its limits."[62] Thereby we will interweave a theology of the cross with full involvement in the life of the world.[63]

Amid this affirmation of life, we must never forget that Old Testament wisdom, like Jesus, clearly teaches a doctrine of *two ways*. The two houses of Proverbs 8 can profitably be compared with Jesus' two houses of Matthew 7. Humans can choose to live against the grain of Yahweh's world: "One might freely ignore this world of force and shape his conduct indifferent to it. But, like a moral order in the universe, or like law in human society, it imposed inevitably the consequences of defiance, and through their unpleasantness induced conformity."[64]

The word for this in Old Testament wisdom—and for Jesus—is "folly," and its consequences are not good. Hence the liminal rhetoric, or what Irwin calls Hebrew ethics' "white heat of urgency."[65] There is a great deal at stake in whether one chooses wisdom or folly. At the heart of the distinction between folly and wisdom is one's relation to the creation; does one receive it with joy and wonder as the Lord's gift, or does one make oneself the center around which one relates to the world? The classic term for the latter approach is idolatry. Søren Kierkegaard gets at this distinction in his vivid images of the knight of infinite resignation and the knight of faith. The latter relinquishes his hold on the world but receives it all back as gift and lives accordingly. The world is made for our enjoyment, but the wise person knows that true joy is found in appropriating the creation responsibly as pure gift.

## WISDOM AND THE DARK NIGHT OF THE SOUL

Clearly a theology of suffering must take account of the wealth of biblical material dealing with this theme. At the heart of the New Testament is the cross, and disciples are called to take up their cross and follow Jesus. The major theme of James, written by Jesus' brother, is

---

[62]Ibid., p. 254.
[63]See ibid., p. 255.
[64]Irwin, "Man in the World," in Frankfort et al., *Intellectual Adventure*, p. 303.
[65]Ibid., p. 311.

wholeness or integrality, and a key to this is suffering (Jas 1:2-4). In this section we will, however, concentrate on Job and Ecclesiastes because of their profound contribution to a theology of suffering.

Ecclesiastes and Job do not represent a crisis in wisdom but focus on exceptions to the general character-consequence theme of Proverbs. But there is more going on than this; indeed, "exceptions" may turn out to be quite the wrong word to describe the sorts of experiences of Job and Qohelet. Both, in their distinctive ways, go through dark nights of the soul, and as the Christian tradition of spirituality teaches us, a dark night of the soul is more than a mere "exception."

The phrase "dark night of the soul" comes from Saint John of the Cross, a sixteenth-century Carmelite mystic who suffered terribly through two incarcerations by fellow Carmelites. John distinguishes between two nights: the night of the senses (book 1) and the night of the Spirit (book 2). This reflects his Thomistic anthropology in understanding the soul to be divided up into the senses and the spirit. The first night is common to many believers, whereas the second, which purges the spirit and paves the way for union with God, is much rarer. Both nights are tough, but the second is the one we generally associate with the dark night of the soul, and it is far harder than the first.

For example, Saint John says of the second night, "The soul feels itself to be perishing and melting away, in the presence and sight of its miseries, in a cruel spiritual death, even as if it had been swallowed by a beast and felt itself being devoured in the darkness of its belly, suffering such anguish as was endured by Jonas in the belly of that beast of the sea."[66] Not surprisingly Saint John refers to such biblical books as Job, Jonah and Lamentations to describe this experience.

We think Saint John is onto something very important in his theology of the dark night of the soul; his book is a classic for good reason. For our purposes we will take the dark night as a metaphor for a profound experience of suffering in which God seems to be absent but is in fact deeply at work.[67]

---

[66]St. John of the Cross, *Dark Night of the Soul*, trans. E. Allison Peers (Garden City, N.Y.: Doubleday, 1959), p. 111.

[67]Work needs to be done on St. John's Thomist anthropology, on how it shapes his theology of

Wisdom is all about how to live life and negotiate its challenges wisely. How does one live profound suffering wisely? Is this question even worth asking? Is the very notion of wise suffering an oxymoron? It certainly seems like it when one is in the midst of suffering, which as we all know is by its nature exceedingly messy. Jerry Sittser, in his remarkable book *A Grace Disguised*, describes how, as he faced the sudden, tragic loss of his wife, mother and daughter in a car crash caused by a drunken driver, the darkness closed in: "I remember the realization sweeping over me that I would soon plunge into a darkness from which I might never again emerge as a sane, normal, believing man."[68]

Ecclesiastes, and Job in particular, provide us with insight into wisdom and suffering that goes far beyond suffering as an exception to the character-consequence theme. We will articulate their theology of suffering in terms of five characteristics: storied, individual, messy, protracted and uncontrollable, and graced.

*1. Storied.* Both Ecclesiastes and Job have a strong narrative shape. Neither book is easy, just like suffering. Ecclesiastes is performatively enigmatic, *just like suffering,* and Job is long, at times tedious, with all those speeches, *just like suffering.* Both books deal with *particular* individuals, just like suffering. Ecclesiastes lets us enter into the journey of one Qohelet as he wrestles with the question "What do people gain from all the toil at which they toil under the sun?" Of course, this question backs into the larger question of whether life is meaningful at all. Job lets us enter into the story of a wise man who fears the LORD and has been wonderfully blessed and then is hit by catastrophe after catastrophe: grief beyond measure, bereavement, complete loss of all wealth and status, and bodily suffering.

The horror of Job's suffering is clear. However, scholars generally fail to take note of how excruciating is Qohelet's journey. Qohelet's journey is of a more intellectual—but no less devastating—struggle over the meaning of life. The excruciating tension in Qohelet's quest

---

the dark night, how this might be reformulated in the context of a different anthropology and so on. There is also the question of his two stages or two nights. Is this the invariable pattern or can the spiritual journey and the suffering involved be more complex? We do not have space to attend to these issues here.

[68]Jerry Sittser, *A Grace Disguised,* expanded ed. (Grand Rapids: Zondervan, 2004), p. 26.

is seen in the fact that juxtaposed throughout Ecclesiastes next to strong *hebel* conclusions are the carpe diem passages, which in Old Testament fashion affirm life and its goodness. Ecclesiastes is indeed characterized by what Meir Sternberg calls contradictory juxtaposition; "Greek Qohelet" cannot find meaning no matter where he looks and no matter what he experiments with. "Hebrew Qohelet" knows confessionally and deep within that life is fundamentally good. The result is that an excruciating tug of war pervades the book as Qohelet searches desperately for meaning—head and heart are set in constant tense warfare with each other, pressing Qohelet to abandon hope.

Thus neither book tries to or indeed allows us to find quick and easy answers to suffering. As is so often the case with suffering, it is others' stories that are most helpful rather than a glib answer to what God is up to in our pain. The Old Testament's response to wisdom and suffering is to provide us with two very different narratives of suffering, and in order to read these and to really listen to them we have to enter into them deeply and wrestle back and forth with them.

*2. Individual.* Suffering has a unique dimension to it. Job and Ecclesiastes are so very different. Job is not an Israelite, Qohelet is. Both are wise and wealthy. We know what caused Job's suffering; we have no idea how Qohelet came to be in his impasse. Job's suffering is profoundly existential—overwhelmed almost literally with grief and agony and the destruction of his life as he has known it. Qohelet's suffering is far more located, at least as it manifests itself, in his mind. Both go through hell, but in very different ways. God is profoundly at work in both but in very different ways. There are common elements but aspects that are unique to their journeys.

This is very instructive—suffering and dark nights of the soul have common elements, but suffering of the deep sort is invariably unique. Think of Abraham en route to Mount Moriah to sacrifice Isaac (Gen 22)—this exemplifies the solitariness that always comes, we think, with deep suffering.

*3. Messy.* Thomas Merton's advice to dealing with the dark night of the soul is as follows:

> The most important thing of all is to get some realization of what God is doing in your soul. . . .
>
> Do not then stir yourself up to useless interior activities. Avoid everything that will bring unnecessary complications into your life. Live in as much peace and quiet and retirement as you can, and do not go out of your way to get involved in labors and duties, no matter how much glory they may seem to give to God. . . .
>
> Love and serve him peacefully and in all your works preserve recollection.[69]

This may be excellent advice, but amid deep suffering we doubt its relevance unless perhaps for a remarkably mature believer. What Job and Ecclesiastes teach is that suffering is downright messy. Qohelet verges continually on blasphemy. Job starts by making a remarkable confession in Job 1:21, and then it takes him some forty-one chapters to return to that starting point of trust and faith.

In that time:

- His wife suggests he curse God and die, that is, that he commit suicide

- His friends arrive and sit with him seven long days and nights in silence

- He curses the day he was born

- He longs for death

- He is subject to the unhelpful advice of his three friends, who all have a lot to say

- He becomes a scapegoat in his society[70]

- He seeks a lawsuit with God

And so on—endless chapters of anger, despair, pain and hell. Rather different from Merton's suggestions!

*4. Protracted and uncontrollable.* For both Job and Ecclesiastes the experience is open-ended—they have surrendered or been forced to

---

[69]Thomas Merton, *The Inner Experience: Notes on Contemplation*, ed. William H. Shannon (San Francisco: HarperSanFrancisco, 2003), pp. 95, 97.

[70]See René Girard, *Job: The Victim of His People* (Stanford, Calif.: Stanford University Press, 1987).

surrender to it, but from there, who knows? For both of them it is out of control intellectually, theologically and existentially. The counsel of wife and friends does not work (Job); excessive activity does not work (Qohelet); and for both God is silent.

This disorienting, uncontrollable nature of their experience is, we think, what Saint John fingers in his dark night of the soul. Familiar compass points and orientation are gone, stripped away, so that the person is left naked and in pain and completely at a loss as to what to do or think or say.

**5. Graced.** Can you imagine grace being hard? Well here it is: hard, tough, ruthless in ways that we had not imagined. Merton says, as we quoted earlier, "The most important thing of all is to get some realization of what God is doing in your soul."[71] We suspect this is often unrealistic—in the midst of suffering by its very nature we do *not* know what God is up to. Everything we thought we knew has been blown apart. With deep suffering it is impossible for *any* of us to discern clearly what God is up to. So much suffering—and so much mystery.

And yet both Ecclesiastes and Job are adamant that this suffering is graced, full of grace, relentless grace. Qohelet is affirmed in the epilogue as one who taught the people wisdom. His journey, virtually torn apart by it—wisdom! In Job 42:7 the LORD rebukes Job's friends, "You have not spoken of me what is right, as my servant Job has."

"Spoken of me what is right"—that is God's description of what Job has had to say. So we would propose revising Merton to say that it can be helpful in suffering to know that God is at work, deeply. We do not need to know what he is doing or when it will end or how it will work out—that is all entirely out of our control, but that he is at work deeply and graciously, we need to cling to, as we are able.

**Bull's-eye.** How might God be at work in our suffering?

It is always dangerous to generalize about suffering, and we don't want to do that here. But there are things to learn from Job, Ecclesiastes, and Gen 22 and psychologies of suffering. In Craig's commentary on Ecclesiastes he appended a psychological reading of Ecclesiastes,

---

[71]Merton, *Inner Experience*, p. 95.

using Jung's insights.[72] And here again we think Saint John of the Cross is very helpful, for he is clear that there is real purpose and grace beyond measure at work in the dark night.

In brief, the message of Job, Ecclesiastes and Saint John is—at least in part—that we are more in need of deep healing than we imagined. Thomas Green explains Saint John as follows:

> In the night of sense we cut the weeds off at ground level. They no longer appear, so the garden looks beautiful and well tended. But the trouble is that the roots are still there underground. Until they are uprooted, the weeds will surely reappear. Similarly, our sensible failings are just the surface manifestations of a deeper problem. We can chop away at them, but they will resurface unless and until the Lord digs out the roots in our "spirit," our interior faculties of memory, understanding, and will.[73]

Saint John's point is that in the dark night God shines his light on our deepest parts but that the darkness there is such that we find it unbearable and disorienting. What Job and Ecclesiastes and the tradition of spirituality alert us to is that in the dark night God goes, as it were, for the jugular. What happens is often our worst nightmare because it puts its finger precisely where the deepest attention is needed. But it is precisely the area(s) we would most protect because we know we are vulnerable there.

There is evidence of precisely this dynamic in Job. In Job 1:5 we see him going to the utmost degree to ensure the protection of his family. He sacrifices for his children *in case* they had sinned and offended God. Religion can become like that—we use it to protect against areas that are most important to us and where we sense our vulnerabilities. Almost from the outset the book of Job highlights the motif of creation order as the underlying issue of the narrative. Job's terrible and excruciating suffering foregrounds his latent, unconscious tendency—or propels him into a tendency—to position himself at the center of the order of creation. Job's life's meaning was evidently connected to his family,

---

[72]See Craig G. Bartholomew, *Ecclesiastes* (Grand Rapids: Baker Academic, 2009), pp. 377-82.
[73]Thomas H. Green, *Drinking from a Dry Well* (Notre Dame, Ind.: Ave Maria, 1991), pp. 42-43.

his property, his reputation, his health. When he was deprived of these he fell into despair and entered a dark night of the soul. Evidence for this emerges in his imagined, preferred place, namely, to be at rest with the kings and counselors of the earth who rebuild ruins for themselves or with princes who have gold and fill their houses with silver (Job 3:13-15). The small and the great are there (Job 3:19), but clearly Job envisages himself among the great.

Qohelet's problem is the very modern one of human autonomy and trust in reason and experience alone to get him to the truth about the world. For both Job and Qohelet, their suffering and struggle works at their deepest levels and hacks mercilessly away at the things they are most in danger of placing before God. Similarly, Leon Kass says of Abraham's call to sacrifice Isaac in Genesis 22 that

> horrible though it is to say so, the test God devises is perfect: for only if Abraham is willing to do without the covenant (and, as proof, is willing to destroy it himself), out of awe-reverence for the Covenantor, can he demonstrate that he merits the covenant and its promised blessings; only in this way can he demonstrate that he is fit for patriarchy, for both fatherhood and founding.[74]

Mysteriously, in the cases of Job, Qohelet and Abraham, their terrible suffering reveals God at work in the deepest parts of their being. He goes for the bull's-eye, as it were.

*Healing.* In Job 23:3 (cf. Job 23:8-11) Job laments that he does not know the place where God can be found:

> Oh that I knew *where* I might find him,
>     that I might come even to his dwelling!

This anticipates the extraordinary hymn in Job 28, which celebrates humankind's abilities to explore and uncover the most distant and hidden places of the earth. But the amazing capacity of humans to mine and excavate serves merely as the backdrop for human limitations as articulated in the refrain in Job 28:12, 20. Norman Habel notes that for each of the treasures sought in Job 28:1-11 there is a place, a means of

---

[74]Leon R. Kass, *The Beginning of Wisdom: Reading Genesis* (Chicago: University of Chicago Press, 2003), p. 337.

access, a way, a process of discovery.[75] But where is wisdom to be found, where is its place? Job 28:20 intensifies the quest for the place of wisdom by asking not just about its place but its origin. Job's suffering highlights the inestimable value of wisdom (28:15-19), but its place cannot be discovered within the creation: even Abaddon and death have only heard rumors of it! Job cannot see the way, but God understands the way to wisdom (Job 28:23) because he looks and he sees everything under the heavens (Job 28:24). He knows its place![76]

It is through God's speeches in Job 38–41 that resolution comes to Job. Intriguingly they contain more than eighty rhetorical questions, which, as we noted in chapter six, Fox divides up into three main types: *who* questions, which point to God as the source of creation; *what* questions, which probe the limits of Job's knowledge; and *have you ever* questions, which evoke a humble, creaturely response.[77] Resolution comes through Job's encounter with God: "God's response to Job's plea for a legal hearing turns him back to contemplate the implications of creation, and thereby recontextualizes the foundations employed by Job to bring his case forward."[78]

In Job 3:23 Job could not "see the way," but in Job 42:6 he says, "Now my eyes see you." Job is restored and blessed materially and relationally more than he was at the beginning. The narrative arc is one of implacement to displacement to *much deeper* re-implacement. Job, and Ecclesiastes, serve not only to deal with the exceptions to the character-consequence motif of wisdom but also to indicate that the journey into the depth implacement that wisdom calls forth may involve immense suffering. Both Job and Ecclesiastes alert us to the fact that genuine wisdom with all its depths and nuances is not easily attained.

For Qohelet resolution comes gradually, toward the end of the book. Ecclesiastes 11:7 is the first major sign of existential resolution: "Light

---

[75]Norman C. Habel, *The Book of Job*, OTL (Philadelphia: Westminster Press, 1985), pp. 393-96.

[76]On Job 28:27 see S. L. Harris, "Wisdom or Creation: A New Interpretation of Job XXVIII 27," *VT* 33 (1983): 419-27.

[77]Michael V. Fox, "Job 38 and God's Rhetoric," *Semeia* 19 (1981): 53-61.

[78]Ryan O'Dowd, *The Wisdom of Torah: Epistemology in Deuteronomy and the Wisdom Literature*, FRLANT (Göttingen: Vandenhoeck & Ruprecht, 2009), p. 159.

is sweet, and it is pleasant for the eyes to see the sun" (NRSV). This becomes stronger in the exhortation to rejoice and especially in the one to "Remember your creator before . . . before . . . before." Such remembrance turns Qohelet's Greek epistemology on its head; it does not solve all the major problems he has raised in the book, but it provides a creaturely place to stand from where the challenges can be lived with joy and hope but without final answers to all his questions.

The healing that Job and Ecclesiastes point to is *depth* healing, just as Saint John does in his dark night of the soul. It is above all else God's work, but it alerts us to the fact that wisdom, knowing how to live as a creature in God's world, is a profound entity, and a lifetime's journey. Little wonder that Saint John says that not many enter and embrace this dark night of the spirit. Green comments that "if we are generous enough to allow the Lord full freedom to transform us, his scalpel must cut deep into the center of our soul."[79]

*How?* There is no one, easy recipe for dealing with suffering. By its very nature, and ironically its hidden gift, suffering is not something we control. Job and Ecclesiastes serve as reminders that it is under *God's* control and that he is at work in it deeply, albeit in ways we cannot fathom.

Job and Ecclesiastes remind us that we don't need to understand what he is doing, as much as we would love to know and feel. Both Job and Qohelet had to surrender to their journey of pain and struggle and to wait it through. Importantly their waiting is not passive; God commends Job for his protest and anger. One should always seek good counsel, but sometimes, like Job, good counsel is unavailable, and this compounds his suffering. Ultimately suffering does what it is intended to do; it throws us back on God. Jerry Sittser describes how:

> Since I knew that darkness was inevitable and unavoidable, I decided from that point on to walk into the darkness rather than try to outrun it, to let my experience of loss take me on a journey wherever it would lead, and to allow myself to be transformed by my suffering rather than to think I could somehow avoid it. I chose to turn toward the pain,

---

[79]Green, *Drinking from a Dry Well*, p. 43.

however falteringly, and to yield to the loss, though I had no idea at the time what that would mean.[80]

Healing came slowly for Jerry, and with deep suffering it invariably does. But, as you will see if you read his book, eventually he came to see his terrible suffering as a grace disguised.

## CONCLUSION

In this book we have aimed to revive the wisdom tradition in the theology of the church today. In this chapter we have excavated some key areas of Christian life and thought in which taking (Old Testament) wisdom seriously makes a significant difference. Wisdom, after all, is the key to bringing glory to God in every area of human life. Wisdom can never remain an area of study; just like Jesus it must become incarnate in our lives. Gabriel Marcel's words evoke for us the sort of response we would love our readers to make to this book:

> Though I shall certainly cause some dismay and scandal among philosophers and theologians, I would say that in this age of absolute insecurity we live in, true wisdom lies in setting out with prudence to be sure, but also with a kind of joyful anticipation, on the paths leading not necessarily beyond time but beyond our time, to where the technocrats and the statistic worshippers on the one hand, and the tyrants and torturers on the other, not only lose their footing but vanish like mists at the dawn of a beautiful day.[81]

## RECOMMENDED READING

### Theological resources

Clements, Ronald E. *Wisdom in Theology*. Grand Rapids: Eerdmans, 1992.

Ford, David, and Graham Stanton, eds. *Reading Texts, Seeking Wisdom: Scripture and Theology*. Grand Rapids: Eerdmans, 2004.

Rad, Gerhard von. *Wisdom in Israel*. Translated by James D. Martin. London: SCM, 1970.

---

[80]Sittser, *A Grace Disguised*, p. 42.

[81]Gabriel Marcel, *Tragic Wisdom and Beyond*, trans. Stephen Jolin and Peter McCormick (Evanston, Ill.: Northwestern University Press, 1973), pp. 212-13.

## Commentaries

Both of the following commentaries are notable for their exploration of the theological and cultural implications of Old Testament wisdom.

Bartholomew, Craig G. *Ecclesiastes*. BCOTWP. Grand Rapids: Baker Academic, 2009.

Leeuwen, Raymond C. van. "Proverbs." In *The New Interpreter's Bible,* ed. Leander Keck, 5:17-264. Nashville: Abingdon, 1997.

## Scholarly resources

Bartholomew, Craig G. "A Time for War and a Time for Peace: Old Testament Wisdom, Creation and O'Donovan's Theological Ethics." In *A Royal Priesthood: The Use of the Bible Ethically and Politically, A Dialogue with Oliver O'Donovan,* ed. Craig G. Bartholomew, Jonathan Chaplin, Robert Song and Al Wolters, pp. 91-112. Grand Rapids: Zondervan, 2002.

Brueggemann, Walter. *The Creative Word: Canon as a Model for Biblical Education*. Philadelphia: Fortress, 1982.

Leeuwen, Raymond C. van. "In Praise of Proverbs." In *Pledges of Jubilee: Essays on the Arts and Culture, in Honor of Calvin G Seerveld,* ed. Lambert Zuidervaart and Henry Luttikhuizen, pp. 308-27. Grand Rapids, Eerdmans, 1995.

O'Donovan, Oliver. "Response to Craig Bartholomew." In *A Royal Priesthood: The Use of the Bible Ethically and Politically, A Dialogue with Oliver O'Donovan,* ed. Craig G. Bartholomew, Jonathan Chaplin, Robert Song and Al Wolters, pp. 113-15. Grand Rapids: Zondervan, 2002.

———. *The Just War Revisited*. Cambridge: Cambridge University Press, 2003.

# Author Index

# Subject Index

# Scripture Index